Integrating Artificial Intelligence in Education:
Enhancing Teaching Practices for Future Learning

Ricardo Queirós
Polytechnic of Porto, Portugal & CRACS INESC TEC, Portugal

Mário Cruz
Polytechnic of Porto, Portugal & inED, Portugal

Daniela Mascarenhas
School of Education, Polytechnic of Porto, Portugal & inED, Portugal

Published in the United States of America by
IGI Global
701 E. Chocolate Avenue
Hershey PA, USA 17033
Tel: 717-533-8845
Fax: 717-533-8661
E-mail: cust@igi-global.com
Web site: https://www.igi-global.com

Copyright © 2025 by IGI Global. All rights reserved. No part of this publication may be reproduced, stored or distributed in any form or by any means, electronic or mechanical, including photocopying, without written permission from the publisher.
Product or company names used in this set are for identification purposes only. Inclusion of the names of the products or companies does not indicate a claim of ownership by IGI Global of the trademark or registered trademark.

Library of Congress Cataloging-in-Publication Data

Names: Queiros, Ricardo, 1975- editor.
Title: Integrating artificial intelligence in education : enhancing teaching practices for future learning / edited by Ricardo Queirós, Mário Cruz, Carla Pinto, Daniela Mascarenhas.
Description: Hershey, PA : IGI Global, 2025. | Includes bibliographical references and index. | Summary: "This book aims to provide a comprehensive understanding of how AI is influencing and revolutionizing the teaching process. We seek contributions that explore both the opportunities and challenges presented by AI technologies in several educational settings"-- Provided by publisher.
Identifiers: LCCN 2024038677 (print) | LCCN 2024038678 (ebook) | ISBN 9798369339442 (hardcover) | ISBN 9798369349816 (paperback) | ISBN 9798369339459 (ebook)
Subjects: LCSH: Artificial intelligence--Educational applications. | Artificial intelligence--Educational applications--Case studies.
Classification: LCC LB1028.43 .I58627 2024 (print) | LCC LB1028.43 (ebook) | DDC 370.285/63--dc23/eng/20240923
LC record available at https://lccn.loc.gov/2024038677
LC ebook record available at https://lccn.loc.gov/2024038678

Vice President of Editorial: Melissa Wagner
Managing Editor of Acquisitions: Mikaela Felty
Managing Editor of Book Development: Jocelynn Hessler
Production Manager: Mike Brehm
Cover Design: Phillip Shickler

British Cataloguing in Publication Data
A Cataloguing in Publication record for this book is available from the British Library.

All work contributed to this book is new, previously-unpublished material.
The views expressed in this book are those of the authors, but not necessarily of the publisher.

Table of Contents

Preface xiii

Chapter 1
AI in Education: Ethical Challenges and Opportunities 1
    Okechukwu Amah, Lagos Business School, Nigeria
    Victoria Oluwakemi Okesipe, Lagos Business School, Nigeria

Chapter 2
Investigation of Primary School Teacher's Attitudes Towards Artificial Intelligence 27
    Ali Mazı, Ministry of National Education, Turkey

Chapter 3
Artificial Intelligence Experiences of Pre-Service Preschool Teachers 59
    Feyza Aydin Bölükbaş, Aksaray University, Turkey
    Kadriye Selin Budak, Bilecik University, Turkey
    Emine Bozkurt Polat, Kahramanmaraş Sütçü İmam University, Turkey
    Kübra Engin, Gazi University, Turkey
    İlkay Ulutaş, Gazi University, Turkey

Chapter 4
Enhancing High-Quality Pedagogy in Higher Education With MyGPTs: A Case of Tailored Teacher Assistant PedaBuddy 89
    Minna-Maarit Jaskari, University of Vaasa, Finland

Chapter 5
Transforming Teaching and Learning With Natural Language Processing 119
    Luis Coelho, ISEP, Polytechnic of Porto, Portugal
    Sara Reis, ISEP, Polytechnic of Porto, Portugal

Chapter 6
Artificial Intelligence-Supported Meta-Learning Assistant 153
    Serap Sisman-Ugur, Anadolu University, Turkey

Chapter 7
AI based Learning in Biology 177
    Shiwani, Dayalbagh Educational Institute, India
    D. K. Chaturvedi, Dayalbagh Educational Institute, India

Chapter 8
Reshaping Assessment Horizons AI's Evolutionary Impact on Traditional
Methods 199
    C. Indu, Lovely Professional University, India
    Prem Lata Gautam, Lovely Professional University, India
    Mehak Malhotra, Lovely Professional University, India
    Akshat Jain, Lovely Professional University, India

Chapter 9
Machine Learning Integration to Analyze Student Behavior in an Online
Digital Learning System 217
    Somdeep Das, Management Development Institute, Murshidabad, India
    Pinaki Pratim Acharjya, Haldia Institute of Technology, India

Chapter 10
Research Study Results: Integrating Artificial Intelligence Into a Higher
Education Course 243
    Luanne M. Amato, Holy Family University, USA
    Christine Schoettle, Holy Family University, USA

Chapter 11
Artificial Intelligence and Language Learning: Methods, Tools, and
Challenges 267
    Ana Rita Costa, ESTGA, Portugal
    Sandra Vieira Vasconcelos, UNIAG, ESHT, Polytechnic Institute of
        Porto, Portugal
    Ana Balula, University of Aveiro, Portugal

Chapter 12
Exploring the Role of Artificial Intelligence in Second Language Acquisition:
A Focus on English Learning 287
    Ines Rodrigues, Instituto Superior de Ciências Empresariais e Turismo,
        Portugal

Compilation of References 313

About the Contributors 365

Index 375

Detailed Table of Contents

Preface xiii

Chapter 1
AI in Education: Ethical Challenges and Opportunities 1
    Okechukwu Amah, Lagos Business School, Nigeria
    Victoria Oluwakemi Okesipe, Lagos Business School, Nigeria

Educational activities, such as teaching and learning, are inherently knowledge-intensive cognitive processes. AI applications, which are designed for cognition and problem-solving using algorithms and knowledge bases, can effectively support and enhance educators' and learners' abilities in teaching and learning endeavors. This chapter delves into the burgeoning integration of Artificial Intelligence (AI) within the educational sector. We begin by exploring the current applications of AI in various educational segments, highlighting how this technology is transforming the teaching-learning experience. Subsequently, the chapter shows the potential advantages AI offers, from personalized learning to enhanced accessibility. However, discussion progresses by acknowledging the ethical concerns around AI in education. Through an exploratory research approach, drawing on existing literature reviews and supporting publications, the chapter proposes action steps to address these challenges.

Chapter 2
Investigation of Primary School Teacher's Attitudes Towards Artificial Intelligence 27
    Ali Mazı, Ministry of National Education, Turkey

This research aims to ascertain primary school teachers' attitudes towards artificial intelligence (AI) in the direction of age, gender, computer skills, utilization of AI programs and using AI in lessons. The study employed the survey model. The research group is comprised of 200 primary school teachers in capitol city (Ankara) of Turkey. In the collection of the data, the "General Attitudes towards Artificial Intelligence Scale" (GAAIS) was used. ANOVA and independent samples t-test were employed at the examination of the collected data. The research conclusions showed that the primary school teachers' attitudes towards AI varied significantly depending on age, gender, computer skills, utilization of AI programs and using AI in lessons. The use of the same scale in different groups can provide better insights into attitudes towards AI.

Chapter 3
Artificial Intelligence Experiences of Pre-Service Preschool Teachers 59
    Feyza Aydin Bölükbaş, Aksaray University, Turkey
    Kadriye Selin Budak, Bilecik University, Turkey
    Emine Bozkurt Polat, Kahramanmaraş Sütçü İmam University, Turkey
    Kübra Engin, Gazi University, Turkey
    İlkay Ulutaş, Gazi University, Turkey

This section covers artificial intelligence integration in education, artificial intelligence literacy, artificial intelligence in early childhood, and the role of teachers in utilising artificial intelligence, as discussed in the literature. Within this framework, the use of artificial intelligence tools by pre-service teachers has been analyzed based on interviews. Advice on how to effectively utilize artificial intelligence and how to employ artificial intelligence tools and applications ethically is provided. The experiences of pre-service teachers who use artificial intelligence tools whilst organising educational activities are intended to offer guidance at this juncture.

Chapter 4
Enhancing High-Quality Pedagogy in Higher Education With MyGPTs: A
Case of Tailored Teacher Assistant PedaBuddy 89
    Minna-Maarit Jaskari, University of Vaasa, Finland

This chapter examines the development and implementation of custom MyGPTs within higher education, using a teacher assistant 'PedaBuddy' as a detailed case study. It explores the guiding principles behind these generative AI tools, focusing on their potential to enhance teaching and learning experiences, while also addressing the challenges they present. The chapter begins with a review of existing literature on generative AI and MyGPTs in academic settings, followed by an in-depth explanation of the configuration process using OpenAI's GPT builder. Through the case study of PedaBuddy, the chapter showcases the practical applications and outcomes of deploying a tailored MyGPT. The discussion concludes by evaluating the strengths, opportunities, and challenges associated with integrating such AI-driven tools in higher education.

Chapter 5
Transforming Teaching and Learning With Natural Language Processing 119
Luis Coelho, ISEP, Polytechnic of Porto, Portugal
Sara Reis, ISEP, Polytechnic of Porto, Portugal

In higher education (HE), the integration of Natural Language Processing (NLP) stands as a transformative force, reshaping traditional paradigms of teaching and learning. NLP systems are also able to perform tasks such as text summarization, text comparison, and personalized text generation, among others. From the teacher's perspective it is possible to have support or automate in tasks such as essay grading or materials generation, among many others. Moreover, NLP-powered intelligent tutoring systems personalize learning experiences by analyzing students' language use, identifying misconceptions, and offering targeted feedback and explanations. The adoption of NLP technology in HE holds the promise of optimizing learning outcomes, enhancing institutional efficiency, and promoting greater accessibility and inclusivity. However, despite its potential benefits, the successful implementation of NLP in HE necessitates careful consideration of ethical, privacy, and equity concerns, as well as ongoing research to address technical challenges and refine pedagogical strategies.

Chapter 6
Artificial Intelligence-Supported Meta-Learning Assistant 153
Serap Sisman-Ugur, Anadolu University, Turkey

In the twenty-first century, when technology has had a profound impact on every aspect of our lives, learning has also changed, revealing the need for a dramatic reorganization of education systems. Individuals have the ability to learn with the possibilities offered by technology, and they play a critical role in the new development of these learning services. In light of artificial intelligence technologies and metaverse universes, the possibility to provide learning experiences in which individuals shape their learning adventures based on their own traits should be considered as an innovation that will take place in the future of learning. When configuring this service, it is essential to identify the proper artificial intelligence algorithms, correlate them with individual differences, and determine the processes that the individual can direct. The development of artificial intelligence-assisted learning assistants in the form of meta-human will provide a new dimension to learning and teaching processes.

Chapter 7
AI based Learning in Biology 177
    Shiwani, Dayalbagh Educational Institute, India
    D. K. Chaturvedi, Dayalbagh Educational Institute, India

This chapter develops an AI based learning system to investigate the incorporation of AI in education. The chapter addresses the advantages of AI in education, including personalized learning programs and reduced teacher workload, in light of its expanding significance in the field. Proving theorems and problem-solving are the two base pillars of AI based learning systems. Partitioning domain-specific knowledge after the inference engine is a fundamental component of these learning systems. The chapter focuses on the design and development of an AI based learning system (on Biology content), detailing the knowledge acquisition, representation, and developmental phases. Systematic explanations of acquiring information from subject matter experts, representing that knowledge using MATLAB, and creating an inference engine. Emphasis is placed on the evaluation phase, demonstrating how the system can evaluate student knowledge in a variety of ways. By including professional evaluations, revisions, and comments, the refinement process guarantees accuracy and trustworthiness.

Chapter 8
Reshaping Assessment Horizons AI's Evolutionary Impact on Traditional Methods 199
    C. Indu, Lovely Professional University, India
    Prem Lata Gautam, Lovely Professional University, India
    Mehak Malhotra, Lovely Professional University, India
    Akshat Jain, Lovely Professional University, India

The incorporation of Artificial Intelligence (AI) in educational evaluation signifies a revolutionary transition from conventional techniques to automated systems driven by sophisticated algorithms. AI frees up teachers to concentrate on individualized instruction by streamlining tasks like item creation and feedback provision. Intelligent tutoring programs tailor lessons to each student's needs and increase interest by personalizing the learning process. But there are issues that need to be carefully considered, like algorithmic bias and privacy concerns. Working together, engineers, legislators, and educators can fully utilize AI's potential while reducing its perils. Continued research is necessary to improve algorithms and guarantee their effectiveness in a variety of scenarios. Beyond its immediate uses, AI-driven evaluation helps to design educational policies that support critical thinking and lifetime learning, as well as evidence-based decision-making.

Chapter 9
Machine Learning Integration to Analyze Student Behavior in an Online
Digital Learning System 217
    Somdeep Das, Management Development Institute, Murshidabad, India
    Pinaki Pratim Acharjya, Haldia Institute of Technology, India

This chapter highlights the various means of digital learning systems, its impact on the school level students of various age groups, the psychology of learning and its behavioral impact on their outcome, and Prognostic Analysis of the behavior on the ISCED level 1 students. This chapter also put forth the significance of not only establishing the technological transformation as a 'change' of Education System, but also carefully designing a holistic learning environment for future, specifically the cognitive and emotional engagement of students of the age group ranging from 6-12 years whose behavioral aspects varies with their varied levels of education.

Chapter 10
Research Study Results: Integrating Artificial Intelligence Into a Higher
Education Course 243
    Luanne M. Amato, Holy Family University, USA
    Christine Schoettle, Holy Family University, USA

Artificial Intelligence (AI) became known as a technological breakthrough in the 1990s but its impact on higher education was minimal. In the current academic climate, AI is now considered a significant force that affects students, faculty, and administrators, but with a dearth of information validated by research, on how to respond. This chapter details a pilot mixed methods research study that examines the education and use of AI, in the form of chatbots, in a live course. The chapter provides a background of AI, the current experience of administrators, faculty, and students, and introduces the research objectives, questions, population, and process. This chapter provides insights of students and faculty based on a survey and a focus group to validate the need for informed professional development for faculty and ethics training for students in order that they may successfully navigate AI in higher education course work.

Chapter 11
Artificial Intelligence and Language Learning: Methods, Tools, and Challenges 267

    Ana Rita Costa, ESTGA, Portugal
    Sandra Vieira Vasconcelos, UNIAG, ESHT, Polytechnic Institute of Porto, Portugal
    Ana Balula, University of Aveiro, Portugal

Artificial Intelligence (AI) has shifted from an emerging trend to a mainstream topic in education, impacting various educational settings, including teacher training. This chapter emphasizes the need to equip teachers with competencies to integrate AI into their practices, particularly in foreign language teaching and learning. By compiling a comprehensive list of AI platforms and tools, the authors aim to support teachers by offering options that can be tailored to different learning designs and outcomes, moving away from "one size fits all" solutions. The chapter provides an annotated list of AI tools, highlighting their features, applications, benefits, and limitations. Referencing Mollick and Mollick's (2023) approaches to AI in education, it includes language chatbots, generative AI, machine translation, and personalized textbooks, showcasing practical examples and reflecting on recent trends. As a result, the chapter seeks to inform and inspire future initiatives in language learning and teaching, helping other practitioners to effectively incorporate AI into their practices.

Chapter 12
Exploring the Role of Artificial Intelligence in Second Language Acquisition:
A Focus on English Learning 287
    Ines Rodrigues, Instituto Superior de Ciências Empresariais e Turismo,
       Portugal

As technology advances, the integration of Artificial Intelligence (AI) in education is prompting a paradigm shift. This chapter explores AI's impact on English as a second language (ESL) acquisition, focusing on its role in developing listening, writing, reading, and speaking skills among students in Portugal. The study highlights the importance of considering students as active participants in shaping their learning environments and ensuring their perspectives influence educational practices. Data were gathered through an online questionnaire targeting secondary school students from public schools in Portugal. Although AI is still emerging in Portuguese schools, students generally view AI-powered tools positively for both English learning and daily tasks. Importantly, they do not see AI as compromising the teacher's role, recognizing the irreplaceable value of empathy and human connection. The study calls for further research into students' perceptions of AI in education.

Compilation of References 313

About the Contributors 365

Index 375

Preface

As we stand at the confluence of education and technology, we are witnessing a paradigm shift where Artificial Intelligence (AI) is emerging as a catalyst for change, offering new possibilities in the realm of teaching and learning. The intersection of these two fields presents a unique opportunity to reimagine education, not as a static tradition but as a dynamic process that evolves in response to the needs and challenges of our time.

The integration of AI into education is not merely an enhancement but a transformation that promises to redefine how educators approach their practice and how students engage with learning. The potential of AI to personalize education, automate routine tasks, provide real-time feedback, and offer insights into student learning patterns is immense. However, with these opportunities come significant challenges. Ethical considerations, data privacy, the potential for bias, and the readiness of educators and institutions to adapt to these changes are critical issues that must be addressed.

This book, *Integrating Artificial Intelligence in Education: Enhancing Teaching Practices for Future Learning,* is our contribution to the ongoing dialogue about the future of education in an AI-driven world. It brings together a collection of perspectives that explore the integration of AI across various educational settings, from traditional classrooms to online platforms. Each chapter offers insights into the practical applications of AI, the challenges faced in implementation, and the future directions for research and practice.

Our contributors include educators, researchers, and practitioners who are at the forefront of this integration. They offer a comprehensive overview of the current state of AI in education, providing both theoretical frameworks and practical examples that can serve as a guide for those looking to harness the power of AI in their own educational contexts.

SECTION 1: FOUNDATIONS OF AI IN EDUCATION

In Chapter 1, the exploration of Artificial Intelligence (AI) in education is approached through a comprehensive analysis of its current applications across various educational sectors. This chapter discusses how AI is transforming teaching and learning, offering advantages such as personalized learning experiences and improved accessibility. However, it also brings to light the ethical concerns surrounding AI in education. Through an exploratory research approach, this chapter proposes actionable steps to address these challenges, laying the groundwork for responsible and effective AI integration in education.

Chapter 2 focuses on a study that investigates primary school teachers' attitudes towards AI, analyzing how these attitudes vary based on factors such as age, gender, computer skills, and the use of AI in teaching. Using the "General Attitudes towards Artificial Intelligence Scale" (GAAIS), the chapter presents findings from a survey conducted with 200 primary school teachers in Ankara, Turkey. The results reveal significant variations in attitudes towards AI, offering insights into how different teacher demographics perceive and engage with AI technology. This chapter underscores the importance of understanding these attitudes to better inform AI integration in primary education.

In Chapter 3, the integration of AI in early childhood education is examined, with a particular focus on pre-service teachers' use of AI tools. Through interviews and literature review, the chapter provides a nuanced analysis of how pre-service teachers interact with AI during their training, offering practical advice on the ethical use of AI in educational settings. This chapter highlights the role of educators in effectively utilizing AI, emphasizing the need for teacher preparedness and the ethical considerations that come with the integration of AI in education.

SECTION 2: AI TOOLS AND APPLICATIONS IN EDUCATIONAL SETTINGS

Chapter 4 presents a detailed case study on the development and implementation of a custom MyGPT, named 'PedaBuddy,' within higher education. The chapter explores the guiding principles behind generative AI tools and their potential to enhance teaching and learning experiences. By detailing the configuration process and practical applications of PedaBuddy, the chapter showcases the benefits and challenges of deploying AI-driven tools in higher education. The discussion concludes with an evaluation of the strengths, opportunities, and challenges associated with such AI integration, providing valuable insights for educators and institutions looking to adopt similar technologies.

In Chapter 5, the transformative potential of Natural Language Processing (NLP) in higher education is explored. The chapter discusses how NLP can support and even automate tasks such as essay grading and materials generation, while also enhancing personalized learning through intelligent tutoring systems. Despite its many benefits, the chapter also addresses the ethical, privacy, and equity concerns that accompany the adoption of NLP in education. The chapter calls for ongoing research and careful consideration to ensure that NLP is implemented in ways that optimize learning outcomes and promote inclusivity.

Chapter 6 delves into the evolving landscape of learning in the twenty-first century, where AI and metaverse technologies are reshaping educational systems. This chapter emphasizes the need for a dramatic reorganization of education, considering individual learning traits and the potential of AI-assisted learning assistants in the form of meta-humans. The chapter discusses the importance of selecting appropriate AI algorithms and correlating them with individual differences to create personalized learning experiences. By envisioning the future of learning through AI and metaverse integration, this chapter offers a forward-looking perspective on how education can evolve to meet the demands of the digital age.

SECTION 3: DESIGNING AI-ENHANCED LEARNING ENVIRONMENTS

In Chapter 7, the development of an AI-based learning system is examined, focusing on its application in teaching Biology. This chapter outlines the advantages of AI in education, such as personalized learning programs and reduced teacher workload, and details the design and development process of the learning system. By explaining the knowledge acquisition, representation, and evaluation phases, the chapter demonstrates how AI can enhance student learning. The chapter also emphasizes the importance of professional evaluations and feedback in refining AI-based systems, ensuring their accuracy and reliability in educational contexts.

Chapter 8 discusses the revolutionary shift in educational evaluation brought about by AI. The chapter explores how AI-driven systems can automate tasks like item creation and feedback provision, allowing teachers to focus on individualized instruction. It also highlights the potential of intelligent tutoring programs to personalize learning experiences. However, the chapter also raises concerns about algorithmic bias and privacy, calling for collaboration among engineers, legislators, and educators to fully realize AI's potential while mitigating its risks. The chapter concludes by advocating for continued research to refine AI algorithms and ensure their effectiveness in diverse educational scenarios.

Chapter 9 highlights the impact of digital learning systems on school-level students, particularly focusing on the cognitive and emotional engagement of students aged 6-12. The chapter discusses the importance of creating a holistic learning environment that considers the psychological and behavioral aspects of learning, especially in the context of technological transformation. Through a prognostic analysis of student behavior, the chapter emphasizes the need to carefully design educational systems that not only incorporate technological advances but also support the cognitive and emotional development of young learners.

SECTION 4: AI'S ROLE IN TEACHER TRAINING AND LANGUAGE LEARNING

Chapter 10 details a pilot study on the use of AI, specifically chatbots, in higher education. The chapter provides an overview of the background of AI in education and presents the research objectives, questions, and methodology of the study. Through surveys and focus groups, the chapter gathers insights from students and faculty about their experiences with AI, highlighting the need for informed professional development for faculty and ethics training for students. The chapter underscores the importance of preparing both educators and students to navigate the challenges and opportunities presented by AI in higher education.

Chapter 11 explores the role of AI in the acquisition of English as a second language, focusing on its impact on developing listening, writing, reading, and speaking skills among secondary school students in Portugal. The chapter presents findings from an online questionnaire that reveals students' positive perceptions of AI-powered tools for language learning. However, it also notes that students value the empathy and human connection provided by teachers, which AI cannot replicate. The chapter calls for further research into students' perceptions of AI in education, advocating for a balanced approach that integrates AI while maintaining the essential human elements of teaching and learning.

Chapter 12 presents a study on the integration of Artificial Intelligence (AI) in English as a second language (ESL) education in Portugal, highlighting AI's impact on developing key language skills—listening, writing, reading, and speaking. Using data from an online questionnaire targeting secondary school students, the chapter explores students' perspectives on AI-powered tools for learning English and their daily lives. Despite the emerging presence of AI in Portuguese schools, students view these tools positively while acknowledging the irreplaceable role of teachers for their empathy and human connection. The chapter calls for further research into students' perceptions of AI in education.

This book is intended for a diverse audience, including educators, researchers, policymakers, and technology practitioners. Whether you are just beginning to explore the possibilities of AI in education or are already working in this field, we hope this book will serve as a valuable resource that informs and inspires your efforts to enhance teaching practices for future learning.

As editors, we are deeply grateful to the contributors for their rigorous scholarship and innovative thinking. We are also thankful to the many educators, students, and institutions whose experiences and challenges have shaped the discussions in this book. It is our belief that by embracing AI with a thoughtful and critical approach, we can help shape an educational future that is equitable, effective, and enriching for all.

Ricardo Queirós
Polytechnic of Porto, Portugal & CRACS INESC TEC, Portugal

Mário Cruz
Polytechnic of Porto, Portugal & inED, Portugal

Daniela Mascarenhas
School of Education, Polytechnic of Porto, Portugal & inED, Portugal

Chapter 1
AI in Education:
Ethical Challenges and Opportunities

Okechukwu Amah
https://orcid.org/0000-0002-6574-6941
Lagos Business School, Nigeria

Victoria Oluwakemi Okesipe
https://orcid.org/0009-0009-2782-6498
Lagos Business School, Nigeria

ABSTRACT

Educational activities, such as teaching and learning, are inherently knowledge-intensive cognitive processes. AI applications, which are designed for cognition and problem-solving using algorithms and knowledge bases, can effectively support and enhance educators' and learners' abilities in teaching and learning endeavors. This chapter delves into the burgeoning integration of Artificial Intelligence (AI) within the educational sector. We begin by exploring the current applications of AI in various educational segments, highlighting how this technology is transforming the teaching-learning experience. Subsequently, the chapter shows the potential advantages AI offers, from personalized learning to enhanced accessibility. However, discussion progresses by acknowledging the ethical concerns around AI in education. Through an exploratory research approach, drawing on existing literature reviews and supporting publications, the chapter proposes action steps to address these challenges.

INTRODUCTION

Significant technological progress has propelled remarkable advancements within the educational sector, reshaping the landscape of teaching and learning (Baako & Abroampa, 2023). The Educause (2019) Horizon Report outlines several emerging technologies with the potential to shape the future of education. Among these, Artificial Intelligence (AI) stands out as one of the most promising (EDUCAUSE, 2019). As technology evolves Artificial Intelligence (AI) plays an increasingly crucial role in revolutionizing teaching practices and shaping the future of education (Sharma et al., 2019). AI is not only helping to enhance the learning experience, but is also creating a borderless platform for teaching and learning without any geographical barrier (Rudolph et al., 2023). Bozkurt et al. (2021) identified five research themes in their study on artificial intelligence and the educational landscape, one of which focused on the utilization of AI for online learning (Bozkurt et al., 2021). Similarly, AI, with its potential to enhance personalized learning, automate assessments, and provide valuable insights into student behavior offers unprecedented opportunities for educators and learners alike (Akgun & Greenhow, 2022). However, alongside these advancements come concerns regarding privacy, surveillance, bias, and discrimination (Akgun & Greenhow, 2022). This means the integration of AI in education not only promises to enhance learning experiences essentially but also raises important ethical considerations that demand a thorough examination.

This book chapter explores the integration of AI in Education, addressing ethical challenges and opportunities it presents to shape the future of learning. The structure of the book chapter will be as follows: First, we examine the current utilization of AI in Education and explore the segments of Education that employ this technology. Next, we explore the potential advantages AI may offer to the educational sector. Finally, we address the ethical concerns surrounding AI in Education and provide diverse perspectives on potential solutions. This chapter employed a qualitative research approach by reviewing existing literature review and other supporting publications to effectively guide and achieve its purpose.

AI IN EDUCATION, USES AND SEGMENTS OF EDUCATION THAT EMPLOY THIS TECHNOLOGY

The emergence of AI in education has significantly transformed traditional teaching and learning methods, revolutionizing the educational landscape across various segments. Initially, AI technology gained momentum in administrative tasks, such as grading, scheduling, and other time-consuming processes, which helped to reduce the workload on educators or educational administrators. Similarly, Chen et al (2020) examined the impact of Artificial Intelligence on education, focusing on its application and effects in administration, instruction, and learning (Chen et al., 2020; Mon et al., 2023). Another study by Bozkurt et al. (2021) identified five key research themes in AI studies in education, including adaptive learning, deep learning algorithms, human-AI interaction, AI-generated data usage, and AI in higher education, while noting a lack of focus on ethics in AI research (Bozkurt et al., 2021). The advancements and developments, which have led to the development and use of AI, have given the education sector, especially academic institutions, an opportunity to harness and utilize AI (Chen et al., 2020). This success paved the way for more comprehensive integration, with AI now being used to enhance instructional practices, personalized learning experiences, and student support systems. Researchers use AI to conduct experiments, analyze data, and assist in writing research papers before publishing their findings. AI has also been used in many other areas, including translation and language, writing, early childhood education, content creation, and adaptive tutoring systems.

The question, "How is Artificial Intelligence used in Education" remains relevant and demands a careful answer. In this chapter, we will focus more on what AI in Education is, how it is being used in the educational sector, and the segment of educational sector that employ this technology.

AI: Definition and Uses

The term "artificial" in "artificial intelligence" signifies its human-made origin and deliberate design. Unlike naturally occurring phenomena, AI emerges through intentional human creativity and programming, rather than biological or evolutionary processes (Fetzer, 1990). This distinction underscores the departure from the natural order and emphasizes the intentional construction of intelligent systems. In simple terms, Fetzer (1990) explained that 'intelligence' in artificial intelligence (AI) refers to the ability of a system to learn, understand, and solve problems. It encompasses acquiring knowledge, adapting to new situations, and reasoning effectively. When applied to inanimate machines, the concept of intelligence should not be dismissed solely based on their lack of biological origin; it's about their capacity to perform tasks intelligently (Fetzer, 1990). Ertel (2018) mentioned meaningful questions to be asked when trying to understand Artificial Intelligence. "What is intelligence?", "How can one measure intelligence?" or "How does the brain work?" (Ertel, 2018).

John McCarthy, an Emeritus Professor in Stanford University coined the term "AI" in 1955 and defined the goal of AI as to develop machines that behave as though they were intelligent (Mccarthy, 2004; McCarthy et al., 2006; Rainer et al., 2020). Also, Alan Turing made the concept widely known that computing machines might one day be able to think like humans (Turing et al., 2009). He believed that in the future, automated computers would be capable of performing computations that humans couldn't complete effectively. The insufficiency in this definition was addressed in the Encyclopedia Britannica definition. AI is the ability of digital computers or computer-controlled robots to solve problems that are normally associated with the higher intellectual processing capabilities of humans (Encyclopedia Britannica, 1991). This definition led to a dilemma that every computer is an AI system. Elaine Rich then came up with another definition that Artificial Intelligence is the study of how to make computers do things at which, at the moment, people are better (Rich, 1985). Rich's definition summarizes the ongoing work of AI researchers in understanding and developing intelligent systems, a definition that will remain relevant well into the future, such as in 2050. AI often describes machines capable of performing cognitive tasks similar to those of the human mind, like problem-solving and learning (Legg & Hutter, 2007).

Segments of Education that Employ Artificial Intelligence

Artificial Intelligence (AI) has sparked a transformative wave across education, reshaping how we teach and learn in profound ways (Popenici & Kerr, 2017). With its rapid expansion, AI has become a focal point in the educational sector, offering innovative solutions to age-old challenges. The integration of AI technologies into learning and teaching processes is on the rise, with its applications evolving to meet the dynamic needs of educators and learners (Aggarwal, 2023; Luckin & Holmes, 2016; North & Nord, 2018; Siemens & Baker, 2012). AI algorithms and educational robots have become essential components of learning management and training systems, offering assistance for various teaching and learning tasks (Costa et al., 2017; García et al., 2007).

One of the most significant impacts of AI in education is its ability to personalize learning experiences through intelligent tutors. These AI-driven tutors adapt content and pacing to suit each student's unique learning style, fostering engagement and enhancing learning outcomes. According to the Horizon research of 2018, AI applications in education were projected to grow by 43% between 2018 and 2022, indicating a growing recognition of AI's potential in education (North & Nord, 2018). Moreover, AI facilitates collaborative learning experiences by breaking down geographical barriers, allowing students to collaborate on projects and assignments in virtual environments. This fosters communication skills and teamwork, creating a vibrant learning community (North & Nord, 2018).

Another exciting aspect of AI in education is its use of immersive technologies like virtual reality (VR). These intelligent VR environments offer interactive and engaging learning experiences, where students can explore complex concepts in a dynamic and immersive setting. Guided by virtual agents, students can delve into simulations and practical exercises, enhancing their understanding and retention of information (Luckin & Holmes, 2016). Furthermore, AI-powered assessment (González-Calatayud et al., 2021) and feedback systems provide real-time insights into student progress, offering personalized feedback and interventions to support their learning journey ((Perez et al., 2017). By analyzing vast amounts of data, these systems predict learning outcomes and identify areas for improvement, enabling educators to tailor their teaching to meet individual student needs effectively (Perez et al., 2017).

In other words, AI is revolutionizing education by offering innovative tools and methods that cater to the diverse needs of students and educators. Its integration into education is not just a trend but a necessity to keep pace with the demands of the modern world. As AI continues to evolve, its potential to transform education for the better is limitless, promising a future where learning is engaging, and effective for all. It is therefore important to reemphasize that AI is not there to replace teachers or render impotent traditional teaching methodology, it is just an efficiency tool. It is to make education better for kids and then for teachers. AI helps us to rethink our whole education system. Artificial Intelligence in Education (AIED) is being embraced by learners, teachers, and educational institutions. Statistics show that 43% of college students in the US use AI tools like ChatGPT, and half of instructors use AI to develop their lessons.[1] AIED has demonstrated its efficacy and effectiveness, with adaptive learning improving student test results by 62%, and AI usage in general enhancing student performance by 30% and reducing anxiety by 20%.[1] Wang et al. (2024) in their study categorized AIED applications into four main groups, each with its own sub-categories: (1) Adaptive learning and personalized tutoring, (2) Intelligent assessment and management, (3) Profiling and prediction, and (4) Emerging technologies or products. Among these applications, their study showed that adaptive learning and personalized tutoring were the most studied (40% of papers in their sample), followed by intelligent assessment and management (24.8%), profiling and prediction (20%), and emerging products in education (15.2%) (Wang et al., 2024). We therefore discuss the role of AI in Education to learners, educators in the following paragraphs.

Use of AI to Learners

Education is a domain where AI is currently and will continue to have a substantial impact. AI Technology in Education, grants students access to an extensive array of information and educational resources, extending beyond traditional textbooks. Interactive elements within educational technology, such as multimedia content, engage students and create more stimulating learning experiences. Features like gamification, simulations, videos, and interactive tools motivate students to actively participate and immerse themselves in the subject matter. AI can facilitate the growth of critical thinking skills among students by presenting them with challenging problems and supporting them to find creative solutions (Aggarwal, 2023).

Moreover, technology enables personalized learning experiences tailored to each student's strengths, weaknesses, and learning styles. Adaptive learning platforms and AI-driven tools adjust content and pace to suit individual student needs, enhancing comprehension and retention. A good example is Khan Academy which provides Khanmigo, an AI tutor utilizing GPT-4 capabilities, to offers personalized learning assistance and intelligent feedback across multiple subjects such as mathematics, programming, and language learning. Duolingo is an example of a language learning platform that employs AI systems to enhance learner experiences (Bicknell et al., 2023). Additionally, technology fosters seamless collaboration among students, educators, and peers, breaking down geographical barriers. Online discussion forums, video conferencing, and collaborative tools facilitate communication and teamwork skills, enriching the educational experience (Aggarwal, 2023).

In the future, when kids spend time in school, they will focus on exploration, creativity, and communication skills but the major emphasis will be on problem-solving. This is crucial, and at some time we can bring in AI to give a more differentiated and more individualized learning experience. Many Learning Platforms are being developed that are AI-driven, with learning, testing and feedback incorporated. For example, the Math learning app, Thinkster identifies areas students are not good at, where they need support, and the platform suggests exercises and areas the student should concentrate on. Individual student's learning experience is customized. Some of the very basic learning-knowledge transfer that teachers have to do, we can also give some of these to AI. The use of AI will enable us to have universal access to learning. Anywhere in the world, students can have access to quality tutoring through large language modelled products in the world. It has evolved beyond buzzwords.

The global AI market size is around 200 billion dollars in 2023 and is expected to grow well beyond that to over 1.8 trillion U.S. dollars by 2030.[2] Furthermore, the implementation of cognitive computing and customization has enabled the individualization and adaptation of syllabi and materials to cater to the unique needs of learners. This personalized approach has promoted greater engagement, absorption, and an enriched learning environment for students overall (Mon et al., 2023).

Use of AI to Educators/Teachers

AI has huge relevance to teaching-learning practices in general. AI should not be considered as a threat to teachers or educators. AI helps to perform administrative tasks such as enrollment and record-keeping, allowing educators to concentrate more on tasks (like teaching and interacting with students) that provide more value.

Educators have utilized AI tools to improve instructional methods and simplify administrative tasks. AI-powered systems can be used to grade multiple-choice exams, or grader assignments. It can also be used to evaluate students more efficiently and quickly (Mon et al., 2023). Generative AI tools can be used to summarize an entire book, if properly instructed and user is patient to give the best prompts that can produce desired results. AI allows educators to collect and analyze student to improve their performance and engagement. AIED applications are designed to assist in teaching and learning tasks, including content creation and sharing, interactions and collaboration, and performance evaluation (Chassignol et al., 2018; Perrotta & Selwyn, 2020).

Another interesting use of AI is the continuous learning opportunity it offers to educators. Continuous learning, also known as lifelong learning, is the concept of constantly acquiring new knowledge, skills, and competencies throughout one's life. With AI, educators now have powerful tools at their disposal to facilitate and enhance continuous learning experiences for both themselves and their students. One way AI supports continuous learning is through personalized professional development. AI algorithms can analyze educators' strengths, weaknesses, and areas for growth based on various data points, such as teaching evaluations, student performance data, and professional achievements. With this information, AI can recommend tailored learning resources, courses, and workshops to help educators improve their teaching practices and stay updated with the latest pedagogical trends and technologies. Furthermore, AI-powered learning platforms offer adaptive and personalized learning experiences for educators too. These platforms use machine learning algorithms to adjust content, pacing, and assessments based on educators' individual learning styles, preferences, and progress. Whether it's exploring new teaching methodologies, mastering classroom management techniques, or going into educational research, AI ensures that educators receive customized learning experiences that meet their specific needs and interests.

Another intriguing use of AI for continuous learning is in the provision of virtual mentorship and spontaneous help. AI chatbots (Okonkwo & Ade-Ibijola, 2021) and virtual assistants can provide educators with on-demand support, guidance, and resources whenever they need it. These virtual mentors can answer questions, offer advice on classroom challenges, suggest teaching strategies, and even provide feedback on lesson plans and assignments right on demand. By leveraging AI-driven virtual mentorship, educators can access professional support and development opportunities anytime, anywhere, bringing about a culture of continuous improvement and innovation in education.

Moreover, AI facilitates collaborative learning communities among educators. Professional online platforms and social networks powered by AI algorithms such as Linkedin connect educators from around the globe, enabling them to share ideas, resources, best practices, and experiences. Through these virtual communities, educators can engage in discussions, participate in webinars and online workshops, and collaborate on projects and research initiatives. By connecting with peers and experts in their field, educators can broaden their perspectives, expand their knowledge, and stay inspired to continuously enhance their teaching practices.

POTENTIAL ADVANTAGES OF AI IN EDUCATION

The rapid growth of understanding in Artificial Intelligence (AI), spans across multiple disciplines like mathematics, engineering, computer science, philosophy, and linguistics. AI has had a significant impact on various sectors, including education, by addressing issues such as content accessibility and teacher shortages. The emphasizes that the implementation and adoption of AI in education are inevitable, with technologies like smart learning, tutoring systems, social robots, virtual facilitators, online learning environments, learning management systems, and learning analytics being part of this transformation. Additionally, as machines acquire learning capabilities, they may soon become super-intelligent (Okello, 2023).

Studies have found that AI has been extensively adopted in education, evolving from computer technologies to web-based intelligent systems and humanoid robots. These technologies, including web-based chatbots (Okonkwo & Ade-Ibijola, 2021), have enabled instructors to perform administrative functions more effectively and efficiently, such as reviewing and grading assignments, leading to higher teaching quality. Additionally, AI systems have personalized curriculum and content to meet students' needs, enhancing uptake, retention, and overall learning quality (Chen et al., 2020). With ongoing research and innovation, we can anticipate even more exciting advancements in AI, making education more accessible, engaging, and effective for learners around the world. This section discusses some future perspectives of AI in Education as summarized into three major forms: Personalized Learning (Akgun & Greenhow, 2022; Bicknell et al., 2023), Global Connectivity (Rudolph et al., 2023), and Lifelong Learning (Maghsudi et al., 2021) and Reskilling.

In terms of personalized learning: AI-driven learning platforms have the potential to equip educators with data detailing their students' learning preferences, aptitudes, and developmental trajectories, facilitating the customization of teaching approaches to cater to each student's unique needs. Speaking of global connectivity, AI also has the potential to democratize global access to education by breaking down traditional barriers to learning and providing opportunities for individuals from diverse backgrounds to access high-quality educational resources and experiences. Finally, AI has the potential to enhance lifelong learning and reskilling by providing consistent access to personalized learning paths, adaptive learning experiences, micro learning opportunities, skills assessment tools, personalized recommendations, and real-time support. Consequently, individuals can continuously acquire new knowledge and skills throughout their careers, adapt to changing job market demands, and pursue lifelong personal and professional growth. AI can make learning much more of a life-long learning process, across the entire life where we see applications (such as Coursera, edX, etc) offering massive online courses. They are starting to leverage AI in what they do. AI has the real potential to transform teaching practices and make it better for both teachers and learners.

CHALLENGES, ETHICAL CONSIDERATIONS AND WHAT TO DO

While the integration of AI in education has numerous advantages, it also raises ethical concerns, including issues of (data) privacy, bias, surveillance, and discrimination (Akgun & Greenhow, 2022; Boulay, 2022; Wells, 2023). Authors have identified various challenges associated with AI in education. Maghsudi et al. (2021) highlighted technical issues such as content production and recommendation, personal challenges like lifelong learning and assessment, and social concerns such as learning networks and algorithm fairness (Maghsudi et al., 2021). Perrotta and Selwyn (2020) addressed challenges linked to deep learning in education, including data quality, the reductionist nature of deep learning approaches, and integrating educational knowledge into application development (Perrotta & Selwyn, 2020).

The digital divide may be a significant issue, with many individuals lacking access to the internet and modern technology, thus hindering their educational and career opportunities. Bridging this ever-widening gap and ensuring equitable access to educational resources is a pressing challenge for policymakers and educators. It is crucial to strike a balance between harnessing AI's potential and safeguarding our collective personal information and rights. Luckin & Holmes (2016) emphasized the need for partnerships between AI developers, educators, and researchers to create effective AIED applications, stressing the importance of human-centered design and considering stakeholders' motivations, involvement, and expertise (Luckin & Holmes, 2016)

Addressing the ethical complexities inherent in the integration of Artificial Intelligence (AI) into education, prompts the following profound ethical questions; what ethical dilemmas arise from historic biases, sociocultural inequalities, and moral quandaries inherent in AI's use in education (Porayska-Pomsta et al., 2023)? Additionally, how do concerns about privacy breaches and biases in AI, as emphasized by Akgun and Greenhow (2022), affect the ethical landscape of AI in education? Furthermore, how do worries about job loss and the possible reduction of human interaction in education cast shadows over AI's role in learning (Akgun &

Greenhow, 2022)? These questions underscore the need to carefully consider issues like data privacy, address existing disparities in education, and understand how AI might worsen inequalities in learning.

In facilitating actionable insights and strategies for promoting ethical and responsible AI use in education, our book chapter will propose novel answers to the following crucial questions. How can we effectively balance the potential benefits of AI-driven educational technologies with the imperative to protect individuals' privacy and data security? What measures can be implemented to ensure compliance with privacy regulations and standards, thereby safeguarding sensitive personal information collected and utilized by AI systems? Furthermore, how do we navigate the inherent biases present in AI algorithms to promote fairness and inclusivity in educational practices and decision-making processes? It is imperative to advocate for initiatives that mitigate bias and promote equitable access to AI technologies and educational resources for all learners, especially those from marginalized or underserved communities. By demanding robust safeguards for privacy and data security, advocating for fairness and inclusivity, and supporting initiatives that prioritize equitable access, we can foster responsible and effective integration of AI in education, ensuring that its benefits are maximized while mitigating potential ethical pitfalls.

Data Privacy

One of the most important ethical issues surrounding the use of AI in education relates to Data privacy concerns (Regan & Jesse, 2019; Remian, 2019; Stahl & Wright, 2018). While data offers valuable insights that can improve educational experiences, it's crucial to prioritize student privacy (Reidenberg & Schaub, 2018). The sheer volume of data that can be potentially collected by AI systems is astounding. These types of data include personal information, academic records, behavioral and biometric data. For instance, data like names, addresses, and birthdays can be used for identity theft, opening fraudulent accounts, or even financial crimes. Also, Phishing attacks become particularly dangerous when attackers use this information to construct personalized emails or messages that trick students into revealing sensitive information.

In the same way unauthorized access to academic records, which contain sensitive details about a student's performance, behavior, and achievements, can be exploited for malicious purposes. This could lead to unfair treatment, discrimination, or stigmatization based on past performance. Perhaps most concerning is the violation of privacy rights that occurs with unauthorized disclosure, potentially damaging a student's reputation and future opportunities. Case in point is InBloom (Weber, 2016), a company offering a cloud-based platform for storing student data, which faced severe criticism for its data collection practices. InBloom's databases were revealed to contain a vast amount of student data, often exceeding 400 unique pieces of information. This significantly surpassed the traditional data collected in student and administrative records. Parents and educators expressed concerns about the vast amount of student information being collected, including test scores, disciplinary records, and health data. The lack of transparency about how this data would be used and shared with third parties fueled privacy anxieties, ultimately leading to InBloom's demise.

The analysis of behavioral data collected through AI systems also raises significant privacy concerns. This data can be used to create detailed profiles of students' preferences, habits, and interests, which can then be exploited for targeted advertising, selection or content recommendations without their consent. For instance, universities increasingly rely on algorithms to analyze student applications and predict academic success (Reidenberg & Schaub, 2018). However, concerns exist that these algorithms may perpetuate existing biases based on factors like race, socioeconomic background, or zip code. This can disadvantage certain students and raise questions about fairness and equal opportunity in college admissions.

Data Privacy and Security Weaknesses

AI systems in education, powered by student data, raise significant security concerns. These concerns are fueled by potential vulnerabilities that can be exploited through both malicious intent and unintentional missteps. On the malicious side, school databases or the AI systems themselves, can be attacked, using sophisticated techniques to gain unauthorized access. This infiltration could expose valuable student information, including names, addresses, birth dates, grades, and even behavioral data. In the same vein, even personnel with official access to student data can pose a serious threat. An example is the Shine Learning data breach. Where a company that provides online curriculum and assessment tools to schools, experienced a data breach that exposed the personal information of millions of students and teachers. This included names, addresses, phone numbers, and even some Social Security numbers. The breach highlighted the risks associated with third-party vendors who handle student data and the importance of robust data security practices.

Similar threats, whether intentional or accidental, can lead to misuse or sale of student data on the black market. Case in point is a controversy that surrounds Google Apps for Education (Marcinkowski et al., 2020). Many schools and users believed, based on service agreements and statements by Google representatives, that their emails wouldn't be scanned for advertising purposes. However, Google admitted in a lawsuit that it scans all Gmail accounts, including those in educational settings, regardless of a user's advertising preference. This scanning involves analyzing email content (key-word analysis) and combining it with user data from other Google services (aggregation) to potentially target users with ads.

In many cases, the security weaknesses extend beyond the personnel at schools. This is because schools often share student data with third-party vendors who develop or maintain the AI systems. Unclear or poorly defined legal contracts with these vendors can leave student data vulnerable if these third-parties lack robust security protocols. Moreover, the potential for secondary use of data creates a significant privacy concern. Data collected for educational purposes could be repurposed for targeted advertising, profiling, or even credit scoring without students or their families ever being informed or offering consent. For example, a school district in Georgia installed cameras on school buses to monitor student behavior. However, it was later discovered that the cameras were also capturing footage of students' homes along the bus routes. This raised concerns about privacy violations and potential for misuse of student data collected outside of school grounds.

Bias and Fairness

Data-driven algorithms in general, learn biases from the data they're trained on (Hrastinski et al., 2019). This can lead to unfair treatment, like favoring certain groups over others. It can also happen because the data used to train the AI might not include enough information about certain groups of people. This can mean unfair results for people who aren't well-represented in the data. Biased algorithms can perpetuate stereotypes, discriminate against certain groups, and reinforce systemic disparities in educational opportunities and outcomes. However, studies on the effects of educational technology on student learning are inconclusive, with some showing a potential for widening achievement gaps (Boser, 2013; Warschauer et al., 2004) while others show the opposite (Kizilcec et al., 2020; Roschelle et al., 2016; Theobald et al., 2020).

Types of Bias: Data Bias

There are different types of bias in data driven AI algorithms. For this discussion we will first be looking at biases in data. These biases are the measurement, omitted-variables, representation and aggregation biases. Measurement bias occurs when the data collection or interpretation of data is flawed (Harini Suresh & John V. Guttag., 2019). Case in point is when standardized tests are culturally biased, favoring students from certain backgrounds familiar with the test format and question styles. This could lead to the AI underestimating the abilities of students from different backgrounds and recommending learning paths that are not challenging enough. An example of this is asking students with Middle Eastern backgrounds questions that require a contextual understanding of snow.

Another type of Bias is the Omitted Variable Bias. This occurs when important factors influencing the outcome of the algorithmic process are left out of the analysis (David B. Mustard., 2003; Kevin A. Clarke., 2005; Stephanie K. Riegg., 2008). For example, imagine an AI designed to predict student success in a specific online course. It considers variables like past grades in similar subjects, prior performance on online learning platforms, and study time reported by students. The AI might miss crucial variables like a student's access to reliable internet and a quiet study environment at home. These two important variables may cause a capable student to struggle with the online course even if they have the academic background to succeed. The AI could misjudge these student's' potential, flagging them as at risk of failure despite their capabilities.

Next, we have representation bias. Representation bias arises from improper sampling from a population during data collection process. Non-representative samples distort the diversity of the population, with missing subgroups and other anomalies. In 2019, a study showed that facial recognition software from major tech companies had significantly higher error rates when identifying people of color compared to white people (Udefi et al., 2023). This bias stemmed from the datasets used to train the software, which were found to be predominantly composed of images of white individuals (Xi Yin et al., 2019).

Aggregation bias, also known as the ecological fallacy, occurs when incorrect assumptions about individuals are based solely on data about the entire population (Harini Suresh & John V. Guttag., 2019). For instance, an AI system analyzing historical data might correlate a specific learning style (e.g., visual aids) with high test scores in a particular subject (e.g., mathematics) across the student population. This could lead to the assumption that all struggling mathematics students benefit from visual materials, neglecting individual learning styles within subgroups. Students who learn best through auditory explanations or hands-on activities might consistently be recommended the wrong materials, hindering their progress. To mitigate this bias, educational AI systems should incorporate data beyond average scores, such as student preferences and past performance in different learning formats, while remaining cautious about generalizing population patterns to specific subgroups without additional evidence.

Two other biases namely the longitudinal data fallacy and the linking bias also exist (Alexandra Olteanu et al., 2019; Samuel Barbosa et al., 2016). The two biases that can arise when analyzing data over time or through connections. Longitudinal data fallacy occurs when researchers use a single snapshot (cross-sectional analysis) of a changing population, leading to misleading conclusions. Linking bias appears in network analysis when user connections (e.g., friendships) don't accurately reflect actual user behavior. This can be caused by factors like how the network is sampled and how connections are defined.

Types of Bias: Algorithmic Bias

Unlike data bias, where prejudice is present in the information used to train the system, algorithmic bias arises from the design choices made by designers of AI systems (Azadeh Nematzadeh et al., 2017; Batya Friedman & Helen Nissenbaum, 1996; David Danks & Alex John London, 2017; Introna L. & Nissenbaum, 2000; Ricardo Baeza-Yates., 2018). These choices can introduce unfairness into the algorithm. One way this can happen is through the specific design choices made in the creation of the AI algorithm. The optimization functions used, how the algorithm handles different data groups, and the selection of statistical tools can all influence how the algorithm makes decisions. For instance, an algorithm designed to predict loan eligibility might be biased against applicants from certain neighborhoods if the developers focused heavily on factors like the cost of living in different areas and not the actual income of the applicants.

Another source of algorithmic bias is user interaction. This can be caused by two factors: the user interface itself and user behavior. A poorly designed interface might nudge users towards certain choices, while a user's own pre-existing biases can influence their interactions with the system. For example, search engines often display results with higher click-through rates at the top. This can create a situation where users only see a limited range of information, even if more relevant results exist lower in the rankings. Similarly, a user with a bias against a particular group might be more likely to interact with negative information about that group when presented with a neutral search result.

Algorithmic bias can also emerge over time as users interact with the system. As user demographics, cultural values, and societal norms evolve, the system's behavior can start to reflect these changes in unintended ways. This can lead to the system reinforcing existing biases or becoming less effective for certain user groups. Finally, bias can also be introduced during the evaluation process. If the benchmarks used to assess an AI system are themselves flawed or biased, the evaluation won't accurately reflect the system's true performance in the real world. For instance, a facial recognition system might be evaluated on a dataset with a limited range of skin tones and genders. This could lead to the system performing poorly when used in a more diverse population.

Types of Bias: User-Generated Bias

While data bias, inherent in the training data itself, has received significant attention, user-generated bias arises from a complex interplay between user behavior and the design of AI algorithms. User-generated bias, has the potential to perpetuate inequalities and distort algorithmic outputs. One prominent form of user-generated bias is called historical bias (Harini Suresh & John V. Guttag., 2019). Even with ideal sampling techniques, societal inequalities can become embedded in the data generated by users. For instance, a search engine query for "female CEOs" might predominantly yield images of men, reflecting the underrepresentation of women in leadership positions. This raises a critical question: Should algorithms simply mirror reality, even if it perpetuates stereotypes, or should they strive to present a more balanced view?

Another type of user-generated bias is the population bias that arises when the user demographics of a platform deviate significantly from the intended target population (Alexandra Olteanu et al., 2019). AI-powered assessment tools can be susceptible to population bias if the data used to develop them reflects existing stereotypes. For instance, an AI system biased towards a certain writing style might unfairly penalize students from cultural backgrounds that use different writing conventions. This can lead to inaccurate assessments and discourage students from diverse backgrounds.

Self-selection bias, a well-established concept in research methodology, also manifests in the AI algorithms. Consider an online poll measuring political candidate support – individuals most passionate about a particular candidate are more likely to participate, skewing the results towards the more vocal supporters. Similarly, user reviews and ratings on online platforms can be susceptible to self-selection bias, as users with strong opinions (positive or negative) are more likely to leave feedback. Beyond individual user behavior, social bias also plays a role. Our judgments can be influenced by the actions of others. For instance, encountering a plethora of positive reviews for a product might lead us to hesitate to leave a negative review, even if it reflects our genuine experience. This herd mentality can distort user-generated data and subsequently influence algorithmic outputs.

Furthermore, behavioral bias arises from the diverse ways users interact with different platforms and contexts. A simple example lies in emoji usage, which can vary significantly across platforms. Misinterpretations and communication errors can arise due to these discrepancies, leading to biased data collection. Temporal bias, another facet of user-generated bias, considers how user behavior and demographics evolve over time. The use of hashtags on social media platforms exemplifies this concept – a hashtag might initially be used to garner attention for a specific event, but its use might continue within discussions long after the initial event itself. This temporal shift can introduce inconsistencies in user-generated data.

Finally, content production bias stems from the inherent differences in the way users generate content. Studies have shown variations in language use across genders and age groups. These linguistic nuances can lead to biases in how algorithms interpret user-generated content. The intricate nature of user-generated bias necessitates a multi-pronged approach for mitigation. Employing diverse datasets during algorithm development and evaluation is crucial to ensure that algorithms are not simply reflecting the biases present in the user base. Additionally, platform design can play a vital role in mitigating bias. For instance, interfaces can be designed to minimize the influence of social bias by anonymizing user reviews or ratings.

AI Surveillance

Despite the benefits of Artificial Intelligence in education, there lurks significant ethical concerns, particularly regarding AI-powered surveillance systems that gather detailed student and teacher data. (Jiang, 2019) asserts that the pervasive nature of surveillance poses significant concerns about the privacy of both teachers and learners. This section delves into the potential pitfalls of such systems, exploring issues of privacy, autonomy, and the perpetuation of social biases.

One major concern lies in the sheer volume of data these systems collect. AI tracking goes beyond mere monitoring of activities; it utilizes algorithms and machine-learning models to analyze student actions, preferences, and even predict future behaviors and learning patterns. This raises a red flag: how can students feel safe and empowered to learn if they know their every move is being scrutinized by AI (Jiang, 2019)? Case in point is the 2020 student facial recognition controversy in Illinois. This case involved a suburban Chicago school district piloting the use of facial recognition technology to identify students entering and exiting lunchrooms. The program sparked significant privacy concerns from parents and advocates who worried about the potential for misuse and the lack of transparency about how the data would be stored and secured. While the pilot program was ultimately scrapped, it highlights the growing debate surrounding the use of biometric data in educational settings.

Consider the parallel with teachers who utilize social networking platforms for educational purposes. Research highlights concerns surrounding privacy boundaries, student-teacher relationships, and the teacher's responsibility to be constantly available online. While monitoring student activity online can be a tool to intervene in cyberbullying or exposure to inappropriate content, it can also morph into a form of intrusive surveillance that undermines student privacy. The constant tracking of online conversations and actions can stifle student participation and discourage them from taking ownership of their ideas. An environment of fear and suspicion hardly fosters a thriving learning space.

Furthermore, these AI-powered surveillance systems threaten student and teacher autonomy, the ability to act independently based on their own values and interests. Predictive algorithms can limit this autonomy by dictating future trajectories based on collected data. When algorithms predict individual actions based on pre-existing information, questions arise about fairness and the freedom to forge one's own path.

The potential for perpetuating existing social biases further complicates the picture. Biases inherent in the data used to train these algorithms can lead to discriminatory outcomes, reinforcing social stratification and marginalizing certain student groups. For instance, an AI system designed to identify students at risk of academic failure might disproportionately flag students from low-income backgrounds, perpetuating pre-existing inequalities.

In conclusion, the use of AI-powered surveillance systems in education raises serious ethical concerns. The potential violation of student and teacher privacy, the curtailing of autonomy, and the risk of reinforcing social biases demand careful consideration. As we move forward with AI in education, it is crucial to prioritize transparency, develop clear data protection protocols, and ensure that AI serves to empower students and teachers, not surveil and control them.

AI Discrimination in Education

Discrimination can be defined as any unfavorable treatment based on features like race, ethnicity, gender, or color that hinders equality in educational opportunities. As mentioned earlier, one of the primary concerns lies in the data used to train AI algorithms. Datasets often reflect the biases present in society, leading to discriminatory outcomes. For instance, an AI system designed to identify students at risk of dropping out might rely heavily on data points like socioeconomic background and standardized test scores. This system could disproportionately flag students from low-income families or minority backgrounds, perpetuating the myth that these groups are inherently less academically capable.

Furthermore, AI-powered educational platforms that personalize instruction based on student performance can worsen existing inequalities. Imagine an AI system that adjusts difficulty levels and learning materials based on a student's past answers. If a student from a historically underserved community has consistently received a subpar education, the AI might place them on a lower learning track, hindering their potential for growth. This creates a self-fulfilling prophecy, where the AI reinforces the very inequalities it was supposed to address.

Another area of concern is facial recognition technology, used in some AI-powered classrooms to monitor student engagement (Zhang et al., 2021; Zhao, 2021). Studies have shown that facial recognition algorithms have higher error rates when identifying people of color (Udefi et al., 2023). In an educational setting, this could lead to students from these backgrounds being misidentified as disengaged or distracted, potentially leading to unfair disciplinary actions.

An interesting perspective to the issue of discrimination is that AI can't eliminate pre-existing teacher biases. If a teacher consciously or unconsciously favors certain students, the AI might pick up on those cues and amplify them in its recommendations or feedback.

Advice to Policymakers and AI Researchers

While AI holds immense promise for education, ethical considerations must be addressed to ensure its responsible and fair implementation. Policymakers can play a crucial role by establishing clear data privacy guidelines, promoting transparency in AI decision-making, and prioritizing equity throughout the development process. Funding research into bias detection and mitigation techniques for educational AI is also vital. Additionally, supporting teacher training on the ethical implications of AI empowers educators to navigate this new landscape effectively.

For AI researchers, the focus should lie on utilizing diverse datasets that accurately represent student populations. Developing explainable AI techniques that promote transparency in decision-making is also crucial. Collaboration with educators throughout the design and development process ensures AI systems align with pedagogical best practices and meet the needs of the classroom. Also, conducting ethical impact assessments before deployment is important in identifying potential risks for bias, discrimination, and student privacy. Finally, fostering open access to research findings and promoting collaboration between researchers will accelerate the development of ethical and responsible AI for the future of education.

CONCLUSION

This book chapter has examined artificial intelligence in education by addressing challenges and ethical considerations to promote responsible and effective integration of AI. This was done with the aim of enhancing teaching-learning processes and educational experiences for all stakeholders involved in the education process. Overall, AI has revolutionized research in the educational sector by accelerating the pace of discovery, improving research quality, and making the research process more efficient and accessible. Moreover, in the realm of education, AI's impact has been profound. Integration of AI with education has led to adaptive learning, a personalized approach that tailors instruction, content, and assessment to individual students' needs. By harnessing AI, adaptive learning platforms offer personalized learning experiences, keeping students engaged, motivated, and empowered in their learning journey. However, the successful integration of AI in education requires addressing challenges and ethical considerations. Educators and stakeholders must ensure the quality of AI algorithms and design of learning materials while maintaining human involvement to provide guidance and insights. Ethical concerns such as privacy, surveillance, and discrimination must also be taken into account. Designers must check existing data, algorithms and user-generated data for Bias on a regular basis. By doing so, we can responsibly harness AI's potential to revolutionize education, offering inclusive and effective learning experiences for all.

REFERENCES

Aggarwal, D. (2023). Integration of Innovative Technological Developments and AI with Education for an Adaptive Learning Pedagogy. *China Petroleum Processing and Petrochemical Technology Catalyst Research*, 23(2), 709–714. DOI: 10.5281/zenodo.7778371

Akgun, S., & Greenhow, C. (2022). Artificial intelligence in education: Addressing ethical challenges in K-12 settings. *AI and Ethics*, 2(3), 431–440. DOI: 10.1007/s43681-021-00096-7 PMID: 34790956

Baako, I., & Abroampa, W. K. (2023). Research trends on ICT integration in Education: A bibliometric analysis. In *Cogent Education* (Vol. 10, Issue 2). Taylor and Francis Ltd. DOI: 10.1080/2331186X.2023.2281162

Barbosa, S., Cosley, D., Sharma, A., & Cesar Jr, Roberto M. (2016). Averaging gone wrong: Using time-aware analyses to better understand behavior. *InProceedings of the 25th International Conference on World Wide Web*. 829–841. DOI: 10.1145/2872427.2883083

Bicknell, K., Brust, C., Settles, B., Svrcek, M., & Brock, D. C. (2023). How Duolingo's AI learns what you need to learn. *Accessed*, (Apr), 25.

Boser, U. (2013). *Are Schools Getting a Big Enough Bang for Their Education Technology Buck?* Center for American Progress.

Boulay, B. (2022). Artificial Intelligence in Education and Ethics. In *Handbook of Open, Distance and Digital Education* (pp. 1–16). Springer Nature Singapore. DOI: 10.1007/978-981-19-0351-9_6-2

Bozkurt, A., Karadeniz, A., Baneres, D., Guerrero-Roldán, A. E., & Rodríguez, M. E. (2021). Artificial intelligence and reflections from educational landscape: A review of AI studies in half a century. *Sustainability (Basel)*, 13(2), 1–16. DOI: 10.3390/su13020800

Chassignol, M., Khoroshavin, A., Klimova, A., & Bilyatdinova, A. (2018). Artificial Intelligence trends in education: A narrative overview. *Procedia Computer Science*, 136, 16–24. DOI: 10.1016/j.procs.2018.08.233

Chen, L., Chen, P., & Lin, Z. (2020). Artificial Intelligence in Education: A Review. *IEEE Access : Practical Innovations, Open Solutions*, 8, 75264–75278. DOI: 10.1109/ACCESS.2020.2988510

Clarke, K. A. (2005). The phantom menace: Omitted variable bias in econometric research. *Conflict Management and Peace Science*, 22(4), 341–352. DOI: 10.1080/07388940500339183

Costa, E. B., Fonseca, B., Santana, M. A., de Araújo, F. F., & Rego, J. (2017). Evaluating the effectiveness of educational data mining techniques for early prediction of students' academic failure in introductory programming courses. *Computers in Human Behavior*, 73, 247–256. DOI: 10.1016/j.chb.2017.01.047

Danks, D., & London, A. J. (2017). Algorithmic bias in autonomous systems. *In Proceedings of the International Joint Conference on Artificial Intelligence.*, 4691–4697.

EDUCAUSE. (2019). *EDUCAUSE Horizon Report 2019: Higher Education Edition*.

Encyclopedia Britannica. (1991). *Encyclopedia Britannica Verlag*.

Ertel, W. (2018). *Introduction to Artificial Intelligence*. Springer.

Fetzer, J. H. (1990). What is artificial intelligence? *In: Artificial Intelligence: Its Scope and Limits*. (Vol. 4). Studies in Cognitive Systems, Springer, Dordrecht. https://doi.org/https://doi.org/10.1007/978-94-009-1900-6_1

Friedman, B., & Nissenbaum, H. (1996). Bias in computer systems. *ACM Trans. Inf. Syst. 14, 3 (July 1996), (pp.330–347). DOI:*Https://Doi.Org/10.1145/230538.230561

García, P., Amandi, A., Schiaffino, S., & Campo, M. (2007). Evaluating Bayesian networks' precision for detecting students' learning styles. *Computers & Education*, 49(3), 794–808. DOI: 10.1016/j.compedu.2005.11.017

González-Calatayud, V., Prendes-Espinosa, P., Roig-Vila, R., & Carpanzano, E. (2021). applied sciences Review Artificial Intelligence for Student Assessment: A Systematic Review. *Applied Sciences (Basel, Switzerland)*, 5467. Advance online publication. DOI: 10.3390/app

Hrastinski, S., Olofsson, A. D., Arkenback, C., Ekström, S., Ericsson, E., Fransson, G., Jaldemark, J., Ryberg, T., Öberg, L.-M., Fuentes, A., Gustafsson, U., Humble, N., Mozelius, P., Sundgren, M., & Utterberg, M. (2019). Critical imaginaries and reflections on artificial intelligence and robots in postdigital K-12 education. *Postdigital Science and Education*, 1(2), 427–445. DOI: 10.1007/s42438-019-00046-x

Introna, L., & Nissenbaum, H. (2000). Defining the Web: The politics of search engines. *Computer 33, 1 (Jan. 2000), (pp.54–62). DOI:*Https://Doi.Org/10.1109/2.816269

Jiang, S. (2019). Rejecting surveillance cameras on campus. *Teachers'. Perspectives*, 2019(12), 2.

Kizilcec, R. F., Reich, J., Yeomans, M., Dann, C., Brunskill, E., Lopez, G., & Tingley, D. (2020). Scaling up behavioral science interventions in online education. *Proceedings of the National Academy of Sciences of the United States of America*, 117(26), 14900–14905. DOI: 10.1073/pnas.1921417117 PMID: 32541050

Legg, S., & Hutter, M. (2007). A collection of definitions of intelligence. *Frontiers in Artificial Intelligence and applications* (Vol. 157).

Luckin, R., & Holmes, W. (2016). Intelligence unleashed: An argument for AI in education.

Maghsudi, S., Lan, A., Xu, J., & van Der Schaar, M. (2021). Personalized education in the artificial intelligence era: What to expect next. *IEEE Signal Processing Magazine*, 38(3), 37–50. DOI: 10.1109/MSP.2021.3055032

Marcinkowski, F., Kieslich, K., Starke, C., & Lünich, M. (2020). Implications of AI (un-) fairness in higher education admissions: the effects of perceived AI (un-) fairness on exit, voice and organizational reputation. *InProceedings of the 2020 Conference on Fairness, Accountability, and Transparency*, 122–130. DOI: 10.1145/3351095.3372867

Mccarthy, J. (2004). WHAT IS ARTIFICIAL INTELLIGENCE? http://www-formal.stanford.edu/jmc/

McCarthy, J., Minsky, M. L., Rochester, N., & Shannon, C. E. (2006). A Proposal for the Dartmouth Summer Research Project on Artificial Intelligence.

Mon, B. F., Wasfi, A., Hayajneh, M., & Slim, A. (2023). A Study on Role of Artificial Intelligence in Education. *In2023 International Conference on Computing, Electronics & Communications Engineering (ICCECE)*IEEE., (pp.133–138). DOI: 10.1109/iCCECE59400.2023.10238613

Mustard, D. B. (2003). Reexamining criminal behavior: The importance of omitted variable bias. *The Review of Economics and Statistics*, 85(1), 205–211. DOI: 10.1162/rest.2003.85.1.205

Nematzadeh, A., Ciampaglia, G. L., Menczer, F., & Flammini, A. (2017). How algorithmic popularity bias hinders or promotes quality. *ArXiv Preprint ArXiv:1707.00574(2017)*.

North, C., & Nord, C. (2018). *Ten facts about artificial intelligence in teaching and learning*. University of California.

Okello, I. (2023). Analyzing the Impacts of Artificial Intelligence on Education. *IAA Journal of Education*, 9(3), 8–13. DOI: 10.59298/IAAJE/2023/2.10.1000

Okonkwo, C. W., & Ade-Ibijola, A. (2021). Chatbots applications in education: A systematic review. *Computers and Education: Artificial Intelligence,*.

Olteanu, A., Castillo, C., Diaz, F., & Kıcıman, E. (2019). Social data: Biases, methodological pitfalls, and ethical boundaries. *Frontiers in Big Data*, 2, 13. DOI: 10.3389/fdata.2019.00013 PMID: 33693336

Perez, S., Massey-Allard, J., Butler, D., Ives, J., Bonn, D., Yee, N., & Roll, I. (2017). Identifying productive inquiry in virtual labs using sequence mining. In *Artificial Intelligence in Education: 18th International Conference, AIED 2017*, Wuhan, China, June 28–July 1, 2017, Proceedings 18. Springer International Publishing., (pp.287–298). DOI: 10.1007/978-3-319-61425-0_24

Perrotta, C., & Selwyn, N. (2020). Deep learning goes to school: Toward a relational understanding of AI in education. *Learning, Media and Technology*, 45(3), 251–269. DOI: 10.1080/17439884.2020.1686017

Popenici, S. A. D., & Kerr, S. (2017). Exploring the impact of artificial intelligence on teaching and learning in higher education. *Research and Practice in Technology Enhanced Learning*, 12(1), 22. Advance online publication. DOI: 10.1186/s41039-017-0062-8 PMID: 30595727

Porayska-Pomsta, K., Holmes, W., & Nemorin, S. (2023). The ethics of AI in education. In *Handbook of Artificial Intelligence in Education*. Edward Elgar Publishing. DOI: 10.4337/9781800375413.00038

Rainer, R. K., Prince, B., Sánchez-Rodríguez, C., Splettstoesser-Hogeterp, I., & Ebrahimi, S. (2020). *Introduction to information systems*. John Wiley & Sons.

Regan, P. M., & Jesse, J. (2019). Ethical challenges of edtech, big data and personalized learning: Twenty-first century student sorting and tracking. *Ethics and Information Technology*, 21(3), 167–179. DOI: 10.1007/s10676-018-9492-2

Reidenberg, J. R., & Schaub, F. (2018). Achieving big data privacy in education. *Theory and Research in Education*, 16(3), 263–279. DOI: 10.1177/1477878518805308

Remian, D. (2019). Augmenting education: ethical considerations for incorporating artificial intelligence in education.

Baeza-Yates, Ricardo . (2018). Bias on the web. *Commun.* ACM 61, 6 (May 2018), (pp.54–61). DOI:Https://Doi.Org/10.1145/3209581

Rich, E. (1985). *Artificial Intelligence and the Humanities* (Vol. 19, Issue 2).

Riegg, S. K. (2008). Causal inference and omitted variable bias in financial aid research: Assessing solutions. *Review of Higher Education*, 31(3), 329–354. DOI: 10.1353/rhe.2008.0010

Roschelle, J., Feng, M., Murphy, R. F., & Mason, C. A. (2016). Online mathematics homework increases student achievement. *AERA Open*, 2(4), 2332858416673968. DOI: 10.1177/2332858416673968

Rudolph, J., Tan, S., & Tan, S. (2023). ChatGPT: Bullshit spewer or the end of traditional assessments in higher education? *Journal of Applied Learning and Teaching*, 6(1), 342–363. DOI: 10.37074/jalt.2023.6.1.9

Sharma, R. C., Kawachi, P., & Bozkurt, A. (2019). The landscape of artificial intelligence in open, online and distance education: Promises and concerns. *Asian Journal of Distance Education*, 14(2), 1–2.

Siemens, G., & Baker, R. S. D. (2012). Learning analytics and educational data mining: towards communication and collaboration. *InProceedings of the 2nd International Conference on Learning Analytics and Knowledge*, 252–254. DOI: 10.1145/2330601.2330661

Stahl, B. C., & Wright, D. (2018). Ethics and privacy in AI and big data: Implementing responsible research and innovation. *IEEE Security and Privacy*, 16(3), 26–33. DOI: 10.1109/MSP.2018.2701164

Suresh, H., & Guttag, J. V. (2019). A framework for understanding unintended consequences of machine learning. *ArXiv Preprint ArXiv:1901.10002(2019)*.

Theobald, E. J., Hill, M. J., Tran, E., Agrawal, S., Arroyo, E. N., Behling, S., Chambwe, N., Cintrón, D. L., Cooper, J. D., Dunster, G., Grummer, J. A., Hennessey, K., Hsiao, J., Iranon, N., Jones, L.II, Jordt, H., Keller, M., Lacey, M. E., Littlefield, C. E., & Freeman, S. (2020). Active learning narrows achievement gaps for underrepresented students in undergraduate science, technology, engineering, and math. *Proceedings of the National Academy of Sciences of the United States of America*, 117(12), 6476–6483. DOI: 10.1073/pnas.1916903117 PMID: 32152114

Turing, A. M., Ford, K., Glymour, C., & Hayes, P. (2009). *Computing Machinery and Intelligence*. Springer Netherlands. DOI: 10.1007/978-1-4020-6710-5_3

Udefi, A. M., Aina, S., Lawal, A. R., & Oluwarantie, A. I. (2023). An Analysis of Bias in Facial Image Processing: A Review of Datasets. *International Journal of Advanced Computer Science and Applications*, 14(5). Advance online publication. DOI: 10.14569/IJACSA.2023.0140593

Wang, S., Wang, F., Zhu, Z., Wang, J., Tran, T., & Du, Z. (2024). Artificial intelligence in education: A systematic literature review. *Expert Systems with Applications*, 252, 124167. DOI: 10.1016/j.eswa.2024.124167

Warschauer, M., Knobel, M., & Stone, L. (2004). Technology and equity in schooling: Deconstructing the digital divide. *Educational Policy*, 18(4), 562–588. DOI: 10.1177/0895904804266469

Weber, A. S. (2016). The big student big data grab. *International Journal of Information and Education Technology (IJIET)*, 6(1), 65–70. DOI: 10.7763/IJIET.2016.V6.660

Wells, R. E. (2023). Strong AI vs. weak AI: What's the difference? Strong AI can do anything a human can do, while weak AI is limited to a specific task. LifeWire. *Retrieved August 22, 2023 from*Https://Www.Lifewire.Com/Strong-Ai-vs-Weak-Ai-7508012

Yin, X., Yu, X., Sohn, Kihyuk, Liu, Xiaoming, & Chandraker, Manmohan. (2019). Feature transfer learning for face recognition with under-represented data. *InIEEE Conference on Computer Vision and Pattern Recognition (CVPR)*, 2019. *2, 3*. DOI: 10.1109/CVPR.2019.00585

Zhang, Y., Qiu, C., Zhong, N., Su, X., Zhang, X., Huang, F., & Wang, L. (2021). AI education based on evaluating concentration of students in class: Using machine vision to recognize students' classroom behaviour. *InProceedings of the 2021 5th International Conference on Video and Image Processing*, 126–133. DOI: 10.1145/3511176.3511196

Zhao, S. (2021). Facial recognition in educational context. *In2021 International Conference on Public Relations and Social Sciences (ICPRSS 2021)(Pp. 10-17)*. Atlantis Press.

ENDNOTES

[1] *Business Solution : Best Online Business Tips and Strategies*. (2023, July 16). businesssolution.org. https://businessolution.org/ai-in-education-statistics/ https://businessolution.org/ai-in-education-statistics/

[2] Artificial Intelligence - Global | Statista Market Forecast. (n.d.). Statista. https://www.statista.com/outlook/tmo/artificial-intelligence/worldwide

Chapter 2
Investigation of Primary School Teacher's Attitudes Towards Artificial Intelligence

Ali Mazı
https://orcid.org/0000-0001-9188-8583
Ministry of National Education, Turkey

ABSTRACT

This research aims to ascertain primary school teachers' attitudes towards artificial intelligence (AI) in the direction of age, gender, computer skills, utilization of AI programs and using AI in lessons. The study employed the survey model. The research group is comprised of 200 primary school teachers in capitol city (Ankara) of Turkey. In the collection of the data, the "General Attitudes towards Artificial Intelligence Scale" (GAAIS) was used. ANOVA and independent samples t-test were employed at the examination of the collected data. The research conclusions showed that the primary school teachers' attitudes towards AI varied significantly depending on age, gender, computer skills, utilization of AI programs and using AI in lessons. The use of the same scale in different groups can provide better insights into attitudes towards AI.

INTRODUCTION

The advent of new technologies has led to the integration of artificial intelligence (AI) into our daily lives since 1956 (Grzybowski, Pawlikowska–Łagód & Lambert, 2024). AI is defined as a machine that processes information (Ma & Sun, 2020), using

DOI: 10.4018/979-8-3693-3944-2.ch002

Copyright © 2025, IGI Global. Copying or distributing in print or electronic forms without written permission of IGI Global is prohibited.

the characteristics attributed to humans (Triguero et al., 2024), to fulfil its task by following logical processes such as understanding the problem, producing solutions (Nishant, Schneckenberg & Ravishankar, 2024), reaching the result and generalizing this result and making inferences from past experiences (Nabiyev, 2012). The goal of AI is to create a theory that computer-assisted replicates the conscious behaviors of living beings in nature (Charniak & McDermot, 1985). The accomplishment of a task by AI is underpinned by the learning ability possessed by living beings. Just as living things cannot do a job without learning it, the working logic of AI also involves learning that job (Spector & Ma, 2019). The most important contribution of AI is its ability to apply what it has learned in the most accurate way and very quickly (Öztürk & Şahin, 2018).

Many countries support the utilization of AI by including it in their education policies (Dahri et al., 2024; Fatima, Desouza & Dawson, 2020; Galindo-Domínguez et al., 2024; Mannuru et al., 2024). However, in the "European Union AI Regulation Proposal" (2021), it is stated that AI is considered a clear and serious threat to people's rights, with individual security being the most important problem. Since countries' use of AI in the social field poses a very high level of risk, it is predicted that the use of such applications will be banned or subjected to serious sanctions (Neuwirth, 2024). Infrastructure, health, basic public services, judicial law enforcement services and judicial proceedings, immigration, employment and education are among the areas with high risk (Singil, 2022). In the field of education, while the potential for personalized learning experiences and data-driven feedback is considerable, there are also a number of risks involved (Wu, Duan & Mi, 2024). Firstly, the collection and processing of student data gives rise to significant concerns pertaining to privacy and data security (Bukar et al., 2024). In particular, the risk of misuse or unauthorized access to personal and academic information necessitates the rigorous implementation of data protection protocols (Vaza, et al., 2024). Furthermore, the vulnerability of AI algorithms to biases and systematic errors gives rise to injustices in education and errors in performance assessments (Tejani, et al., 2024). This situation is of paramount importance in terms of ensuring fair assessment and support of students

When employment and education, which are areas involving high risk, are investigated together, it can be seen that the effectiveness of AI-driven computers and machines in work environments has led to reduced demand for human physical labor (Gunay & Sisman, 2019). However, there is a need to train qualified human resources that can use AI systems (Aguinis, Beltran & Cope, 2024; Chowdhury et al., 2024). As AI applications develop, various changes are becoming apparent in the qualities of individuals produced by educational systems (Demir, 2019). The integration of AI applications into society and the business world impacts the entire population, from the education system to the business sector (Coskun & Gulleroglu, 2021). It is seen that scientists are very interested in this subject and are trying to explore its areas of use in education (Russel & Norvig, 2010; Bostrom & Yudkowsky, 2014; Müller, 2016; Stefan & Sharon, 2017; Popenici & Kerr, 2017; Khare, Stewarti & Khare, 2018; Tasci & Celebi, 2020).

The advent of new educational paradigms has led to a corresponding evolution in human characteristics (Xu, Gao & Ge, 2024). In order to align with the objectives and operational dynamics of contemporary education, educators of the future are expected to possess the capacity to leverage AI applications within the context of an evolving educational landscape (Demir, 2019). In this connection, the problem statement of the current research is "What are primary school teachers' attitudes towards AI?" the sub-problem of the research is "Do primary school teachers' attitudes towards AI vary significantly by gender, age, computer skills, utilization of AI programs and using AI in lessons?" Determining primary school teachers' opinions about AI usage is expected to add to the body of knowledge by enabling education policymakers to assess the outcomes of the educational system.

BACKGROUND

The acceleration of scientific and technological progress has a profound impact on educational and social systems (Akaev & Rudskoi, 2017; Ayeni et al., 2024). Information and technology play a pivotal role in the advancement of the educational process, while also contributing to the dynamism of the economy (Usman, et al., 2024; Ximei, et al., 2024). The rapid evolution of information technology has led to profound changes in social structures and the emergence of information societies (Volti & Croissant, 2024). In addition to monitoring the developments in science and technology that affect social order, it has become imperative to adapt these developments to the social sphere (Gurol, 1990). Another factor affecting social life is the rapid increase in the number of students (Marais, 2016). This situation has made it necessary to change the educational process and quality, and to integrate information technologies into educational environments (Keles, 2007).

The societal changes that have occurred have led to a decline in the quality of education as a result of the increase in the number of students included in the education system and the increase in the number of students per teacher (Koc & Celik, 2015). In addition to the emerging teacher shortage, the content that needs to be taught to students has become more complex as a result of the rapid development of information and technology (Barbour & Hodges 2024). Despite the existence of this problem, the demand for education has continuously increased (Ong & Annamalai, 2024). The desire of students to benefit more from quality education opportunities has made individual teaching more important (Arnon & Reichel, 2007). The increasing need for quality education has led to the view that the use of instructional materials containing technology in education is essential (Judijanto, Atsani & Chadijah, 2024). Furthermore, the fact that teaching materials containing technology motivate students more, support lifelong education, and increase flexibility in curricula has also been put forward as a justification for this situation in education (Gurol 1990).

The integration of technology into the educational process has been a subject of study for scholars for over 30 years (Delgado et al., 2015). The use of teaching materials containing technology in schools has been rapid (Ali, Aini & Alam, 2024). Currently, the manner and purpose of the use of technological teaching materials, such as computer software or artificial intelligence, in the education system varies according to the policies of countries (Mouta, Torrecilla-Sánchez & Pinto-Llorente, 2024). Prior to the utilization of technological tools and software as an educational instrument, it is imperative to ascertain the subjects deemed crucial for instruction in the present and immediate future, and to delineate the methodologies by which the identified pedagogical content should be conveyed to the students (Al-khresheh, 2024). Furthermore, it is essential to plan the delivery of the requisite education in a meticulous manner, with particular attention to the present and prospective technological developments (Castellan 1987). The integration of computers into the educational system has led to significant alterations in the structure and content of educational programs. The introduction of digital technology has transformed the way information is disseminated, prompting a radical transformation in the structure and functioning of educational systems (Numanoglu, 1990).

The definition of artificial intelligence is understood to be an attempt to develop computer processes that will reveal the similarity of human thinking (Wang, 2019). This is done by understanding the structure of human thinking or the attempt of a programmed computer to think (Keles, 2007). The concept of artificial intelligence was first introduced in a conference in 1956 by McCarthy, who proposed investigating the idea of developing integrated programs with intelligence as a program technique (Simon, 1983). Minsky (1995) defines artificial intelligence as one of the ways of studying and researching intelligent behaviors, and its place in technology is stated as a new branch of science open to development. One of the most significant research topics in the field of artificial intelligence is the study of learning (Ezzaim et al., 2024). This process, which can be defined as the acquisition of knowledge and skills by artificial intelligence systems, encompasses a range of factors, including technical and theoretical knowledge, common sense, definition, and determination. The development of these systems' capabilities, as a result of the acquired knowledge, encompasses the ability to organize information and effective execution. Artificial intelligence, which has the potential to transform the way computer programs are written, employs a learning process that is analogous to the way humans learn (Chen, Chen & Lin, 2024). This process involves acquiring new information and applying it to future situations. The modelling of this process in a computer environment is known as machine learning. There are two fundamental concepts in machine learning: learning and understanding ability (Oztemel, 1992). A review of the areas where artificial intelligence is employed reveals that the studies of artificial intelligence institutes are supported to a significant extent with substantial budgetary resources provided by a range of sources, including space, defense, industry, education, computer and other scientific research funds (Keles, 2007). The advent of artificial intelligence has profoundly altered the way in which people live their lives. Although the impact of the use of artificial intelligence applications in education is more limited compared to other sectors, studies in this field have increased in recent years, with notable contributions from (Bhutoria, 2022; Chassignol, Khoroshavin, Klimova & Bilyatdinova; Murphy, 2019). The advent of artificial intelligence has brought with it the concept of "Intelligent, adaptive or personalized learning systems" to the classroom environment. It is thought that the effectiveness and quality of artificial intelligence applications will be enhanced by the collection of more data from more students and the subsequent analysis of this information in the process carried out for these concepts (Murphy, 2019). Due to the global epidemic, the concept of distance education has been incorporated into the education system of countries (Al Lily et al., 2020; Ali, 2020; Ennam, 2024; Gupta et al., 2024). Educational artificial intelligence-supported computer software represents one of the many methods employed in distance education (de Queiroz et al., 2024; Dogan, Goru Dogan & Bozkurt, 2023; Lin & Yu, 2024; Maphoto et al., 2024). It has been established that the artificial intelligence software utilized in our country is based on repetition and practice. However, after a certain point, repetition can result in the learner becoming bored. In order to address this issue, simulation and game-like methods are employed (Keles, 2007).

The objective of utilizing artificial intelligence in the field of education can be defined as the introduction of novel elements to the learning environment, thereby facilitating the acquisition of knowledge and enhancing the quality of education while optimizing the efficiency of individuals engaged in educational pursuits. The contributions of artificial intelligence applications in the field of education to education and training can be enumerated as follows (Bhutoria, 2022);

- The application of artificial intelligence allows the generation of personalized learning materials and exercises according to the specific learning requirements of an individual student. Furthermore, it enables the evaluation of these materials.
- Artificial intelligence applications have the potential to inform educators about students who may be experiencing learning disabilities, exhibiting negative behaviors, or demonstrating a decline in academic performance. These

applications can also be employed to identify students' learning styles and interests, as well as the underlying reasons that may contribute to students at risk of dropping out of school.
- It is possible to respond to queries by imitating the human speech skills.
- The interactive structure of artificial intelligence applications enables the feedback received to be used to determine the needs and requirements of students. Based on these determinations, the applications play an active role in determining the most appropriate learning options for individuals.
- The field of artificial intelligence applications is one that lends itself to the development of diverse teaching materials.
- The advent of virtual assistants has enabled educators to create instructional designs that can be characterized as complex. Image recognition technologies have the potential to facilitate the correction of assignments in a relatively short time, thereby allowing educators to dedicate more of their attention to teaching. Furthermore, robot assistants, which are defined as human-machine interaction, can empower students to devise solutions to common problems.
- The utilization of virtual reality tools enables students with special needs to participate in applied teaching in a home or classroom environment. The integration of artificial intelligence applications into the educational process facilitates the provision of diverse learning environments, including distance learning, open education, e-learning, and others. This approach is conducive to the realization of equal educational opportunities.
- The utilization of artificial intelligence applications enables the reduction of time spent on various paperwork processes that school administrations are required to manage, with the processes being completed automatically.
- The potential applications of AI are vast and include the ability to extend learning environments beyond the confines of a physical classroom. AI can facilitate communication with individuals from different learning environments around the world. This enables the provision of education from a variety of sources, including those situated in other countries and delivered through diverse cultural, academic, and linguistic contexts. In this regard, AI is seen to play a significant role in supporting lifelong learning and offering a multitude of opportunities.
- It is possible to utilize personal assistants and chatbots to facilitate translation across different languages, correct spelling mistakes and edit article abstracts.

The evaluation of AI applications in education has identified a number of reasons for their perceived ineffectiveness. These include a lack of relevant learning resources to provide individualized/adaptive learning, a lack of AI in education research on socio-emotional aspects, a lack of educational perspectives in AI in education research, and negative attitudes towards AI among students and teachers. It has been suggested that teacher attitudes towards artificial intelligence applications play a significant role in determining the effective use of these applications (Chiu, Xia, Zhou, Chai & Cheng). In this context, it is first necessary to define the term "attitude".

The term "attitude" is defined as "permanent systems that include cognitive and affective elements as well as a behavioral orientation" (Freedman, Sears & Carlsmith, 1993). Concurrently, it is also posited as a state of readiness that elicits a continuous positive or negative emotional response in individuals regarding an object or situation that has not undergone any value judgement in a psychological process (Sherif & Sherif, 1996). While defining attitude, it is said to be a reaction towards some elements (Kagitcibasi, 1999). Among these, the affective elements of attitude include evaluative reactions, such as liking or disliking an object. The cognitive elements are the reactions related to beliefs, ideas and opinions about the object of attitude. In addition, the behavioral elements can be stated as responses involving behavioral intentions and action tendencies. In a study examining teacher attitudes towards artificial intelligence applications in the field of education, Chocarro, Cortinas, and Marcos-Matas (2021) investigated teachers' attitudes towards AI-supported chatbots. The study found that teachers' ability to influence the design and communication capabilities of chatbots would be beneficial in accepting developments in education. In the study conducted by Belanche, Casalo, and Flavian (2019), it was determined that those who use roboconferencing, one of the artificial intelligence applications, use the application more effectively when they are familiar with robotic systems and their perceptions are high. In the study conducted by Roll and Wylie (2016), it was stated that artificial intelligence applications will undergo a kind of evolution process that cooperates with teachers in the future.

The methodology employed in this research, which examined teachers' attitudes towards artificial intelligence, is outlined below.

METHOD

In this part of the research, research model, study group, measurement tool, procedure and data analysis are explained.

Model

In the current study, survey model, one of the quantitative research methods, was used. This model allows the generalization of the results of the study, since data are collected from a large population (Fraenkel, Wallen & Hyun, 2012). Survey research, which is conducted on relatively larger samples than other forms of research, is defined as a study in which the views of the participants on a subject or event or their interests, skills, abilities, attitudes, etc. are determined. Survey researches are generally characterised by three key attributes (Buyukozturk, Kilic Cakmak, Akgun, Karadeniz & Demirel, 2021).

- The objective of this methodology is to describe the views, or characteristics (beliefs, knowledge, attitudes, concerns, interests, etc.) of a large community in regard to a particular subject. To that end, a subset of the community, comprising individuals who can effectively represent the entire community is selected.
- The process of data collection for the research is based on the responses provided by the individuals who are the data sources to the questions posed to them.
- The collection of data is not conducted on each individual member of the community whose characteristics are to be described. Rather, it is carried out on a representative part of this community, namely a sample.

Survey research can be categorized into four main types: Instantaneous, cross-sectional, longitudinal and historical. Instantaneous survey research is defined as studies conducted to describe the current situation as it exists at a specific point in time. In cross-sectional studies, the variables to be described (such as developmental characteristics, reading comprehension skills, voting behaviors, attitudes) are measured at a single point in time. Cross-sectional studies are generally studies in which the sample size is large and covers a community with a wide range of characteristics. In longitudinal survey research, repeated measurements are made at different times to examine the time-dependent changes of research variables. This type of research can be conducted to determine trends, to examine a group with common characteristics, or to investigate the time-dependent changes and trends of the same people. Historical survey studies are based on the opinions and statements of people who experienced the events in the past (Karasar, 2002; Buyukozturk et al., 2021) In this study, primary school teachers' attitudes towards artificial intelligence are an example of instantaneous survey research.

Sampling

The study group comprises 200 classroom teachers employed in public primary schools in the Akyurt district of Ankara Province, Turkey. In the 2023-2024 academic year, approximately 400 classroom teachers are employed in the Akyurt district of

Ankara. In this context, the sample size is deemed sufficient. Demographic data of the participants is given in Table 1.

Table 1. Demographic information of the participants

Variable		N	Frequency	Percent
Gender	Male	200	35	17.5
	Female		165	82.5
Computer Skills	Moderate	200	105	52.5
	Good		78	39
	Advanced		17	8.5
Use of Artificial Intelligence Programs	Yes	200	75	37.5
	No		125	62.5
Use of Artificial Intelligence Applications in Lessons	Yes	200	58	29
	No		142	71
Age	20-25	200	132	66
	26-30		28	14
	31-35		20	10
	36 years old and older		20	10

As seen in Table 1, a total of 200 primary school teachers, 35 (17.5%) males and 165 (82.5%) females, participated in the study. When the participants' computer skills are examined, it can be said that 105 (52.5%) participants have moderate computer skills, 78 (39%) participants have good computer skills, and 17 (8.5%) participants have advanced computer skills. Of the participants, 75 (37.5%) use AI programs, while 125 (62.5%) do not use AI programs. While 58 (29%) participants stated that they use AI applications in their lessons, 142 (71%) stated that they do not make use of AI applications in their lessons. Finally, 132 (66%) participants are in the 20-25 age group, 28 (14%) are in the 26-30 age group, 20 (10%) are in the 31-35 age group, 20 (10%) are in the age group of 38 and older.

Measurement Tools

In this part of the study, information about the measurement tools is given.

Personal Information Form

The researcher improved the form to gather information about the participants' gender, age, computer skills, utilization of AI applications in their lessons and using AI programs.

General Attitudes Towards Artificial Intelligence Scale (GAAIS)

In this study, the "General Attitudes towards AI Scale" was used that was adapted to Turkish by Kaya, Aydin Schepman, Rodway, Yetisensoy and Demir Kaya (2022) from the original version of Schepman and Rodway (2020). The scale was translated into Turkish and checked by 4 experts.

In the research conducted by Schepman and Rodway (2020), GAAIS was used on 100 participants. The study by Schepman and Rodway (2022) consists of two steps. The first step of the study was a replicate study conducted on 304 participants. In the second step, the relationship of the scale with different variables was studied. The validity of the scale was found to increase with the increasing number of participants.

Reliability

The scale of Schepman and Rodway (2020) has 20 items. It is a 5-point Likert scale. The coefficient of internal consistency was calculated as $\alpha=0.88$ for the dimension of positive attitude and $\alpha=0.83$ for the dimension in the first stage of the study Schepman & Rodway (2022) and $\alpha=0.85$ for the dimension of positive attitude and $\alpha=0.82$ for the dimension in the second phase of the research.

The scale, adapted to Turkish by Kaya et al. (2022), has 20 items and 2 factors. A total of 350 people participated in the adaptation research. The scale is a 5-point Likert scale. The internal consistency coefficient was found to be $\alpha=.82$ for the dimension of positive attitude and $\alpha=.84$ for the dimension of negative attitude. The internal consistency was calculated as $\alpha=.79$ in the current study. Consequently, it may be concluded that the research is reliable (Dogan, 2019).

Construct Validity

In this part of the study, information about the confirmatory and exploratory factor analyses of General Attitudes towards Artificial Intelligence Scale (GAAIS) is given.

Exploratory Factor Analysis (EFA)

To establish the construct validity in the research, first, an exploratory factor analysis was performed. Schepman and Rodway (2020) applied exploratory factor analysis during the scale development stage on 100 participants. The scale initially consisted of 32 items. After the exploratory factor analysis, the number of items was downsized to 20. The scale has two dimensions called positive attitude and negative attitude. The first 12 items are in the positive attitude dimension while the last 8 items are in the positive attitude dimension. The Kaiser-Meyer-Olkin test value was found to be .87 and Bartlett's Test of Sphericity was calculated as significant (p=.00). The total variance explained is 47.4%. Schepman and Rodway (2022) conducted an exploratory factor analysis on 304 participants in the first stage of their study and found the Kaiser-Meyer-Olkin test value as .90 and Barlett's Test of Sphericity as significant (p=.00). In the second stage of their study, Schepman and Rodway (2022) conducted an exploratory factor analysis on 300 participants and found the Kaiser-Meyer-Olkin test value as .89 and Bartlett's Test of Sphericity as significant (p=.00). In the current research, an exploratory factor analysis was also performed. Table 2 displays the analysis's findings.

Table 2. Results of Exploratory Factor Analysis (EFA)

Item	Factor 1 (Positive)	Factor 2 (Negative)
I3	.79	
I7	.78	
I5	.76	
I2	.75	
I9	.73	
I8	.72	
I11	.70	
I4	.68	
I6	.62	
I12	.61	
I10	.57	
I1	.52	
I16		.76
I15		.73
I13		.72
I17		.69
I19		.64
I18		.60
I14		.60
I20		.56
Kaiser-Meyer-Olkin Test and Bartlett's Test of Sphericity	.89	.00
Total Variance Explained	53.62	

The results of the EFA in the current study using a different sample are consistent with the EFAs conducted by Schepman and Rodway (2020) and Schepman and Rodway (2022) in terms of dimensions and items obtained. Item factor loadings were also found to be very close to each other. This demonstrates that the GAAIS developed by Schepman and Rodway (2020) is a highly replicable scale (Osborne & Fitzpatrick, 2012).

Confirmatory Factor Analysis (CFA)

Before proceeding with the confirmatory factor analysis, the sample size was checked. It was understood that the study group was large enough to conduct a confirmatory factor analysis (Anderson & Gerbing, 1984; Boomsma, 1985; Goodwin, 1999; Muthén & Muthén, 2002; Stevens, 2002, Tanaka, 1987).

To ensure the construct validity in the current study, the results of the confirmatory factor analyses of the research of Schepman and Rodway (2020), Schepman and Rodway (2022), Kaya et al. (2022) on GAAIS and that of the current study are given below. Kaya et al. (2022) used NNFI as the model fit index in their study. In the current study, TLI index was used instead of NNFI. Furthermore, in the study by Schepman and Rodway (2020), CFI and SRMR indices were not reported. Finally, the number of participants was added to Table 3 for the reader to better distinguish the studies.

Table 3. Results of the Confirmatory Factor Analysis (CFA)

Index	Schepman and Rodway (2020)	Schepman and Rodway (First) (2022)	Schepman and Rodway (Second) (2022)	Kaya et al. (2022)	Current study	Result (Fit)
χ^2/sd	1.5	1.32	1.03	1.51	1.94	Perfect
CFI	-	.98	.99	.97	.92	Acceptable
TLI	.88	.98	.99	.97	.91	Acceptable
SRMR	-	.06	.05	.06	.06	Acceptable
RMSEA	.08	.03	.01	.03	.06	Acceptable
Participant	100	304	300	350	200	Adequate

According to the model fit indices in Table 3, the values of CFI, TLI are at an acceptable level. χ^2/sd value indicates a perfect fit. An RMSEA index below .05 indicates a close fit. In addition, the RMSEA index being close to .08 is stated as an acceptable level (Browne & Cudeck, 1993). Thus, it can be said that the scale used in the current study is a valid scale (Kline, 2016).

Data Collection and Analysis

In the selection of the participants, simple random sampling was used. The sampling method in which units are selected at random with each unit having an equal probability of selection is known as simple random sampling. This method ensures that each sample is selected with equal probability from the sample space. In this sampling method, all units in the universe have an equal and independent chance to be selected for the sample. In other words, all individuals have an equal probability of being selected, and the selection of one individual does not affect the selection of other individuals. Random sampling is therefore the most valid and optimal method for selecting a representative sample (Cingi, 1994; Buyukozturk et al., 2021). The data for this study were collected in December 2023.

In this section, the information is given about how the data were collected and analysed to answer to the study question "What are primary school teachers' attitudes towards AI?". The online scale prepared to collect the data of this study has two parts. In the first part of the measurement tool, there are items to elicit demographic information and in the second part, there are items to elicit information about their attitudes towards AI (Gosling & Mason, 2015). In addition, the consent of all the participants was obtained before they completed the measurement tool. In this study, a normality test was first carried out on the data collected through GAAIS to decide whether a parametric or a non-parametric test would be utilized in the data analysis. Table 4 displays the results of the normality test.

Table 4. Normality Analysis of the GAAIS

Score	N	Mean	Sd	Skewness	Kurtosis
Total	200	3.24	.50	.46	1.45

As seen above, Skewness and Kurtosis values of GAAIS are between -1.5 and +1.5 and are within the normal distribution limits (Tabachnick & Fidell, 2014). Then, the Q-Q Plot shape of the data was examined. After the normality test, the homogeneity of the data obtained from GAAIS was looked at with Levene's test and the scale items are seen to be homogeneous according to this test. As a result, when the normality test values of GAAIS were examined, it was observed that the data were normally distributed (Morgan, Leech, Gloeckner & Barrett, 2004). Thus, the normality and homogeneity criteria required to use parametric tests were met (Koklu, Buyukozturk & Bokeoglu, 2007). As a result, independent samples t-test and one-way ANOVA test were executed. Furthermore, Cohen's d values were used to ascertain the effect size (Kilic, 2014). The research findings were subjected to a statistical analysis at the $p < .05$ level of significance. SPSS 26 and MPLUS 7 statistical program packages were used to analyze the collected data.

Validity and Reliability

The following section outlines the procedures employed to ensure the validity and reliability of the research.

Firstly, it is necessary to conduct both the exploratory factor analysis and the confirmatory factor analysis in order to guarantee the internal validity of the research. The external validity of the research was ensured by employing the simple random sampling technique. The results of the research therefore have a high degree of generalizability to large groups.

The reliability of the study was determined using the Cronbach's Alpha coefficient. The resulting Cronbach's Alpha value of the study data was .79; thus, the research can be considered quite reliable. Consequently, the research can be considered to be both valid and reliable.

Findings

In this section of the study, information about the findings is given, Table 5 displays mean attitude score of the participants

Table 5. Mean Attitudes Score

Score	N	x̄	Sd
Total	20	3.24	.50

As seen in Table 5, the mean attitude score of the participants is 3.24. Thus, the participants' general attitude towards AI can be expressed as something between "Undecided" and "Agree". This might indicate that the participants have already developed some attitude towards AI.

An independent samples t-test was run to seek an answer for the sub-problem of the research "Do primary school teachers' attitudes towards AI vary significantly by gender, utilization of AI programs and using AI in lessons?" and the results are presented in Table 6.

Table 6. Independent Samples of the t-Test

Score	Variable		N	Mean	Sd	df	t	p	Cohen's d
Total	Gender	Male	35	3.52	.64	41.34	2.99	.00	.61
		Female	165	3.18	.45				

continued on following page

Table 6. Continued

Score	Variable		N	Mean	Sd	df	t	p	Cohen's d
Total	Use of AI Programs	Yes	75	3.37	.43	198	2.86	.00	.42
		No	125	3.16	.53				
Total	Use of AI in Lessons	Yes	58	3.36	.44	198	2.34	.02	.37
		No	142	3.18	.52				

As seen in Table 6, the participants' attitudes towards AI differ significantly according to gender (p<.05) and the effect size is medium (d=.61). The mean attitude score of the male participants was observed to be significantly higher than that of the female participants. This is thought to be due to the different levels of technology use of men and women in daily life.

The participants' attitudes towards AI were found to vary significantly depending on the utilization of AI programs (p<.05) and the effect size is small (d=.42). The mean attitude score of the participants who make use of AI programs was found to be significantly higher than that of the participants who do not use AI programs. This is thought to be due to the rapid development of AI to meet the needs of society.

The participants' attitudes towards AI were found to vary significantly depending on the utilization of AI applications in their lessons (p<.05) and the effect size is small (d=.37). The mean attitude score of the participants who use AI applications in the courses they take is significantly higher than that of the primary school teachers who do not use AI applications in the courses they take. This is thought to be due to the fact that most of the AI programs are open source and educational AI programs are added to the course contents by lesson programme creators.

The results of the one-way ANOVA run to seek an answer to the sub-problem of the research "Do primary school teachers attitudes towards AI vary significantly depending on the variables of age and computer skills?" are given in Table 7.

Table 7. Results of the One-Way ANOVA

Score	Variable		N	X	Groups	f	SS	F	p	Scheffe Test	η^2
Total	Skills	Moderate	105	3.10	Between Groups	2	4.19	8.87	.00	1-2*	.08
		Good	78	3.40	Within Groups	97	46.53				
		Advanced	17	3.35	Total	99	50.72				

continued on following page

Table 7. Continued

Score	Variable		N	X	Groups	f	SS	F	p	Scheffe Test	η^2
Total	Age	20-25	132	3.26	Between Groups	3	2.58	3.51	.01	2-3*	.05
		26-30	28	3.03	Within Groups	96	48.14				
		31-35	20	3.47	Total	99	50.72				
		36 and older	20	3.13							

As seen in Table 7, depending on how proficient they are with computers, the participants' perspectives regarding AI change considerably (p<.05). This difference is between the participants having a moderate level of computer skills and the participants having a good level of computer skills in favor of the participants having a good level of computer skills. The square value indicates a small effect size. This is thought to be due to the fact that attitudes towards AI change positively as participants' computer skills improve.

The participants' attitudes towards AI were found to vary significantly depending on age (p<.05). This differentiation was found to be between the participants who are in the 26-30 age group and the participants who are in the 31-35 age group in favor of the primary school teachers who are in the age group of 31-35. Eta square value indicates a small effect size. This might be because the participants between the ages of 31 and 35 realized that they could benefit more from learning-teaching activities using AI.

RESULTS, DISCUSSION AND SUGGESTIONS

In the current research, the aim is to understand the attitudes of primary school teachers towards AI. The findings showed that gender, age, computer skills, utilization of AI programs and using AI applications in lessons are variables having significant effects on primary school teachers' attitudes towards AI.

The first result is that the teachers demonstrated positive attitudes towards AI. Studies with comparable findings have been published in the pertinent literature (Ahmed et al., 2022; Alghamdi & Alashban, 2023; Al-Medfa et al., 2023; Fietta et al., 2022; Jeong et al., 2023; Zhang et al., 2023). It has been reported that participants in various countries, including Italy, Pakistan, Saudi Arabia, Bahrain, South Korea, China, and different sample groups, hold positive attitudes towards artificial intelligence. The current study was conducted in Turkey, and the attitudes of the participants towards artificial intelligence were found to be similar. It is thought that this situation will contribute to the literature.

A study has revealed that male primary school teachers exhibit greater positive attitudes towards artificial intelligence than female teachers. According to Ahmed et al. (2022), the gender of the participants does not affect their attitudes towards AI. However, in the study conducted by Schepman and Rodway (2022) in the United Kingdom, the male participants were found to have more positive attitudes towards AI. In a similar study, Zhang and Dafoe (2022) stated that the attitudes of the male participants were higher in their study in China. Similarly, a number of studies have indicated that male participants tend to hold more favorable attitudes towards artificial intelligence. (Figueiredo, 2019; Fatemi, 2020; Fietta et al., 2022; Sindermann et al., 2021). It is thought that this result of the study will contribute to the relevant literature.

The middle-aged teachers were observed to have more positive attitudes towards AI. In their study conducted in Bahrain, Al-Medfa and Al-Ansari (2023) stated that the ages of the participants and their attitudes towards AI were close to each other. In their study conducted in Bahrain, Al-Medfa and Al-Ansari (2023) stated that the ages of the participants do not have a significant effect on their attitudes towards AI. When the literature related to this result is compared, it can be seen that there are research (Gillespie et al., 2021; Hauk et al., 2018; Mariano et al., 2022; Zhang & Dafoe, 2019) stating that the attitudes of young participants towards AI are more positive. Moreover, there are studies in which it was found that ages of the participants do not affect their attitudes (Al-Medfa & Al-Ansari, 2023; Chocarro et al., 2022; Kaya et al., 2022). Conversely, Park et al. (2022) found that relatively older individuals have a higher tendency to accept AI-assisted information technologies and as individuals age, they become more receptive to new technology. It is postulated that the results of the current research will contribute to the related literature.

Another result of the current study is that those who have better computer skills have more positive attitudes towards AI. Zhang and Dafoe (2019) stated in their study in China that those with good computer skills are more supportive of new AI applications. Kaya et al. (2022) explained in their study that computer users have more positive attitudes towards AI. According to Vu and Lim (2022) and Martin et al. (2020), computer use positively affects the attitude towards AI. The results of these studies are in parallel with the results of the present study. It is believed this situation will contribute to the development of the existing literature.

The attitudes of the primary school teachers who used AI applications in the lesson they took were found to be more positive. In the literature, it was determined that university professors had positive attitudes towards AI and its teaching in courses (Irshad, 2020). The final result of the current research is that the attitudes of the primary school teachers who use programs requiring AI are more positive. Similar results have been reported in the literature (Kim & Lee, 2020; Park et al., 2022Belanche et al., 2019; Mantello et al., 2021). In accordance with the findings of this study, a number of recommendations were put forth to researchers and practitioners for future studies. It is recommended that new courses be created at the university to utilize artificial intelligence, and that the existing course contents be updated. In order for female teachers to develop positive attitudes towards the use of artificial intelligence in the classroom, it is recommended that in-service training activities be provided. Qualitative research can be conducted on the problems encountered by primary school teachers regarding AI and it can be determined what kind of problems they face. Also, experimental studies can be planned using AI applications in the field of education.

Limitations and Implications

The present study aimed to analyze the attitudes of primary school teachers towards artificial intelligence. While the research yielded significant insights, it is important to acknowledge the limitations of the study. Firstly, this research was conducted exclusively with classroom teachers, which represents a limitation of the study in that it does not encompass the perspectives of other teacher branches. Secondly, teacher attitudes towards artificial intelligence were determined through a scale, although it is possible to collect teacher attitudes through other means, such as interviews or observations. Finally, the fact that the study group was conducted only in Ankara province of Turkey represents a limitation of the research.

The practical implications of the use of artificial intelligence in the context of educational settings encompass a broad range of considerations, from teachers' technology adoption processes to classroom management. The development of a positive attitude towards AI programs by teachers can facilitate the effective utilization of such programs, thereby conferring benefits such as the personalization of teaching processes and an increase in efficiency. AI programs such as GPT have the potential to offer personalized learning experiences by analyzing student performance and providing instant feedback to teachers, thereby enabling them to offer support that is tailored to individual needs. Furthermore, such programs allow teachers to spend more time on pedagogical interaction, which can help to reduce the amount of paperwork they are required to complete. However, economic constraints in the use of these programs affect teachers' resource allocation and access to training materials. In this context, the support of education policymakers is needed to increase the level of access.

The ethical implications of teacher attitudes towards the use of artificial intelligence (AI) in education are manifold and include data privacy, bias and professional role reversals. The potential of AI to monitor student performance and deliver personalized learning experiences is significant; however, it also raises serious concerns about privacy and security. These relate to the collection, storage and use of both student and teacher data. It is imperative that teachers assume an active role in the design and implementation of AI tools to guarantee the protection of student data and to establish a just and equitable educational environment. Furthermore, the integration of AI in certain instructional processes may result in a transformation of the teacher's professional role, potentially jeopardizing their values and autonomy in the field of education. Consequently, it is essential to conduct a comprehensive assessment of teachers' attitudes towards AI, with the objective of maintaining a student-centered approach while addressing ethical concerns.

REFERENCES

Aguinis, H., Beltran, J. R., & Cope, A. (2024). How to use generative AI as a human resource management assistant. *Organizational Dynamics*, 53(1), 101029. DOI: 10.1016/j.orgdyn.2024.101029

Ahmed, Z., Tariq, A., Tahir, M. J., Tabassum, M. S., Bhinder, K. K., Mehmood, Q., Malik, M., Aslam, S., Asghar, M. S., & Yousaf, Z. (2022). Knowledge, attitude, and practice of artificial intelligence among doctors and medical students in Pakistan: A cross-sectional online survey. *Annals of Medicine and Surgery (London)*, 76. Advance online publication. DOI: 10.1016/j.amsu.2022.103493 PMID: 35308436

Akaev, A. A., & Rudskoi, A. I. (2017). Economic potential of breakthrough technologies and its social consequences. In Devezas, T., Leitão, J., & Sarygulov, A. (Eds.), *Industry 4.0. Studies on entrepreneurship, structural change and industrial dynamics*. Springer., DOI: 10.1007/978-3-319-49604-7_2

Al-khresheh, M. H. (2024). Bridging technology and pedagogy from a global lens: Teachers' perspectives on integrating ChatGPT in English language teaching. *Computers and Education: Artificial Intelligence*, 6, 100218. DOI: 10.1016/j.caeai.2024.100218

Al Lily, A. E., Ismail, A. F., Abunasser, F. M., & Alqahtani, R. H. A. (2020). Distance education as a response to pandemics: Coronavirus and Arab culture. *Technology in Society*, 63, 101317. DOI: 10.1016/j.techsoc.2020.101317 PMID: 32836570

Al-Medfa, M. K., Al-Ansari, A. M., Darwish, A. H., Qreeballa, T. A., & Jahrami, H. (2023). Physicians' attitudes and knowledge toward artificial intelligence in medicine: Benefits and drawbacks. *Heliyon*, 9(4), e14744. Advance online publication. DOI: 10.1016/j.heliyon.2023.e14744 PMID: 37035387

Alghamdi, S. A., & Alashban, Y. (2023). Knowledge, attitudes and practices towards artificial intelligence (AI) among radiologists in Saudi Arabia. *Journal of Radiation Research and Applied Sciences*, 16(2), 100569. Advance online publication. DOI: 10.1016/j.jrras.2023.100569

Ali, M., Aini, M. A., & Alam, S. N. (2024). Integrating technology in learning in madrasah: Towards the digital age. [INJOE]. *Indonesian Journal of Education*, 4(1), 290–304.

Ali, W. (2020). Online and remote learning in higher education institutes: A necessity in light of COVID-19 pandemic. *Higher education studies*, 10(3), (pp.16-25). https://doi.org/DOI: 10.5539/hes.v10n3p16

Anderson, J. C., & Gerbing, D. W. (1984). The effect of sampling error on convergence, improper solutions, and goodness-of-fit indices for maximum likelihood confirmatory factor analysis. *Psychometrika*, 49(2), 155–173. DOI: 10.1007/BF02294170

Arnon, S., & Reichel, N. (2007). Who is the ideal teacher? Am I? Similarity and difference in perception of students of education regarding the qualities of a good teacher and of their own qualities as teachers. *Teachers and Teaching*, 13(5), 441–464. DOI: 10.1080/13540600701561653

Ayeni, O. O., Al Hamad, N. M., Chisom, O. N., Osawaru, B., & Adewusi, O. E. (2024). AI in education: A review of personalized learning and educational technology. *GSC Advanced Research and Reviews*, 18(2), 261–271. DOI: 10.30574/gscarr.2024.18.2.0062

Barbour, M. K., & Hodges, C. B. (2024). Preparing teachers to teach online: A critical issue for teacher education. *Journal of Technology and Teacher Education*, 32(1), 5–27. https://www.learntechlib.org/primary/p/223927/

Belanche, D., Casalo, L. V., & Flavian, C. (2019). Artificial intelligence in FinTech: Understanding robo-advisors adoption among customers. *Industrial Management & Data Systems*, 119(7), 1411–1430. DOI: 10.1108/IMDS-08-2018-0368

Bhutoria, A. (2022). Personalized education and artificial intelligence in United States, China, and India: A systematic review using a human-in-the-loop model. *Computers and Education: Artificial Intelligence*, 3, 1–18. DOI: 10.1016/j.caeai.2022.100068

Boomsma, A. (1985). Nonconvergence, improper solutions, and starting values in Lisrel maximum likelihood estimation. *Psychometrika*, 50(2), 229–242. DOI: 10.1007/BF02294248

Bostrom, N., & Yudkowsky, E. (2014). The ethics of artificial intelligence *The Cambridge handbook of artificial intelligence*. Cambridge: Cambridge University Press.

Browne, M. W., & Cudeck, R. (1993). Alternative ways of assessing model fit. In *K. A. Bollen ve S. Long (Der.) Testing structural equation models* (pp. 131–161). Sage Publications.

Bukar, U. A., Sayeed, M. S., Razak, S. F. A., Yogarayan, S., & Sneesl, R. (2024). Decision-making framework for the utilization of generative artificial intelligence in education: A case study of ChatGPT. *IEEE Access : Practical Innovations, Open Solutions*, 12, 95368–95389. DOI: 10.1109/ACCESS.2024.3425172

Buyukozturk, Ş., Kilic Cakmak, E., Akgun, Ö. E., Karadeniz, Ş., & Demirel, F. (2021). *Scientific research methods in education*. Pegem Academy.

Castellan, N. J.Jr. (1987). Computers and the shape of the future: Implications for teaching and learning. *Education and Computing*, 3(1-2), 39–48. DOI: 10.1016/S0167-9287(87)80483-1

Charniak, E., & McDermot, D., (1985). *Introduction to Artificial Intelligence*. Boston: Addison-Wesley company.

Chassignol, M., Khoroshavin, A., Klimova, A., & Bilyatdinova, A. (2018). Artificial intelligence trends in education: A narrative overview. *Procedia Computer Science*, 136, 16–24. DOI: 10.1016/j.procs.2018.08.233

Chen, L., Chen, P., & Lin, Z. (2020). Artificial intelligence in education: A review. *IEEE Access : Practical Innovations, Open Solutions*, 8, 75264–75278. DOI: 10.1109/ACCESS.2020.2988510

Chiu, T. K., Xia, Q., Zhou, X., Chai, C. S., & Cheng, M. (2022). Systematic literature review on opportunities, challenges, and future research recommendations of artificial intelligence in education. *Computers and Education: Artificial Intelligence*, 4(100118), 1–15. DOI: 10.1016/j.caeai.2022.100118

Chocarro, R., Cortinas, M., & Marcos-Matas, G. (2021). Teachers' attitudes towards chatbots in education: A technology acceptance model approach considering the effect of social language, bot proactiveness, and users' characteristics. *Educational Studies*, ●●●, 1–19. DOI: 10.1080/03055698.2020.1850426

Chowdhury, S., Dey, P., Joel-Edgar, S., Bhattacharya, S., Rodriguez-Espindola, O., Abadie, A., & Truong, L. (2023). Unlocking the value of artificial intelligence in human resource management through AI capability framework. *Human Resource Management Review*, 33(1), 100899. DOI: 10.1016/j.hrmr.2022.100899

Cingi, H. (1994). *Sampling method*. Hacettepe University press.

Coskun, F., & Gulleroglu, H. D. (2021). Yapay zekanın tarih içindeki gelişimi ve eğitimde kullanılması. [JFES]. *Ankara University Journal of Faculty of Educational Sciences*, 54(3), 947–966. DOI: 10.30964/auebfd.916220

Coskun, F., & Gulleroglu, H. D. (2021). Yapay zekânın tarih içindeki gelişimi ve eğitimde kullanılması. [JFES]. *Ankara University Journal of Faculty of Educational Sciences*, 54(3), 947–966. DOI: 10.30964/auebfd.916220

Creswell, J. W. (2014). *A concise introduction to mixed methods research*. SAGE publications.

Dahri, N. A., Yahaya, N., Al-Rahmi, W. M., Vighio, M. S., Alblehai, F., Soomro, R. B., & Shutaleva, A. (2024). Investigating AI-based academic support acceptance and its impact on students' performance in Malaysian and Pakistani higher education institutions. *Education and Information Technologies*, •••, 1–50. DOI: 10.1007/s10639-024-12599-x

de Queiroz, D. C., do Nascimento, J. L. G., de Oliveira Nunes, P. H., Gomes, A. M. P., de Souza, J. T., & de Oliveira, I. N. (2024). Artificial intelligence in education: An overview of distance education courses. *Revista de Gestão Social e Ambiental*, 18(5), e08125–e08125. DOI: 10.24857/rgsa.v18n5-169

Delgado, A. J., Wardlow, L., McKnight, K., & O'Malley, K. (2015). Educational technology: A review of the integration, resources, and effectiveness of technology in K-12 classrooms. *Journal of Information Technology Education*, 14, 397–416. http://www.jite.org/documents/Vol14/JITEv14ResearchP397416Delgado1829.pdf. DOI: 10.28945/2298

Demir, O. (2019). Sürdürülebilir kalkınma için yapay zeka. In Telli, G. (Ed.), *Yapay zeka ve gelecek* (pp. 44–63). Doğu Kitapevi.

Dogan, M. E., Goru Dogan, T., & Bozkurt, A. (2023). The use of artificial intelligence (AI) in online learning and distance education processes: A systematic review of empirical studies. *Applied Sciences (Basel, Switzerland)*, 13(5), 3056. DOI: 10.3390/app13053056

Dogan, N. (2019). Measurement and evaluation in education Ankara: Pegem academy.

Ennam, A. (2024). Assessing Covid-19 pandemic-forced transitioning to distance e-learning in Moroccan universities: An empirical, analytical critical study of implementality and achievability. *Journal of North African Studies*, 29(1), 153–177. DOI: 10.1080/13629387.2021.1937138

Ezzaim, A., Dahbi, A., Aqqal, A., & Haidine, A. (2024). AI-based learning style detection in adaptive learning systems: A systematic literature review. *Journal of Computers in Education*, (pp.1-39). https://doi.org/DOI: 10.1007/s40692-024-00328-9

Fatemi, F. (2020). Bridging the gender gap in AI. *Forbes*. https://www.forbes.com/sites/falonfatemi/2020/02/17/bridging-the-gender-gap-in-ai/

Fatima, S., Desouza, K. C., & Dawson, G. S. (2020). National strategic artificial intelligence plans: A multi-dimensional analysis. *Economic Analysis and Policy*, 67, 178–194. DOI: 10.1016/j.eap.2020.07.008

Fietta, V., Zecchinato, F., Stasi, B. D., Polato, M., & Monaro, M. (2022). Dissociation between users' explicit and implicit attitudes toward artificial intelligence: An experimental study. *IEEE Transactions on Human-Machine Systems*, 52(3), 481–489. DOI: 10.1109/THMS.2021.3125280

Figueiredo, M. M. (2019). Artificial Intelligence acceptance: morphological elements of the acceptance of Artificial Intelligence. (Doctoral dissertation). http://hdl.handle.net/10400.14/28555

Fraenkel, J. R., Wallen, N. E., & Hyun, H. H. (2012). *How to design and evaluate research in education*. McGraw-hill.

Freedman, J. L., Sears, D. O., & Carlsmith, J. M. (1993). *Social psychology*. Prentice Hall.

Galindo-Domínguez, H., Delgado, N., Losada, D., & Etxabe, J. M. (2024). An analysis of the use of artificial intelligence in education in Spain: The in-service teacher's perspective. *Journal of Digital Learning in Teacher Education*, 40(1), 41–56. DOI: 10.1080/21532974.2023.2284726

Gillespie, N., Lockey, S., & Curtis, C. (2021). Trust in artificial intelligence: A five country study. https://doi.org//DOI: 10.14264/e34bfa3

Goodwin, L. D. (1999). The role of factor analysis in the estimation of construct validity. *Measurement in Physical Education and Exercise Science*, 3(2), 85–100. DOI: 10.1207/s15327841mpee0302_2

Gosling, S. D., & Mason, W. (2015). Internet research in psychology. *Annual Review of Psychology*, 66(1), 877–902. DOI: 10.1146/annurev-psych-010814-015321 PMID: 25251483

Grzybowski, A., Pawlikowska–Łagód, K., & Lambert, W. C. (2024). A history of artificial intelligence. *Clinics in Dermatology*, 42(3), 221–229. DOI: 10.1016/j.clindermatol.2023.12.016 PMID: 38185196

Gunay, D., & Sisman, B. (2019). *Bilgi ve egitim teknolojileri okuryazarlığı.*, In *Egitimde ve endustride 21. yüzyil becerileri* (ss. 257-275Ankara: Pegem Akademi.

Gupta, A. K., Aggarwal, V., Sharma, V., & Naved, M. (2024). Education 4.0 and Web 3.0 technologies application for enhancement of distance learning management systems in the post–COVID-19 era. In *the role of sustainability and artificial intelligence in education improvement* (pp. 66-86Chapman and Hall/CRC.

Gurol, M. (1990). Eğitim aracı olarak bilgisayar ilişkin öğretmen görüş ve tutumları. (Unpublished Master's Thesis). Fırat Üniversitesi, Elazığ.

Guvercin, A. (2006). Examining the depression levels of the mothers and their children who see an earthquake according to some variables. https://www.proquest.com/dissertations-theses/depremzede-anneler-ve-çocuklarının-depresyon/docview/2564166661/se-2

Hauk, N., Hüffmeier, J., & Krumm, S. (2018). Ready to be a silver surfer? A meta-analysis on the relationship between chronological age and technology acceptance. *Computers in Human Behavior*, 84, 304–319. DOI: 10.1016/j.chb.2018.01.020

Irshad, H. (2020). Attitude of university students and teachers towards instructional role of artificial intelligence. *International Journal of Distance Education and E-Learning (IJDEEL)*. 5(2). https://doi.org/DOI: 10.36261/ijdeel.v5i2.1057

Jeong, H., Han, S. S., Kim, K. E., Park, I. S., Choi, Y., & Jeon, K. J. (2023). Korean dental hygiene students' perceptions and attitudes toward artificial intelligence: An online survey. *Journal of Dental Education*, 87(6), 804–812. Advance online publication. DOI: 10.1002/jdd.13189 PMID: 36806223

Judijanto, L., Atsani, M. R., & Chadijah, S. (2024). Trends in the development of artificial intelligence-based technology in education. *International Journal of Teaching and Learning*, 2(6), 1722–1723. https://injotel.org/index.php/12/article/view/197

Kagitcibasi, C. (1999). *New person and people*. Evrim publishing.

Karasar, N. (2002). *Scientific research method*. Nobel publishing.

Kaya, F., Aydin, F., Schepman, A., Rodway, P., Yetisensoy, O., & Demir-Kaya, M. (2022). The roles of personality traits, AI anxiety, and demographic factors in attitudes toward artificial intelligence. *International Journal of Human-Computer Interaction*. Advance online publication. DOI: 10.1080/10447318.2022.2151730

Keles, A. (2007). Artificial intelligence and web based intelligent tutoring system design in learning teaching process and "An application in mathematics teaching". (Doctoral Dissertation). Atatürk University. Erzurum.

Khare, K., Stewart, B., & Khare, A. (2018). Artificial intelligence and the student experience: An institutional perspective. *IAFOR Journal of Education*, 6(3).

Kilic, S. (2014). Effect size. *Journal of Mood Disorders*, 4(1), 44–46. DOI: 10.5455/jmood.20140228012836

Kim, S. W., & Lee, Y. (2020). Attitudes toward artificial intelligence of high school students' in Korea. *Journal of the Korea Convergence Society*, 11(12), 1–13. DOI: 10.15207/JKCS.2020.11.12.001

Kline, R. B. (2016). *Principles and practice of structural equation modelling*. Guilford Press.

Koc, N., & Celik, B. (2015). The impact of number of students per teacher on student achievement. *Procedia: Social and Behavioral Sciences*, 177, 65–70. DOI: 10.1016/j.sbspro.2015.02.335

Koklu, N., Buyukozturk, S., & Bokeoglu, C. O. (2007). *Statistic for Social Sciences*. Pegem.

Lin, Y., & Yu, Z. (2024). A bibliometric analysis of artificial intelligence chatbots in educational contexts. *Interactive Technology and Smart Education*, 21(2), 189–213. DOI: 10.1108/ITSE-12-2022-0165

Ma, L., & Sun, B. (2020). Machine learning and AI in marketing–connecting computing power to human insights. *International Journal of Research in Marketing*, 37(3), 481–504. DOI: 10.1016/j.ijresmar.2020.04.005

Mannuru, N. R., Shahriar, S., Teel, Z. A., Wang, T., Lund, B. D., Tijani, S., Pohboon, C. O., Agbaji, D., Alhassan, J., Galley, J. K. L., Kousari, R., Ogbadu-Oladapo, L., Saurav, S. K., Srivastava, A., Tummuru, S. P., Uppala, S., & Vaidya, P. (2023). Artificial intelligence in developing countries: The impact of generative artificial intelligence (AI) technologies for development. *Information Development*, 02666669231200628. Advance online publication. DOI: 10.1177/02666669231200628

Mantello, P., Ho, M. T., Nguyen, M. H., & Vuong, Q. H. (2021). Bosses without a heart: Socio-demographic and cross-cultural determinants of attitude toward Emotional AI in the workplace. *AI & Society*, •••, 1–23. DOI: 10.1007/s00146-021-01290-1 PMID: 34776651

Maphoto, K. B., Sevnarayan, K., Mohale, N. E., Suliman, Z., Ntsopi, T. J., & Mokoena, D. (2024). Advancing students' academic excellence in distance education: Exploring the potential of generative AI integration to improve academic writing skills. Open Praxis, 16(2), 142-159. https://search.informit.org/doi/10.3316/informit.T2024041000014190886861950

Marais, P. (2016). We can't believe what we see": Overcrowded classrooms through the eyes of student teachers. *South African Journal of Education*, 36(2), (pp.1–10). https://hdl.handle.net/10520/EJC189909. DOI: 10.15700/saje.v36n2a1201

Mariano, J., Marques, S., Ramos, M. R., Gerardo, F., Cunha, C. L., Girenko, A., Alexandersson, J., Stree, B., Lamanna, M., Lorenzatto, M., Mikkelsen, L. P., Bundgård-Jørgensen, U., Rego, S., & de Vries, H. (2022). Too old for technology? Stereotype threat and technology use by older adults. *Behaviour & Information Technology*, 41(7), 1503–1512. DOI: 10.1080/0144929X.2021.1882577

Martin, B. A., Jin, H. S., Wang, D., Nguyen, H., Zhan, K., & Wang, Y. X. (2020). The influence of consumer anthropomorphism on attitudes towards artificial intelligence trip advisors. *Journal of Hospitality and Tourism Management*, 44, 108–111. DOI: 10.1016/j.jhtm.2020.06.004

Minsky, M. (1995). *Smart machines. The third culture*. Simon & Shuster.

Morgan, G. A., Leech, N. L., Gloeckner, G. W., & Barrett, K. C. (2004). *SPSS for introductory statistics: Use and interpretation*. Psychology Press. DOI: 10.4324/9781410610539

Mouta, A., Torrecilla-Sánchez, E. M., & Pinto-Llorente, A. M. (2024). Design of a future scenarios toolkit for an ethical implementation of artificial intelligence in education. *Education and Information Technologies*, 29(9), 10473–10498. DOI: 10.1007/s10639-023-12229-y

Müller, V. C. (2016). *Risks of artificial intelligence*. Chapman & Hall. DOI: 10.1201/b19187

Murphy, R. F. (2019). Artificial intelligence applications to support K-12 teachers and teaching: A review of promising applications, opportunities, and challenges. *Perspective* Rand Corporation. https://www.rand.org/pubs/perspectives/PE315.html

Muthén, L. K., & Muthén, B. O. (2002). How to use a Monte Carlo study to decide on sample size and determine power. *Structural Equation Modeling*, 9(4), 599–620. DOI: 10.1207/S15328007SEM0904_8

Nabiyev, V. V. (2012). *Artificial Intelligence: Human-Computer Interaction*. Seçkin Yayıncılık.

Neuwirth, R. J. (2023). Prohibited artificial intelligence practices in the proposed EU artificial intelligence act (AIA). *Computer Law & Security Report*, 48(105798), 1–14. DOI: 10.1016/j.clsr.2023.105798

Nishant, R., Schneckenberg, D., & Ravishankar, M. N. (2024). The formal rationality of artificial intelligence-based algorithms and the problem of bias. *Journal of Information Technology*, 39(1), 19–40. DOI: 10.1177/02683962231176842

Numanoglu, M. (1992). Milli eğitim bakanlığı bilgisayar destekli eğitim projesi: Bilgisayar destekli eğitim yazılımlarında bulunması gereken eğitsel özellikler. (Unpublished Master's Thesis) Ankara University. Ankara.

Ong, Q. K. L., & Annamalai, N. (2024). Technological pedagogical content knowledge for twenty-first century learning skills: The game changer for teachers of industrial revolution 5.0. *Education and Information Technologies*, 29(2), 1939–1980. DOI: 10.1007/s10639-023-11852-z

Osborne, J. W., & Fitzpatrick, D. C. (2012). Replication analysis in exploratory factor analysis: What it is and why it makes your analysis better. *Practical Assessment, Research & Evaluation*, 17(15), 1–8.

Oztemel, E. (1992). Integrating expert systems and neural networks for intelligent on-line statistical process control. (Doctoral Dissertation). University of Wales. Cardiff.

Park, I., Kim, D., Moon, J., Kim, S., Kang, Y., & Bae, S. (2022). Searching for new technology acceptance model under social con-text: Analyzing the determinants of acceptance of intelligent information technology in digital transformation and implications for the requisites of digital sustainability. *Sustainability (Basel)*, 14(1), 579. DOI: 10.3390/su14010579

Popenici, S. A., & Kerr, S. (2017). Exploring the impact of artificial intelligence on teaching and learning in higher education. *Research and Practice in Technology Enhanced Learning*, 22(12), 22. Advance online publication. DOI: 10.1186/s41039-017-0062-8 PMID: 30595727

Roll, I., & Wylie, R. (2016). Evolution and revolution in artificial intelligence in education. *International Journal of Artificial Intelligence in Education*, 26(2), 582–599. DOI: 10.1007/s40593-016-0110-3

Russel, S., & Norvig, P. (2010). *Artificial intelligence - a modern approach*. Pearson Education.

Schepman, A., & Rodway, P. (2020). Initial validation of the general attitudes towards Artificial Intelligence Scale. *Computers in Human Behavior Reports*, 1, 100014. Advance online publication. DOI: 10.1016/j.chbr.2020.100014 PMID: 34235291

Schepman, A., & Rodway, P. (2022). The general attitudes towards artificial intelligence scale (GAAIS): Confirmatory validation and associations with personality, corporate distrust, and general trust. *International Journal of Human-Computer Interaction*. Advance online publication. DOI: 10.1080/10447318.2022.2085400

Sherif, M., & Sherif, C. W. (1996). Introduction to social psychology 2. (Tra. Mustafa Atakay & Aysun Yılmaz). İstanbul: Sosyal.

Simon, H. A. (1983). Why should machines learn? In *Machine learning*. Morgan Kaufmann., DOI: 10.1016/B978-0-08-051054-5.50006-6

Sindermann, C., Sha, P., Zhou, M., Wernicke, J., Schmitt, H. S., Li, M., Sariyska, R., Stavrou, M., Becker, B., & Montag, C. (2021). Assessing the attitude towards artificial intelligence: Introduction of a short measure in German, Chinese, and English language. *Kunstliche Intelligenz*, 35(1), 109–118. DOI: 10.1007/s13218-020-00689-0

Singil, N. (2022). Artificial intelligence and human rights. *Public and Private International Law Bulletin*, 42(1), 121–158. DOI: 10.26650/ppil.2022.42.1.970856

Spector, J. M., & Ma, S. (2019). Inquiry and critical thinking skills for the next generation: From artificial intelligence back to human intelligence. *Smart Learning Environments*, 6(1), 1–11. DOI: 10.1186/s40561-019-0088-z

Stefan, A. D. (2017). Exploring the impact of artificial intelligence on teaching and learning in higher education. *Research and Practice in Technology Enhanced Learning*, 1(1), 3–13. DOI: 10.1186/s41039-017-0062-8

Stevens, J. (2002). *Applied multivariate statistics for the social sciences*. Lawrence Erlbaurn Associates.

Tabachnick, B. G., & Fidell, L. S. (2013). *Using multivariate statistics* (6th ed.). Pearson.

Tanaka, J. S. (1987). How big is big enough?": Sample size and goodness of fit in structural equation models with latent variables. *Child Development*, 58(1), 134–146. DOI: 10.2307/1130296

Tasci, G., & Celebi, M. (2020). A new paradigm in education: "Artificial intelligence in higher education. *OPUS International Journal of Society Researches*, 16(29), 2346–2370. DOI: 10.26466/opus.747634

Tejani, A. S., Ng, Y. S., Xi, Y., & Rayan, J. C. (2024). Understanding and mitigating bias in imaging artificial intelligence. *Radiographics*, 44(5), e230067. DOI: 10.1148/rg.230067 PMID: 38635456

Triguero, I., Molina, D., Poyatos, J., Del Ser, J., & Herrera, F. (2024). General purpose artificial intelligence systems (GPAIS): Properties, definition, taxonomy, societal implications and responsible governance. *Information Fusion*, 103, 102135. DOI: 10.1016/j.inffus.2023.102135

Usman, F. O., Kess-Momoh, A. J., Ibeh, C. V., Elufioye, A. E., Ilojianya, V. I., & Oyeyemi, O. P.Favour Oluwadamilare UsmanAzeez Jason Kess-MomohChidera Victoria IbehAkinola Elumakin ElufioyeValentine Ikenna IlojianyaOluwaseun Peter Oyeyemi. (2024). Entrepreneurial innovations and trends: A global review: Examining emerging trends, challenges, and opportunities in the field of entrepreneurship, with a focus on how technology and globalization are shaping new business ventures. *International Journal of Science and Research Archive*, 11(1), 552–569. DOI: 10.30574/ijsra.2024.11.1.0079

Vaza, R. N., Parmar, A. B., Mishra, P. S., Abdullah, I., & Velu, C. M. (2024). Security and privacy concerns in Ai-enabled IOT educational frameworks: An in-depth analysis. *Educational Administration: Theory and Practice*, 30(4), 8436–8445. DOI: 10.53555/kuey.v30i4.2742

Volti, R., & Croissant, J. (2024). *Society and technological change*. Waveland press.

Vu, H. T., & Lim, J. (2022). Effects of country and individual factors on public acceptance of artificial intelligence and robotics technologies: A multilevel SEM analysis of 28-country survey data. *Behaviour & Information Technology*, 41(7), 1515–1528. DOI: 10.1080/0144929X.2021.1884288

Wang, P. (2019). On defining artificial intelligence. *Journal of Artificial General Intelligence*, 10(2), 1–37. DOI: 10.2478/jagi-2019-0002

Wu, X., Duan, R., & Ni, J. (2024). Unveiling security, privacy, and ethical concerns of ChatGPT. *Journal of Information and Intelligence*, 2(2), 102–115. DOI: 10.1016/j.jiixd.2023.10.007

Ximei, L., Latif, Z., Danish, , Latif, S., & waraa, K. (2024). Estimating the impact of information technology on economic growth in south Asian countries: The silver lining of education. *Information Development*, 40(1), 147–157. DOI: 10.1177/02666669221100426

Xu, W., Gao, Z., & Ge, L. (2024). New research paradigms and agenda of human factors science in the intelligence era. *Acta Psychologica Sinica*, 56(3), 363. DOI: 10.3724/SP.J.1041.2024.00363

Yaslioglu, M. M. (2017). Factor analysis and validity in social sciences: Application of exploratory and confirmatory factor analyses. *Istanbul University Journal of the School of Business*, 46, (pp.74-85). https://dergipark.org.tr/tr/download/article-file/369427

Zhang, B., & Dafoe, A. (2019). Artificial Intelligence: American attitudes and trends. *SSRN*. http://dx.doi.org/DOI: 10.2139/ssrn.3312874

Zhang, T., Lu, X., Zhu, X., & Zhang, J. (2023). The contributions of AI in the development of ideological and political perspectives in education. *Heliyon*, 9(3), e13403. Advance online publication. DOI: 10.1016/j.heliyon.2023.e13403 PMID: 36879973

ADDITIONAL READING

Kaya, F., Aydin, F., Schepman, A., Rodway, P., Yetisensoy, O., & Demir-Kaya, M. (2022). The roles of personality traits, AI anxiety, and demographic factors in attitudes toward artificial intelligence. *International Journal of Human-Computer Interaction*. Advance online publication. DOI: 10.1080/10447318.2022.2151730

Schepman, A., & Rodway, P. (2020). Initial validation of the general attitudes towards Artificial Intelligence Scale. *Computers in Human Behavior Reports*, 1, 100014. Advance online publication. DOI: 10.1016/j.chbr.2020.100014 PMID: 34235291

Schepman, A., & Rodway, P. (2022). The general attitudes towards artificial intelligence scale (GAAIS): Confirmatory validation and associations with personality, corporate distrust, and general trust. *International Journal of Human-Computer Interaction*. Advance online publication. DOI: 10.1080/10447318.2022.2085400

KEY TERMS AND DEFINITONS

Artificial Intelligence: Artificial intelligence (AI) is the ability of a machine to simulate human intelligence. This includes the ability to learn, reason, solve problems, and make decisions. AI research has been highly successful in developing effective techniques for solving a wide range of problems, from game playing to medical diagnosis.

Attitude: Attitude is a learned predisposition to respond to a person, object, or event in a consistently favorable or unfavorable way.

Primary School: A state-authorized institution, operating for a minimum of four years, was established for the purpose of providing basic education for boys and girls of a school-going age.

Teacher: A teacher, also called a schoolteacher or formally an educator, is a person who helps students to acquire knowledge, competence, or virtue, via the practice of teaching.

Education: Direct or indirect assistance, inside or outside of the school, for children and young people to acquire the knowledge, skills and understanding necessary for them to take their place in the life of.

Chapter 3
Artificial Intelligence Experiences of Pre-Service Preschool Teachers

Feyza Aydin Bölükbaş
Aksaray University, Turkey

Kadriye Selin Budak
 https://orcid.org/0000-0002-8161-7074
Bilecik University, Turkey

Emine Bozkurt Polat
 https://orcid.org/0000-0002-1821-028X
Kahramanmaraş Sütçü İmam University, Turkey

Kübra Engin
 https://orcid.org/0000-0003-2590-1115
Gazi University, Turkey

İlkay Ulutaş
 https://orcid.org/0000-0002-2234-0773
Gazi University, Turkey

ABSTRACT

This section covers artificial intelligence integration in education, artificial intelligence literacy, artificial intelligence in early childhood, and the role of teachers in utilising artificial intelligence, as discussed in the literature. Within this framework, the use of artificial intelligence tools by pre-service teachers has been analyzed

DOI: 10.4018/979-8-3693-3944-2.ch003

based on interviews. Advice on how to effectively utilize artificial intelligence and how to employ artificial intelligence tools and applications ethically is provided. The experiences of pre-service teachers who use artificial intelligence tools whilst organising educational activities are intended to offer guidance at this juncture.

INTRODUCTION

In recent years, research on artificial intelligence technologies in early childhood has also increased (Su & Yang 2022). Artificial intelligence shows that the use of voice assistants, smart toys (William et al. 2019), and education in children's daily lives is a potentially powerful tool (Zhang & Chen 2022). Although children can easily experience these tools in social environments, they require guided teaching processes for the targeted acquisition of calculative thinking. In this context, in order to support children's AI literacies, it is necessary to support the AI literacies of experts, teachers, and pre-service teachers who interact with children.

The limited number of studies conducted with pre-service teachers in the research conducted actually reveals a limitation in the literature, and it is thought that pre-service teachers are also an important stakeholder in this process (Holmes et al., 2019). It is considered necessary to structure educational processes to support digital literacies in higher education institution curricula.

Changes Brought by Technology in Education

As a social discipline, education is viewed as a field that examines and directs the process of educating individuals, transferring knowledge and values, gaining skills, and transferring cultural heritage. Consequently, this discipline includes various theories, methods, and practices to contribute to the development of individuals and society. In the social dimension of education, issues such as how people learn within social structures, the social effects of this learning, and the interaction of education systems with social structures are examined. Particularly in line with technological advances, the interaction between education and technology becomes inevitable, and in this transformation, the interaction occurs bilaterally. Today, the advancement of digital technology and the frequent occurrence of global crises such as pandemics and civil wars have made it a duty to protect education as a fundamental human right (Coccia, 2019; Taylor et al., 2021). Especially in times of crisis and conflict, the physical inaccessibility of educational institutions has increased the importance of digital education tools. In this context, as a social responsibility, making education accessible through digital platforms is considered an important step to ensure that everyone has equal educational opportunities (Holmes et al., 2021). In the modern world, digital technology is seen not only as a tool but also as a living environment that opens up new opportunities. Non-governmental organizations around the world, such as UNESCO, in their reports, support various measures to expand educational opportunities and improve the relevance and quality of learning processes, to promote lifelong learning, and for this, digital innovation involving the use of information and communication technologies (ICT) is necessary. It also emphasizes the strengthening of education and learning management systems and the use of digital tools for effective monitoring of learning processes. This approach aims to create a more comprehensive and accessible environment in the field of education (Holmes et al., 2021). The change and transformation towards artificial intelligence in education is taking place in the academic world based on various research and applications. One of the most important aspects of this transformation is the use of artificial intelligence to improve learning processes. For example, AI techniques such as machine learning and data analytics can be used to assess children's performance, identify learning disabilities, and personalize teaching materials (Chen et al., 2020). In this way, learning environments that better respond to the needs of students can be created. Moreover, technological developments such as artificial intelligence are now considered among the preferred and supported digital innovations in terms of providing equal opportunities, offering adaptive learning systems, and providing children with opportunities for a customized experience according to their individual needs (Sunitha & Gunavardhan, 2023).

What is Artificial Intelligence?

In line with the definition obtained by including many skills within the scope, artificial intelligence is an umbrella term covering technology-based applications that can make commands and tasks intelligently applicable. When the skills are analyzed, it is the study of artificial neural networks with qualities similar to a human brain such as learning, creativity, reasoning, problem solving and creativity, and is defined as the brain of computers, robots and other smart technologies (European Parliament, 2023). Artificial intelligence definitions, also referred to as "the science of creating intelligent machines" Akgun & Greenhow, 2021; refers to the science and engineering of producing intelligent machines that solve different types of problems in the context of new updates, with exciting technological innovations, especially capable of performing cognitive tasks such as learning and problem solving (Wang, 2019).

As in other basic disciplines, artificial intelligence study areas that offer a context that attracts the attention of experts, especially in the field of education, provide great benefit and convenience for learners to personalize their experiences (Sabzalieva & Valentini, 2023). It is aimed at developing artificial intelligence literacy in line with the goals of moving from consumption to production (Ng et al., 2021). In line with this transformation, artificial intelligence is taking its place in education. In this transformation process, digital tools are changing in the direction of interacting with tablets and toys with much more computing power. New technology related to data-based change in computing has been adapted for use in all segments of life, including work, entertainment, social relationships and learning (Vartianianen et al., 2023).

Virtual assistants like Alexa, Siri, and Cortana have been in use for quite some time. However, in recent years, the emergence of productive artificial intelligence has led to the development of applications such as OpenAI ChatGPT. ChatGPT is a chatbot specifically designed to engage in close language interactions with humans and provide answers to questions. Additionally, alongside language-based generative AI programs, there are image-based applications like Dall-E, DreamStudio, and Lexica IA that are also being utilized. With these advancements, the integration of artificial intelligence into educational processes has become inevitable (Álvarez-Herrero, 2024; Chen et al., 2020). Research indicates that the use of artificial intelligence by both children and teachers improves teaching-learning processes (Choi et al., 2023; Su & Yang, 2022). Artificial intelligence has the capacity to grant access to numerous resources and learning materials in the education sector. It also offers support by providing answers to questions and supplementary information, and it can address individual children's needs through various assessment tools. Furthermore, AI provides teachers with support tools for personalized assessment of children and feedback. Through the analysis of big data using AI tools, teachers can obtain valuable information to enhance their teaching practices (Álvarez-Herrero, 2024).

Further research is necessary to better comprehend and mitigate uncertainties regarding the impact of AI on education, as well as to understand how it can benefit educational practices. The swift integration of AI technologies into educational processes poses challenges in terms of implementing infrastructure and preparation processes within schools and universities (Holmes et al., 2021; Hussin, 2018). To effectively navigate this integration and establish a clear framework for competencies related to AI technologies, the concept of AI literacy is employed. AI literacy pertains to the ability to correctly identify, utilize, and assess AI-related tools while adhering to ethical standards. Moreover, AI literacy does not necessitate individuals to be experts in the underlying theories and developments of AI. Rather, individuals are deemed AI literate if they can competently and judiciously utilize AI products (Wang et al., 2023).

Artificial Intelligence Literacy

As each of the changes in media and communication occur, the mentality of the consuming, enjoying, learning society appears to change with them. This alteration also modifies the needs of individuals. Whilst in the past the acquisition of basic literacy skills was emphasized, today terms such as digital literacy, media literacy, artificial intelligence literacy have taken their place. Artificial intelligence literacy is significantly related to digital literacy, attitudes towards robots and the use of artificial intelligence in individuals' social lives (Wang, Rau & Yuan, 2023). In order for individuals to live in the digital world, learning and acquiring these literacies has become a fundamental priority (Long & Magerto, 2020). In the process of acquiring this literacy, it is considered necessary to critically evaluate these technologies rather than accepting them without question. Additionally, it is seen that it is important for every individual, including children, to have knowledge about artificial intelligence and be able to use it, as it encompasses a set of competencies that enable individuals to communicate and collaborate (Su et al., 2023; Druga and Ko 2021). In summary, the process involves acquiring a series of functions such as the ability to use, understand, and interact with these technologies in line with their intended purpose (Ng et al., 2021). Upon closer examination of these abilities, skills such as understanding how these systems operate, analyzing data, interpreting machine learning algorithms, and awareness of AI ethics and security issues emerge. It is emphasized that the ability to critically evaluate the reliability, credibility, and validity of information is crucial (Li & Zaki, 2024), particularly due to the risk posed by artificial intelligence tools providing false and misleading information or suggestions, which could threaten individuals' safety. Effective management of people's fears and concerns, especially in a rapidly evolving field, is achieved through adept utilization and administration of these technologies. Understanding the potential impact of these technologies is especially important for individuals, as it enhances their ability to assess and adapt to technological developments' effects on human life. Therefore, being capable of evaluating and managing the impacts of these technologies can instill individuals with greater confidence in facing the future (Druga et al., 2019). Ongoing studies on artificial intelligence education for young children without prior knowledge highlight the current nature of this field of research. Educational research predominantly focuses on older children, which presents a significant limitation in the realm of education (Ng & Chu, 2021; Kong et al., 2021). The limited focus on artificial intelligence solely with older age groups underscores the need for broader exploration across all age ranges. There's a recognized importance in fostering various literacies from early childhood, as the quality of this period significantly influences individuals' ability to become productive members of society. To ensure that society benefits from technology integration and individuals attain productive roles, it's imperative to support digital literacy and artificial intelligence literacy from an early age, alongside embracing the cognitive principles underpinning these systems.

Artificial Intelligence in Education In the transition from an industrial society to an information society, social requirements and the needs of individuals are changing. Teachers need to include technology integration and artificial intelligence in their professional development processes and adapt to this process known as education 4.0 (Napoleon & Ramanujam, 2022; Li & Zaki, 2024). Acquiring 21st-century skills, which are considered essential for individuals to effectively utilize digital transformation and artificial intelligence in education, is important in terms of adapting to changing social conditions. In recent studies, researchers emphasize that 'Artificial Intelligence Literacy' should be a 21st-century skill that should be acquired to underline the importance of integrating artificial intelligence into 21st-century digital literacy skills from a young age (Ng et al., 2021). Artificial intelligence impacts educational processes in various ways, presenting both applications and challenges (Figure 1).

Figure 1. The multifaceted impact of artificial intelligence in education

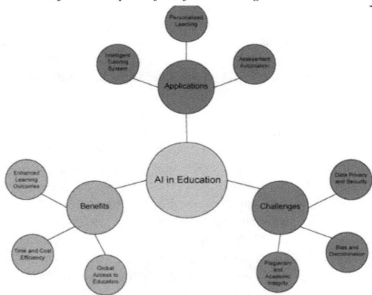

AI applications in education encompass personalized learning, intelligent tutoring systems, assessment automation, and fostering teacher-student collaboration. Whilst integrating AI into education yields positive outcomes, there are accompanying concerns regarding data privacy, security, bias, and the preservation of teacher-student relationships. Addressing these concerns is pivotal for ensuring the ethical advancement of the integration process. Incorporating AI literacy and ethics into the education curriculum is essential for facilitating qualified integration amidst the rapid changes brought about by artificial intelligence (Kamalov et al., 2023). It is crucial to highlight the impact of teachers and pre-service teachers utilizing artificial intelligence technologies on both pre-service and in-service educational processes. There is a growing need for innovative approaches in digital learning platforms, personalized learning environments, increased internet usage, and the integration of cutting-edge technologies like augmented reality and artificial intelligence (Tapan Broutın, 2024). Pre-service teachers play a pivotal role in shaping the integration of AI technologies into educational settings. Their acceptance of AI is believed to significantly impact the future development and implementation of AI in education. Given the challenges that AI presents in education, pre-service teachers hold a crucial position in addressing these issues and finding effective methods to incorporate these tools into the classroom (Zhang et al., 2023).

Artificial Intelligence in Early Childhood

As artificial intelligence (AI) becomes increasingly prevalent across various fields such as healthcare, automotive, social media, and entertainment, it significantly alters people's lives. Consequently, there is a growing need to provide education on AI literacy, particularly during the acquisition process of artificial intelligence literacy, which has become accessible to individuals of all ages today. These educational efforts should be particularly geared towards enabling individuals to adapt to these technologies effectively. Given the rapidly evolving digital landscape, it is anticipated that supporting the development of AI literacy and literacy acquisition, especially during early childhood, will become essential as individuals encounter AI applications throughout their lives (Su & Yang, 2022; Ng et al., 2021). Understanding the fundamental functions of AI, learning how these systems operate, and effectively utilizing AI applications are expected to become fundamental components of technologically advancing societies. It is important to acknowledge both the positive and negative impacts of implementing AI in early childhood education. While AI offers benefits such as personalized learning and interactive support, concerns about its excessive and improper use in educational settings exist (Chen & Lin, 2023). Rather than merely discussing the drawbacks of AI technologies, it is essential to take measures to mitigate risks and ensure quality interactions for children. This entails establishing appropriate technological integrations to provide children with high-quality experiences both at home and in educational settings. Key considerations include selecting and structuring AI applications based on children's developmental characteristics and ages, ensuring accessibility beyond text-based interactions to accommodate children who do not yet possess literacy skills, and providing purposeful guidance to help children understand, use, and evaluate AI. While children may interact with AI in various social settings, it is important to recognize that they may not necessarily develop computational thinking skills, even if they engage with AI-driven interactions. Therefore, they need guidance from individuals proficient in AI literacy to support their understanding and utilization of these tools (Druga et al., 2017). In this regard, individuals with AI literacy should provide support and convey usage criteria to children. Given the complexity of AI-based applications and children's developmental stage in understanding and using these technologies, teachers play a crucial role in guiding students through this process. By imparting knowledge about the logic, functionality, and ethical use of AI applications, teachers enable students to use these technologies more conscientiously. Additionally, teaching AI-based applications and elucidating their usage areas and potential benefits to students enhance their motivation and foster a positive attitude towards technology. Consequently, teachers' ability to teach AI-based applications to children effectively strengthens students' digital literacy, preparing them for the digital age. However, for teachers to acquire this competence, there is a need to develop programs that cultivate AI literacy among teacher candidates during their higher education training.

Teacher and Artificial Intelligence

As digital technologies continue to reshape educational dynamics, the roles of teachers are also evolving. All educational stakeholders emphasize the integration of technology into educational processes, highlighting the importance of guiding children's knowledge acquisition in this paradigm shift (Mensah & Ampadu, 2024). Teachers are tasked with supporting students in embracing technological innovations, considering children's natural inclination towards these advancements. The integration of new technological developments into education should encompass methodological shifts and incorporate a scientific approach, necessitating adjustments in teaching methods and assessment techniques to align with technology (Li & Zaki, 2024). In the educational sphere, AI holds potential to assist teachers in predicting students' learning progress and performance, recommending learning materials, and automating assessments. This can enhance students' learning experiences through intelligent agent systems, concept instruction, chatbots, and recommendation systems (Williams et al., 2019).

DigCompEdu provides a framework that provides guidelines to help educators integrate technological tools and applications in a qualified way in the educational process (Ng., et al., 2023). In the context of the European Digital Competence Framework for Educators (DigCompEdu), it states that educators are at the center of successfully adopting AI systems and realizing the potential benefits of digital data in education. Therefore, teachers' understanding of the opportunities and challenges of using AI systems is also crucial for more efficient and ethical use of AI systems in education. This model includes a wide range of components organized in six main areas: (1) professional engagement, (2) digital resources, (3) teaching and learning, (4) assessment, (5) empowering students, (6) facilitating students' digital competitiveness (European Commission, 2022) (see Figure 2).

Table 1. DigCompEdu framework for teachers' AI competency

Area	Capability Elements	Potential Indicators
1. Professional Participation	Critically identify the implications of using AI and data in education	Ø Active participation in continuous professional learning Ø Evaluating the ethical implications of AI systems in school Ø Promote the ethical use of AI and data
2. Digital Resources	Data management	Ø Being aware of the types of personal data Ø To know the responsibilities regarding data security and confidentiality Ø Understand that the processing of personal data is subject to regulations
3. Teaching and Learning	Managing digital technologies in education	Ø Participate in the development of AI-supported learning practices Ø Explain how AI systems serve educational goals Ø Discuss the use of ethical AI in education
4. Evaluation	Use of AI in student assessment	Ø Understanding student responses to automatic feedback Ø Evaluating sources of bias in AI systems Ø Understanding AI's capacity to assess creativity and social capabilities
5. Empowering Students	Personalizedd learning tailored to student needs	Ø Ability to adapt the behavior of personalized learning systems Ø To be able to meet the needs of different student groups Ø Continuous monitoring of the results of the use of AI

continued on following page

Table 1. Continued

Area	Capability Elements	Potential Indicators
6. Facilitating Digital Capabilities	Students' ethical use of digital technologies	Ø To teach students the ethical aspects of AI and data use Ø Guiding students in digital content creation and problem solving

(European Commission, 2022)

This table contains outlined indicators for the development of educators' AI capabilities so that it can help them to better manage technological integration processes. Each domain describes the skills and know-how required by educators to effectively support teaching and learning processes in the digital age.

Social relationships between teachers and students, such as emotional intelligence, social interaction, inspiration, motivation, etc. are components of the teaching and learning process. Since AI has difficulty in imitating interpersonal relationships, it is considered appropriate to be used to support the learning environment instead of being tools to replace teachers (Guan et al., 2020; Shen et al., 2020).

Teachers' roles in the integration process are of great importance. Teachers' competencies are very important for the quality of technology integration in education. It has been determined that teachers face difficulties in artificial intelligence knowledge, skills, and confidence in artificial intelligence applications due to the lack of curriculum design and teaching guidelines (Su & Yang, 2022; Su et al., 2023).

Artificial intelligence offers teachers opportunities such as improving the teaching process, providing individualized learning experiences and facilitating administrative tasks (Zawacki-Richter et al., 2019). For this reason, it is important to include content related to artificial intelligence and its use in education in the education processes of pre-service teachers in order to support professional development. Artificial intelligence tools that facilitate and accelerate stages such as evaluation and planning (Baker et al., 2017) can support the learning process by providing more time for teacher-student interaction. In addition, the functions of AI tools provide an interactive learning environment by supporting and improving learning strategies (Johnson et al., 2016). Artificial intelligence tools can adapt learning according to individual needs (Kulik & Fletcher, 2016). Pre-service teachers can enrich and develop learning contents and tools by taking ideas from these tools. Practices to be carried out in learning environments created with virtual simulation provided by artificial intelligence can support pre-service teachers' practical skills by providing them with experiences in classroom management and implementation of teaching strategies (Harris et al., 2019).

Situations such as not all institutions or students not having access to artificial intelligence tools, not complying with measures to ensure data security, not developing artificial intelligence literacy skills for accessing correct/ethical data may pose a risk in issues such as inability to ensure equality between students during applications, data loss, and information pollution (Selwyn, 2016; Miller, 2018; O'Neil, 2016). For this reason, there are some important points that teachers should pay attention to during the integration of artificial intelligence into education. Since it is impossible for artificial intelligence to provide interpersonal interactions with the current technology, it is aimed to support the learning environment instead of replacing teachers in educational processes. Therefore, teachers should continue to support students socially and emotionally by maintaining their role as motivators and guides in the process (Williamson & Piattoeva, 2020). Since artificial intelligence is a new technology, teachers may need support in acquiring adequate skills related to its use and integration into the educational process (Holmes et al., 2019). In this context, teacher training programs should be structured in a way to introduce the features of new technologies, provide experiences with these technologies and provide practice on integration into education.

Artificial intelligence processes user data as well as many other data. For this reason, it is necessary to take the necessary precautions to ensure the information privacy of itself and its students and to act in accordance with the laws (Binns et al., 2020). For this reason, it is important for the teacher to have prior knowledge about information privacy, ethical rules, working principles of artificial intelligence and laws regarding its use, and to inform his/her students about this issue during the integration process.

Artificial intelligence has limitations. The data obtained through artificial intelligence should be analyzed with a critical approach to eliminate these limitations (Williamson & Piattoeva, 2020). Teachers should be aware of the limitations, have the AI literacy skills to critically evaluate them, and aim to provide these skills to their students.

To adequately prepare pre-service teachers for the challenges they will face in their professional careers, it is essential that they are equipped with technological skills and gain valuable experiences in this area. As such, this research aims to investigate the experiences of pre-service teachers regarding artificial intelligence. Specifically, it seeks to explore the experiences of pre-service teachers who are actively engaged with and utilize technological innovations as part of their university education.

RESEARCH MODEL

The research is a survey design study from quantitative research methods. Survey research aims to describe certain characteristics of the participants such as opinions, attitudes, etc., regarding a subject, concept, event, or situation (Büyüköztürk et al.,

2020). Since the current research aims to reveal the use of artificial intelligence by pre-service preschool teachers, it is conducted within the survey model.

Study Group

The study group of the research comprises 132 pre-service teachers who are studying in the preschool education departments of four universities in Turkey and who agreed to participate in the study. The study group was determined through convenience sampling. Convenience sampling is defined as collecting data from data sources that researchers can easily access, and it allows for cost reduction (Büyüköztürk et al., 2020). The researchers accessed the students studying in the preschool education departments of the universities they had access to, and the prospective teachers who volunteered to participate in the study completed the form. Demographic data about the participants are presented in Table 2.

Table 2. Demographic data of participants

	f	%
Gender		
Man	21	15,9
Woman	111	84,1
Age		
19 and below	15	11,4
20	27	20,5
21	35	26,5
22	23	17,4
23 and above	32	24,2
Experience with Artificial Intelligence		
No Experience	47	35,6
Limited	71	53,8
I Use Often	14	10,6
Use of Artificial Intelligence Tools		
ChatGbt	58	44
Virtual Assistant on the Phone	16	12,12
Other	8	6,06

Of the participants of the study, 15.9% were male and 84.1% were female. 11.4% of the pre-service teachers were 19 years old or younger, 20.5% were 20 years old, 26.5% were 21 years old, 17.4% were 22 years old and 24.2% were 23 years old or older. Among the participants, 35.6% stated that they had no experience with artificial intelligence, 53.8% stated that they had limited experience and 10.6% stated that they frequently used artificial intelligence. 44% of the candidates stated that they used ChatGPT, 12.12% stated that they used virtual assistants and 6.06% stated that they used other artificial intelligence tools.

Data Collection Tools

To collect the data for the study, researchers developed a questionnaire on Pre-service Preschool Teachers' Artificial Intelligence Integration in Education. During the questionnaire development, the literature was utilized, and the developed questionnaire was presented to the opinions of five field experts. After the corrections were made based on the expert opinions, the questionnaire was finalized. The first part of the questionnaire contains questions that reveal the demographic data of the participants, including the university of education, age, gender, and grade level. The second part of the questionnaire contains 15 questions that explore the views of pre-service teachers on the use of artificial intelligence in education, have multiple choice answers and allow more than one answer to be selected. Some of the questions in the questionnaire are as follows: 'How would you like to use artificial intelligence in the educational process?', 'What advantages do you think integrating artificial intelligence into your educational processes provides?', 'Which artificial intelligence tools do you believe can improve children's learning experience?', 'What kind of training or resources do you think will be necessary for pre-service teachers to prepare for the use of artificial intelligence tools in education?', 'At which level of education do you think artificial intelligence tools will be more effective?', 'For what purposes do you use artificial intelligence tools?'

Data Collection

The questions in the questionnaire were transferred to the online platform via Google Forms and the link created was sent to the pre-service teachers studying in the preschool teaching department of the universities to which the researchers had access via social media and email groups. The pre-service teachers answered the survey questions online on a voluntary basis.

Data Analysis

The data obtained through Google Forms were transferred to the SPSS software package. As the tool used was not a standard measurement tool, descriptive analyzes were applied to the questions. Percentage and frequency features are indicated.

Findings

The findings obtained in the research conducted to determine the experiences of pre-service preschool teachers about artificial intelligence were analyzed and presented under three themes: 'pre-service preschool teachers' purposes and competencies of using artificial intelligence', 'pre-service preschool teachers' views on the integration of artificial intelligence into education', and 'pre-service preschool teachers' artificial intelligence needs'. Findings related to pre-service teachers' purposes and competencies of using artificial intelligence are given in Table 3."

Table 3. Findings related to pre-service preschool teachers' aims and competences for using artificial intelligence

Categories	Subcategories	f	%
Purposes of Using Artificial Intelligence	Academic writing	44	7.54
	Coding	25	4.28
	Text Generation	51	8.74
	Writing Assistants	29	4.97
	Video editing	68	11.65
	Photo editing	68	11.65
	Text Editing	57	9.77
	Design / Design	60	10.28
	Presentation	90	15.44
	Content Editing	52	8.92
	Music instruments	27	4.63
	Story Creation	45	7.72
	None of them	2	0.34
	Total	598	100
Proficiency in the ability to apply artificial intelligence tools in the classroom	Very adequate	9	6.82
	Adequate	35	26.52
	Slightly adequate	54	40.91
	Less is enough	20	15.15
	I'm not sure at all	14	10.61
	Total	132	100
Use of artificial intelligence in the education process	In the process of activity preparation	100	34.60
	During the activity implementation process	69	23.87
	During the evaluation process	55	19.03
	Individualised learning adaptation	64	22.15
	Other	1	0.35
	Total	289	100

When Table 2 was analyzed, it was seen that pre-service teachers mostly used artificial intelligence in preparing presentations (f=90), and they also stated that they frequently used artificial intelligence tools in video editing (f=68) and photo editing (f=68). Pre-service teachers stated that they used artificial intelligence tools at least in coding. Very few of the pre-service teachers who participated in the study stated that they did not use artificial intelligence tools. In addition, when the competencies of pre-service teachers regarding their ability to apply artificial intelligence tools in the classroom are examined, it is seen that the majority of them consider themselves "somewhat sufficient" (f=54). In addition, while pre-service teachers often saw themselves as "sufficient" (f=35), very few of them stated that they were "very sufficient" (f=9). In addition, when the pre-service teachers' use of artificial intelligence in the education process is analyzed, it is seen that pre-service teachers frequently use artificial intelligence in the process of preparing activities (f=100). In addition, a large number of pre-service teachers stated that they also used artificial intelligence in the activity implementation process (f=69) and individualized learning adaptation (f=64). One of the pre-service teachers (PT64) stated that he would not use artificial intelligence in the specified categories and that he would use it to get ideas:

"I prefer to use artificial intelligence to have an idea about how I can do activities on a subject. As I mentioned, I use it only for the sake of having an idea. I do not want to use it at the stages mentioned above. Because I think it may cause my creativity and lack of knowledge on issues such as what is an activity and how to prepare it as a prospective teacher."

The findings related to pre-service preschool teachers' views on the integration of artificial intelligence into education are given in Table 4.

Table 4. Findings related to pre-service preschool teachers' views on the integration of artificial intelligence into education

Categories	Subcategories	f	%
Advantages of integrating artificial intelligence into education processes	Time saving	96	26.67
	Active participation of children	65	18.06
	Data-based assessment to improve teaching strategies	76	21.11
		44	12.22
	Individualized learning for children	68	18.89
	Increasing children's interest and motivation	1	0.28
	Other (Please specify):	10	2.78
	I do not think there are advantages.	360	100
	Total		
Disadvantages of integrating artificial intelligence into the education process	Failure to ensure data reliability	74	25.87
	Blunting cognitive skills	68	23.78
	Ethical violations	61	21.33
	Inability to control artificial intelligence	69	24.13
	Other	2	0.70
	I don't think there are disadvantages	12	4.20
	Total	286	100
The ability of artificial intelligence tools to improve children's learning experience	Adaptive learning platforms that adjust to the individual needs of children	81	28.03
	Intelligent tutoring systems for one-to-one support	62	21.45
	Evaluation and feedback systems	64	22.15
	Virtual reality experiences for engaging learning	81	28.03
	Other	1	0.35
	Total	289	100

When Table 3 is analyzed, it is seen that pre-service teachers stated that artificial intelligence would provide the most time saving (f=96) in integrating artificial intelligence into educational processes. In addition, they frequently stated that it can be used in data-based evaluation (f=76) to develop teaching strategies. Very few of the pre-service teachers (f=10) do not think that artificial intelligence has advantages in the education process. Apart from these subcategories, one of the pre-service teachers stated that he sometimes used artificial intelligence to design creative open-ended questions for the assessment process.

The pre-service teachers stated that not being able to ensure data security (f=74) was the most disadvantageous factor in integrating artificial intelligence into the education process. In addition, they stated that not being able to control artificial intelligence (f=69) and using artificial intelligence blunting cognitive skills (f=68) were disadvantages. 12 of the candidates think that there is no disadvantage of artificial intelligence. In addition, 2 pre-service teachers expressed opinions outside the determined subcategories. One of the pre-service teachers who expressed opinions outside these subcategories stated that he found artificial intelligence scary, while the other expressed his opinion as follows: *"Since it is easy, it dulls mental thinking skills, in a way, we can say thinking instead of the person, which is a negative thing."*

In addition, it is seen that pre-service teachers mostly stated that adaptive learning platforms adjusted to the individual needs of children can be used to improve children's learning experience (f=81) and pre-service teachers stated that artificial intelligence can provide virtual reality experiences for engaging learning (f=81). In addition, they also stated that evaluation and feedback systems (f=64) and smart lesson experiences can be provided for one-to-one support to children (f=62), but one of the participants stated that artificial intelligence should not be used in children:

> *"I believe that it should be kept away from children, I think it would be more correct for the teacher to use it and integrate it into children accordingly, it is definitely wrong for children to use it directly because ready-made information gradually damages the creativity of the individual."*

The findings related to the artificial intelligence needs of pre-service preschool teachers are given in Table 5.

Table 5. Findings related to the artificial intelligence needs of pre-service preschool teachers

Categories	Subcategories	f	%
The learning level where artificial intelligence tools are thought to be more effective	Pre-school education	93	28.46,
	Primary education	84	25.69,
	Secondary education	91	27.84,
	Special Education	56	17.14
	Other	3	0.92
	Total	327	100
Training or resources that may be necessary to prepare prospective teachers for the use of artificial intelligence tools in education	Formal course work on artificial intelligence	69	23.55
	Workshops and seminars	52	17.75
	Online trainings and resources	79	26.98
	Hands-on experience with artificial intelligence tools	91	31.05
	Other	2	0.68
	Total	293	100
Challenges in integrating artificial intelligence into the classroom	Lack of infrastructure (e.g. hardware, software)	105	23.54
	Insufficient training or knowledge	85	17.75
	Resistance from parents or managers	43	26.98
	Ethical concerns regarding data privacy	61	31.03
	Other	2	0.68
	Total	293	100
Measures to reduce biases or inequalities related to AI in education	Regular audits of artificial intelligence systems should be carried out in terms of bias	61	17.94
	There should be a variety of datasets to train AI models	56	16.47
		64	18.82
	Ethical standards should be incorporated into the development of artificial intelligence	84	24.71
	Training on AI ethics for educators	75	22.06
	Organise trainings on artificial intelligence	-	
	Other		
	Total	340	100

When Table 4 is analyzed, it is seen that pre-service preschool teachers think that artificial intelligence tools will be most effective in preschool education (f=93) and secondary education (f=91). In addition, it was frequently stated that it can also be used in primary education (f=84). In addition, 3 pre-service teachers thought that artificial intelligence would be more effective to be used in higher education and master's degree level outside of the determined categories.

When the training or resources that may be necessary for pre-service teachers to prepare for the use of artificial intelligence tools in education are analyzed, it is seen that pre-service teachers mostly think that providing hands-on experience with artificial intelligence tools (f=91) can be effective. In addition, they frequently stated that online training and resources (f=79) can also be used. In addition, two pre-service teachers expressed opinions outside of these categories, one of the pre-service teachers stated that artificial intelligence can be given as an additional course in universities, while the other pre-service teacher expressed his opinion as follows: *"It would be much more effective to read a single article with one's own effort in-*

stead of obtaining thousands of information with artificial intelligence. Artificial intelligence restricts access to metacognitive knowledge, that is, learning to learn.

Preschool teacher candidates stated that the most common difficulty in integrating artificial intelligence into the classroom is the lack of infrastructure (f=105). In addition, they mostly stated that insufficient education or knowledge (f=85) is one of the difficulties that can be encountered. 2 pre-service teachers expressed opinions outside the determined subcategories, and one of the pre-service teachers expressed his opinion on this issue as follows: *"I would not prefer to use artificial intelligence, I would rather do the real thing outside than putting glasses on children and putting them in the mud. If simulation is deemed necessary for an activity that cannot be done, I will pretend to do it."*, while the other pre-service teacher expressed her concern as *"I am not against change, I will apply it if positive learning will be provided, but I do not yet know the qualities of artificial intelligence or what it can do."*.

Pre-service preschool teachers stated that the most effective measure to be taken to reduce prejudices or inequalities related to artificial intelligence in education is to provide training on artificial intelligence ethics for educators (f=84). In addition, they frequently stated that training on artificial intelligence should be organized (f=75).

In addition, when the pre-service teachers' willingness to take part in the processes of developing or testing artificial intelligence tools for education was analyzed; 58.59% of the pre-service teachers stated that "yes, I would be very interested" (f=75), 33.59% stated that "maybe I would like to learn more before the study" (f=43); 7.81% stated that *"no, I am not interested"* (f=10).

DISCUSSION AND RESULTS

The objective of this study is to explore the perspectives and experiences of pre-service preschool teachers regarding artificial intelligence. The rapid advancement of artificial intelligence accelerates technological progress, underscoring the growing significance of pre-service teachers' insights and experiences in the integration of artificial intelligence into education (Le et al., 2024; Tapan Broutın, 2024). While research on artificial intelligence in teacher education has predominantly focused on in-service teachers, there has been limited exploration of its impact on pre-service teachers (Zhang et al., 2023). Therefore, this study seeks to capture the viewpoints of pre-service teachers regarding the integration of artificial intelligence in education.

The study revealed that pre-service teachers primarily utilized artificial intelligence tools for preparing presentations in their educational processes as intended. Alongside presentation preparation, they also indicated a preference for video and photo editing. It was noted that coding was the area in which they least utilized artificial intelligence. Additionally, only a small number of prospective teachers reported not using artificial intelligence tools at all. The predominant use of artificial intelligence tools for presentation preparation suggests that pre-service teachers perceive artificial intelligence as a valuable aid in enhancing the visual and organizational aspects of educational materials (Gabriska & Pribilová, 2023).

It was determined that the majority of pre-service teachers believe they possess sufficient skills to integrate artificial intelligence into classroom settings. Additionally, it was found that most pre-service teachers utilized artificial intelligence tools when preparing activities, and they also favored their use during implementation and for individualized learning adaptation. Similarly, Sun et al. (2020) noted in their research that AI-supported teaching platforms enhance learning processes by providing personalizedd learning experiences. Xue and Wang (2022) concluded that artificial intelligence reduces teachers' workload, enhances information literacy, and contributes to their professional development. Conversely, Ekizce et al. (2022) found that pre-service teachers generally have below-average awareness of Industry 4.0 concepts. While pre-service teachers in this study displayed positive attitudes towards integrating artificial intelligence in education, it is evident that they would benefit from comprehensive training programs addressing the multidimensional aspects of artificial intelligence integration.

When examining the views of teacher candidates regarding the integration of artificial intelligence into educational processes, it was noted that they mentioned its ability to save time. Furthermore, it was found that artificial intelligence could be utilized for data-driven assessment to enhance teaching strategies. Sánchez-Prieto et al. (2019) conducted a study focusing on artificial intelligence-based evaluation. In their research, it was emphasized that for teachers to utilize artificial intelligence, especially in the assessment phase, it is essential for them to first accept the technology. Thus, it is imperative for teachers to have a level of acceptance towards technology, particularly in processes that yield crucial outcomes in educational assessment. Moreover, this acceptance of technology should extend to various technological integrations. Therefore, it is believed that providing support for the acceptance of new technology integrations like artificial intelligence, followed by training across different application areas, is necessary. The study concluded that very few pre-service teachers expressed the view that artificial intelligence lacks benefits in the education process. This perspective may stem from individuals' unease with technology from another standpoint. Misuse of technology can manifest its negative effects on both adults and children (Li & Huang, 2020). Naturally, teachers' firsthand experiences of these drawbacks reinforce their belief that artificial intelligence offers no advantages in education. Another notable finding echoed this sentiment, as pre-service teachers highlighted concerns such as the inability to ensure data security, lack of control over artificial intelligence, and potential cognitive dulling as disadvantages in integrating artificial intelligence into education. Zawacki-Richter et al. (2019) reinforce these findings, highlighting the significance of addressing ethical concerns and adopting suitable pedagogical approaches in the integration of artificial intelligence into education. While the considerable pedagogical potential of AI is acknowledged (Gunawan et al., 2021), there's a suggestion for employing AI-supported educational tools and strategies to simplify complexities (Rogers, 1985). Wang et al.'s (2021) study delves into various criteria governing the use of artificial intelligence tools by pre-service teachers. Particularly, the ease of use and utility of these tools significantly influence their adoption. Furthermore, factors like anxiety, self-efficacy, and attitudes towards artificial intelligence are identified as key determinants shaping the acceptance of this technology.

Furthermore, it was found that pre-service teachers could offer support for adaptive learning platforms tailored to individual children's needs, enhancing their learning experiences. Additionally, they can facilitate virtual reality experiences to foster engaging learning environments, implement evaluation and feedback systems, and provide smart lesson experiences for personalizedd support. The integration of artificial intelligence tools into educational processes offers numerous benefits, emphasizing the importance of their qualified integration. Providing training that encompasses artificial intelligence literacy will help mitigate potential drawbacks while allowing artificial intelligence to realize its full potential (Rütti-Joy et al., 2023). When examining the training or resources necessary for pre-service teachers to prepare for using artificial intelligence tools in education, it was concluded that hands-on experience with these tools would be most effective. Additionally, online training and resources were identified as viable means to familiarize pre-service teachers with artificial intelligence tools.

Preschool teacher candidates were found to encounter challenges in integrating artificial intelligence into the classroom, primarily due to inadequate infrastructure. Insufficient education or knowledge was also identified as a common obstacle. These issues are prevalent in developing countries, as highlighted in UNESCO's report, which emphasizes potential infrastructure deficiencies related to artificial intelligence. Consequently, countries should prioritize decisions regarding the establishment of physical infrastructure for technology integration within their education policies (Holmes et al., 2021). Moreover, it's essential not only to support physical infrastructure but also to provide training for individuals tasked with implementing these integrations. Equipping them with the necessary skills through educational experiences ensures effective utilization of technology in both educational settings and their personal lives.

Moreover, when examining pre-service teachers' willingness to engage in the development or testing of artificial intelligence tools for education, it was found that the majority expressed interest. Some indicated a preference for being briefed prior to participation, while a small minority showed no interest. Consistent with these findings, Haseski (2019) concluded that pre-service teachers assigned varied meanings to artificial intelligence and believed it could yield both positive and negative impacts on education. The allure of emerging technologies captures individuals' attention and bolsters their motivation. Studies indicate that the integration of these tools into education enhances children's interest and motivation (Baykara et al., 2017).

In summary, efforts to promote AI in early childhood can contribute significantly to establishing a digital inclusion ecosystem, integrating programs and policies to address society's diverse needs for digital access and utilization. The role of teachers is pivotal in fostering a digital ecosystem during early childhood. Teachers guide children to explore the digital realm safely and effectively, while highlighting AI's beneficial aspects and promoting its responsible use. They aid in developing children's AI literacy, offering guidance on ethical, privacy, and security concerns associated with AI, thus shielding them from potential risks. Through these efforts, teachers assist children in embracing the digital world healthily from an early age, preparing them to thrive as future digital citizens. It's crucial that individuals of all ages, especially those in disadvantaged and vulnerable areas, have access to digital literacy training and the utilization of digital technologies, including AI. Moreover, integrating quality technological education into educational processes is essential for developing countries to bridge the gap and achieve economic and developmental standards comparable to those of developed nations.

RECOMMENDATIONS

For Prospective Teachers

In order to increase AI literacy, it is important to introduce children to the basic concepts of AI and computer science at an early age and to provide them with the opportunity to explore the relationships between AI applications and the basic principles of these applications. In this direction, it is especially important that teachers working at the preschool education level show the necessary dedication to technology integration. The basis of digital literacy and artificial intelligence literacy lies in the individual's own dedication, curiosity about technology and having a positive attitude towards these constructs. While the pre-service teachers in this study have positive attitudes towards the integration of artificial intelligence into education, they have opinions that they can benefit from comprehensive training programs that address the multidimensional aspects of artificial intelligence integration. In this context, it is important for pre-service teachers to explore artificial intelligence tools in order to support their own development and to gain experience in using them in different fields. With the development of technology, many paid and free artificial intelligence applications have been produced. It is recommended that pre-service teachers should investigate the usage areas of these applications and experience them in order to facilitate their personal lives. In addition, there are many online trainings on these applications. The effective use of these trainings by pre-service teachers will contribute to the development of their artificial intelligence literacy and support their professional development. In particular, the knowledge and skills they will acquire by participating in these trainings will enable them to use artificial intelligence creatively not only in course presentations but also in other dimensions of education and training processes. Such competences that they will acquire through their own efforts will help them make a difference in their future teaching careers.

For Policymakers and For Researchers

It is a recommendation to higher education institutions and researchers that teachers should be provided with AI literacy at the undergraduate education level, and that undergraduate courses on AI literacy for children should be included in higher education programs. Policy makers should prioritize including AI literacy training modules in their curricula so that prospective teachers can effectively use AI technologies as a pedagogical tool.

Artificial intelligence literacy includes not only access to and use of information, but also critical thinking, ethical awareness and the ability to interact in the digital world. In this context, the inclusion of content that will support digital literacy and artificial intelligence literacy in higher education curricula will enable students to grow as better equipped individuals in both their academic and professional lives. Therefore, it is of great importance that artificial intelligence literacy is accepted as a priority educational goal in higher education and structured educational processes are developed in this direction. In particular, it is important that the curricula are structured both for the professional development of the teacher candidate and for integration in the education process with children in order to support the process as a whole. In the context of structured trainings and curriculum arrangements, the advantages and limitations of artificial intelligence applications, effective usage methods and ethical principles are seen as issues that should be at the basis of content arrangements. Particular attention should be paid to the integration of these trainings into educational experiences, and devotion should be shown to the evaluation process of integration. It is thought that these trainings and curriculum arrangements will be the basis for teachers and prospective teachers to acquire artificial intelligence literacy.

Pre-service teachers generally use artificial intelligence tools only for preparing presentations. This situation shows that the wide range of opportunities offered by artificial intelligence cannot be sufficiently utilized in education. Researchers can develop practical applications and methods on how artificial intelligence tools can be used in a wider range of educational contexts. At the same time, policy makers should plan educational processes that encourage pre-service teachers to use AI effectively in various stages of pedagogical processes, not only in preparing presentations. This will enable pre-service teachers to use AI in a more comprehensive and creative way.

In addition, it is important to support practice areas where pre-service teachers can acquire the targeted artificial intelligence literacy skills in practice. It is known that providing them with experience with artificial intelligence-supported educational tools and resources is critical for them to learn how to integrate these technologies in their teaching processes. In practice areas, pre-service teachers should be encouraged to gain experience on how to monitor and evaluate children's development and develop individualised teaching strategies by using artificial intelligence applications effectively. Thus, pre-service teachers will not only be limited to theoretical knowledge, but will also have the opportunity to reinforce their professional skills by putting what they have learnt into practice. This process will enable them to see AI literacy not only as a concept but as an integral part of their daily teaching practices.

REFERENCES

Akgun, S., & Greenhow, C. (2022). Artificial intelligence in education: Addressing ethical challenges in K-12 settings. *AI and Ethics*, 2(3), 431–440. DOI: 10.1007/s43681-021-00096-7 PMID: 34790956

Álvarez-Herrero, J. F. (2024). Opinion of Spanish Teachers About Artificial Intelligence and Its Use in Education. In *IoT, AI, and ICT for Educational Applications: Technologies to Enable Education for All* (pp. 163–172). Springer Nature Switzerland. DOI: 10.1007/978-3-031-50139-5_8

Baker, R. S., Inventado, P. S., & Corbett, A. T. (2017). *"Educational Data Mining and Learning Analytics." Cambridge Handbook of the Learning Sciences* (2nd ed.). Cambridge University Press.

Baykara, M., Gürtürk, U., Atasoy, B., & Perçin, İ. (2017). "Augmented reality based mobile learning system design in preschool education'', 72-77. *2017 International Conference on Computer Science and Engineering (UBMK)*. IEEE. DOI: 10.1109/UBMK.2017.8093560

Binns, R., Veale, M., Van Kleek, M., & Shadbolt, N. (2020). The Ethics of AI in Education: A Review of Current Practices. *Journal of Educational Technology*, 15(2), 123–138.

Büyüköztürk, Ş., Kılıç-Çakmak, E., Akgün, Ö., Karadeniz, Ş., & Demirel, F. (2020). *Bilimsel araştırma yöntemleri*. Pegem Akademi.

Chen, J., & Lin, J. (2023). Artificial intelligence as a double-edged sword: Wielding the power principles to maximize its positive effects and minimize its negative effects. *Contemporary Issues in Early Childhood*, 25, 1. DOI: 10.1177/14639491231169813

Chen, L., Chen, P., & Lin, Z. (2020). Artificial Intelligence in Education: A Review. *IEEE Access : Practical Innovations, Open Solutions*, 8, 75264–75278. DOI: 10.1109/ACCESS.2020.2988510

Chiu, T. K., Xia, Q., Zhou, X., Chai, C. S., & Cheng, M. (2023). Systematic literature review on opportunities, challenges, and future research recommendations of artificial intelligence in education. *Computers and Education: Artificial Intelligence*, 4, 100118. DOI: 10.1016/j.caeai.2022.100118

Choi, S., Jang, Y., & Kim, H. (2023). Influence of pedagogical beliefs and perceived trust on teachers' acceptance of educational artificial intelligence tools. *International Journal of Human-Computer Interaction*, 39(4), 910–922. DOI: 10.1080/10447318.2022.2049145

Coccia, M. (2019). Why do nations produce science advances and new technology? *Technology in Society*, 59, 101124. DOI: 10.1016/j.techsoc.2019.03.007

Druga, S., & Ko, A. J. (2021). "How do children's perceptions of machine intelligence change when training and coding smart programs?", In *Interaction design and children*, (pp. 49–61).

Du Boulay, B. (2016). Artificial intelligence as an effective classroom assistant. *IEEE Intelligent Systems*, 31(6), 76–81. DOI: 10.1109/MIS.2016.93

Ekizce, H. N., Anılan, B., & Atalay, N. (2022). Pre-service science teachers' levels of awareness of industry 4.0 concepts. *Journal of Innovative Research in Teacher Education*, 3(2), 192–208. DOI: 10.29329/jirte.2022.464.9

European Commission. (2022). Ethical guidelines on the use of artificial intelligence (AI) and data in teaching and learning for Educators. Retrieved November 11, 2022, from https://education.ec.europa.eu/news/ethical-guidelines-on-the-use-of-artificial-intelligence-and-data-in-teaching-and-learning-for-educators

Gabriska, D., & Pribilová, K. (2023). Artificial intelligence in education, issues and potential of use in the teaching process. *2023 21st International Conference on Emerging eLearning Technologies and Applications (ICETA)*, (pp.141-146). https://doi.org/DOI: 10.1109/ICETA61311.2023.10344286

Guan, C., Mou, J., & Jiang, Z. (2020). Artificial intelligence innovation in education: A twenty-year datadriven historical analysis. *International Journal of Innovation Studies*, 4(4), 134–147. DOI: 10.1016/j.ijis.2020.09.001

Gunawan, K. L., Kaniawati, I., & Setiawan, W. (2021). The responses to artificial intelligence in teacher integrated science learning training program. *Journal of Physics: Conference Series*, 2098(1), 012034. Advance online publication. DOI: 10.1088/1742-6596/2098/1/012034

Harris, A., & Jones, M. (2019). Virtual Reality and Augmented Reality in Teacher Training: An Innovative Approach. *Journal of Educational Technology & Society*, 22(3), 34–45.

Haseski, H. (2019). What Do Turkish Pre-Service Teachers Think About Artificial Intelligence? *Int. J. Comput. Sci. Educ. Sch.*, 3(2), 3–23. DOI: 10.21585/ijcses.v3i2.55

Holmes, W., Bialik, M., & Fadel, C. (2019). *Artificial Intelligence in Education: Promises and Implications for Teaching and Learning*. Harvard Education Press.

Hussin, A. A. (2018). Education 4.0 made simple: Ideas for teaching. *International Journal of Education and Literacy Studies*, 6(3), 92–98. DOI: 10.7575/aiac.ijels.v.6n.3p.92

Johnson, L., Adams Becker, S., & Cummins, M. (2016). *The NMC Horizon Report: 2016 Higher Education Edition*. New Media Consortium.

Kamalov, F., Santandreu Calonge, D., & Gurrib, I. (2023). New era of artificial intelligence in education: Towards a sustainable multifaceted revolution. *Sustainability (Basel)*, 15(16), 12451. DOI: 10.3390/su151612451

Kong, S. C., Cheung, W. M. Y., & Zhang, G. (2021). Evaluation of an artificial intelligence literacy course for university students with diverse study backgrounds. *Computers and Education: Artificial Intelligence*, 2, 100026. DOI: 10.1016/j.caeai.2021.100026

Kulik, C.-L. C., & Fletcher, J. D. (2016). Effectiveness of Intelligent Tutoring Systems: A Meta-Analysis. *Review of Educational Research*, 86(3), 430–456. DOI: 10.3102/0034654315581420

Le, A. N. N., Nguyen, V. N., Nguyen, M. T. X., & Bo, L. K. (2024). Exploring the Use of ChatGPT as a Tool for Developing Eportfolios in ESL Classrooms. In *IoT, AI, and ICT for Educational Applications: Technologies to Enable Education for All*, (pp. 51-76).

Li, X., & Zaki, R. (2024). Harnessing the Power of Digital Resources in Mathematics Education: The Potential of Augmented Reality and Artificial Intelligence. In *IoT, AI, and ICT for Educational Applications: Technologies to Enable Education for All* (pp. 191–223). Springer Nature Switzerland. DOI: 10.1007/978-3-031-50139-5_10

Long, D., & Magerko, B. (2020, April). What is AI literacy? Competencies and design considerations. In *Proceedings of the 2020 CHI Conference on Human Factors in Computing Systems* (pp. 1–16). DOI: 10.1145/3313831.3376727

Mensah, F. S., & Ampadu, E. (2024). Benefits, Challenges and Opportunities of Using Computer-Assisted Instruction in Mathematics Education. In *IoT, AI, and ICT for Educational Applications: Technologies to Enable Education for All*, (pp. 31-49).

Miao, F., Holmes, W., Huang, R., & Zhang, H. (2021). *AI and education: A guidance for policymakers*. UNESCO Publishing.

Miller, T. (2018). "Ethics of Artificial Intelligence and Robotics." *Stanford Encyclopedia of Philosophy*. Retrieved from https://plato.stanford.edu

Napoleon, D., & Ramanujam, V. (2022). Education 4.0: Curriculum Development for the Educational Framework. In *Industry 4.0 Technologies for Education* (pp. 275-291). Auerbach Publications.

Ng, D. T. K., & Chu, S. K. W. (2021). Motivating Students to Learn AI Through Social Networking Sites: A Case Study in Hong Kong. *Online Learning : the Official Journal of the Online Learning Consortium*, 25(1), 195–208. DOI: 10.24059/olj.v25i1.2454

Ng, D. T. K., Leung, J. K. L., Chu, S. K. W., & Qiao, M. S. (2021). Conceptualizing AI literacy: An exploratory review. *Computers and Education: Artificial Intelligence*, 2, 100041.

Ng, D. T. K., Leung, J. K. L., Su, J., Ng, R. C. W., & Chu, S. K. W. (2023). Teachers' AI digital competencies and twenty-first century skills in the post-pandemic world. *Educational Technology Research and Development*, 71(1), 137–161. DOI: 10.1007/s11423-023-10203-6 PMID: 36844361

O'Neil, C. (2016). *Weapons of Math Destruction: How Big Data Increases Inequality and Threatens Democracy*. Crown Publishing Group.

Open, A. I. (2023a). GPT-4 (June 21 version) [Large language model]. https://chat.openai.com/

Open, A. I. (2023b). ChatGPT (September 29 version) [Large language model]. https://chat. openai.com/

Rogers, J. (1985). Artificial intelligence in education (panel session)., 52. https://doi.org/.DOI: 10.1145/320435.320454

Rütti-Joy, O., Winder, G., & Biedermann, H. (2023). Building AI Literacy for Sustainable Teacher Education. *Zeitschrift für Hochschulentwicklung*, 18(4), 175–189. DOI: 10.21240/zfhe/18-04/10

Sabzalieva, E., & Valentini, A. (2023). ChatGPT and artificial intelligence in higher education: quick start guide.

Sánchez-Prieto, J. C., Cruz-Benito, J., Therón, R., & García-Peñalvo, F. J. [Francisco J.] (2019). How to Measure Teachers' Acceptance of AI-driven Assessment in eLearning. In González, M. Á. C., Sedano, F. J. R., Llamas, C. F., & García-Peñalvo, F. J. (Eds.), *Proceedings of the Seventh International Conference on Technological Ecosystems for Enhancing Multiculturality* (pp. 181–186). ACM. https://doi.org/ DOI: 10.1145/3362789.3362918

Selwyn, N. (2016). *Education and Technology: Key Issues and Debates*. Bloomsbury Academic.

Shen, J., Wu, H., Reeves, P., Zheng, Y., Ryan, L., & Anderson, D. (2020). The association between teacher leadership and student achievement: A meta-analysis. *Educational Research Review*, 31, 100357. DOI: 10.1016/j.edurev.2020.100357

Su, J., Ng, D. T. K., & Chu, S. K. W. (2023). Artificial intelligence (AI) literacy in early childhood education: The challenges and opportunities. *Computers and Education: Artificial Intelligence*, 4, 100124. DOI: 10.1016/j.caeai.2023.100124

Su, J., & Yang, W. (2022). Artificial intelligence in early childhood education: A scoping review. *Computers and Education: Artificial Intelligence*, 3, 100049. DOI: 10.1016/j.caeai.2022.100049

Sun, Z., Anbarasan, M., & Kumar, D. (2020). Design of online intelligent English teaching platform based on artificial intelligence techniques. *Computational Intelligence*, 37(3), 1166–1180. DOI: 10.1111/coin.12351

Sunitha, D. B., & Gunavardhan, E. (2023). Artificial Intelligence based Smart Education System. *2023 4th International Conference on Electronics and Sustainable Communication Systems (ICESC)*, (pp.1346-1350). https://doi.org/DOI: 10.1109/ICESC57686.2023.10193720

Tapan Broutın, M. S. T. (2024). Exploring Mathematics Teacher Candidates' Instrumentation Process of Generative Artificial Intelligence for Developing Lesson Plans. *Yükseköğretim Dergisi*, 14(1), 165–176.

Taylor, M., Fudge, A., Mirriahi, N., & de Laat, M. (2021). *Use of digital technology in education: Literature review. Prepared for the South Australian Department for Education on behalf of The Centre for Change and Complexity in Learning*. The University of South Australia.

UNESCO. (2022). K-12 AI Curricula: A mapping of government-endorsed AI curricula. Paris, FranceUNESCO. https://unesdoc.unesco.org/ark:/48223/pf0000380602Z

Vartiainen, H., Tedre, M., & Valtonen, T. (2020). Learning machine learning with very young children: Who is teaching whom? *International Journal of Child-Computer Interaction*, 25, 100182. DOI: 10.1016/j.ijcci.2020.100182

Wang, B., Rau, P. L. P., & Yuan, T. (2023). Measuring user competence in using artificial intelligence: Validity and reliability of artificial intelligence literacy scale. *Behaviour & Information Technology*, 42(9), 1324–1337. DOI: 10.1080/0144929X.2022.2072768

Wang, P. (2019). On defining artificial intelligence. *Journal of Artificial General Intelligence*, 10(2), 1–37. DOI: 10.2478/jagi-2019-0002

Wang, Y., Liu, C., & Tu, Y.-F. (2021). Factors affecting the adoption of ai-based applications in higher education: An analysis of teachers' perspectives using structural equation modeling. *Journal of Educational Technology & Society*, 24(3), 116–129. Retrieved June 8, 2023, from https://www.jstor.org/stable/27032860

Williams, R., Park, H., Oh, L., & Breazeal, C. (2019). PopBots. *Designing an Artificial Intelligence Curriculum for Early Childhood Education*, 33(1), 9729–9736. DOI: 10.1609/aaai.v33i01.33019729

Williamson, B., & Piattoeva, N. (2020). Education Governance and the Role of AI: New Directions in Educational Research. *Educational Policy Review*, 29(4), 567–585.

Xue, Y., & Wang, Y. (2022). Artificial Intelligence for Education and Teaching. *Wireless Communications and Mobile Computing*, 2022, 1–10. Advance online publication. DOI: 10.1155/2022/4750018

Yu, H., & Guo, Y. (2023). Generative artificial intelligence empowers educational reform: Current status, issues, and prospects. [). Frontiers Media SA.]. *Frontiers in Education*, 8, 1183162. DOI: 10.3389/feduc.2023.1183162

Zawacki-Richter, O., Marín, V., Bond, M., & Gouverneur, F. (2019). Systematic review of research on artificial intelligence applications in higher education – where are the educators? *International Journal of Educational Technology in Higher Education*, 16(1), 39. Advance online publication. DOI: 10.1186/s41239-019-0171-0

Zhang, C., Schießl, J., Plößl, L., Hofmann, F., & Gläser-Zikuda, M. (2023). Acceptance of artificial intelligence among pre-service teachers: A multigroup analysis. *International Journal of Educational Technology in Higher Education*, 20(1), 49. DOI: 10.1186/s41239-023-00420-7 PMID: 36743849

Zhang, S., & Chen, X. (2022, December). Applying Artificial Intelligence into Early Childhood Math Education: Lesson Design and Course Effect. In *2022 IEEE International Conference on Teaching, Assessment and Learning for Engineering (TALE)* (pp. 635-638). IEEE. DOI: 10.1109/TALE54877.2022.00109

Chapter 4
Enhancing High-Quality Pedagogy in Higher Education With MyGPTs:
A Case of Tailored Teacher Assistant PedaBuddy

Minna-Maarit Jaskari
https://orcid.org/0000-0002-5412-7176
University of Vaasa, Finland

ABSTRACT

This chapter examines the development and implementation of custom MyGPTs within higher education, using a teacher assistant 'PedaBuddy' as a detailed case study. It explores the guiding principles behind these generative AI tools, focusing on their potential to enhance teaching and learning experiences, while also addressing the challenges they present. The chapter begins with a review of existing literature on generative AI and MyGPTs in academic settings, followed by an in-depth explanation of the configuration process using OpenAI's GPT builder. Through the case study of PedaBuddy, the chapter showcases the practical applications and outcomes of deploying a tailored MyGPT. The discussion concludes by evaluating the strengths, opportunities, and challenges associated with integrating such AI-driven tools in higher education.

DOI: 10.4018/979-8-3693-3944-2.ch004

INTRODUCTION

Higher education is currently experiencing turbulent times in many ways. Student populations are more diverse than ever, encompassing varied cultural backgrounds, learning styles, and educational needs, including those of neurodivergent students. This diversity presents unique challenges that require educators to adopt adaptive teaching methods suited to a broad spectrum of learning preferences and abilities. Unfortunately, educators often face significant time constraints due to the pressure to publish, limiting their ability to provide individualized attention and supervision.

There is often an implicit assumption that students will autonomously find their way through and understand course materials, however, this is not always the case. Also, evaluation and feedback processes can be opaque and difficult for students to understand, particularly when feedback is not tailored to their specific learning goals and diverse needs. Such lack of clarity can hinder students' learning progress, motivation, and engagement, posing challenges in meeting their learning objectives effectively. Due to the high volume of work and the diversity of student needs, educators may struggle to consistently provide feedback that is both accessible and actionable. However, constructive feedback is crucial for students' learning.

The significance of artificial intelligence in education is rapidly increasing (Dwidevi et al., 2023), and it is expected to address many of the challenges described above. The growing use of generative AI is playing an important role. These technologies allow for the creation of tailored tools to specific educational contexts, which can significantly support teachers in tasks like customizing curricula and developing educational materials. This not only enhances the efficiency and personalization of teaching but also frees up educators to focus on more human-centered aspects of their work. Generative AI technologies even allow the creation of tailored, pre-configured chatbots, so called MyGPTs, for specific needs.

This chapter explores the development and testing of tailored MyGPTs in higher education, using PedaBuddy as a specific example. It begins by reviewing previous literature on generative AI and MyGPTs in higher education. Next, it explains the configuration process of MyGPTs using OpenAI's GPT builder. The chapter then presents a detailed case study of 'PedaBuddy', a tailored teachers assistant for higher education, highlighting its development and practical applications. Finally, it concludes with a discussion of the strengths, opportunities, and challenges associated with customized MyGPTs.

Readers of this chapter will gain insight into both the advantages and challenges of building MyGPTs in educational settings, as well as a hands-on guide for constructing AI assistants. This makes the chapter a valuable resource for educators, policymakers, and educational technology developer as well as others interested in tailoring and configuring chatbots for assistance.

GENERATIVE AI IN HIGHER EDUCATION

The growing use of artificial intelligence (AI) is driving significant digital transformation, which is a key factor causing disruption in various sectors (Chintalapati & Pandey, 2022), not least in higher education (Dwivedi et al., 2023). Scholars argue that AI has a critical role in modern education, significantly enhancing the efficiency, accessibility, and personalization of learning environments (Chan & Colloton, 2024). Indeed, today educational AI applications range from automating administrative processes to providing adaptive learning technologies, fundamentally altering teaching practices and student engagement strategies. The relevance of AI extends into the job market as well, where many positions, such as in marketing management, increasingly demand proficiency with various AI technologies and capabilities (Davenport et al, 2020; Elhajjar, 2024; Elhajjar et al., 2020).

Generative AI (GenAI) represents a specialized branch within artificial intelligence, uniquely focused on the creation of new data or content. The term 'generative' highlights this AI's capability to produce novel outputs, rather than simply replicating, categorizing, processing, or analyzing existing inputs. Its range of capabilities is broad, enabling the generation of diverse content forms, including text, images, audio, videos, and even complex computer code. This extensive functionality is detailed in recent studies by Adesola & Adepoju (2023) and Chan (2024a).

ChatGPT, a Chat Generative Pre-Trained Transformer, has rapidly gained popularity in various fields, including education, since its debut in November 2022 (Chan, 2024a; Gimpel et al., 2023) This AI tool is highly adept at understanding and generating text that closely mimics human language with remarkable speed (Baber et al., 2023). Its effectiveness stems from being trained on an extensive dataset, which enables it to master patterns, styles, and complexities of human language (Chan, 2024a). ChatGPT's ability to generate language, translate text, summarize content, and manage question-and-answer interactions has made a significant impact on the tech industry (Zaveri, 2023). Although ChatGPT was the first conversational agent of its kind, competitors soon emerged, including Microsoft's Copilot (formerly Bing) and Google's Gemini (formerly Bard), which also excel in text generation. Meanwhile, Midjourney stands out as particularly efficient in creating visuals. MyGPTs are specialized and customized versions of these systems, designed to provide specific assistance tailored to users' needs, making them particularly valuable in academic contexts.

In their systematic literature review, Baber et al. (2023) identify two primary ways in which ChatGPT can support education in broad terms. First, it serves as a valuable tool for creating personalized lesson plans. This individualized approach can lead to a more targeted, effective, and even memorable educational experience. Second, generative AI has been suggested to use in closing the achievement gap, reducing educational disparities by ensuring that students from less privileged backgrounds receive the same personalized attention and support as their more advantaged counterparts. However, it is important to acknowledge the digital divide, which highlights the unequal access to technology. Many students do not have the same availability of technological resources and high-speed internet, leading to disparities in learning opportunities. As a result, students from less privileged backgrounds may encounter substantial barriers to utilizing AI-enhanced educational tools, potentially deepening educational inequalities (Baber et al., 2023; Nah et al., 2023).

Generative AI agents are increasingly utilized in education, offering significant benefits to both students and lecturers (Gimpel et al., 2023; UNESCO, 2023). For students, these tools can identify learning gaps, provide personalized feedback, and support the development of academic skills, such as research, writing, and generating literature reviews (Zawacki-Richter et al., 2019; Aljanabi et al., 2023; Aydin, 2022). For lecturers, AI can be used in curriculum design, it can automate tasks such as assessments and administration, saving time that can then be redirected towards more empathetic, human-focused teaching (Colloton, 2024; UNESCO, 2023). Additionally, AI assistants can aid in lesson planning and material creation across different learning levels, enhancing educational efficiency (Rudolph et al., 2023; Schön et al., 2023).

Indeed, generative AI-powered chatbot technologies have demonstrated the potential to enhance learning experiences and improve student outcomes in higher education. Research shows that these tools can increase student interaction and streamline the learning process (Muñoz et al., 2023). Winkler and Söllner (2018) specifically highlighted that chatbot technology positively impacts the quality of learning and student achievements. Additionally, chatbots are seen as beneficial in boosting student motivation and engagement, which are crucial for successful learning outcomes (Deng & Yu, 2023). ChatGPT can aid in creating lesson plans, developing educational resources such as scripts, slides, and quizzes, grading assignments, and offering feedback to students (Chan, 2024b; Nah et al., 2023). Other potential advantages of using generative AI in education include streamlining administrative tasks through automation as well as enhancing the efficiency of data analysis (Baber et al., 2023).

However, reaching a consensus among educators about the use of AI technologies like ChatGPT poses a persistent challenge (Adeshola & Adepoju, 2023; Firat, 2023). Despite many advantages, several studies highlight concerns about the potential decline in critical analytical abilities, the spread of misinformation, the reinforcement of biases, and the challenges posed to academic integrity such as cheating and plagiarism (Baber et al., 2023, Nah et al., 2023). Also, several ethical concerns arise with the use of large language model (LLM) based generative AI tools in general, not only in ChatGPT (Schön et al., 2023). These language models often reflect human biases found in their training data, potentially leading to biased or discriminatory responses that could harm users psychologically. Additionally, the quality of responses can vary with the language of the prompt, indicating a language-based quality bias. LLMs like ChatGPT do not provide attribution for the texts they use to generate responses, raising issues related to ownership, copyright, and intellectual rights. Another concern is the character of the AI; ChatGPT tends to trust easily, making it susceptible to manipulation, and it often responds with unwarranted confidence, which may mislead users if the information is incorrect. Furthermore, there are significant privacy concerns, as LLMs are trained on web documents without explicit consent, possibly leading to breaches in personal or institutional privacy. The unclear ownership and copyright status of ChatGPT's output further complicates how society or institutions should manage AI-generated content, whether it should be considered the property of the user who prompted it or attributed to the AI itself (Baber et al., 2023; Nah et al., 2023; Schön et al., 2023).

Thus, the use of generative AI in education also requires careful management of competencies, ethical considerations, and awareness of AI's limitations, such as the potential for generating incorrect or misleading information. Both students and lecturers need to critically evaluate AI outputs and ensure that human oversight remains a central aspect of educational use of AI (Nah et al., 2023; Schön et al., 2023; UNESCO, 2023).

A STEP DEEPER - MYGPTS AS AI ASSISTANTS

While there is a rapidly growing number of academic articles about the use of ChatGPTs in education, MyGPTs are not specifically explored earlier. MyGPTs are customized versions of the GPT (Generative Pre-trained Transformer) models developed by OpenAI. These customized models are tailored to specific user needs or applications, enhancing their relevance and effectiveness in particular contexts. Users can fine-tune and train these AI models on domain-specific data, adjust parameters, and integrate unique functionalities to meet their specific objectives. To illustrate, a MyGPT assistants developed for educational purposes could function as a virtual tutor or academic mentor, understanding and responding to student queries, generating educational content, or facilitating learning activities. This level of customization makes MyGPTs invaluable in sectors where specialized knowledge and interaction are required. (OpenAI, 2024).

The Process of Developing MyGPT's in OpenAI Platform

In November 2023 OpenAI introduced the possibility to create custom versions of ChatGPT (OpenAI, 2024). Prior to this, users could build so-called AI assistants their own applications. Custom GPTs operate within ChatGPT framework and hosted by OpenAI, without requiring coding for integration. GPT Builder tool allows users to customize models by training on specific datasets relevant to the tasks and interactions that AI is needed to handle. Users can train and fine-tune the model, iteratively enhancing its responses based on trial and feedback. Developers of MyGPTs can choose whether to keep them for personal use, share them with a link, or make them available in the OpenAI GPT store (OpenAI, 2024).

In the GPT builder the user can configure GPT in two ways. They can either "create" GPT through chatting with GPT4 or they can "configure" it by themselves. The configuration can be tested and reconfigured multiple times. The easiest way to start creating a new GPT is with the Create function. There GPT Builder asks you to start to chat with the text: "Hi! I'll help you build a new GPT. You can say something like, "make a creative who helps generate visuals for new products" or "make a software engineer who helps format my code." What would you like to make?" Once the idea is submitted, GPT builder starts to configure the new GPT. The chat continues and GPT Builder asks questions that helps it to configure the GPT. From the configuration tab the final configuration can be viewed. The GPT can be tested from the preview window all the time. This process can be continued as long as needed. The Appendix 1 showcases a configuration of MyGPT 'Pedagogy Partner' (different from PedaBuddy) using the create-function.

GPTs can also be customized through direct configurations in the "Configure" tab. Users can set a unique name for the GPT, provide a concise short description to outline the GPT's purpose, and craft detailed instructions to guide its interactions. Adding conversation starters also helps ensure a smooth initiation of interaction, making the GPT accessible and user-friendly from the start. For instance, integrating knowledge bases relevant to higher education, such as a university's education strategy or the formatting guidelines for course descriptions, can significantly enhance the GPT's utility in a specific academic setting. In the similar way marketing departments can add their brand handbooks to ensure that the output is according to these guidelines. This customization not only allows the GPT to meet but also anticipate the specific needs of its users.

Next, a detailed case study on the configuration process of MyGPT PedaBuddy is presented, along with examples showcasing its use.

Case Study: PedaBuddy, Your Support that Helps You to Rock the Classroom

PedaBuddy is a generative AI tool (MyGPT) specifically designed to enhance the pedagogical capabilities of university educators by assisting in several critical areas of course development. As a publicly available MyGPT targeted at university lecturers, PedaBuddy can be accessed through the GPT Store or directly via this link: https://chatgpt.com/g/g-TiWBcFpCr-pedabuddy for anyone registered with ChatGPT. Initially launched in February 2024, PedaBuddy has been continuously developed and updated using the principles of action research. Building on my prior experience in developing AI assistants, this case study details the process behind PedaBuddy's creation and ongoing refinement.

Description of PedaBuddy

PedaBuddy's functionalities are tailored to improve educational quality and effectiveness through structured support in setting learning objectives, constructing curricula, planning assessments, and fostering engaging interactions. It aims to integrate research-based teaching principles into different tasks that teachers meet in their daily jobs, such as planning assignments or giving constructive feedback.

PedaBuddy guides instructors in formulating clear and measurable intended learning objectives (ILO's), which are fundamental to the educational design process. The tool provides suggestions based on curriculum standards and educational goals specific to the subject area. By ensuring that objectives are aligned with both course content and assessment strategies, PedaBuddy helps create a cohesive educational experience that drives student engagement and learning.

With PedaBuddy, educators can also design curricula that integrate various teaching methodologies and content alignments. Utilizing the principle of constructive alignment (Biggs, 1996), the tool ensures that all aspects of the curriculum — from lectures and materials to activities and assessments — systematically support the learning objectives. This method promotes coherence between teaching strategies and desired outcomes, making learning more effective.

Recognizing the importance of interaction in the meaningful learning process, PedaBuddy provides strategies for increasing student engagement through active learning techniques. These include flipped classrooms, experiential learning opportunities, and transformative learning projects. By facilitating more interactive and participatory learning environments, PedaBuddy helps teachers foster a more dynamic and inclusive educational atmosphere.

Assessment is another area where PedaBuddy can be used. The tool aims to assist teachers in developing diverse evaluation methods (both formative and summative) that measure student learning relative to the set objectives. From traditional exams and quizzes to innovative formative assessments like peer reviews and reflective journals, PedaBuddy can be used to tailor different options. It also provides guidance on aligning these assessments with the overall educational goals, ensuring that they are fair, comprehensive, and conducive to learning.

PedaBuddy aids instructors in crafting constructive feedback that is both encouraging and developmental. The tool can offer templates and examples of feedback that are specific to the tasks and objectives of the course, enabling educators to provide personalized responses that guide students towards improved performance and deeper understanding.

PedaBuddy provides teachers with valuable examples, opportunities, and options to consider in their instructional planning. However, it is essential for teachers to remain as human supervisors, carefully evaluating and selecting the suggestions that best align with their specific teaching situations.

To sum up, MyGPT PedaBuddy aims to act as a friend and "buddy" to teachers supporting their ability to design, implement, and refine pedagogical strategies for ever diverse students.

Objectives Behind the Development of PedaBuddy

The development of PedaBuddy began in a context where the author serves as a program manager for a master's program and as a teacher-researcher at an accredited Finnish business university. This role requires maintaining high standards of research-based teaching across the program's curriculum. Accreditation bodies such as the Association to Advance Collegiate Schools of Business (AACSB) provide standards to ensure high-quality teaching in business education. Universities are expected to demonstrate active engagement in creating and maintaining a learning-supportive environment, which includes rigorous practices in curriculum development, assessment of learning outcomes, and the continuous improvement of educational methods. Moreover, it is expected to ensure that faculty are well-qualified and engage in ongoing professional development to sustain high teaching practices (AACSB, 2024).

However, typically faculty at research universities may not be well-versed in pedagogical research and often perceive teaching as a "necessary evil" that diverts time from their research activities. Concurrently, student populations are becoming increasingly diverse, complicating the task of designing high-quality instructional methods. Still, the governmental educational strategies emphasize that no less than 50% of the population has a higher education degree.

Contemporary educational trends strive for open, transparent, and sustainable teaching practices, further underscoring the importance of teachers' ability to clearly articulate their pedagogical intentions and rationales. The struggle that many researchers face is indeed real. How do they meet the conflicting objectives, and how do they manage the challenges posed by these competing goals?

This backdrop informed the initiation of an action research project focused on "meaningful learning experiences," driven by insights from future competence needs in business and marketing, the widening gap between theory and practice, Finnish Ministry of Education's future goals, the university's updated strategy, and student feedback. A central component of this project is teacher support, which is designated as one of the working packages, specifically focusing on the development of MyGPT teaching assistant, PedaBuddy.

The Configuration Process of PedaBuddy

PedaBuddy was developed using the OpenAI MyGPT Builder, initially grounded in resources from ChatGPT4 and OpenAI. The tool was specifically designed to support university-level education. Its pedagogical philosophy was carefully articulated early in the development process. PedaBuddy aims to be the 'best buddy' for university teachers, enhancing their classroom experience. The persona of PedaBuddy is crafted to be humorous, approachable, and fun. This character is visually represented by a rock'n'roll inspired teddy bear in its profile picture (created using Midjourney) to maintain a friendly and engaging image. The concept of 'rocking the classroom's stems from the author's personal brand and reflects the collaborative relationship she seeks to foster with teachers. Although PedaBuddy was later made publicly available, these distinctive characteristics were retained.

PedaBuddy was configured using the configuration tab and the following aspects were defined:

- **Name:** PedaBuddy
- **Short Description:** Rock the Classroom – Make Every Lesson an Encore!
- **Instructions:** The instructions focused on general instructions on what PedaBuddy is targeted to do and pedagogical guidelines that need to be followed. Also, instructions were given about interaction guidelines with users. The character of PedaBuddy was described including the tone of voice. In each phase explicit examples were given.
- **Conversation Starters:** Typical questions that users were expected to ask were set as conversation starters. At the moment these include: "Please help give constructive feedback based on my notes", "Please help me plan a course curriculum that follows the guidelines of constructive alignment", "Please

help me plan an interactive assignment based on my topic" and "Please help me plan transparent assessment for my course".
- **Knowledge:** There is a possibility to upload files that GPT uses in conversation. However, PedaBuddy was not given any specific knowledge bases since it is opened for public use. However, suitable knowledge base could include a) university's educational strategy, b) explicit customer value proposals, c) intended learning outcomes for the specific program d) teaching and learning philosophy, and e) other guidelines or specific requirements agreed with teachers.
- **Capabilities**: PedaBuddy was given capabilities of web browsing, DALL.E image generation and code interpreter.
- **Actions:** PedaBuddy was not advised for any actions.

The development of PedaBuddy is a continuous trial and error - process that involves regular updates and improvements. PedaBuddy has been actively tested and used to enhance teaching and learning activities. We have tested the configuration changes using ChatGPT multiple times to make sure it works well and asked ChatGPT to analyze the configuration. The chatbot has been made available for teachers as well as publicly in LinkedIn and Facebook. Feedback is collected and used to keep making the configuration better.

Examples of Interactive and Engaging Teaching Enhancements Provided by PedaBuddy

The following examples aim to illustrate how PedaBuddy answers typical questions asked from it. The examples are copy-pasted from chat with PedaBuddy. The link to these chats can be found at https://chat.openai.com/share/074c053d-7caf-414c-b043-2df72a86519b.

Example 1: Feedback Generation

The first example focuses on formulating constructive feedback.

> **User:** *Hi, I am in a hurry and I need to write some feedback to online forum to the students. Here are the first bullet points: interesting topic, good purpose. Text is still too much referencing and describing earlier studies. Needs more critical analysis. The holistic view is missing. A framework figure could be good. Needs more work to enhance systematic work.*
>
> **PedaBuddy:** *Here's a quick draft for your feedback that maintains a constructive and encouraging tone:*
> **Feedback on Forum Submission**
> *Hi everyone,*
> *Great job on choosing such an interesting topic and clearly defining your purpose! These are strong foundations for a compelling discussion.*
> *However, I've noticed that the text heavily references and describes earlier studies. While these references are valuable, incorporating more critical analysis could really deepen the insights. Try to engage more critically with these sources rather than just describing them. What are the implications of these findings? Are there any contradictions or areas left unexplored by these studies?*
> *Additionally, a more holistic view could tie together the different threads of discussion more coherently. Consider creating a framework figure to visually organize your thoughts and findings, which could also aid in developing a more systematic approach to your analysis.*
> *There's definitely more work to be done, but you're on the right track. Enhancing your systematic work will not only strengthen your arguments but also make your conclusions more robust. Keep up the good work!*
>
> *This feedback should be specific enough to guide improvements while encouraging further development. If you need more detailed suggestions or have other areas you'd like feedback on, feel free to ask!*

Example 2: Asking for Advice to Supervision Challenge

The following examples illustrates a typical supervision challenge and PedaBuddy's suggestion to solve it.

> **User:** *I am supervising bachelor thesis and I really struggle how to explain the students about critical analysis of earlier literature. My students sometimes don't use good enough academic articles and even if they do, they tend to describe and reference them and don't reach critical analysis nor argumentative voice. What would you suggest, how I could supervise them?*
>
> **PedaBuddy:**
> *Guiding students to conduct critical analysis of literature can indeed be challenging, especially if they're accustomed to simply summarizing sources. Here's a step-by-step approach you could use to enhance their skills in this area:*
>
> *1.**Emphasize the Importance of Source Quality**: Start by helping students understand what makes a source credible and relevant. Encourage them to use peer-reviewed academic articles from respected journals. You can provide a list of criteria for evaluating sources, such as the reputation of the journal, the credentials of the authors, and the recency of the publication.*
>
> *2.**Teach Critical Reading Skills**: Before they can write critically, students need to read critically. Teach them to ask questions as they read, such as:*
> - *What are the main arguments?*
> - *How do these arguments compare with those in other studies?*
> - *What evidence is used, and is it convincing?*
> - *What are the limitations of this research?*
>
> *3.**Model Critical Analysis**: Provide examples of critical analysis from good papers or your own work. Show how scholars build upon or challenge previous studies, and how they position their arguments within the existing literature. Demonstrating how to integrate source material with their own analysis can be very helpful.*
>
> *4.**Practice with Structured Exercises**: Give them exercises that require critical engagement with texts. For instance, have them write a critique of an article's methodology or a comparative analysis of two papers with opposing viewpoints.*
>
> *5.**Foster an Argumentative Voice**: Encourage them to develop their own academic voice. This includes making their own arguments and supporting them with evidence. You might start with small assignments where they argue a point in a paragraph using sources.*
>
> *6.**Use Workshops or Peer Reviews**: Arrange sessions where students can present their literature reviews and receive feedback from peers and yourself. This not only helps them understand different perspectives but also allows them to critique others, reinforcing critical thinking skills.*
>
> *7.**Continuous Feedback**: Provide regular, constructive feedback on their drafts, pointing out where they are just summarizing versus analyzing. Highlight good instances of critical analysis to show them what to aim for.*
>
> *8.**Encourage Revision**: Make them understand that writing is a process, and revision is a key part of strengthening their argumentative skills. Encourage them to revise their drafts focusing on deepening the analysis based on feedback.*
>
> *Implementing these steps should help your students advance from merely describing literature to critically analyzing it and developing their own argumentative voice. If you'd like more detailed strategies or specific resources to use in your supervision, I'm here to help!*

Example 3: Planning an Exercise

The following example illustrates a typical question about planning an exercise for a class. Note that the question is based on the earlier chat.

User: *I really like the idea no 4 practicing with structured exercises. Can you give an example of this kind of exercise and also add peer learning or some kind of collaborative aspect the exercise?*

PedaBuddy: *Absolutely! Structured exercises that include peer learning or collaborative elements can significantly enhance students' critical analysis skills. Here's an example of an exercise that you could implement:*

Exercise: Comparative Article Analysis
Objective: To develop critical analysis skills by comparing and contrasting two scholarly articles, identifying strengths, weaknesses, and the interplay of different research perspectives.
Materials Needed:
- Two academic articles that address similar topics but take different perspectives or reach different conclusions.
- A set of guiding questions to help frame the analysis.

Instructions:
1. Preparation:
- Divide the students into small groups (3-4 members).
- Assign each group the same pair of articles to ensure consistency in discussions and outputs.
- Provide each group with a set of guiding questions to structure their analysis, such as:
    o What are the main arguments presented in each article?
    o How do the methodologies differ and what are the implications of these differences?
    o How does each author support their arguments? What types of evidence are used?
    o What are the strengths and weaknesses of each article?
    o How do these articles contribute to the broader field of study?

2. Group Discussion:
- Allow the groups time to read and discuss the articles based on the guiding questions.
- Each group should prepare a comparative analysis that addresses each question, citing specific examples from the texts.

3. Peer Review:
- After the groups complete their analyzes, pair each group with another group. Each group presents their findings to the other.
- During the presentations, encourage the listening group to provide feedback, focusing on the depth of the analysis and how effectively the group supported their arguments with evidence from the articles.

4. Reflection and Revision:
- After the peer review, give groups time to revise their analyzes based on the feedback received.
- Each group submits a final document that outlines their comparative analysis, incorporating insights gained from the peer review process.

5. Class Discussion:
- Conclude the exercise with a full class discussion, allowing each group to share key findings and reflections on the process.
- Discuss how these skills can be applied to their own research and thesis work.

Benefits:
- Collaborative Learning: Students benefit from seeing how their peers approach the same texts, which can introduce new analytical perspectives.
- Critical Engagement: The structured questions and requirement to compare articles push students to go beyond surface-level reading and engage critically with the content.
- Feedback Integration: The peer review process encourages students to critique and be critiqued, fostering a more nuanced understanding of critical analysis.

This exercise not only helps students develop critical thinking and analysis skills but also encourages collaboration and communication, essential skills in academic and professional settings. If you'd like more exercises or variations on this one, feel free to ask!

Example 4: Formulating Review and Exam Questions

The following example illustrates how PedaBuddy can be used to come up with questions that can be used in class discussion, debates, quizzes, or exams. In the example a pre-version of a later published article about design thinking written by the author (Jaskari, 2024) was submitted to PedaBuddy. First, time was given to read the document. Then PedaBuddy was asked to formulate review questions, debate topics and multiple-choice questions. A short illustration of this chat follows.

User: Please read the following document and tell when you have read it.

PedaBuddy: I've read the document on using design thinking as a pedagogical approach to foster sustainability in higher education. How can I assist you further with this information?

User: Please come up with 10 review questions that can be used in class discussion.

PedaBuddy: Certainly! Here are 10 review questions that can be used for a class discussion on the topic of design thinking as a pedagogical approach to foster sustainability:

Define Design Thinking: How would you define design thinking based on the readings? What are the core principles that underlie this approach?

Human-Centric Design: Why is empathy considered a crucial component in the design thinking process? Can you provide an example of how empathy towards users can lead to better problem-solving outcomes?

Iterative Process: Discuss the iterative nature of design thinking. How does this non-linear approach enhance the development of sustainable solutions?
[list continues...]

User: Thank you. Based on the article, could you come up with interesting topics for class debates?

PedaBuddy: Certainly! Based on the document on design thinking as a pedagogical tool for sustainability, here are some interesting debate topics that can engage students in meaningful discussions:

Effectiveness of Design Thinking vs. Traditional Problem-Solving Methods in Education:

Pro: Design thinking promotes creativity, empathy, and iterative learning which are crucial for modern challenges.
Con: Traditional problem-solving methods are more structured and predictable, offering a straightforward approach to learning and outcomes.

Is an Interdisciplinary Approach Essential for Teaching Sustainability through Design Thinking?

Pro: Interdisciplinary approaches enrich students' perspectives and foster innovative solutions to complex problems.
Con: Specialized, discipline-specific approaches provide deeper, more focused expertise that is necessary for addressing specific sustainability issues.
[list continues...]

User: Thank you so much! Could you also come up with 10 multiple choice questions that are based on the article?

PedaBuddy: Certainly! Here are 10 multiple-choice questions based on the article discussing design thinking as a pedagogical approach to foster sustainability. These questions can help assess students' understanding of key concepts and details from the document:

What is a key characteristic of design thinking?
   A) Linearity
   B) Predictability
   C) Iterative process
   D) Single-discipline focus

Which of the following is NOT one of the 4C's emphasized in the document?
   A) Creativity
   B) Compliance
   C) Collaboration
   D) Communication

According to the document, what is the role of empathy in design thinking?
   A) To provide financial insight
   B) To understand user needs and experiences
   C) To simplify the design process
   D) To speed up product development
[list continues...]

These examples above illustrate what are thought to be the typical use cases of PedaBuddy GPT. Each example shows the prompt that has been written and PedaBuddy's answer to that prompt. Each of these answers were generated in few seconds. Indeed, the strength of PedaBuddy is the speed in which it can generate content, where teachers can review what is useful and what is not. For example, in the first example about feedback, PedaBuddy uses a typical structure on how feedback is written. Teachers can use this as a starting point and modify the text to sound as them. In other examples, PedaBuddy's power to quickly ideate and suggest different option can be a very useful tool when planning teaching and learning activities.

DISCUSSION

The development of PedaBuddy and other MyGPT agents has revealed various strengths and opportunities, as well as challenges. These aspects will be discussed next.

Integrating MyGPTs such as PedaBuddy as AI assistants in higher education offers several opportunities for teachers. Serving as a "right hand" or colleague to educators, MyGPTs can facilitate a more personalized and engaging educational environment. MyGPTs can be efficiently used in creating individualized learning paths that cater to the diverse needs of students, thereby enhancing learner-centeredness. Additionally, MyGPTs contribute to the scalability of teaching, allowing educators to effectively manage larger groups of students without a drop in the quality of instruction. This scalability ensures that every student receives the necessary attention and support, fostering an inclusive educational atmosphere.

MyGPTs may also bring about significant efficiency gains and help address resource constraints within educational institutions. By helping from ideation to planning and automating routine tasks, they may free up valuable time and resources that faculty can then redirect for example towards research. Furthermore, the multilingual capabilities of MyGPTs provide a substantial advantage in international settings – whether talking about faculty or students - where they can offer support and resources in various languages, thereby broadening access and participation.

The adoption of MyGPTs in educational settings is not without its challenges. In addition to the common hurdles associated with generative AI, such as data privacy concerns, ethical issues, and the necessity for digital literacy, new technological tools demand significant time investment for learning. The initial use of tools like ChatGPT is often intuitive and straightforward, but as applications become more complex, the importance of proficiency in AI usage grows. Users must engage in a trial-and-error process to develop sufficient skills to effectively benefit from using GPTs. Also, there often is a need for training to effectively use these tools.

Another challenge lies in the cost of software licensing. The development of tailored MyGPTs requires a ChatGPT Plus subscription. While the price of ChatGPT Plus (20€ per month) may not seem prohibitive for individual users, expenses can become substantial when scaled to hundreds of users. It is evident that not all higher education institutions have the financial resources to afford these licenses for their faculty.

Thirdly, although efforts have been made to steer PedaBuddy towards using modern pedagogical methods like constructive alignment, experiential learning, flipped learning, and interactive learning, it does not eliminate the need for teachers to understand the pedagogical foundations of their teaching. Thus, it is crucial to recognize that PedaBuddy is meant to serve as an assistant or a support tool, not to replace teachers.

Lastly, generative AI tools require human oversight to ensure that their outputs are suitable for the intended purposes. While MyGPT can generate a large volume of ideas, plans, exercises, assessment rubrics and other content quickly, the accuracy and relevance of this content must continually be checked, since generative AI can hallucinate and often wants to please its user. Thus, human supervision is critical to guarantee that the AI-generated content meets the academic standards.

CONCLUSIONS

This chapter has explored the development and testing of custom MyGPTs in higher education context, specifically through the case study of PedaBuddy. It began by reviewing the existing literature on generative AI and MyGPTs, highlighting their transformative potential in educational settings. The discussion then detailed how MyGPTs are configured using OpenAI's GPT builder, followed by an in-depth case study of PedaBuddy, which showcased its development process and practical applications.

The development of PedaBuddy alongside other MyGPT agents has revealed several advantages and possibilities for improving higher education. These AI assistants act as an extension of the teaching faculty, fostering a more tailored and dynamic educational experience. They are instrumental in crafting customized learning trajectories that address the varied requirements of students, thereby prioritizing student-centric education. Furthermore, MyGPTs enhance the ability of teachers to handle larger classes effectively without compromising educational quality. This ability to scale helps ensure that more individual attention is maintained across a broader range of students, supporting an inclusive learning environment.

On the flip side, incorporating MyGPTs like PedaBuddy into educational settings is fraught with challenges. Issues such as concerns over data privacy, ethical dilemmas, and the necessity for digital literacy skills accompany the deployment of generative AI technologies. Additionally, these sophisticated tools require significant time to master and necessitate ongoing education to utilize effectively. Financially, the costs associated with software licensing may strain educational institutions' budgets, especially when extended to a large number of users. While MyGPTs can support contemporary pedagogical approaches, they do not eliminate the need for educators to deeply understand and engage with these methods themselves. Moreover, the output produced by MyGPTs must be meticulously supervised to ensure it aligns with educational standards and goals.

There are several interesting future research ideas to understand the impact of MyGPTs in higher education, specifically from teacher and faculty perspective. First, investigating the effectiveness of AI teaching assistants could provide valuable insights into how these tools influence student engagement and learning. Second, exploring the customization and personalization capabilities of these AI tools would be valuable. Third, examining the training requirements and digital literacy needed for effective use of AI tools like MyGPTs provides interesting passages for future research. Together, these research directions could significantly contribute to optimizing MyGPTs and generative AI's potential in delivering high-quality teaching and learning experiences in higher education.

REFERENCES

AACSB. (2024). AACSB Accreditation. Available at: https://www.aacsb.edu/educators/accreditation Accessed on May 12, 2024.

Adeshola, I., & Adepoju, A. P. (2023). The opportunities and challenges of ChatGPT in education. *Interactive Learning Environments*, •••, 1–14. DOI: 10.1080/10494820.2023.2253858

Aljanabi, M., Ghazi, M., Ali, A. H., & Abed, A. (2023). ChatGPT: Open possibilities. *Iraqi Journal for Computer Science and Mathematics*, 4(1), 62–64. DOI: 10.52866/20ijcsm.2023.01.01.0018

Aydin, Ö. (2022). OpenAI ChatGPT Generated Literature Review: Digital Twin in Healthcare. Available online at: https://papers.ssrn.com/sol3/papers.cfmabstract_id = 4308687 (accessed April 10, 2024).

Baber, H., Nair, K., Gupta, R., & Gurjar, K. (2023). The beginning of ChatGPT – a systematic and bibliometric review of the literature. *Information and Learning Science*, 125(7/8), 587–614. DOI: 10.1108/ILS-04-2023-0035

Biggs, J. (1996). Enhancing teaching through constructive alignment. *Higher Education*, 32(3), 347–364. DOI: 10.1007/BF00138871

Chan, C. K. Y. (2024a). Introduction to Artificial Intelligence in Higher Education. In Chan & Colloton (eds) Generative AI in Higher Education: The ChatGPT Effect (1st ed.). Routledge, (pp.1-23). https://doi.org/DOI: 10.4324/9781003459026-1

Chan, C. K. Y. (2024b). Redesigning Assessment in the AI Era. In Chan & Colloton (eds) Generative AI in Higher Education: The ChatGPT Effect (1st ed.). Routledge, (pp.87-127). DOI: 10.4324/9781003459026-4

Chan, C. K. Y., & Colloton, T. (2024). *Generative AI in Higher Education: The ChatGPT Effect* (1st ed.). Routledge., DOI: 10.4324/9781003459026

Chintalapati, S., & Pandey, S. K. (2022). Artificial intelligence in marketing: A systematic literature review. *International Journal of Market Research*, 64(1), 38–68. DOI: 10.1177/14707853211018428

Colloton, T. (2024). Strengths and Weaknesses in Embracing ChatGPT in Curriculum Design. In Chan & Colloton (eds) Generative AI in Higher Education: The ChatGPT Effect (1st ed.). Routledge, (pp.44-86). https://doi.org/DOI: 10.4324/9781003459026-3

Davenport, T., Guha, A., Grewal, D., Bressgott, T., & Davenport, T. (2020). How artificial intelligence will change the future of marketing. *Journal of the Academy of Marketing Science*, 48(1), 24–42. DOI: 10.1007/s11747-019-00696-0

Deng, X., & Yu, Z. (2023). A meta-analysis and systematic review of the effect of Chatbot technology use in sustainable education. *Sustainability (Basel)*, 15(4), 2940. DOI: 10.3390/su15042940

Dwivedi, Y. K., Kshetri, N., Hughes, L., Slade, E. L., Jeyaraj, A., Kar, A. K., Baabdullah, A. M., Koohang, A., Raghavan, V., Ahuja, M., Albanna, H., Albashrawi, M. A., Al-Busaidi, A. S., Balakrishnan, J., Barlette, Y., Basu, S., Bose, I., Brooks, L., Buhalis, D., & Wright, R. (2023). "So what if ChatGPT wrote it?" Multidisciplinary perspectives on opportunities, challenges and implications of generative conversational AI for research, practice and policy. *International Journal of Information Management*, 71, 102642. DOI: 10.1016/j.ijinfomgt.2023.102642

Elhajjar, S. (2024). The current and future state of the marketing management profession. *Journal of Marketing Theory and Practice*, 32(2), 233–250. DOI: 10.1080/10696679.2023.2166535

Elhajjar, S., Karam, S., & Borna, S. (2020). Artificial intelligence in marketing education programs. *Marketing Education Review*, 31(1), 2–13. DOI: 10.1080/10528008.2020.1835492

Firat, M. (2023). What ChatGPT means for universities: Perceptions of scholars and students. *Journal of Applied Learning and Teaching*, 6(1). Advance online publication. DOI: 10.37074/jalt.2023.6.1.22

Gimpel, H., Hall, K., Decker, S., Eymann, T., Lämmermann, L., Mädche, A., & Vandrik, S. (2023). Unlocking the power of generative AI models and systems such as GPT-4 and ChatGPT for higher education: A guide for students and lecturers (No. 02-2023). *Hohenheim Discussion Papers in Business, Economics and Social Sciences*. https://nbn-resolving.de/urn:nbn:de:bsz:100-opus-21463

Jaskari, M.-M. (2024). Academic Design Thinking Pedagogy as an Approach to Foster Sustainability Skills in Higher Education. In Goi, C. (Ed.), *Teaching and Learning for a Sustainable Future: Innovative Strategies and Best Practices* (pp. 69–90). IGI Global., DOI: 10.4018/978-1-6684-9859-0.ch004

Muñoz, S. A. S., Gayoso, G. G., Huambo, A. C., Tapia, R. D. C., Incaluque, J. L., Aguila, O. E. P., & Arias-Gonzales, J. L. (2023). Examining the impacts of ChatGPT on student motivation and engagement. *Social Space*, 23(1), 1–27.

Nah, F. F.-H., Zheng, R., Cai, J., Siau, K., & Chen, L. (2023). Generative AI and ChatGPT: Applications, challenges, and AI-human collaboration. *Journal of Information Technology Case and Application Research*, 25(3), 277–304. DOI: 10.1080/15228053.2023.2233814

Open, A. I. (2024). GPT's. Accessed at May, 12, 2024. https://help.openai.com/en/collections/8475420-gpts

Rudolph, J., Tan, S., & Tan, S. (2023). ChatGPT: Bullshit spewer or the end of traditional assessments in higher education? *Journal of Applied Learning & Teaching*, 6(1), 343–363. DOI: 10.37074/jalt.2023.6.1.9

Schön, E. M., Neumann, M., Hofmann-Stölting, C., Baeza-Yates, R., & Rauschenberger, M. (2023). How are AI assistants changing higher education? *Frontiers of Computer Science*, 5, 1208550. Advance online publication. DOI: 10.3389/fcomp.2023.1208550

UNESCO. (2023). ChatGPT and artificial intelligence in higher education: quick start guide. Available at https://unesdoc.unesco.org/ark:/48223/pf0000385146

Winkler, R., & Söllner, M. (2018). Unleashing the potential of chatbots in education: A state-of-the-art analysis. *Proceedings - Academy of Management*, 1(1), 15903. Advance online publication. DOI: 10.5465/AMBPP.2018.15903abstract

Zaveri, P. (2023, February 3). Microsoft's landmark deal with OpenAI shows that ChatGPT is going to be the defining technology of 2023. Business Insider. Retrieved May 12, 2024, from https://www.businessinsider.com/why-generative-ai-chatgpt-the-defining-tech-of-this-year-2023-1?r=US&IR=T

Zawacki-Richter, O., Marin, V. I., Bond, M., & Gouverneur, F. (2019). Systematic review of research on artificial intelligence applications in higher education–where are the educators? *International Journal of Educational Technology in Higher Education*, 16(1), 1–27. DOI: 10.1186/s41239-019-0171-0

APPENDIX

Illustrative case of building MyGPT *"Pedagogy Partner"* using Open AI ChatBuilder

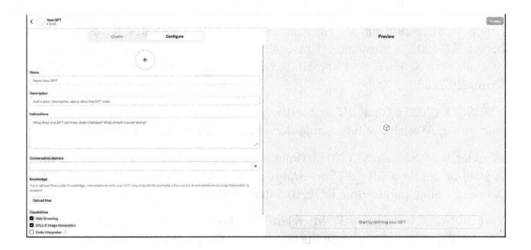

111

GPT Builder

Hi! I'll help you build a new GPT. You can say something like, "make a creative who helps generate visuals for new products" or "make a software engineer who helps format my code."

What would you like to make?

You

I would like to make a GPT that helps university teachers to make excellent, high quality teaching that is based on research-based pedagogy.

GPT Builder

Great choice! Now, let's give your GPT a name. How about **Pedagogy Partner**? Does this sound good to you, or do you have another name in mind?

You

I think that is a great name

GPT Builder

Here is the initial profile picture for **Pedagogy Partner**. How do you like it? Would you like to make any changes to this image?

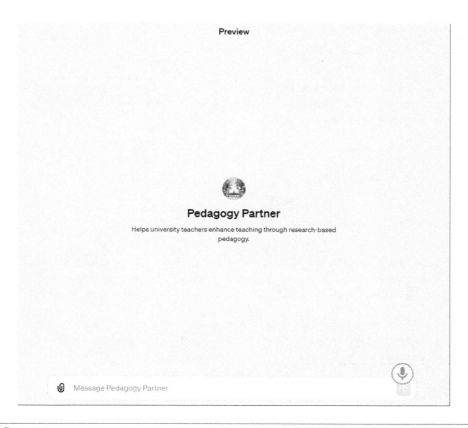

You
I think this picture is more about reading than pedagogy. Could you make a picture that takes into account teachers point of view. Also, please use colors of blue ocean and yellow sun.

GPT Builder

Here's the updated profile picture that better reflects the teacher's perspective and includes the colors of blue ocean and yellow sun. Does this better match what you were looking for?

You
No, I preferred the earlier one. Please use that one.

GPT Builder
We've reverted to the original profile picture. Now, let's refine the GPT's behavior further. What kind of teaching topics should it focus on? For example, should it cover a wide range of subjects or specialize in certain areas like STEM or humanities?

You
The GPT is mainly targeted to university teachers teaching at the university of business studies. However, many topics in business studies cover subjects areas in other disciplines such as economics, sociology and psychology. So maybe it should cover a wide range of subjects. Or what do you think?

GPT Builder
That sounds like a balanced approach. By covering a wide range of subjects related to business studies and overlapping disciplines, **Pedagogy Partner** can offer comprehensive support. This will allow the GPT to be more versatile and useful across different areas of study within the university setting.

What specific types of interactions or responses should it prioritize to be most helpful to university teachers? For example, should it focus more on providing resources, suggesting teaching strategies, or something else?

You
I would like that it gives teachers very specific instructions, suggestions and even templates to be used when they encounter specific challenges. For example, if they want to five constructive feedback to the students but have only some bullet points in their mind, the GPT would write feedback in a constructive manner and help teachers to give feedback that is easier to understand.

GPT Builder
That's a practical focus! **Pedagogy Partner** will now be able to offer specific guidance, such as converting brief notes into detailed, constructive student feedback.

Would you like to add any features related to how this GPT interacts, such as a particular tone or style in its responses? For example, should it maintain a formal academic tone, or perhaps a more conversational and supportive style?

You

Yes, I would like this GPT to be easy to approach in many levels. It should be fun to use and have a friendly tone in its answers. It should remember that while Pedagogy Partner knows everything about high quality teaching and learning, the teachers that use the chat may not know everything. Still, it should not be too nurturing or childish towards teachers. Just encouraging.

GPT Builder

That sounds like a great balance for **Pedagogy Partner**—friendly and encouraging without being overbearing. It's now set up to be an engaging and supportive companion for teachers.

Would you like to try interacting with **Pedagogy Partner** in the preview to see how it performs? You can also suggest any further refinements based on that experience.

Testing GPT in preview

You

I just reading a mid-report of bachelor thesis and I have no idea how to formulate my feedback in a good way. The structure of the thesis is not good, it is just bits and pieces put together. The earlier literature is just short descriptions of what has been done, but there is not thinking or argumentation based on those. This student clearly has not used enough time to really know what she has been writing. I must fail him if he doesn't step up his work. Can you write a feedback.

Pedagogy Partner

Absolutely, providing clear and constructive feedback is essential for helping your student improve. Here's a draft of how you might structure your feedback to be both encouraging and instructive:

I have reviewed the mid-report of your bachelor thesis, and I want to thank you for the effort you've put into this project so far. I'd like to offer some feedback that I hope will guide you in refining your thesis to meet the academic standards required.

Structure: Currently, the structure of the thesis appears fragmented, with sections that seem somewhat disconnected from each other. A coherent structure is critical in a thesis as it helps guide the reader through your argumentation and findings. I suggest creating a clear outline that defines the main argument or thesis statement and systematically builds on it with each section. This will help in presenting your research in a logical and persuasive manner.

Literature Review: The literature review should do more than summarize previous works; it needs to critically engage with existing research to set a strong foundation for your own study. Each piece of literature you discuss should clearly tie back to your research question, showing how it supports or challenges your work. Consider revisiting the literature with a critical eye, analyzing the methodologies, findings, and arguments of previous studies, and positioning your research within these academic conversations.

Depth of Understanding: It is essential that your thesis demonstrates a deep understanding of the topic you are exploring. This means going beyond surface-level descriptions and engaging critically with the material you are discussing. Please make sure you fully understand and interpret the sources you cite, reflecting on their implications for your research question.

Next Steps: I encourage you to allocate dedicated time to review your work critically. It might be hel[pful] to schedule a meeting to discuss your thesis in more detail. This would also be a great opportunity t[o] clarify any doubts you might have and ensure you're on the right track.

Please remember, the goal of this thesis is not only to fulfill an academic requirement but also to contribute meaningfully to the topic you are passionate about. I believe in your ability to enhance yo[ur] thesis and am here to support you through this process. Let's aim to discuss these points in our nex[t] meeting, and please bring any questions or areas where you need further clarification.

Looking forward to your revisions and to seeing how your thesis develops.

Best regards,

[Your Name]

This feedback aims to be specific about what needs improvement while also offering support and guidance on how to enhance their work. Adjust the tone and content as you see fit to match your personal style and the relationship you have with the student.

You

Well, that was a very long feedback. Can you please summarize it to one paragraph?

Pedagogy Partner

Certainly! Here's a more concise version of the feedback:

Dear [Student's Name],

I've reviewed your bachelor thesis mid-report and recommend focusing on improving its structure and depth. The thesis currently reads as disjointed and lacks critical engagement with the literature. Please refine your structure to create a coherent narrative and deepen your analysis of the sources to demonstrate a robust understanding of the topic. Consider revisiting and critically analyzing the literature to more effectively support your research. Let's schedule a meeting to discuss your progress and any challenges you're facing.

Best regards,

[Your Name]

You
Please translate the feedback in Finnish.

Pedagogy Partner
Certainly! Here is the feedback translated into Finnish:

Hei [Opiskelijan nimi],

Olen lukenut kandidaatintutkielmasi väliraportin ja suosittelen keskittymään sen rakenteen ja syvyyden parantamiseen. Tutkielma vaikuttaa tällä hetkellä sirpaleiselta eikä sisällä kriittistä perehtymistä kirjallisuuteen. Ole hyvä ja hio rakennetta luodaksesi yhtenäisen kerronnan ja syvennä analyysiäsi lähteistä osoittaaksesi vankka ymmärrys aiheesta. Harkitse kirjallisuuden uudelleentarkastelua ja kriittistä analysointia tukemaan tehokkaammin tutkimustasi. Asettakaamme tapaaminen keskustellaksemme edistymisestäsi ja kohtaamistasi haasteista.

Parhain terveisin,

[Nimesi]

This translation maintains the professional and supportive tone of the original message.

Chapter 5
Transforming Teaching and Learning With Natural Language Processing

Luis Coelho
https://orcid.org/0000-0002-5673-7306
ISEP, Polytechnic of Porto, Portugal

Sara Reis
https://orcid.org/0000-0002-3416-2257
ISEP, Polytechnic of Porto, Portugal

ABSTRACT

In higher education (HE), the integration of Natural Language Processing (NLP) stands as a transformative force, reshaping traditional paradigms of teaching and learning. NLP systems are also able to perform tasks such as text summarization, text comparison, and personalized text generation, among others. From the teacher's perspective it is possible to have support or automate in tasks such as essay grading or materials generation, among many others. Moreover, NLP-powered intelligent tutoring systems personalize learning experiences by analyzing students' language use, identifying misconceptions, and offering targeted feedback and explanations. The adoption of NLP technology in HE holds the promise of optimizing learning outcomes, enhancing institutional efficiency, and promoting greater accessibility and inclusivity. However, despite its potential benefits, the successful implementation of NLP in HE necessitates careful consideration of ethical, privacy, and equity concerns, as well as ongoing research to address technical challenges and refine pedagogical strategies.

DOI: 10.4018/979-8-3693-3944-2.ch005

1 INTRODUCTION

1.1 Background and Context

In higher education, Natural Language Processing (NLP) is emerging as a revolutionary tool, significantly altering conventional teaching and learning methods. As a branch of artificial intelligence focused on the interaction between computers and humans using language, NLP comes to provide diverse solutions and applications designed to address several challenges in higher education while creating opportunities to improve the education processes.

NLP algorithms have recently reached a very mature state of development, being able to understand not only the interlocutor's intention but also to generate an appropriate response and even hold a conversation (from a human perspective). In addition, NLP systems can perform tasks such as text summarization, text comparison, and personalized text generation, among others. Such abilities came to transform teaching and learning approaches, allowing us to enhance various aspects of the process, while offering a myriad of applications.

From the teacher's perspective, one notable application is in automated essay grading, where NLP systems analyze the content, coherence, and grammar of student essays, providing quick and consistent feedback. This capability not only aids educators in efficiently handling large class sizes but also empowers students with valuable insights for improvement (Shermis and Hamner 2012). Similar algorithms can even be extendable to STEM domains where written language is combined with numbers, symbols or drawings, making it possible to tackle disciplines such as computer science (Combéfis 2022; Paiva, Leal, and Figueira 2022), physics (Zhai et al. 2020), chemistry (Maestrales et al. 2021) and mathematics (Botelho et al. 2023; Moreno and Pineda 2020).

Moreover, NLP-powered intelligent tutoring systems personalize learning experiences by analyzing students' language use, identifying misconceptions, and offering targeted feedback and explanations. By adapting to individual learning styles and needs, these systems optimize student engagement and comprehension (VanLehn 2011).

Text summarization and information extraction are additional areas where NLP shines in education. By summarizing large volumes of text or extracting key information from educational materials, NLP techniques enable students to grasp complex topics more efficiently while assisting educators in preparing course materials tailored to students' needs (Nenkova and McKeown 2011).

Furthermore, NLP-based tools can also play a crucial role in language learning and assessment by providing language practice exercises, assessing proficiency, and offering personalized learning recommendations. These tools cater to individual strengths and weaknesses, facilitating more effective language acquisition (Yannakoudakis, Briscoe, and Medlock 2011).

NLP systems can also have a role as virtual assistants, either for providing personalized support or to handle massified courses. Educational virtual assistants and chatbots offer on-demand support to students, answering questions, providing guidance, and facilitating communication between students and instructors. This real-time assistance fosters a supportive learning environment and enhances students' overall educational experience (Graesser et al. 2018).

Lastly, NLP techniques enhance search engines and recommendation systems in educational settings by understanding the semantics of user queries and content. By providing more relevant and personalized search results and recommendations, these systems streamline information retrieval and support students in accessing resources aligned with their learning objectives (Tang et al. 2019).

The integration of Natural Language Processing (NLP) as an affective interaction tool in educational contexts represents a groundbreaking advancement in pedagogy and student engagement. Unlike traditional methods of instruction, which often lack personalized feedback and emotional awareness, NLP-driven systems have the capability to understand and respond to students' affective states in real-time. By analyzing linguistic cues, sentiment, and tone of voice, NLP tools can detect indicators of student emotions such as frustration, confusion, or engagement. This novel approach enables educators to tailor their instructional strategies and interventions based on students' emotional needs, fostering a supportive and empathetic learning environment. Moreover, NLP facilitates more natural and conversational interactions between students and educational technology, promoting deeper engagement and comprehension. As such, the incorporation of NLP as an affective interaction tool in education holds promise for enhancing student motivation, learning outcomes, and overall well-being in the classroom.

1.2 Scope and Objectives

The adoption of NLP technology in higher education holds the promise of optimizing learning outcomes, enhancing institutional efficiency, and promoting greater accessibility and inclusivity. However, despite its potential benefits, the successful implementation of NLP in higher education necessitates careful consideration of ethical, privacy, and equity concerns, as well as ongoing research to address technical challenges and refine pedagogical strategies. This chapter seeks to explore the current landscape of NLP in higher education, providing insight about its transformative potential, inherent limitations, and pointing directions for future research and application.

2 OVERVIEW OF NATURAL LANGUAGE PROCESSING

2.1 Definition and Core Concepts

Natural Language Processing (NLP) is a field of artificial intelligence (AI) focused on the interaction between computers and humans through natural language. The primary goal of NLP is to enable computers to understand, interpret, and generate human language in a manner that is meaningful and useful. This field combines elements from linguistics, computer science, and machine learning to develop algorithms and models capable of performing tasks such as language translation, sentiment analysis, speech recognition, and text generation.

NLP systems are composed of several subsystems, usually with high levels of complexity, that exchange information in several linguistic layers (Ferreira et al. 2023). In Figure 1, a general pipeline for an NLP system is represented, having as input a normalized text string. This input string must be prepared in a previous text normalization stage (not represented) where all non-letter representing characters existent in the raw text have been removed or replaced by a text equivalent (e.g. recognizing and converting to text entities such as numbers, dates, acronyms, among others) and all special characters are removed. In Figure 1, the presented functional blocks sequence can be rearranged, or the blocks can have additional interdependencies depending on the approach.

Figure 1. General pipeline for a natural language processing system

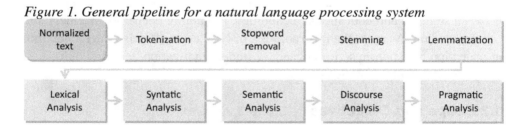

One of the foundational aspects of NLP is text preprocessing, which involves preparing text data for analysis. This includes tokenization, the process of breaking down text into smaller units like words or sentences, and stop word removal, which eliminates common words that do not add significant meaning to the text, such as "and", "the", and "is". Additionally, stemming and lemmatization are techniques used to reduce words to their root forms; stemming removes suffixes, while lemmatization considers the context to convert words to their base forms.

Lexical or morphological analysis are crucial for understanding the grammatical structure of text. Morphemes are identified and words are converted to their root form. Part-of-speech (POS) tagging associates the grammatical categories of words, such as nouns, verbs, and adjectives. Dependency parsing analyzes the grammatical structure to establish relationships between words, like subjects and objects, while constituency parsing breaks down sentences into sub-phrases or constituents, such as noun phrases and verb phrases. Constituency parsing then analyzes the hierarchical structure of each sentence by creating a parse tree.

Semantic analysis in NLP involves understanding the meaning of text. Named Entity Recognition (NER) identifies and classifies entities within text, including names of people, organizations, locations, and dates. Word Sense Disambiguation (WSD) determines the correct meaning of a word based on its context, especially for words with multiple meanings (Braga, Coelho, and Resende 2007; Wang, Wang, and Fujita 2020). Coreference resolution is another important technique that identifies when different words refer to the same entity.

Depending on the purpose of the NLP application, different functional blocks can be involved. To tackle language beyond the sentence level, discourse analysis is performed. This aims to understand how sentences are integrated and sequenced to create a coherent and meaningful text, considering factors like context, conversation flow, and unspoken rules. This helps NLP applications like question answering and summarization. Furthermore, text classification and categorization are essential for organizing and making sense of large volumes of text. Pragmatic analysis can cover additional communication information that is beyond the text itself. For example, sentiment analysis determines the sentiment expressed in a piece of text, categorizing it as positive, negative, or neutral. Topic modeling identifies the main themes or topics within a set of documents, often using techniques like Latent Dirichlet Allocation (LDA). Document classification assigns documents to predefined categories based on their content, a common example being spam detection in emails.

Advanced techniques have further enhanced the capabilities of NLP. Transformers (Vaswani et al. 2017), allow for parallel processing of words, significantly improving efficiency. BERT (Bidirectional Encoder Representations from Transformers), developed by Google, uses bidirectional training to understand the context of words in all directions, providing deeper language understanding. Word embeddings represent words as vectors in a continuous vector space where semantically similar words are closer together, with popular models including Word2Vec (Mikolov et al. 2013), GloVe (Pennington, Socher, and Manning 2014), and FastText (Bojanowski et al. 2017).

2.2 Historical Evolution

The development of Natural Language Processing (NLP), as depicted in Figure 2, has progressed through several significant milestones, each representing a technological breakthrough.

Figure 2. Chronology NLP systems evolution

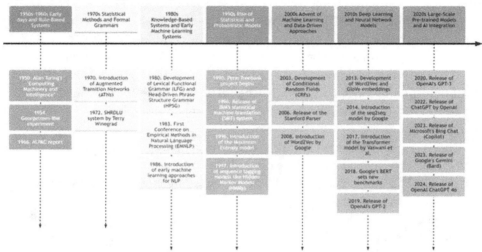

In the 1950s and 1960s, the early days of NLP were characterized by rule-based systems. Alan Turing's 1950 paper "Computing Machinery and Intelligence" laid the conceptual groundwork by proposing the Turing Test as a measure of machine intelligence. In 1954, the Georgetown-IBM experiment demonstrated the potential of machine translation by successfully translating 60 Russian sentences into English using rule-based methods. However, progress slowed following the 1966 ALPAC report, which criticized the lack of practical advancements in machine translation, leading to decreased funding and interest.

The 1970s saw the introduction of statistical methods and formal grammar. Augmented Transition Networks (ATNs) helped to provide a framework for parsing natural language (Woods 1970). Terry Winograd's SHRDLU system in 1972 showcased natural language understanding within a limited domain, marking a significant step forward.

The 1980s brought knowledge-based systems and early machine learning approaches. Developments such as Lexical Functional Grammar (LFG) and Head-Driven Phrase Structure Grammar (HPSG) in 1980 advanced the understanding of syntax and semantics (Kaplan 2004). The first Conference on Empirical Methods in

Natural Language Processing (EMNLP) in 1983 highlighted the growing importance of statistical and data-driven methods, and by 1986, machine learning approaches like decision trees and rule induction began to emerge.

The 1990s were characterized by the rise of statistical and probabilistic models. The Penn Treebank project, initiated in 1990, provided a large, annotated corpus crucial for training and evaluating NLP models (Taylor, Marcus, and Santorini 2003). IBM's release of the first statistical machine translation (SMT) system in 1996 utilized probabilistic models to improve translation quality. The introduction of the Maximum Entropy model offered a flexible statistical framework for various NLP tasks (Berger, Pietra, and Pietra 1996). Additionally, the introduction of sequence tagging models such as Hidden Markov Models (HMMs) in 1997 further advanced the field.

The 2000s marked the advent of machine learning and data-driven approaches. Conditional Random Fields (CRFs), developed in 2003, achieved state-of-the-art performance for sequence labeling tasks. The Stanford Parser, released in 2006, provided a highly accurate probabilistic parser for syntactic analysis. The development of Word2Vec by Google in 2008 revolutionized the field by introducing efficient algorithms for learning word embeddings that capture semantic relationships.

The 2010s saw the rise of deep learning and neural network models, significantly transforming NLP. Word2Vec (Mikolov et al. 2013) and GloVe (Global Vectors for Word Representation) (Pennington et al. 2014) provided high-quality word embeddings. Google's seq2seq (sequence-to-sequence) model (Sutskever, Vinyals, and Le 2014) brought significant improvements in machine translation and text generation. The introduction of the Transformer model (Vaswani et al. 2017) enhanced performance and efficiency through self-attention mechanisms. Google's BERT (Bidirectional Encoder Representations from Transformers) in 2018 set new benchmarks by providing deep bidirectional context for words. OpenAI's GPT-2 (Generative Pre-trained Transformer 2), showcased the power of large-scale pre-training for text generation (Radford et al. 2019).

The 2020s have been marked by the development of large-scale pre-trained models and their integration into various applications. OpenAI's GPT-3, released in 2020, with 175 billion parameters, demonstrated impressive capabilities in text generation, understanding, and interaction. BERT-inspired models such as RoBERTa, DistilBERT, and T5 further pushed the boundaries of NLP (Sanh et al. 2020). In 2021, OpenAI's DALL-E model expanded NLP applications into multimodal tasks by generating images from textual descriptions. The development of ChatGPT by OpenAI in 2022, leveraging GPT-3, created conversational agents that interact more naturally and coherently with users.

These milestones highlight the significant advancements in NLP, from early rule-based systems to the sophisticated deep learning models that drive today's applications. Each milestone has contributed to the field's growth, enabling a wide range of applications.

2.3 Evaluating NLP Models

Evaluating NLP systems and LLMs is crucial to understanding their capabilities and limitations across various tasks. As LLMs continue to advance rapidly, robust evaluation metrics are needed to compare different models effectively and to be able to analyze their suitability for a given task. A thorough evaluation provides insights into how well an LLM can generate human-like text, respond to prompts accurately, or maintain coherence in its outputs. Furthermore, it aids in ensuring that LLMs adhere to ethical standards, minimizing biases and misinformation. Evaluating LLMs involves examining various error perspectives to ensure comprehensive assessment and improvement. These perspectives include:

- **Answer Relevancy**. Addressing the LLM ability to process a given input in an informative and concise manner. It evaluates how well the model's response aligns with the user's query, focusing on the relevance and utility of the provided information.
- **Correctness**. Assesses whether an LLM output is factually correct based on some ground truth. Ensuring correctness is crucial, especially in applications where accuracy and reliability of information are paramount, such as in educational tools or informational chatbots.
- **Hallucination**. Refers to instances where an LLM output contains fake or made-up information. Identifying and minimizing hallucinations is vital to maintain the trustworthiness and credibility of the model, particularly in contexts where users rely on the generated content for decision-making.
- **Contextual Relevancy**. In the setting of RAG (Retrieval-Augmented Generation)-based LLM systems, this metric determines whether the retriever is able to extract the most relevant information for the LLM as context, ensuring that the model's responses are grounded in accurate and pertinent data.
- **Responsible Metrics**. These metrics include assessing bias and toxicity in LLM outputs. They determine whether an LLM output contains generally harmful and offensive content, ensuring that the model adheres to ethical standards and promotes a positive user experience. Addressing issues of bias and toxicity is crucial for creating inclusive and respectful AI systems.

- **Other Task-Specific Metrics**. These are tailored to specific use cases, such as summarization. Each task might have custom criteria that define success, reflecting the unique requirements and goals of different applications. For instance, summarization metrics might focus on coherence, completeness, and conciseness of the generated summaries.

By incorporating these diverse error perspectives, evaluators can gain a better understanding of LLM performance, identifying areas their limitations and ensuring that these models meet the specific needs and ethical standards required for their intended applications.

Evaluating LLMs poses several challenges. One significant issue is the inherent randomness and creativity in their outputs due to prompt engineering, which can make consistent evaluation difficult. Additionally, LLMs are computationally expensive, necessitating efficient evaluation metrics that do not require extensive resources. Evaluating aspects such as coherence, factual accuracy, and bias requires going beyond simple word-matching metrics, demanding more sophisticated and comprehensive approaches. These complexities make it imperative to develop and utilize diverse metrics that can capture the multifaceted nature of LLM outputs.

To address the complexities of evaluating LLMs, several key metrics are often employed, from which the following are more popular:

- **BLEU (Bilingual Evaluation Understudy)**. This metric measures the precision of word n-grams between the generated text and reference texts. It is widely used for its simplicity and efficiency, providing a quick estimate of how closely a model's output matches a given reference.
- **ROUGE (Recall-Oriented Understudy for Gisting Evaluation)**. Unlike BLEU, ROUGE focuses on the recall of word n-grams and longest common sequences. It is particularly useful for tasks such as summarization, where capturing all relevant information is crucial. ROUGE-L and ROUGE-N are variant of this method.
- **METEOR (Metric for Evaluation of Translation with Explicit ORdering)**. METEOR incorporates both recall and precision, along with additional semantic matching based on stems and paraphrasing. This metric aims to provide a more nuanced evaluation by considering semantic similarities.
- **BERTScore**. This metric leverages BERT's contextual embeddings to match words and phrases at a token-level granularity, offering a deeper understanding of meaning and paraphrasing. BERTScore is particularly valuable for evaluating the semantic fidelity of generated text.

Each evaluation metric has its strengths and limitations, making it essential to use them in conjunction to achieve a comprehensive evaluation of LLMs. BLEU and ROUGE are statistical metrics that are simple and fast to calculate, making them suitable for initial evaluations. However, they rely solely on word matching, which can overlook the semantic accuracy and coherence of the generated text. METEOR incorporates semantic matching and paraphrasing, being able to capture some level of semantic similarity, and leading to a more accurate assessment when it is required to go beyond exact word matches. BERTScore is a model-based metric that addresses the shortcomings of word-matching metrics, allowing to evaluate the semantic content of the text. It can cover paraphrased text and contextually accurate sentence generation. Covering several levels of linguistic context comes at the expense of computational power, implying more complex algorithms and effort.

Using a set of metrics, combined, offers a balanced approach and a better understanding of the model's advantages and limitations.

2.4 Current State of the Art in Natural Language Processing

NLP has seen remarkable advancements in recent years, driven by breakthroughs in machine learning, particularly deep learning. These advancements have enabled significant progress in understanding and generating human language, resulting in applications.

The paper "Attention is All You Need" by Vaswani et al. (2017) introduced the transformer model, which relies on self-attention mechanisms to process input data in parallel rather than sequentially. This architecture addresses many limitations of previous recurrent neural network (RNN) models, such as long-range dependencies and computational inefficiency. Transformers have become the foundation for state-of-the-art models, especially when using pre-trained language models (PLMs), enabling learning contextual representations from large corpora of text data.

BERT (Bidirectional Encoder Representations from Transformers) (Devlin et al. 2019), is a landmark example that uses bidirectional training of transformers on a large text corpus to achieve deep contextual understanding. This model has been pre-trained on vast amounts of text and can be fine-tuned on specific tasks, demonstrating exceptional performance in tasks like named entity recognition (NER), question answering, and text classification.

OpenAI's GPT (Generative Pre-trained Transformer) (Radford and Narasimhan 2018), particularly GPT-4, has further pushed the boundaries by employing even larger model sizes and more extensive training data. GPT-4, with its 1T parameters, exhibits remarkable capabilities in generating coherent and contextually relevant text, performing zero-shot, few-shot, and multi-turn interactions effectively. These models' ability to generalize across various tasks without task-specific training represents a significant leap in NLP.

Multilingual models like mBERT (Libovický, Rosa, and Fraser 2019) and XLM-R (Conneau et al. 2020) have extended the benefits of PLMs to multiple languages, enabling cross-lingual transfer learning. These models are trained on multilingual corpora and can perform well on tasks in different languages, even those with limited training data. Such models have been crucial in bridging the language gap, allowing NLP technologies to be accessible to non-English speakers and facilitating research in low-resource languages.

Another important aspect of modern NLP systems is few-shot and zero-shot learning. These have emerged as promising techniques to address to overcome the need for large annotated datasets. Models like GPT-3 leverage their extensive training on diverse text to perform tasks with minimal examples (few-shot) or even without any specific examples (zero-shot). This capability is transforming how NLP systems are designed and deployed, making them more adaptable and easier to customize for new tasks and domains.

The latest evolution in NLP covers a multimodal model where text, image and context are combined using information fusion with the purpose of achieving a full perception of the context (Ebrahimi 2024), which have set new benchmarks in various tasks.

Technological landmarks such as transformers, the ability to use pre-trained models, multilingual and multimodal models and few/zero shot learning allowed to bring to natural language processing system near-human abilities and these advancements have led to a wide array of applications. However, these advancements also raise ethical considerations. The deployment of powerful language models has highlighted issues related to bias, misinformation, and privacy. Models trained on large, unfiltered datasets may propagate and amplify biases present in the data. Moreover, the ability of models like GPT-3 to generate human-like text raises concerns about the potential for misuse in generating fake news or impersonating individuals. These are critical ethical challenges that must be addressed for a responsible development and deployment of NLP technologies. Raising the awareness of software developers about the impacts that their creations can have on the world is of particular importance (Reis et al. 2023).

3 APPLICATIONS OF NLP IN HIGHER EDUCATION

Modern AI supported NLP systems are valuable tools in higher education. In this context, large Language Models (LLMs), capable of several NLP tasks, are predominantly used for virtual assistants, code explanation/correction, question generation and answer grading (García-Méndez, de Arriba-Pérez, and Somoza-López 2024).

3.1 Intelligent Tutoring Systems

In higher education, NLP and AI-powered NLP allowed to boost the development of intelligent tutoring systems (ITS), which provide personalized and adaptive learning experiences for students. These systems leverage NLP to understand and interpret students' natural language inputs and understanding their intents while considering an underlying theoretical context (that can be driven by the teacher). Discourse pragmatics, in the form of emotion classification, can be also explored as an additional source of information (Feng et al. 2020; Koufakou et al. 2022). These possibilities allow for more interactive and responsive educational tools. In addition, by analyzing students' written and spoken language, ITS can assess their knowledge levels, identify misconceptions, and provide immediate, tailored feedback. NLP-powered ITS can also facilitate natural language dialogues, guiding students through complex problem-solving processes and offering hints and explanations in real-time (Steenbergen-Hu and Cooper 2014; Wang et al. 2023).

Computer programming code explanation and correction is also a popular use of such system among students and that modern NLP systems can not only address natural language but also computer programming languages (Denny et al. 2024).

Before the release of major LLM's chatbots (e.g. ChatGPT) the use of NLP for educational purposes was viewing as an interesting approach with many open possibilities (Civaner et al. 2022) while after, NLP is reported as an invaluable tool with successful applications in education (Gordon et al. 2024; Narayanan et al. n.d.; Sun et al. 2023).

3.2 Automated Assessment and Feedback

In education, NLP significantly enhances automated assessment and feedback systems, streamlining the evaluation process and providing timely, detailed responses to students. By leveraging NLP techniques, these systems can analyze and grade large volumes of written assignments, essays, and short answers with high accuracy and consistency. NLP algorithms evaluate the content for grammar, coherence, relevance, and originality, offering constructive feedback on areas such as argument strength, clarity, and writing style. This immediate, personalized feedback helps students understand their strengths and areas for improvement, fostering a more effective and self-directed learning process. Additionally, automated assessment systems powered by NLP reduce the grading workload for educators, allowing them to focus more on instructional activities and direct student interaction.

3.3 Academic Research and Writing Assistance

Producing high quality documents, based on well-established methodologies, and supported by strong scientific support is a central aspect of academia. The involved process follows several stages where NLP tools are being successfully introduced.

3.3.1 Literature Review

A literature review is a critical analysis of existing research that establishes the context and identifies gaps in knowledge. NLP algorithms are transforming the literature review process by automating and enhancing the way researchers gather, analyze, and synthesize vast amounts of academic literature. Their ability to handle large sets of information allow to automatically extract key information from a large corpus of research papers, including abstracts, conclusions, and references. This process, defined as "text summarization" allows to generate concise summaries of larger texts while retaining key information, which can be done extractively by selecting sentences or abstractively by generating new sentences. In addition, by categorizing and summarizing findings across numerous studies, NLP aids researchers in quickly identifying relevant works and understanding the broader context of their research area (Sarmet et al. 2023). This automation not only saves time but also ensures a more comprehensive and systematic review, enabling researchers to stay current with the latest developments and build on existing knowledge effectively (Khalifa and Albadawy 2024).

3.3.2 Reference Management

The mentioned benefits extend to reference exploration and management. NLP-powered tools can automatically extract citation information from academic papers and manage bibliographic data accurately. These tools help researchers organize references, generate citations in various formats, and integrate seamlessly with writing software (e.g. as a plugin). By recognizing patterns and contexts within the text, NLP algorithms can identify relevant sources and suggest citations, ensuring proper attribution and adherence to citation standards. Connection between papers can now be found based on content similarity, overcoming the limitations of citation based connections (Sarmet et al. 2023). These tools employ techniques such as topic modeling or sentiment analysis to identify prevailing themes, trends, and gaps in the literature. Such automation reduces the manual effort involved in reference management, minimizes errors, and enhances the overall workflow for researchers, allowing new forms of exploration of the academic literature landscape.

3.3.3 Writing Assistant

NLP and AI writing assistance tools can be used to directly help to improve clarity, coherence, and style of academic writing, ensuring high quality standards. These intelligent tools provide real-time feedback on grammar, style, and structure, helping students and researchers improve the clarity and quality of their writing. NLP-based writing assistants can suggest synonyms, rephrase sentences for better readability, and detect complex issues like coherence and argument strength. This can be of particular relevance for nonnative speakers of English, the *lingua franca* in academic writing. NLP tools are not just helpful but now have a crucial role in improving the efficiency and quality of academic writing. Their use allows writers to fully focus on the ideas and innovative aspects of research (Golan et al. 2023).

3.3.4 Plagiarism Detection

Advanced NLP algorithms can scan vast databases of academic content to identify similarities and potential instances of plagiarism in student submissions and research papers. These systems go beyond simple keyword matching by understanding the context and semantics of the text, making it possible to detect paraphrased or modified plagiarized content. NLP tools provide detailed reports highlighting the suspect sections and their original sources, helping educators maintain academic integrity. This robust detection process not only deters plagiarism but also educates students about proper citation practices and the importance of originality in academic writing (Chong 2013; Elkhatat, Elsaid, and Almeer 2023).

In summary, NLP supported services and tools help individuals navigate the complexities of academic research, from literature reviews to the organization and presentation of their findings. By providing guidance on research methodologies, citation management, and adherence to academic standards, these resources can help to ensure that academic and research work is thorough, credible, and well-documented.

3.4 Language Learning and Translation

NLP has revolutionized language learning through the development of intelligent tutoring systems (ITS) and adaptive learning platforms. These computational technologies provide algorithms that are able to analyze learner's input and provide customized feedback, making the learning process more interactive and personalized. For instance, platforms like Duolingo[1] and Babbel[2] use NLP to tailor exercises to individual user proficiency levels, providing real-time feedback that helps learners correct mistakes and improve their language skills. Such applications not only enhance the efficiency of language acquisition but also make learning more engaging, while accessing a global audience.

The use of acoustic speech processing systems is a cornerstone of modern language learning tools, enabling not only the development of applications that can understand spoken language but also to evaluate the phonemic quality by comparison against native speaker models. Automatic speech recognition (ASR) converts spoken words into text, allowing learners to practice pronunciation and receive immediate feedback on their accuracy. Pronunciation assessment tools, such as those integrated into language learning apps, utilize ASR like algorithms to help learners fine-tune their pronunciation. Convergence to pleasant speaking styles can also be achieved by targeting specific durations, pauses and styles (Pinto-Coelho et al. 2009) These technologies, using underlying NLP algorithms, have been particularly effective in helping learners develop their speaking and listening skills in a new language (Huang, Hew, and Fryer 2022).

In addition, grammar checkers and writing enhancement tools, also powered by NLP, proved to be invaluable resources for language learners or even for native speakers to enrich their style. Tools like Grammarly[3] analyze text for grammatical errors, stylistic issues, and contextual spelling mistakes, offering suggestions for improvement. Part-of-speech taggers and syntactic parsers are examples of the components that help to identify the context of the text and provide accurate corrections.

Traditional language learning often relies on the simulation of interactions. With NLP, computer-based language learning, using conversational agents and chatbots, can provide similar contexts, conveying opportunities to practice language skills through simulated conversations. For example, chatbots can engage learners in role-playing scenarios, offering a safe environment to practice language skills without the fear of making mistakes. This interaction not only enhances conversational skills but also helps learners build confidence in using the language in real-life situations. When combined with AI, these systems can offer a multitude of situations and dialogue sequences, always exposing the learner to new variations or challenges.

Assessment and feedback, for the mentioned aspects of writing, such as coherence, cohesion, or grammatical accuracy, can be performed by automated systems. NLP techniques provide consistent and objective assessments, along with personalized feedback that guides learners on how to improve their writing. This can be done in real-time but also opens the possibility to handle large-scale language instruction, where human grading can be time-consuming and subject to bias.

Another area that has seen significant advancements over the years, is Mation Translation, that has transitioned from rule-based approaches to statistical methods, and more recently, to neural machine translation (NMT), in particular deep learning based machine translation (Popel et al. 2020). These systems can capture complex linguistic patterns and nuances and achieve translation quality comparable to human professionals. When working in real-time, translation tools facilitate communication between speakers of different languages, breaking down language barriers and promoting cross-cultural collaboration.

Despite the described advancements, machine translation still faces some challenges. Handling idiomatic expressions and cultural nuances can be hard to handle, as these elements often require deep contextual understanding and cultural awareness that machines lack. Domain-specific translation also poses difficulties, as technical jargon and specialized language require precise terminology and context-sensitive interpretation (Gilmartin et al. 2018). These are challenges that require further research and development to enhance language learning and translation systems.

4 BENEFITS OF NLP IN HIGHER EDUCATION

Students self-perception of in-class instruction is viewed more positively but their actual performance can be better in online modes (Palvia and Matta 2023). In fact, both synchronous and asynchronous online teaching methods demonstrated improvements in learning outcomes and high levels of student satisfaction (Hung et al. 2024). Engagement and personalization are key factors in this process. Interactive tools such as digital simulations, educational games, and virtual reality environments create immersive learning experiences that captivate students' attention and enhance their comprehension of complex subjects. Studies show that these interactive platforms increase student motivation and participation, leading to deeper engagement with the material (Reis et al. 2018; Shemshack and Spector 2020). Additionally, real-time feedback and assessments provided by educational technologies allow students to identify and address their learning gaps promptly, thereby improving their overall understanding and retention of information. In addition, adaptive learning technologies tailor educational content to meet the unique needs of each student, creating personalized learning paths that optimize individual progress. Students' performance can be monitored even without a formal evaluation and the curriculum can be adjusted accordingly. This personalized approach ensures that students receive the appropriate level of challenge and support, preventing both boredom and frustration (Dockterman 2018). Hence, despite the complexity of the education process (Coelho and Reis 2023), NLP can add a layer of personalization. This enhances the learning experience by making it more engaging and effective, suited to individual learning paces and styles, ultimately improving educational outcomes.

From the teachers' perspective, NLP can be used to support the automation of repetitive tasks. Automated grading systems, for example, can quickly and accurately evaluate student assignments, quizzes, and exams, freeing up valuable time for educators to focus on curricula development, or more interactive and personalized teaching activities. When supported by AI, NLP tools can also provide novel interactions situations and introduce variations based on the teachers' guidelines (Troussas et al. 2023). For larger audiences, NLP can provide the necessary scalability to implement high-quality education standards. Massive Open Online Courses (MOOCs) exemplify this scalability, offering courses from renowned universities to learners worldwide at minimal costs. As a result, technology-driven scalability democratizes education, providing equal learning opportunities to students regardless of their geographical location.

The incorporation of assistive technologies and language support tools in educational settings enhances accessibility for non-native speakers and students with disabilities. Language translation applications and bilingual dictionaries support non-native speakers in overcoming language barriers, facilitating their comprehension and participation in class activities. For students with disabilities, assistive technologies such as screen readers, speech recognition software, and alternative input devices enable them to engage with educational content effectively. These tools not only provide necessary accommodations but also foster an inclusive learning environment where all students can thrive (Burgstahler 2015).

5 CHALLENGES AND LIMITATIONS

The use of language processing in teaching and learning presents both opportunities and challenges. On one hand, the availability of large sets of data, such as corpora and social media posts, offers the potential to track learner performance, identify patterns, and predict future performance (Kamalov, Santandreu Calonge, and Gurrib 2023). However, the technical challenge of data quality and quantity is a significant concern. While large language models (LLMs) can streamline complex processes, their efficacy diminishes with more complex teaching practices (Xu et al.

2024). This requires a balance between the benefits of LLMs and human expertise (Tu et al. 2024).

The effectiveness of NLP models hinges on the quality and availability of training data, posing a substantial challenge, particularly for less-resources languages or specialized domains. Furthermore, the use of data analysis in language learning requires careful monitoring to ensure transparency and fairness (Godwin-Jones 2021).

A larger amount of data allows models to capture a wider range of linguistic variations and contexts (Naveed et al. 2024). Instead of this fact, we can´t neglect its quality. The quality of data is fundamental to ensuring that the suggestions and responses provided by NLP are accurate and reliable (Dwivedi et al. 2023). Data that has poor quality, or even incorrect, can lead to errors that directly jeopardize student learning and undermine the trust in technology.

To maximize the impact of NLP in education, it is essential to balance the quality and quantity of data. High-quality data that is accurate, diverse, and free of bias, combined with a large quantity of examples, allows for the development of effective and adaptative educational tools.

Recent research has highlighted the limitations and biases in NLP models. (Dayanik, Vu, and Padó 2022) and (Santy et al. 2023) both emphasize the need for more robust statistical analysis and the consideration of multiple bias variables, with Dayanik proposing the use of multivariate regression models. Santy introduces the NLPositionality framework, which characterizes design biases and quantifies the positionality of NLP datasets and models. Wal (2024) further discusses the challenges of psychometric concepts such as construct validity and reliability, with methodological tools for designing better bias measures (Wal et al. 2024).

5.1 Ethical and Privacy Concerns

The use of NLP in data privacy and security has been a topic of significant research. (Katz and Graveman 1991) and (Martinovic and Ralevich 2007) emphasized the need for appropriate privacy functionality and the combination of technical security procedures with legal restrictions and policies to protect sensitive information. We have no idea how much private and sensitive information can be exposed. The lack of literacy in the use of systems based on artificial intelligence is evident. (Canfora et al. 2018) demonstrated this gap, concluding that the preservation of privacy can be conditioned by: (1) users don´t believe they are exposed to risks; (2) users believe they have skills greater than those they demonstrate; (3) users are unable to assess the most relevant risks because they are unaware of them. Therefore, in addition to the need to educate users about the potential risks related to privacy, it is necessary to create systems that preserve this privacy.

Since the collection of student data can include sensitive information, it must always be ensured that, at least, it is stored securely and that it is collected in accordance with CDPR (General Data Protection Regulation) in Europe or FERPA (Family Educational Rights and Privacy Act) in the United States. FERPA is a federal law that protects the privacy of student education records (Anon 2021). To make the process even safer, it is essential to obtain the informed consent of students/users before collecting their data. In this consent, the information must be clear, so that they understand why their data is being collected, how it will be used and, ultimately, whom it will be shared.

Finally, the robustness of this procedure could be guaranteed by anonymizing the data. Even with consent, it is important to anonymize students to protect their identities, especially if this data is used for training tools. Though transparency is essential, students/users must have access to the collected data so that they can correct false or inaccurate information (Reis et al. 2023).

As discussed above, the integration of artificial intelligence, such as NLP, in education presents both opportunities and ethical challenges. It is necessary to emphasize the need for transparency, accountability, and fairness in AI design and deployment, particularly in addressing privacy, bias, and educational inequalities (Leta and Vancea 2023; Vavekanand 2024). There is a need to further highlight the potential of AI to improve learning outcomes, but also to stress the importance of balanced policies and practices to ensure the ethical adoption of these new methodologies (Bai 2024). Critical concerns should be raised about the limitations and potential harms of AI in education, calling for a recalibration of current debates to prioritize equity and educational benefits.

Addressing these issues in a practical and effective way requires the establishment of inclusive policies. Policymakers must involve educators, students and specialists in the development and implementation of new educational basis. This must ensure equitable access, bridging the digital gap.

The effectiveness of this change may depend on the creation of robust training programs for teachers to effectively integrate AI into their pedagogy. These programs should be combined with the development and adherence to ethical guidelines for the use of AI in education, so that fairness, transparency and respect for privacy are guaranteed. At least, we must not forget that the design of these tools must be human-centered. AI systems must be designed to increase and not to replace the role of teachers, always preserving the human role in education.

Addressing the issues above, the adoption of AI in education can be managed in such a way as to maximize its benefits and minimize potential harm.

6 FUTURE DIRECTIONS AND TRENDS

6.1 Open Challenges and Emerging Technologies

The future of NLP in education holds immense potential as systems' quality continues to improve and new advancements continue to accelerate the interaction ability of machines. However, language variability and the broad scope of language related tasks still hold many open challenges for NLP systems. In Figure 3, an overview of the most relevant evolution vectors for NLP systems is shown, encompassing four main areas: language analysis, language generation, translation and modality interfacing. Text analysis, is still the most challenging area, covering not only a top-level text analysis but also underlying algorithms. Specifically, some of these components and techniques form the foundation of modern NLP systems and constitute fundamental functional blocks for many NLP related tasks. In each case, the approach to follow is often hybrid, first using the well know grammatical rules and other linguistic knowledge to then, explore the ability of AI algorithms to tackle more complex patterns. For example, homographs interpretation, an obvious task for humans, requires disambiguation for computers, and can imply a complex analysis of the text (Braga et al. 2007). To add naturality to computer interaction, a top layer of pragmatic analysis must be present in the NLP system. Emotion analysis and sarcasm or humor detection, crucial aspects of pragmatics, requiring specific algorithms to address all the implied discourse intricacies. This will enable NLP tools to provide more nuanced feedback and support to learners, adapting to their emotional states and learning needs.

Finally, the ability to translate text to/from other data formats is also improving and open new opportunities for machines to interact with humans. The integration of NLP with other emerging technologies like Augmented Reality (AR), Virtual Reality (VR), and the Internet of Things (IoT) can highly change the educational landscape, especially in healthcare related areas (Magalhães et al. 2024). NLP combined with AR/VR can create immersive learning environments where students can interact with virtual objects and simulations using natural language commands, enhancing engagement and retention of complex concepts. For instance, a biology student could explore a virtual human body, asking questions and receiving real-time explanations. Similarly, IoT devices equipped with NLP capabilities can provide personalized learning experiences by analyzing student data and adjusting educational content to fit individual learning styles.

Figure 3. A taxonomy of NLP tasks with open challenges

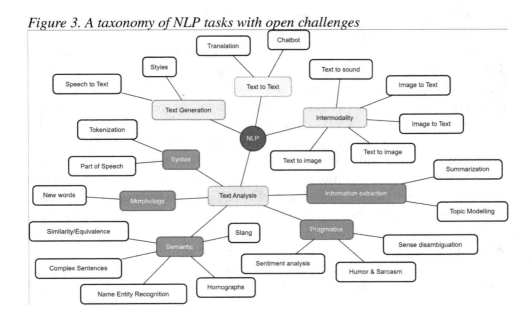

6.2 Guidelines and Policies

As NLP technologies become more prevalent in educational settings, the need for robust guidelines and policies becomes increasingly urgent to address the ethical use of student data and ensuring privacy and security. Policies must also focus on the minimization and mitigation of NLP algorithms biases to provide fair and equitable educational opportunities for all students. Establishing standards for the development and deployment of NLP tools in education can help maintain quality and consistency across different educational platforms. On the teacher's perspective, clear policies are needed to define the role of NLP tools, ensuring that technology enhances rather than replaces human interaction in the learning process. In this way, educational institutions and governments play a critical role in shaping the future of NLP in education. Institutions must accept new technologies and create an environment to promote innovation while fostering collaboration between educators, researchers, and technologists. This can be achieved through dedicated research centers, funding for pilot projects, and professional development programs that equip teachers with the skills to effectively integrate NLP tools into their pedagogy. Governments, on the other hand, should establish regulatory frameworks that support the ethical and effective use of NLP in education. This demands an investment effort in infrastructure but also providing grants for research and development, without forgetting the establishment of public-private partnerships.

The environment is also a part of the equation since the rapid advancement and deployment of artificial intelligence (AI) and large language models (LLMs) have significantly increased energy consumption. As depicted in Figure 4, training and operating sophisticated LLM models require substantial computational power, that has increased at an exponential rate over the years, leading to tremendous electricity usage and carbon emissions. This footprint necessitates a concerted effort to integrate sustainable practices within the AI industry, and measures such as implementing green energy solutions, optimizing algorithms for energy efficiency, or adopting carbon offset strategies are essential steps to mitigate the environmental impact. Policymakers and industry leaders must also collaborate to establish strong regulations and incentives that promote the development and usage of eco-friendly AI technologies. Addressing these challenges is vital to ensuring that the benefits of AI advancements do not come at the expense of the planet's health, aligning technological progress with environmental concerns.

Figure 4. Computation effort required to training for some of the most relevant LLM models, according to their release date (Anon 2024)

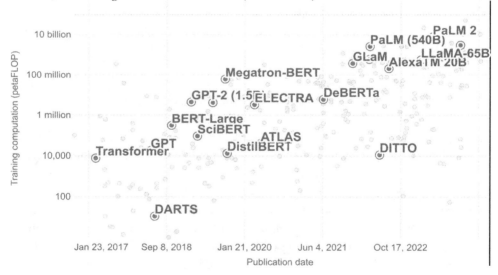

7 IMPLEMENTATION

Considering the previously mentioned aspects, a set of general directives can be developed for preparing a successful implementation of NLP in an educational setting.

7.1 Needs Assessment and Objective Definition

Before implementing NLP tools in an educational setting, it is critical to conduct a thorough needs assessment. Educators should identify specific challenges or opportunities in the teaching and learning process that NLP can address. For example, whether the goal is to improve student critical thinking skills, provide personalized feedback, or enhance problem solving, clear objectives must be defined. For each goal, success metrics must be defined as well as evaluation parameters. This clarity will guide the selection of appropriate NLP tools and technologies. In this phase, it is also important to consider the diversity of learners, ensuring that the chosen NLP solutions are accessible and equitable for all students.

7.2 Selection of NLP Tools

The selection of NLP tools should align with the educational objectives established during the needs assessment. There is a wide range of NLP applications available, from automated essay scoring systems and intelligent tutoring systems to tools for sentiment analysis and plagiarism detection. When choosing these tools, consider factors such as ease of integration with existing educational platforms, user-friendliness, the ability to handle multiple languages, and the level of customization available. It is also important to consider the business model of the provider, either subscription or one-time payment. Additionally, it's essential to evaluate the tool's accuracy and reliability, especially in the context of its application in diverse educational environments. Asking for feedback from previous implementations in similar conditions can prove to be very supportive to a final decision.

7.3 Data Privacy and Ethical Considerations

The implementation of NLP in education involves the collection and processing of large amounts of student data, which raises significant privacy and ethical concerns. Institutions must ensure that they comply with relevant data protection regulations, such as GDPR in Europe or FERPA in the United States. Moreover, transparency with students about how their data will be used is crucial. Educators should also consider the potential biases embedded in NLP algorithms and take steps to mitigate these biases to prevent unfair treatment of any student group. Regular audits of NLP tools can help identify and rectify any bias or ethical issues that may arise.

7.4 Training and Professional Development

For successful integration, students, educators and administrators must be adequately trained to use NLP tools effectively. Professional development programs should be designed to help teachers understand both the capabilities and limitations of NLP technologies. Training should cover not only the technical aspects but also how to interpret the outputs of NLP tools and integrate them into the teaching and learning process. Continuous support and advanced training sessions may be necessary as new features and tools become available.

7.5 Evaluation and Feedback Mechanisms

Implementing NLP in education should be an iterative process, with continuous evaluation and refinement. Establishing feedback mechanisms is essential to assess the effectiveness of NLP tools in meeting educational goals. Teachers and students should be encouraged to provide feedback on their experiences with the tools, which can inform future improvements. Additionally, institutions should use quantitative and qualitative data to evaluate the impact of NLP on learning outcomes, adjusting the implementation strategy as needed to maximize effectiveness. Monitoring usage and performance is paramount to successfully operationalize such tools and ensure their best usage during the entire product life-cycle.

7.6 Scalability and Sustainability

Finally, when planning for the implementation of NLP technologies, scalability and sustainability must be considered. The chosen solutions should not only meet current educational needs but also be scalable to accommodate future growth in student numbers or program offerings. Closed format, lack of API or unsupportive customer teams should be avoided. Additionally, institutions should plan for the long-term sustainability of NLP tools, which includes budgeting for ongoing maintenance, updates, and potential expansions. Collaborations with NLP vendors or open-source communities can also help ensure that the tools remain up-to-date and relevant.

8 CONCLUSION

In conclusion, the integration of NLP in higher education holds immense potential to transform the educational landscape in all aspects. Educators can leverage NLP tools to create more engaging and adaptive curricula, allowing them to focus on higher-level teaching activities. Students benefit from personalized feedback, improved accessibility, and enriched learning experiences tailored to their individual needs. Policymakers, on the other hand, can utilize data-driven insights from NLP applications to make informed decisions that shape future educational strategies and policies.

However, the successful implementation of NLP in higher education requires careful consideration of ethical implications, data privacy, and the need for continuous professional development for educators. Stakeholders must collaborate to ensure that NLP tools are used responsibly without forgetting inclusivity and equity.

As technology continues to evolve, it is recommended that institutions invest in ongoing research and development of NLP technologies, provide training for educators to effectively integrate these tools into their teaching practices, and establish clear guidelines to safeguard implied data. By embracing the opportunities presented by NLP while addressing its challenges, higher education can reach novel paradigms of educational quality allowing students and educators to excel.

REFERENCES

Anon. 2021. "Family Educational Rights and Privacy Act (FERPA)." Retrieved June 18, 2024 (https://www2.ed.gov/policy/gen/guid/fpco/ferpa/index.html)

Anon. 2024. "Computation Used to Train Notable Artificial Intelligence Systems." Our World in Data. Retrieved June 17, 2024 (https://ourworldindata.org/grapher/artificial-intelligence-training-computation)

Bai, X. (2024). THE ROLE AND CHALLENGES OF ARTIFICIAL INTELLIGENCE IN INFORMATION TECHNOLOGY EDUCATION. *Pacific International Journal*, 7(1), 86–92. DOI: 10.55014/pij.v7i1.524

Berger, A. L., Della Pietra, V. J., & Della Pietra, S. A. (1996). A Maximum Entropy Approach to Natural Language Processing. *Computational Linguistics*, 22(1), 39–71.

Bojanowski, Piotr, Edouard Grave, Armand Joulin, and Tomas Mikolov. 2017. "Enriching Word Vectors with Subword Information."

Botelho, A., Baral, S., Erickson, J. A., Benachamardi, P., & Heffernan, N. T. (2023). Leveraging Natural Language Processing to Support Automated Assessment and Feedback for Student Open Responses in Mathematics. *Journal of Computer Assisted Learning*, 39(3), 823–840. DOI: 10.1111/jcal.12793

Braga, D., Coelho, L., & Fernando Gil, V. R. (2007). "Homograph Ambiguity Resolution in Front-End Design for Portuguese TTS Systems." Pp. 1761–64 in *Proc.* [International Speech Communication Association.]. *Interspeech*, •••, 2007.

Burgstahler, S. (2015). *Universal Design in Higher Education* (2nd ed.). Harvard Education Press.

Canfora, G., Di Sorbo, A., Emanuele, E., Forootani, S., & Visaggio, C. A. 2018. "A Nlp-Based Solution to Prevent from Privacy Leaks in Social Network Posts." Pp. 1–6 in *Proceedings of the 13th International Conference on Availability, Reliability and Security, ARES '18*. New York, NY, USA: Association for Computing Machinery. DOI: 10.1145/3230833.3230845

Chong, Man Yan Miranda. 2013. "A Study on Plagiarism Detection and Plagiarism Direction Identification Using Natural Language Processing Techniques."

Civaner, M. M., Uncu, Y., Bulut, F., Chalil, E. G., & Tatli, A. (2022). Artificial Intelligence in Medical Education: A Cross-Sectional Needs Assessment. *BMC Medical Education*, 22(1), 772. DOI: 10.1186/s12909-022-03852-3 PMID: 36352431

Coelho, L., & Reis, S. (2023). Enhancing Learning Experiences Through Artificial Intelligence: Classroom 5.0. In *Fostering Pedagogy Through Micro and Adaptive Learning in Higher Education: Trends, Tools, and Applications*. IGI Global. DOI: 10.4018/978-1-6684-8656-6.ch008

Combéfis, S. (2022). Automated Code Assessment for Education: Review, Classification and Perspectives on Techniques and Tools. *Software*, 1(1), 3–30. DOI: 10.3390/software1010002

Conneau, Alexis, Khandelwal, Kartikay, Goyal, Naman, Chaudhary, Vishrav, Wenzek, Guillaume, Guzmán, Francisco, Grave, Edouard, Ott, Myle, Zettlemoyer, Luke, & Stoyanov, Veselin. 2020. *"Unsupervised Cross-Lingual Representation Learning at Scale."*

Dayanik, E., Vu, N. T., & Padó, S. (2022). Bias Identification and Attribution in NLP Models With Regression and Effect Sizes. *Northern European Journal of Language Technology*, 8(1). Advance online publication. DOI: 10.3384/nejlt.2000-1533.2022.3505

Denny, P., Prather, J., Becker, B. A., Finnie-Ansley, J., Hellas, A., Leinonen, J., Luxton-Reilly, A., Reeves, B. N., Santos, E. A., & Sarsa, S. (2024). Computing Education in the Era of Generative AI. *Communications of the ACM*, 67(2), 56–67. DOI: 10.1145/3624720

Devlin, Jacob, Chang, Ming-Wei, Lee, Kenton, & Toutanova, Kristina. 2019. "BERT: Pre-Training of Deep Bidirectional Transformers for Language Understanding."

Dockterman, D. (2018). Insights from 200+ Years of Personalized Learning. *NPJ Science of Learning*, 3(1), 1–6. DOI: 10.1038/s41539-018-0033-x PMID: 30631476

Dwivedi, Y. K., Kshetri, N., Hughes, L., Slade, E. L., Jeyaraj, A., Kar, A. K., Baabdullah, A. M., Koohang, A., Raghavan, V., Ahuja, M., Albanna, H., Albashrawi, M. A., Al-Busaidi, A. S., Balakrishnan, J., Barlette, Y., Basu, S., Bose, I., Brooks, L., Buhalis, D., & Wright, R. (2023). Opinion Paper: 'So What If ChatGPT Wrote It?' Multidisciplinary Perspectives on Opportunities, Challenges and Implications of Generative Conversational AI for Research, Practice and Policy. *International Journal of Information Management*, 71, 102642. DOI: 10.1016/j.ijinfomgt.2023.102642

Ebrahimi, Sayna. 2024. "LANISTR: Multimodal Learning from Structured and Unstructured Data."

Elkhatat, A. M., Elsaid, K., & Almeer, S. (2023). Evaluating the Efficacy of AI Content Detection Tools in Differentiating between Human and AI-Generated Text. *International Journal for Educational Integrity*, 19(1), 1–16. DOI: 10.1007/s40979-023-00140-5

Feng, X., Wei, Y., Pan, X., Qiu, L., & Ma, Y. (2020). Academic Emotion Classification and Recognition Method for Large-Scale Online Learning Environment—Based on A-CNN and LSTM-ATT Deep Learning Pipeline Method. *International Journal of Environmental Research and Public Health*, 17(6), 1941. DOI: 10.3390/ijerph17061941 PMID: 32188094

Ferreira, R., Gregório, P., Coelho, L., & Reis, S. S. 2023. "Natural Language Processing and Cloud Computing in Disease Prevention and Management." (Pp. 217–40) in *Exploring the Convergence of Computer and Medical Science Through Cloud Healthcare*. IGI Global.

García-Méndez, S., de Arriba-Pérez, F., & María del Carmen, S.-L. (2024). A Review on the Use of Large Language Models as Virtual Tutors. *Science & Education*. Advance online publication. DOI: 10.1007/s11191-024-00530-2

Gilmartin, E., Cowan, B. R., Vogel, C., & Campbell, N. (2018). Explorations in Multiparty Casual Social Talk and Its Relevance for Social Human Machine Dialogue. *Journal on Multimodal User Interfaces*, 12(4), 297–308. DOI: 10.1007/s12193-018-0274-2

Godwin-Jones, Robert. 2021. "Big Data and Language Learning: Opportunities and Challenges."

Golan, R., Reddy, R., Muthigi, A., & Ramasamy, R. (2023). Artificial Intelligence in Academic Writing: A Paradigm-Shifting Technological Advance. *Nature Reviews. Urology*, 20(6), 327–328. DOI: 10.1038/s41585-023-00746-x PMID: 36829078

Gordon, M., Daniel, M., Ajiboye, A., Uraiby, H., Xu, N. Y., Bartlett, R., Hanson, J., Haas, M., Spadafore, M., Grafton-Clarke, C., Gasiea, R. Y., Michie, C., Corral, J., Kwan, B., Dolmans, D., & Thammasitboon, S. (2024). A Scoping Review of Artificial Intelligence in Medical Education: BEME Guide No. 84. *Medical Teacher*, 46(4), 446–470. DOI: 10.1080/0142159X.2024.2314198 PMID: 38423127

Graesser, A. C., Chipman, P., Haynes, B. C., & Olney, A. (2018). Autotutor and ALEKS: A Personalized, Conversational Agent Tutoring System. *International Journal of Artificial Intelligence in Education*, 28(1), 39–62.

Huang, W., Hew, K. F., & Fryer, L. K. (2022). Chatbots for Language Learning—Are They Really Useful? A Systematic Review of Chatbot-Supported Language Learning. *Journal of Computer Assisted Learning*, 38(1), 237–257. DOI: 10.1111/jcal.12610

Hung, C.-T., Wu, S.-E., Chen, Y.-H., Soong, C.-Y., Chiang, C.-P., & Wang, W.-M. (2024). The Evaluation of Synchronous and Asynchronous Online Learning: Student Experience, Learning Outcomes, and Cognitive Load. *BMC Medical Education*, 24(1), 326. Advance online publication. DOI: 10.1186/s12909-024-05311-7 PMID: 38519950

Kamalov, F., Calonge, D. S., & Gurrib, I. (2023). New Era of Artificial Intelligence in Education: Towards a Sustainable Multifaceted Revolution. *Sustainability (Basel)*, 15(16), 12451. DOI: 10.3390/su151612451

Kaplan, Ronald M. 2004. "Lexical Functional Grammar A Formal System for Grammatical Representation."

Katz, J. E., & Graveman, R. F. (1991). Privacy Issues of a National Research and Education Network. *Telematics and Informatics*, 8(1), 71–120. DOI: 10.1016/S0736-5853(05)80096-6

Khalifa, M., & Albadawy, M. (2024). Using Artificial Intelligence in Academic Writing and Research: An Essential Productivity Tool. *Computer Methods and Programs in Biomedicine Update*, 5, 100145. DOI: 10.1016/j.cmpbup.2024.100145

Koufakou, A., Garciga, J., Paul, A., Morelli, J., & Frank, C. 2022. "Automatically Classifying Emotions Based on Text: A Comparative Exploration of Different Datasets." Pp. 342–46 in 2022 IEEE 34th International Conference on Tools with Artificial Intelligence (ICTAI). DOI: 10.1109/ICTAI56018.2022.00056

Leta, F. (2023). Ethics in Education: Exploring the Ethical Implications of Artificial Intelligence Implementation. *Ovidius University Annals, Economic Sciences Series*, XXIII(1), 413–421. DOI: 10.61801/OUAESS.2023.1.54

Libovický, Jindřich, Rosa, Rudolf, & Fraser, Alexander. 2019. "How Language-Neutral Is Multilingual BERT?"

Maestrales, S., Zhai, X., Touitou, I., Baker, Q., Schneider, B., & Krajcik, J. (2021). Using Machine Learning to Score Multi-Dimensional Assessments of Chemistry and Physics. *Journal of Science Education and Technology*, 30(2), 239–254. DOI: 10.1007/s10956-020-09895-9

Magalhães, R., Oliveira, A., Terroso, D., Vilaça, A., Veloso, R., Marques, A., Pereira, J., & Coelho, L. (2024). Mixed Reality in the Operating Room: A Systematic Review. *Journal of Medical Systems*, 48(1), 76. DOI: 10.1007/s10916-024-02095-7 PMID: 39145896

Martinovic, D., & Ralevich, V. (2007). Privacy Issues in Educational Systems. *International Journal of Internet Technology and Secured Transactions*, 1(1/2), 132. DOI: 10.1504/IJITST.2007.014838

Mikolov, Tomas, Chen, Kai, Corrado, Greg, & Dean, Jeffrey. 2013. "Efficient Estimation of Word Representations in Vector Space."

Moreno, J., & Pineda, A. F. (2020). A Framework for Automated Formative Assessment in Mathematics Courses. *IEEE Access : Practical Innovations, Open Solutions*, 8, 30152–30159. DOI: 10.1109/ACCESS.2020.2973026

Narayanan, S., Ramakrishnan, R., Durairaj, E., & Das, A. (2023, November 28). (n.d.). Artificial Intelligence Revolutionizing the Field of Medical Education. *Cureus*, 15(11), e49604. DOI: 10.7759/cureus.49604 PMID: 38161821

Naveed, Humza, Khan, Asad Ullah, Qiu, Shi, Saqib, Muhammad, Anwar, Saeed, Usman, Muhammad, Akhtar, Naveed, Barnes, Nick, & Mian, Ajmal. 2024. "A Comprehensive Overview of Large Language Models."

Nenkova, Ani, & McKeown, Kathleen. 2011. "Automatic Summarization." *Foundations and Trends® in Information Retrieval* 5(2–3): (pp.103–233).

Paiva, José Carlos, José Paulo Leal, and Álvaro Figueira. 2022. "Automated Assessment in Computer Science Education: A State-of-the-Art Review." ACM Transactions on Computing Education 22(3):34:1-34:40. .DOI: 10.1145/3513140

Palvia, S., & Matta, V. (2023). Comparing Student Perceptions of In-Class, Online Synchronous, and Online Asynchronous Instruction. *World Journal on Educational Technology: Current Issues*, 15(3), 303–320. DOI: 10.18844/wjet.v15i3.8656

Pennington, J., Socher, R., & Manning, C. 2014. "GloVe: Global Vectors for Word Representation." Pp. 1532–43 in *Proceedings of the 2014 Conference on Empirical Methods in Natural Language Processing (EMNLP)*, edited by Moschitti, A., Pang, B., & Daelemans, W.. Doha, Qatar: Association for Computational Linguistics. DOI: 10.3115/v1/D14-1162

Pinto-Coelho, L., Horst-Udo, H., Jokisch, O., & Braga, D. 2009. "Towards an Objective Voice Preference Definition for the Portuguese Language." in joint SIG-IL/Microsoft Workshop on Speech and Language Technologies for Iberian Languages. Porto Salvo, Portugal.

Popel, M., Tomkova, M., Tomek, J., Kaiser, Ł., Uszkoreit, J., Bojar, O., & Žabokrtský, Z. (2020). Transforming Machine Translation: A Deep Learning System Reaches News Translation Quality Comparable to Human Professionals. *Nature Communications*, 11(1), 4381. DOI: 10.1038/s41467-020-18073-9 PMID: 32873773

Radford, Alec, & Narasimhan, Karthik. 2018. "Improving Language Understanding by Generative Pre-Training."

Radford, A., & Wu, J. (2019). *R. Child, D. Luan, Dario Amodei, and I. Sutskever*. Language Models Are Unsupervised Multitask Learners.

Reis, S., Coelho, L., Sarmet, M., Araújo, J., & Corchado, J. M. 2023. "The Importance of Ethical Reasoning in Next Generation Tech Education." Pp. 1–10 in 2023 5th International Conference of the Portuguese Society for Engineering Education (CISPEE). DOI: 10.1109/CISPEE58593.2023.10227651

Reis, S., Guimarães, P., Coelho, F., Nogueira, E., & Coelho, L.. 2018. "A Framework for Simulation Systems and Technologies for Medical Training." Pp. 1–4 in 2018 Global Medical Engineering Physics Exchanges/Pan American Health Care Exchanges (GMEPE/PAHCE).

Sanh, V., Debut, L., Chaumond, J., & Wolf, T. (2020). *DistilBERT, a Distilled Version of BERT: Smaller*. Faster, Cheaper and Lighter.

Santy, Sebastin, Liang, Jenny T., Le Bras, Ronan, Reinecke, Katharina, & Sap, Maarten. 2023. "NLPositionality: Characterizing Design Biases of Datasets and Models."

Sarmet, M., Kabani, A., Coelho, L., Seabra dos Reis, S., Zeredo, J. L., & Mehta, A. K. (2023). The Use of Natural Language Processing in Palliative Care Research: A Scoping Review. *Palliative Medicine*, 37(2), 275–290. DOI: 10.1177/02692163221141969 PMID: 36495082

Shemshack, A., & Spector, J. M. (2020). A Systematic Literature Review of Personalized Learning Terms. *Smart Learning Environments*, 7(1), 33. DOI: 10.1186/s40561-020-00140-9

Shermis, Mark D., & Hamner, Ben. 2012. "Contrasting State-of-the-Art Automated Scoring of Essays: Analysis." Pp. 51–82 in *Handbook of Automated Essay Evaluation*.

Steenbergen-Hu, S., & Cooper, H. (2014). A Meta-Analysis of the Effectiveness of Intelligent Tutoring Systems on College Students' Academic Learning. *Journal of Educational Psychology*, 106(2), 331–347. DOI: 10.1037/a0034752

Sun, L., Yin, C., Xu, Q., & Zhao, W. (2023). Artificial Intelligence for Healthcare and Medical Education: A Systematic Review. *American Journal of Translational Research*, 15(7), 4820–4828. PMID: 37560249

Sutskever, Ilya, Vinyals, Oriol, & Le, Quoc V.. 2014. "Sequence to Sequence Learning with Neural Networks."

Tang, X., Huang, Y., Luo, W., Qian, X., & Xie, G. (2019). Personalized Recommendation for Academic Articles Based on NLP Techniques. *Frontiers in Psychology*, 10, 1543.

Taylor, A., Marcus, M., & Santorini, B. (2003). The Penn Treebank: An Overview. In Abeillé, A. (Ed.), *Text, Speech and Language Technology* (Vol. 20, pp. 5–22). Springer Netherlands.

Troussas, C., Papakostas, C., Krouska, A., Mylonas, P., & Sgouropoulou, C. (2023). Personalized Feedback Enhanced by Natural Language Processing in Intelligent Tutoring Systems. In Frasson, C., Mylonas, P., & Troussas, C. (Eds.), *Augmented Intelligence and Intelligent Tutoring Systems* (pp. 667–677). Springer Nature Switzerland. DOI: 10.1007/978-3-031-32883-1_58

Tu, X., Zou, J., Su, W., & Zhang, L. (2024). What Should Data Science Education Do With Large Language Models? *Harvard Data Science Review*, 6(1). Advance online publication. DOI: 10.1162/99608f92.bff007ab

van der Wal, O., Bachmann, D., Leidinger, A., van Maanen, L., Zuidema, W., & Schulz, K. (2024). Undesirable Biases in NLP: Addressing Challenges of Measurement. *Journal of Artificial Intelligence Research*, 79, 1–40. DOI: 10.1613/jair.1.15195

VanLehn, K. (2011). The Relative Effectiveness of Human Tutoring, Intelligent Tutoring Systems, and Other Tutoring Systems. *Educational Psychologist*, 46(4), 197–221. DOI: 10.1080/00461520.2011.611369

Vaswani, A., Shazeer, N., Parmar, N., Uszkoreit, J., Jones, L., Gomez, A. N., Kaiser, Ł., & Polosukhin, I. 2017. "Attention Is All You Need." Pp. 6000–6010 in *Proceedings of the 31st International Conference on Neural Information Processing Systems, NIPS'17*. Red Hook, NY, USA: Curran Associates Inc.

Vavekanand, Raja. 2024. "IMPACT OF ARTIFICIAL INTELLIGENCE ON STUDENTS AND ETHICAL CONSIDERATIONS IN EDUCATION."

Wang, H., Tlili, A., Huang, R., Cai, Z., Li, M., Cheng, Z., Yang, D., Li, M., Zhu, X., & Fei, C. (2023). Examining the Applications of Intelligent Tutoring Systems in Real Educational Contexts: A Systematic Literature Review from the Social Experiment Perspective. *Education and Information Technologies*, 28(7), 9113–9148. DOI: 10.1007/s10639-022-11555-x PMID: 36643383

Wang, Y., Wang, M., & Fujita, H. (2020). Word Sense Disambiguation: A Comprehensive Knowledge Exploitation Framework. *Knowledge-Based Systems*, 190, 105030. DOI: 10.1016/j.knosys.2019.105030

Woods, W. A. (1970). Transition Network Grammars for Natural Language Analysis. *Communications of the ACM*, 13(10), 591–606. DOI: 10.1145/355598.362773

Xu, P., Liu, J., Jones, N., Cohen, J., & Ai, W. (2024). *The Promises and Pitfalls of Using Language Models to Measure Instruction Quality in Education.* Annenberg Institute at Brown University. DOI: 10.18653/v1/2024.naacl-long.246

Yannakoudakis, H., Briscoe, T., & Medlock, Ben. 2011. "A New Dataset and Method for Automatically Grading ESOL Texts." Pp. 180–89 in *Proceedings of the 49th Annual Meeting of the Association for Computational Linguistics: Human Language Technologies-Volume 1*.

Zhai, X., Yin, Y., Pellegrino, J. W., Haudek, K. C., & Shi, L. (2020). Applying Machine Learning in Science Assessment: A Systematic Review. *Studies in Science Education*, 56(1), 111–151. DOI: 10.1080/03057267.2020.1735757

Endnotes

[1] https://www.duolingo.com/

[2] https://www.babbel.com/

[3] https://www.grammarly.com/

Chapter 6
Artificial Intelligence–Supported Meta–Learning Assistant

Serap Sisman-Ugur
https://orcid.org/0000-0002-4211-1396
Anadolu University, Turkey

ABSTRACT

In the twenty-first century, when technology has had a profound impact on every aspect of our lives, learning has also changed, revealing the need for a dramatic reorganization of education systems. Individuals have the ability to learn with the possibilities offered by technology, and they play a critical role in the new development of these learning services. In light of artificial intelligence technologies and metaverse universes, the possibility to provide learning experiences in which individuals shape their learning adventures based on their own traits should be considered as an innovation that will take place in the future of learning. When configuring this service, it is essential to identify the proper artificial intelligence algorithms, correlate them with individual differences, and determine the processes that the individual can direct. The development of artificial intelligence-assisted learning assistants in the form of meta-human will provide a new dimension to learning and teaching processes.

INTRODUCTION

The advancements in computer and mobile technology have shown their effectiveness through artificial intelligence applications in various fields, from health to production, which saves both time and effort. As technology affects every aspect

DOI: 10.4018/979-8-3693-3944-2.ch006

of our life in the twenty-first century, it is inevitable that learning and, naturally, humans will be impacted by these developments. Furthermore, the necessity for artificial intelligence applications to promote lifelong learning with technology and to regulate the learning needs of individuals based on the information they acquire from the individual is becoming increasingly evident. The metaverse, which commenced its journey with a novel published in 1992 and began to be commonly cited in 2021, is the sensation of existing and embodying a virtual space. Metaverse improves the quality of online interactions and facilitates seamless movement across virtual fields containing virtual assets such as interoperability, avatars, and digital objects. The meta-human that emerged with the metaverse will be able to assume different roles for the real person.

In this article, an attempt will be made to define the general features of the artificial intelligence-supported meta-learning assistant application that will be developed to assist the learning of individuals, as well as the features that should be considered while personalizing this assistant. In the research, studies in the literature were examined through descriptive analysis, one of the qualitative research methods.

PERSONAL ASSISTANT

The term personal assistant refers to software that can serve a specific task or person based on user input, location, and the ability to access information from various online sources (Wikipedia, 2018). In other words, they are software that organizes the calendar and makes things easier. Personal software assistants that aid users with tasks such as locating information, organizing calendars, and managing workflow demand customization for each user (Can, 2016). Personal assistants are employed to automate ordinary daily tasks to lessen the cognitive load of their users (Modi, Veloso, Smith, & Oh, 2005).

Smart personal assistants are software developed and offered to users by technology companies in an effort to understand consumer behavior and provide new products and services to consumers. This software allows technology companies to gather information about consumer preferences, travel patterns, and other details about their lives and habits. Siri, Microsoft Cortana, Google Assistant, Amazon Echo, Robin, Jarvis, and Ceyd-A are examples of personal assistant software developed as personal assistants that can work platform-dependent or independently.

In addition, personal assistant applications, widely utilized in the healthcare field, have a significant place in the mobile health industry. Systems that keep patient medical records and allow users to access remote healthcare services have been developed (Kurban, 2006), which implies that systems with a similar structure may be established for educational purposes. Here, it is clear that machine learning enables the collecting of data from the individual and an artificial intelligence application that evaluates the possibilities based on the processing of this data and generates options suited to the individual must be developed. In addition, the most crucial sources for this application will be the "individual-specific" information that it gathers by asking the person and monitoring their actions.

The term "artificial intelligence" (Pirim, 2006), which was first mentioned in the Dartmouth interview in 1956, is a science concerned with having machines develop solutions and make decisions similar to those of humans when presented with a problem. This is typically accomplished through the application of the cognitive and decision-making characteristics of human intelligence in various settings and contexts to the computer as an algorithm (Cohen and Feinghebum, 2014; Ertel, 2018; Koyuncu, 2009). Artificial neural networks, expert systems, fuzzy logic, and genetic algorithms are among the topics and components covered on the axis of artificial intelligence (Pirim, 2006). Today, there are thousands of application areas for artificial intelligence, ranging from production and control to health and logistics. These fields can range from military applications such as autonomous control and targeting to the world of entertainment such as computer games and robotic animals. These practices and approaches can be listed as follows:

1. Knowledge-based expert system approach: These are the systems that solve problems that can be solved by an expert.
2. Artificial neural networks approach: It is a simulation of a basic neuronal model of the brain. It is employed for control and system identification, image and voice recognition, prediction and prediction, fault analysis, medicine, communication, traffic, and production management.
3. Fuzzy logic approach: In place of 0-1 binary logic, these are multivalued thoughts and applications that can apply intermediate values.
4. Non-traditional optimization techniques
    a. Genetic algorithm: It is software that learns in a way similar to that of living systems.
    b. Simulated annealing: It is a stochastic search method based on the similarities to the physical annealing of solids.
    c. Taboo search: It is an iterative research algorithm developed by F. Glover to solve optimization problems.
    d. Hybrid algorithms: These are the algorithms designed to ensure the convergence of the global optimal point in the shortest amount of time and with the least iterations.
5. Object-oriented programming: It is creating applications using objects.

6. Decision support systems: They are computer-based information systems that support business or corporate decision-making processes, which are frequently based on sorting or choosing among alternatives.
7. Soft computing: Expert systems can be employed independently in fuzzy logic, artificial neural networks, and genetic algorithm applications and are also utilized in conjunction with one another in various situations, taking into account the advantages and disadvantages of each method.

Artificial intelligence optimization algorithms, on the other hand, are population-based optimization algorithms inspired by the behavior patterns of living entities, such as living, reproducing, and feeding. Literature reveals that optimization algorithms for artificial intelligence are addressed under the following headings:

- Genetic algorithms: Genetic algorithms are an optimization method that works by imitating the principles of evolution and chromosomal processes in genetic science in a computer environment.
- Swarm intelligence optimization algorithms: Swarm refers to a group of dispersed-built individuals interacting with one another. In swarms, N pieces of representatives work together to realize a purposeful behavior and achieve the goal. This "collective intelligence" arises from frequent repetitive behaviors among agents. The sum of group activity produces a type of self-organization.

Depending on various factors, including the intended use of the application to be developed and the data to be employed, the most suitable of these methods must be chosen. Naturally, discussing machine learning will be necessary at this point. Because the data that will be used to feed an AI application will be collected through machine learning. Machine learning can be defined as systems comprised of techniques that are a sub-discipline of artificial intelligence and model a given problem based on the information it acquires from the environment. There are two methods for machine learning: supervised and unsupervised learning. "Supervised learning" refers to the machine learning method that uses data with previously observed and known results (labeled) and aims to create a function that contains the results of the data alongside these data. On the other hand, the unsupervised learning method can be defined as uncovering the hidden structure within unlabeled data. In other words, it is the process of revealing the existing but invisible relationship between the data (Breiman, 2001; Nizam and Akın, 2014; Onan and Korukoğlu, 2015; Quinlan, 1998). In machine learning, the data set is obtained using algorithms based on artificial intelligence. Applications such as facial recognition, document classification, and spam detection can be cited as examples of machine learning in our everyday lives.

In order to maintain the security and dependability of an artificial intelligence application when machine learning is designed for mobile devices, it may be necessary to pay attention to registration with the local device. Users may be concerned about the security of their data stored in cloud services. Thus, people may prefer to keep their data on their devices, particularly in programs that might save their personal information.

The learning assistant, developed as an artificial intelligence application that will scan and identify education/training programs that may be of interest to the individual by determining their learning needs and preferences based on device data, make suggestions for the individuals, and present these suggestions by compiling them according to the content types of the individual preference, will play a crucial role in the future generation of learning.

In the literature, regarding personalized learning assistants; It is possible to come across different studies for the use of artificial intelligence (Xia, 2021; Fitria, 2021), the use of Natural Learning Processing (Mathew et al, 2021), the use of deep learning (Liu, Chen and Yao, 2021), and the development and use as a chatbot (Chen et al, 2023). In addition, IBM's Watson platform, which provides teachers with insights into student performance and learning trends, allowing them to personalize lesson plans and strategies, has been used by North Carolina State University (NCSU), which has been reported to provide better academic guidance to students. Watson identified which subjects students were struggling with and suggested customized intervention strategies to teachers for these students. During this process, data security and privacy were kept at the highest level (Murtaza et al, 2016; Zadrozny et al, 2015). Georgia State University (GSU) uses adaptive learning technologies to increase student success. This system analyzes student data using AI-based algorithms and offers students individual learning paths. GSU has achieved a significant increase in graduation rates using adaptive learning platforms (Tesene, 2018). All these studies show that artificial intelligence-supported personal assistants are becoming increasingly widespread.

LEARNING ASSISTANT IN OPEN AND DISTANCE LEARNING

With the advancement of technology, smart devices, which are now used by nearly everyone aged 7 to 70, have become indispensable to our daily life. Individuals can use these devices not just to fulfill their communication needs but also to conduct various other tasks, including entertainment, shopping, agenda management, and graphic design. Software created for these devices and designed using the machine learning method can monitor all user activities, save and predict the chosen data, and use that data as input for new operations.

Software that will be developed as a learning assistant should be designed as an artificial intelligence application that will be developed individually and will continue its development by feeding with the data from the individual. Each individual has unique learning methods, styles, strategies, and habits. Even the preferred learning materials for a subject can vary according to the context. In other words, while an individual prefers to watch a documentary to learn history, he/she may prefer to read and take notes on the written text to learn grammar, to watch furniture assembly, or to listen to how to calculate income and expense. In this sense, the algorithm and machine learning method to be selected for artificial intelligence to be used are also crucial.

Learning Map and Artificial Intelligence in Learning Habits

The selection of user data to be collected through machine learning from the device installed for the learning assistant is also important. A data repository can be created to map an individual's learning using the following data:

- The keywords that the user enters when searching the web
- User's posts on social networks
- The posts commented on the user's network
- The page/group/activity etc. that a user likes
- The content reviewed and read by the user
- The user's most-visited pages
- The news user reads
- The educational activities in which the user participated
- Social activities
- The group, blog, and columns followed by a user
- The photo taken/recorded by the user
- The videos watched by the user
- GPS logs of visited locations

As discussed previously, the choice of the machine learning method and artificial intelligence optimization algorithm at this stage is crucial. Indeed, this system must be able to receive information from the individual. Optimization is the process of selecting the most suitable alternative to a problem under certain conditions. The term "optimization problem" can refer to any problem involving the determination of unknown parameter values under specified constraints (Murty, 2003).

There have been many proposed algorithms for optimization problems. In a reasonable amount of time, intuitive algorithms can generate near-optimal solutions to large-scale optimization problems. General-purpose heuristic optimization algorithms are evaluated within eight distinct categories: biology-based, physics-based, swarm-based, social-based, mathematics-based, sports-based, music-based, and chemistry-based. Swarm intelligence-based optimization algorithms have been developed by investigating the behavior of flocks of living entities, such as fish, cats, bees, and birds. Some types of herd intelligence optimization algorithms are listed as follows:

- Firefly Algorithm
- Firefly Swarm Optimization
- Ant Colony Optimization
- Particle Swarm Optimization
- Artificial Fish Swarm Algorithm
- Artificial Bee Colony Algorithm
- Bacterial Food Search Optimization Algorithm
- Wolf Colony Algorithm
- Cat Swarm Optimization

Figure 1. Artificial intelligence optimization algorithms (Source: Altunbey and Alataş, 2015)

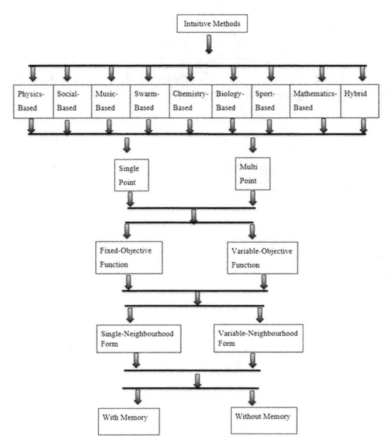

In addition to swarm-based algorithms, learning assistants may also employ social-based algorithms. Social-based artificial intelligence optimization algorithms are listed as follows:

- Imperialist competitive algorithm
- Teaching-learning-based optimization algorithm
- Social-emotional optimization algorithm
- Brainstorming optimization
- Group leaders optimization algorithm
- Hierarchical social algorithm
- Human group formation algorithm

- Social-based algorithm
- Society and civilization algorithm
- Cultural algorithm
- parliamentary optimization algorithm.

Among these algorithms, the learning-teaching-based optimization algorithm, which operates based on the effect of the teacher on the learners, particularly in the classroom, may be considered suitable for the learning assistant. Similarly, human-group, cultural, and social algorithms can be utilized.

Individual Differences Influencing the Design of the Learning Assistant

Once the algorithm configuration for the learning assistant has been defined, the data to be collected from the individual must be determined for the learning assistant. The following aspects can be determined by questions posed to the individual in order to determine their learning patterns:

- the hours during which the mind is most active and most conducive to work
- the subject and learning preference
- learning strategies, styles and habits
- the content and the material

This information can be gathered in the initial round by posing questions to the user before they begin using the program/application/software, during the installation process, or when it is first installed and used. It will provide objective responses to these questions and reveal how well individuals know themselves.

In accordance with the gathered answers, the most prominent individual differences relating to learning that will be considered in the design of a learning assistant who would operate on the basis of the obtained data are as follows:

- Learning habits of individuals
- Studying techniques
- Learning styles
- Learning strategies
- Cognitive strategies

Nonetheless, the demographic characteristics of the users may also play a significant role in the customization of the learning assistant. Other individual characteristics to be considered include the following:

- gender
- age
- level of education
- level of income
- culture
- learning styles
- learning strategies
- cognitive strategies
- prior learning

According to the literature, gender is regarded within the context of physiological/biological gender and social gender, and definitions are formed within this framework. While biological gender indicates physical differences, social gender indicates the roles that are expected, laid, and assumed in social and cultural contexts (Karadeniz, 2017). In both biological and social contexts, the gender of an individual influences their preferences in various domains. Education and learning needs are another domain where diversity can be observed.

Some studies in the literature reveal there are few cognitive differences between men and women, and women's verbal skills and regular working habits are more prominent in planning and behaving organized manner (Alcı and Altun, 2007; Demiray, 2013; Zeytinkaya, 2016). Considering the lifelong learning needs of individuals, it is evident that the gender variable should be integrated into the development of any services aimed at meeting this need.

Similarly, when the age variable is considered, research is carried out to determine whether there are variations between the learning environments chosen by individuals of the Y generation and the Z generation under the current conditions. Examined within the context of intergenerational differences, it is clear that the age factor must be taken into account. While the Y generation may consider augmented reality as an additional service, the X generation (those born in 2000 and later) may consider it indispensable. Considering the attitudes of the X generation (those born between 1961-1980) and Generation Y (those 1980-2000 born / 1983-1995 in Turkey (Yuksekbilgili, 2015)) towards online education technologies, it is possible to assert that; individuals of the X generation have a negative view of the utilization of web-based technology in higher education, compared to those of the Y generation. they believe web-based communication and support services are inadequate and prefer to utilize social networks less; however, they are optimistic about the future of web-based learning technologies and even consider them as an alternate solution to education-related problems (Etlican, 2012). On the other hand, it is anticipated that the new generation, often known as the digital generation or generation Z, will differ from previous generations due to their birth and upbringing in the digital age

(Oblinger & Oblinger, 2005; Prensky, 2001, p.1). Based on research on the more effective and widespread use of augmented reality applications, similar technologies should be incorporated into education given the generation's current technology-oriented and effective use of technology, with the potential to catch the attention of generation z, as well as in response to the search for effective methods/environments to support and enrich education (Somyurek, 2014). In light of this information, it can be expected that age and generational knowledge will be essential sources of data for the learning assistant that will be designed.

Individuals' learning patterns, cognitive structures, information analysis, synthesis processes, evaluation criteria, and preferences for the subject they wish to study may vary as their degree of education increases. When the literature is reviewed, it is possible to find studies in which the opinions of individuals with varying degrees of education regarding the same content are collected, and their differences are revealed. This can be interpreted as an indication of the significance of education level knowledge as one of the crucial components of data that must be collected about the individual when designing the learning assistant.

Whether the platforms that offer users the content they wish to study are paid or free services, services such as MOOC, xMOOC, cMOOC, certificate programs, online courses, YouTube videos, and social media sharing, paid associate degree/undergraduate/master's without thesis, master's with thesis, and doctorates, both within the context of education and income level, may be important. According to the user's payment limit, the learning assistant should be able to scan and generate options accordingly.

The phrase "the world is small" has gained more validity as a result of globalization and many other factors, in particular, advancements in information technologies. The interaction of people from different cultures has become an natural occurrence today(Harris, 2006: Trompenaars and Hampden-Turner, 1997). In an environment where intercultural interaction and multiculturalism are on the rise, cultural differences are one of the most important issues (Yeşil, 2009). Culture is defined as the assumptions and norms that determine how members of a society or group interact with one another and approach their work (DiStefano and Maznevski, 2000). Based on this definition, it may be claimed that data on the characteristics of the culture the individuals belong to and the characteristics of the culture they are a part of will be required in order to predict the interactions that individuals will have in the learning environment provided by the learning assistant.

In learning how to study, learning style (Güven ve Kürüm, 2004), which is claimed to be an inherent trait, and learning styles(Kaplan ve Kies, 1995), a concept that does not change easily throughout a person's life, play a significant role (Carroll, 1998). Kolb, who established the experiential learning theory based on the learning process, defines learning style as an individual's preferred method for receiving and processing information (Jonassen & Grobowski, 1999). Honey and Mumford, on the other hand, define "learning style" as an individual's preferences in learning activities (Ülgen, 1995), whereas Dunn and Dunn (1986) define "learning style" as each student's use of distinct and unique ways when preparing to learn, learning, and recalling new and challenging information. Many researchers, including Grasha, Keefe, Gregorc, and Butler, have carried out studies on learning styles, developed scales, and attempted to define learning styles within the framework of these scales.

According to Felder, there is a predominant way in which individuals prefer to receive and process information, that varies from person to person. For instance, while one person focuses on data, events, and algorithms, another person may require more theoretical and mathematical models for the same information or respond better to visual forms of information such as diagrams, graphs, and pictures. Some may prefer active and participatory learning, whereas others may prefer written and spoken explanations or may prefer to learn more directly and in the light of their own emotions (Felder, 1996).

When an individual is aware of their particular learning style, they can engage in this style during the learning process to learn more easily and successfully (Biggs, 2001). Based on this prediction, it can be stated that the individual's learning style should be a significant data source for the learning assistant. It is important to note, however, that in recent years it has been debated whether learning styles exist or need to be readdressed.

In addition to learning styles, the learning strategies aspect is also addressed. Learning strategies are defined as the methods and instruments required for independent learning (Apps, 1990; Loranger, 1994; Weinstein and MacDonald, 1986). The learner can be viewed as an active information processor, interpreter, and synthesizer who chooses the information to be learned, encrypts it, transfers it to memory, and, when necessary, employs a variety of retrieval mechanisms. (Weinsten and MacDonald, 1986). The two primary groups of learning strategies are: Cognitive strategies and cognitive orientation strategies.

Cognitive strategies perform the functions of:

- memorizing
- sense-making
- and organizing, and enable new knowledge to be stored in memory, interpreted, and recalled when needed

On the other hand, cognition-directing strategies control and manage learning processes under the headings of:

- preparing to understand

- following understanding
- and directing understanding (Gall, Gall, Jacobsen, & Bullock, 1990; Pintrich, 1988)

Since learning strategies are directly related to independent/autonomous learning competence, open and distance learning can be viewed as a natural requirement (Somuncuoğlu and Yıldırım, 1998). There are various studies exploring the extent to which learners use their learning strategies competently within the context of open and distance learning programs and the impact of such use on academic accomplishment.

In addition, navigation strategies might provide as a valuable source of information for the learning assistant. The navigation strategy is used to determine how an individual navigates and obtains information in online settings. There are four distinct development strategies:

- In-depth: It is the strategy in which a user navigates from the home page to subpages via links but returns to the home page when they reach a page with no links.
- Expanded: It is the strategy by which a user returns to a website by first exploring its subpages of the homepage.
- In-depth-expanding: It is the strategy of individual's in-depth navigation to a certain point and then expanding.
- Random: It is the strategy in which the individual visits the pages randomly (De Vocht, 1994).

An individual can use one or more of these strategies. De Bra, Houben, and Kornatzky (1992) state that the strategy that enables individuals to access information most effectively is the in-depth navigation strategy, based on the study that concluded the navigation strategies used by individuals in Internet environments are effective in determining the path they will choose to achieve their learning objectives. In light of this information, it would be accurate to state that the navigation strategy should be one of the primary data sources utilized to identify the user and determine the learning assistant's needs.

The following technologies can be utilized in the design of the learning assistant:

- 3D design
- augmented reality
- virtual reality
- hologram
- meta-human

The utilization of learning assistants can be made more appealing by including the gamification method, which is currently being employed in every field and is supported by scientific research that shows its positive impact on individual motivation. Inclusion of features such as follow-up charts and ranking lists might enhance the desire and motivation of individuals to utilize the assistant.

METAVERSE AND META-HUMAN

Metaverse, which was first mentioned by Neal Stephenson in his novel "Snow Crash" in 1992, is a concept used to describe the digital world in which the real and the virtual merge, allowing people to travel between different universes using different devices and interact in a virtual environment. Wearable technology has accelerated the development of meta-universes where individuals can interact with graphical representations of themselves in the virtual world, also known as digital avatars in virtual reality.

Platforms such as Roblox, Fortnite, Epic Games, and Minecraft, which have facilitated the formation of video game communities in recent years, will play an essential role in the construction of the metaverse world of tomorrow. Moreover, applications such as Sandbox, Zepeto, VRChat, Spatial, OVR, and Decentraland offer users a metaverse universe experience.

The meta-universes, whose significance and application domains are constantly expanding with advancements in virtual reality technologies, offer users an "immersive" experience in the applications they provide, making them feel as though they are actually there. Furthermore, metaverse provides users with the following benefits:

- experience of socializing, meeting new people, deepening existing friendships, and establishing new communities
- experience, unlimited users and universes
- independence from space and time, interaction opportunities
- the ability to be owned and shaped by the individuals who live, interact, create, and engage in it

In the metaverse, it is possible to talk about various human forms. When examining existing applications, there are three distinct formats for human models encountered. These can be defined as following:

- The first is the Digital Avatar, which is based on the preferences of the individual and exists in the real world.

- The second is the Digital Twin, defined as the projection of human beings and is one of the human forms within the scope of transhumanism.
- The third is Digital Human, which is generated using artificial intelligence and modeling and has no real-world counterpart.

The term of Meta-human can be applied generally to all three digital model formats.

Meta Learning Assistant

Metaverse is the post-reality universe, a permanent and ongoing multi-user environment that merges physical reality and digital simulation. Virtual environments such as virtual reality (VR) and augmented reality (AR) are built on the convergence of technologies that allow multisensory interactions with humans and digital objects.

Due to the constantly evolving technology, the doors to an online virtual world that includes augmented reality, virtual reality, 3D holographic avatars, video, and other communication tools are practically open. As the number of platforms providing metaverse universes increases, it is inevitable that coexisting hyper-real alternative worlds will be made available. Through virtual world trips such as concerts, conferences, and business meetings or activities such as studying and playing with friends, service and platform providers expect that users will be constantly connected on the Metaverse platform, where users can move in a digital and reality-enhanced virtual universe and where many elements of technology will push the boundaries.

In contrast to the Internet, which has been in use since the 21st century, users of the Metaverse will be able to experience all changes in real time. In the Metaverse, any modification a person makes will be permanent and visible to almost everyone. The permanence and interoperability of the Metaverse will provide users with more identity and continuity of experience compared to the modern Internet. Therefore, users will be able to be themselves across all channels in the Metaverse and will not need to create different identities for Twitter, "Fortnite," and Reddit.

In these platforms, users will be able to use projections of real people or newly-created characters as learning assistants, as well as the meta-humans that institutions will provide for them as learning assistants. However, it is foreseen that there should be an identity consistency in the metaverse. This identity consistency can be regarded as the primary important factor in determining how Metaverse users receive, learn, and consume content. Consequently, this will also be a determining factor in the learning process of meta-human and the structure of the meta-learning assistant. The advantages and disadvantages of the artificial intelligence-supported meta-learning assistant to be provided by the educational institution or the utility and applicability of the individual-created meta-learning assistant will be the subject of a separate study.

Integrating a Meta-Learning Assistant into Existing Learning Management Systems (LMS)

The following steps can be applied for a meta-learning assistant to be integrated into an existing LMS:

1. Development and Planning Phase

    Needs Analysis: First, the goals of the metaverse-based learning assistant to be added to the LMS should be determined. The needs of the users (students, teachers) and the shortcomings of the existing LMS should be identified. This analysis determines which features the learning assistant should have.

    Technical Infrastructure and Integration Plan: A robust technical infrastructure is needed to develop a learning assistant that runs on Metaverse. It is important that this infrastructure is compatible with the LMS. First, it should be determined which metaverse platforms will be used (e.g. Decentraland, Sandbox) and how to integrate with the LMS. APIs, SDKs and other integration tools are used in this process.

2. Design Phase

    Avatar and Interface Design of the Learning Assistant: In the Metaverse environment, the learning assistant is represented as an avatar. The design of this avatar should be user-friendly and fun. At the same time, an interface should be developed that users can interact with comfortably. At this stage, designs compatible with virtual reality (VR) or augmented reality (AR) glasses and other wearable devices should also be considered.

    Development of Interaction Mechanics: It should be determined how the metaverse-based learning assistant will interact with students. A system that provides text and voice communication using natural language processing (NLP) techniques can be developed. Also, interactive activities (games, simulations) should be designed for learning processes.

3. Integration and Implementation Phase

    Integration of Metaverse and LMS: The learning assistant in the Metaverse environment should be integrated with the existing LMS. This integration should ensure seamless data flow. Student performance data should be transferred from the metaverse platform to the LMS and the content in the LMS should be made accessible in the metaverse environment.

    Data Synchronization: Student data needs to be synchronized between LMS and metaverse. This ensures that students' progress is recorded in both environments. This data synchronization should be instantaneous and provide an equal experience for all users.

Security and Privacy: Security and privacy should be kept at the highest level in Metaverse and LMS integration. Student data should be secured and necessary measures should be taken to protect this data against unauthorized access.

4. Testing and Piloting Phase

    Pilot Implementation and Feedback Collection: The developed system should be tested on a specific group of users. These tests are important to evaluate the system's errors and user experience. During the pilot implementation, feedback from students and teachers should be collected and necessary improvements should be made to the system.

    Performance and Usability Tests: The performance and usability of the learning assistant's integration with the LMS should be tested. At this stage, it is evaluated whether the system is stable and whether users can use the system comfortably.

5. Deployment and Training Phase

    Wide Deployment: After a successful pilot, the metaverse-based learning assistant can be made available to all users. At this stage, the system is deployed to a wide range of users.

    User Training: Students and teachers should be trained to use the new system. These trainings should cover how to navigate the metaverse environment, how to interact with the learning assistant and how the integration with the LMS works.

6. Continuous Monitoring and Improvement Phase

    Feedback Loop: User feedback should continue to be collected after the system has been deployed. This feedback contributes to continuous improvement of the system.

    Artificial Intelligence Updates: The AI algorithms of the learning assistant should be updated and improved according to student data. This process allows the assistant to become smarter and more efficient over time.

CONCLUSION AND RECOMMENDATIONS

The cognitive coaching of learning assistants can be expected to be executed by teachers. From this viewpoint, it can be stated that a learning assistant that can be designed and utilized for open and distance learning should be able to present different web content on topics and subjects that the user is curious about, interested in, needs, or desires. These contents can be presented, for instance, in a bachelor's program or certificate program, a MOOC curriculum, and they can be formal or informal sources. While finding and presenting these resources to the user, the learning assistant should be able to design the content of these resources based on the individual's learning preferences. The learning assistant must perform the following functions:

- Determining the appropriate program/course for the individual
- Enrollment in the program or course
- LMS integration
- Smart content recommendation system
- Individual measurement and evaluation

The learning assistant can be designed as a mobile application that runs on a device or it can be presented as a character or avatar. Additionally, this character's interaction with the user can be ensured. By modeling the character in 3D, holographic technology can be used to display the character. Moreover, meta-human forms can be considered learning assistants in the metaverse universe. The user's character can be edited by himself or by the institution or organization that offers the training.

The learning assistant can be reinforced with gamification elements such as ranking, leveling, and sorting.

- The user can create his own assistant and his own meta-human
- Interact with other users
- Vote on other users
- Create common studying areas
- Interaction can be achieved through meta-humans (digital twins, digital avatars, digital humans)

Meta-learning assistants collect and analyze users' personal data. This data includes information such as users' learning styles, performance, interests and interaction habits. Data ownership raises the question of who controls this data and how it is used.

Users' explicit consent is required for meta-learning assistants to collect and process data. Consent processes should clearly tell users what data is being collected, how it will be used and for what purposes it is being processed. Users should also have the right not to consent to the collection and use of their data.

AI algorithms learn from the data they collect and can reflect biases in that data. If the data is biased on factors such as gender, race, social status, etc., the AI system can learn these biases and make erroneous decisions based on these biases. This could raise serious concerns about fairness and equality.

Strategies such as transparency, user education and continuous monitoring should be developed to overcome these challenges. Protecting the rights of users and ensuring the credibility of the system are critical to the long-term success of such technologies.

REFERENCES

Akyol, S., & Alataş, B. (2012). Güncel Sürü Zekası Optamizasyon Algoritmaları. *Nevşehir Bilim ve Teknoloji Dergisi,* 1(1).

Alcı, B., & ve Altun, S. (2007). Lise Öğrencilerinin Matematik Dersine Yönelik Özdüzenleme Ve Bilişüstü Becerileri Cinsiyete Sınıfa Ve Alanlara Göre Farklılaşmakta Mıdır?.*Çukurova Üniversitesi Sosyal Bilimler Enstitüsü Dergisi,* 16(1).

Alexan, A. I., Osan, A. R., & Oniga, S. (2012, October). Personal assistant robot. In Design and Technology in Electronic Packaging (SIITME)*, 2012 IEEE 18th International Symposium for IEEE.* (pp. 69-72). DOI: 10.1109/SIITME.2012.6384348

Altunbey, F., & Alataş, B. (2015). Sosyal ağ analizi için sosyal tabanlı yapay zekâ optimizasyon algoritmalarının incelenmesi. *International Journal of Pure and Applied Sciences,* 1(1).

Apps, J. W. (1990). *Study skills for today's college student.* McGraw-Hill, Inc.

Biggs, J. (2001). Enhancing Learning: A Matter of Style or Approach. Ed.: Robert J. Sternberg ve Li - Fang Zhang. Perspectives on Thinking, Learning and Cognitive Styles. Lawrance Erlbaum Associates, Mahwah, ss.73 - 102.

Breiman, L. (2001). *Machine Learning*, 45, (pp.5–32), Random Forests.

Butler, K. A. (1987). *Learning Styles - Personel Exploration and Practical Applications.* The Learner's Dimension.

Can 2016. Kişisel Asistan Teknolojisi. https://www.derinogrenme.com/2016/12/28/kisisel-asistan-teknolojisi/ Erişim tarihi: 10.04.2018.

Carroll, A. (1998). *How to Study Better and Faster - Using Your Learning Styles and Strengths-. J.* Weston Walch Publisher.

Chen, Y., Jensen, S., Albert, L. J., Gupta, S., & Lee, T. (2023). Artificial intelligence (AI) student assistants in the classroom: Designing chatbots to support student success. *Information Systems Frontiers,* 25(1), 161–182. DOI: 10.1007/s10796-022-10291-4

Cohen, P. R., & Feigenbaum, E. A. (Eds.). (2014). *The handbook of artificial intelligence* (Vol. 3). Butterworth-Heinemann.

De Vocht, J. (1994). *Experiments for the Characterization of Hypertext Structures. Yayınlanmamış Yüksek Lisans Tezi.* Eindhoven Univ. Of Technology.

Dunn, K., & Dunn, R. (1986). The Look of Learning Styles. *Early Years*, 8, 46–52.

Ertel, W. (2018). *Introduction to artificial intelligence*. Springer.

Etlican, G. (2012). X ve y kuşaklarının online eğitim teknolojilerine karşı tutumlarının karşılaştırılması (Doctoral dissertation).

Felder, R. M. (1996). Matters of style. *ASEE Prism*, 6(4), 18–23.

Fitria, T. N. (2021, December). Artificial intelligence (AI) in education: Using AI tools for teaching and learning process. In *Prosiding Seminar Nasional & Call for Paper STIE AAS* (Vol. 4, No. 1, pp. 134-147).

Gall, M. D., Gall, J. P., Jacobsen, D. R., & Bullock, T. L. (1990). *Tools for Learning*. ASCD Publication.

Jonassen, ve, H. D., & Grobowski, B. L. (1999). *Handbook of Individual Differences, Learning and Instruction*. Lawrance Erlbaum Associates.

Kaplan, E. Joseph ve Daniel A. Kies. (1995). Teaching Styles and Learning Styles. *Journal of Instructional Psychology*, 22(1), 29–34.

Keefe, J. W. (1990). *Learning Style Profile Handbook* (Vol. II). Developing Cognitive Skills. National Association of Secondary School Principals.

Kolb, D. A. (1984). *Experiential Learning: Experience as The Source of Learning and Development*. Prentice-Hall.

Koyuncu, M. (2009). Fuzzy querying in intelligent information systems. In *International Conference on Flexible Query Answering Systems* (pp. 536-547). Springer, Berlin, Heidelberg. DOI: 10.1007/978-3-642-04957-6_46

Kurban, T. (2006). *Kablosuz Taşınabilir Uzaktan Sağlık İzleme Sistemi: Mobil Sağlık Danışmanı*. Yayınlanmamış Yüksek Lisans Tezi.

Liu, Y., Chen, L., & Yao, Z. (2022). The application of artificial intelligence assistant to deep learning in teachers' teaching and students' learning processes. *Frontiers in Psychology*, 13, 929175. DOI: 10.3389/fpsyg.2022.929175 PMID: 36033031

Loranger, A. L. (1994). The study strategies of successful and unsuccessful high school students. *Journal of Reading Behavior*, 26(4), 347–360. DOI: 10.1080/10862969409547858

Mathew, A. N., Rohini, V., & Paulose, J. (2021). NLP-based personal learning assistant for school education. *Iranian Journal of Electrical and Computer Engineering*, 11(5), 4522–4530. DOI: 10.11591/ijece.v11i5.pp4522-4530

Modi, P. J., Veloso, M., Smith, S. F., & Oh, J. (2005). Cmradar: A personal assistant agent for calendar management. In *Agent-Oriented* [Springer, Berlin, Heidelberg.]. *Information Systems*, II, 169–181.

Murtaza, S. S., Lak, P., Bener, A., & Pischdotchian, A. (2016, January). How to effectively train IBM Watson: Classroom experience. In 2016 49th Hawaii International Conference on System Sciences (HICSS) (pp. 1663-1670IEEE.

Nizam, H., & Akın, S. S. (2014). *Sosyal medyada makine öğrenmesi ile duygu analizinde dengeli ve dengesiz veri setlerinin performanslarının karşılaştırılması. XIX*. Türkiye'de İnternet Konferansı.

Oblinger, D., & Oblinger, J. (2005). Is it age or IT: First steps toward understanding the net generation. Educating the net generation, 2(1–2), 20. Prensky, M. (2001). Digital Natives, Digital Immigrants Part 1. *On the Horizon*, 9(5), 1–6.

Onan, A., & Korukoğlu, S. (2016). Makine öğrenmesi yöntemlerinin görüş madenciliğinde kullanılması üzerine bir literatür araştırması. *Pamukkale Üniversitesi Mühendislik Bilimleri Dergisi*, 22(2), 111–122.

Pirim, A. G. H. (2006). Yapay zeka. *Journal of Yaşar University*, 1(1), 81–93.

Quinlan, J. R. (1986). [Induction of Decision Trees.]. *Machine Learning*, 1, 81–106.

Somuncuoğlu, Y., & Yıldırım, A. (1998). Öğrenme stratejileri: Teorik boyutları, araştırma bulguları ve uygulama için ortaya koyduğu sonuçlar. *Eğitim ve Bilim*, 22(110).

Somyürek, S. (2014). Öğretim sürecinde z kuşağının dikkatini çekme: Artırılmış gerçeklik. *Eğitim Teknolojisi Kuram ve Uygulama*, 4(1), 63–80. DOI: 10.17943/etku.88319

Tesene, M. M. (2018). Adaptable selectivity: A case study in evaluating and selecting adaptive learning courseware at Georgia State University. *Current Issues in Emerging Elearning*, 5(1), 6.

Ülgen, G. (1995). *Eğitim Psikolojisi -Birey ve Öğrenme-*. Ankara.

Weinstein, C.E., & MacDonald, J.D. (1986) "Why does a school psychologist need to know about learning strategies?", *Journal of School Psychology*, 24(3), (pp.257-265).

Xia, P. (2021). Design of personalized intelligent learning assistant system under artificial intelligence background. In *The 2020 International Conference on Machine Learning and Big Data Analytics for IoT Security and Privacy: SPIoT-2020*, Volume 1 (pp. 194-200). Springer International Publishing. DOI: 10.1007/978-3-030-62743-0_27

Yeşil, S. (2009). Kültürel farklılıkların yönetimi ve alternatif bir strateji: Kültürel zeka.

Yüksekbilgili, Z. (2015). Türkiye'de Y Kuşağinin Yaş Araliği. *Elektronik Sosyal Bilimler Dergisi*, 14(53), 259–267.

Zadrozny, W. W., Gallagher, S., Shalaby, W., & Avadhani, A. (2015, February). Simulating IBM Watson in the classroom. In *Proceedings of the 46th ACM Technical Symposium on Computer Science Education* (pp. 72-77). DOI: 10.1145/2676723.2677287

Zeytinkaya, D. (2016). Bilişsel Stil Kullanımına Yönelik Bir Araştırma. *Journal of International Social Research*, 9(46).

Chapter 7
AI based Learning in Biology

Shiwani
Dayalbagh Educational Institute, India

D. K. Chaturvedi
https://orcid.org/0000-0002-4837-2570
Dayalbagh Educational Institute, India

ABSTRACT

This chapter develops an AI based learning system to investigate the incorporation of AI in education. The chapter addresses the advantages of AI in education, including personalized learning programs and reduced teacher workload, in light of its expanding significance in the field. Proving theorems and problem-solving are the two base pillars of AI based learning systems. Partitioning domain-specific knowledge after the inference engine is a fundamental component of these learning systems. The chapter focuses on the design and development of an AI based learning system (on Biology content), detailing the knowledge acquisition, representation, and developmental phases. Systematic explanations of acquiring information from subject matter experts, representing that knowledge using MATLAB, and creating an inference engine. Emphasis is placed on the evaluation phase, demonstrating how the system can evaluate student knowledge in a variety of ways. By including professional evaluations, revisions, and comments, the refinement process guarantees accuracy and trustworthiness.

DOI: 10.4018/979-8-3693-3944-2.ch007

1.0. INTRODUCTION

The findings of AI research have drawn progressively more attention over the last years. The first application of AI to be profitable on a commercial scale was knowledge-based systems (Lansdown & Roast, 1987), and this field has drawn numerous interests. The term "knowledge-based system" is typically used to describe data systems that apply emblematic depiction of humanoid knowledge (Chandiok & Chaturvedi, 2018), typically in a manner that mimics human reasoning. The most effective of these knowledge-based systems to date are learning systems. According to Buchanan (1986), "Learning systems are programs that have the ability to provide answers to certain issues in a specific ground or to provide guidance at a level and in a manner that is similar to that of experts in the area. The development of learning systems in certain application areas has even given rise to a whole field of study called knowledge engineering (Shaw & Gaines, 1992).

Learning systems are being created to address challenges in sectors where significant human skill is needed to find solutions (Zhang & Sun, 2024). These problem domains include different fields such as, education sector, financial counseling, product design, and medical diagnosis etc. The majority of learning systems in use today can only handle limited issue domains. However, even in extremely narrow fields, learning systems typically require a vast amount of data (knowledge) to perform on par with actual humanoid expertise in the topic.

In this chapter, author focuses on concept of AI and education, AI and learning systems, features of AI based learning systems, Types of AI based learning systems in education, Importance of Biology education, Design and developmental phase of an AI based learning system, Empirical evidences, Educational Implications and Conclusion.

1.1. AI and Education Sector

"If I had requested persons what they required, they would have said faster horses," is a remark by Henry Ford that Roll and Wylie (2016) draw attention to. At initial glimpse, one may claim that educational institutions have altered into "quicker/fast classes," yielding outcomes more quickly.

Is it necessary to think differently in the 21st century, or will these "fast classes" persist in doing so? Will imparting metacognition, skills & critical intellectuals be adequate as we move closer to the 21st era? Or ought we to arrange new, never-before-considered procedures for the current period? What informative potentials might AI present that would set people aside from robots or driverless cars while preserving their social and emotional characteristics? These problems will most probably soon be at the top of the agenda for decision-makers and practitioners in the area; in detail, there have previously been conversations on whether or not AI can really replace teachers (Felix, 2020).

Good instructors will still be around in the future, according to Manyika et al. (2017), and they will continue to offer lessons that will improve students' communication, creativity, and affective intelligence. These writers contend that advancements in automation and AI will actually make "people more human." The usage of AI in the education sector will make learning more individualized, provide effective learning experiences, allow students to discover their talents, improve their creativity, and lessen the workload of teachers, according to Haseski (2019), who is discussing educational research on artificial intelligence. However, opposing viewpoints also exist.

According to Humble and Mozelius' (2019), artificial intelligence study shows that there may be a risk associated with teachers outsourcing their duties to machines. According to Wogu et al. (2018), states and nations have the responsibility of developing a teacher profile that is compatible with these support systems in order to be ready for this future.

Studies on the theory of general artificial intelligence date back at least to the 14th century, and although artificial intelligence in education has garnered numerous attentions recently, these researches were revived in 1937 thanks to the work of Alan Turing (Humble & Mozelius, 2019). In scientific circles and scholarly writing, they are currently gaining importance. There will likely be significant changes to education systems and procedures when artificial intelligence is used more in the classrooms. Sekeroglu et al., (2019) suggested that artificial intelligence might assist educators in offering more personalized instructions for their pupils in light of the study's findings. According to Pedro et al. (2019), AI has the possibility to offer improved and more suitable learning options for marginalized groups such as refugees, individuals with disabilities, out-of-school youth, and isolated communities. Research demonstrates how intelligent learning environments and artificial intelligence techniques can enhance the presentation of effective, individually personalized approaches (Mohammed & Watson, 2019). Artificial intelligence envisions raising education and quality at all levels, particularly by offering personalization, even though it appears that active participation from human teachers is necessary for successful education (Grosz & Stone, 2018). In terms of individualized education, Pedro et al. (2019) highlights a dual-teacher model with artificial intelligence. Teachers devote many times to routine and other administrative tasks, like repeating information and responding to inquiries on a diverse range of subjects. However, by dipping the quantity of period spent on routine procedures, secondary teachers supported by AI in the class will enable teachers to concentrate more on student guidance and one-on-one communication.

1.2. AI and Learning Systems

The computer (digital) was first intended to designate a numerical processor; a minor assemblage of investigators was working on non-numerical applications as first as the device's development. These researchers' efforts eventually produced AI, the computer science branch that studies learning systems that produce outcomes for which humanoid action would look essential. AI has been around since the 1956 Seminar at Dartmouth Summer (Bonnet, 1985).

Problem solving and proving theorems were the focus of early study in the 1950s. The created computer programs in both domains are distinguished by their intricate algorithms, which function on problems presented in relatively simple primitives and possess the ability to solve problems generally, regardless of a specific problematic area. The domain of theorem proving focuses on the automated verification of theorems based on a defined set of axioms, facilitated by computer algorithms. Theorems and axioms, rooted in logic, undergo logical inference processes to derive theorems from the given axioms. M. Davis pioneered the development of the initial program capable of generating mathematical proofs in number theory as far back as 1954. The substantial progress in theorem proving did not occur until the mid-1960s. Practically, theorem proving didn't get interesting until the resolution inference rule was introduced. The field made additional strides in the 1970s as a result of multiple improvements made to the first resolution principle.

The development of computer-based systems with a broad capability to solve various types of problems was the main emphasis of problem-solving researchers. According to Newell and Simon (1963), the most well-known method was created by A. Newell, H.A. Simon, and J.C. Shaw and is called GPS (General Problem Solver). An initial state, a desired ultimate state, and a series of transitions to change states into new states are used to illustrate a given problem. When such a representation is given using states and operations, GPS creates a series of transitions that, when applied sequentially, change the original state into the specified final state. The success of GPS has been lacking (Shiwani et al, 2021).

It was difficult, to begin with, to translate a non-trivial problem into language that a GPS could understand. Second, GPS proved to be a fairly ineffective technology. Given that GPS was designed to handle problems generally, it was not possible to use specific knowledge about the issue at hand to influence the transition that was chosen for a given state, even if that knowledge suggested a particular transition might result in a more effective solution. GPS generated an exponential temporal complexity by examining every conceivable transition in each phase. GPS started a major push in AI study in the direction of more dedicated systems, despite its very limited performance as a problem solver. This change in focus from broad issue/problem solver to particular systems, where the cognitive process may be observed by employing the problem knowledge, is frequently measured as an advancement in artificial intelligence (Radi & ELHami, 2018).

There aren't any clear answers in the related research for issues that come up in practice across an extensive variety of disciplines. The knowledge possessed by a learning in the field typically isn't documented in precise definitions or explicit algorithms; instead, it resides in practical rules and experiential facts known as - heuristics. Thus, an expert/learning system's database is heavily domain specific. Learning systems' success can be attributed primarily to their capacity to express and use investigative techniques and knowledge on computers. Expert/learning systems may typically provide commentary on their recommendations and solutions based on the knowledge stored within the system. Additionally, learning systems allow for the flexible integration of newly acquired knowledge with preexisting knowledge (Matsuzaka & Yashiro, 2023).

Learning systems, a significant field within artificial intelligence, have their origins in the 1960s and 1970s. They emerged from endeavors to replicate human expertise in addressing intricate problems. Among the earliest and most renowned learning systems stands Dendral (Tawafak et al., 2022), crafted during the 1960s at Stanford University, with the objective of interpreting mass spectrometry data for organic compound analysis. Another notable achievement came in the form of MYCIN, developed at Stanford in the 1970s, tasked with diagnosing bacterial infections and suggesting antibiotics (Copeland, 2018). These pioneering systems operated on rule-based reasoning and symbolic logic to emulate human decision-making processes (Chandiok & Chaturvedi, 2018). Over time, learning systems progressed alongside advances in computing capabilities and methods of knowledge representation, assuming pivotal roles across diverse fields like medicine, education, finance & engineering etc (Gupta, 1990).

1.3. Features of AI Based Learning Systems

Learning systems were typically created in the initial ages using high-level programming languages. Specifically, LISP was often selected as the operation language. However, while employing a high-level programming language as a learning system building instrument, one must focus an excessive amount of attention on the system's implementation details, which are unrelated to the topic that needs to be represented. Furthermore, the algorithms used to automatically apply the specialized/learning knowledge in the sector will be intricately entwined and difficult to distinguish from one another. As a result, once systems were built, they were essentially impossible to modify to account for shifting opinions within the relevant profession. However, learning knowledge is dynamic in nature because experience and knowledge are always changing.

learning system = knowledge base + inference engine

As a result, a learning system usually consists of the subsequent two crucial parts:

- A *knowledge base* made up of domain-specific knowledge which is captured and
- An *inference engine* made up of algorithms for modifying the information included in the *knowledge base*.

These days, writing an AI based learning system in a complex programming language is rare. It is frequently built in an environment that is unique and constrained, known as a learning system shell. Recently, many general tools have become existing for creating learning systems, which are more similar to special purpose programming languages and again enforce this division among inference and knowledge.

Figure 1. AI based learning systems

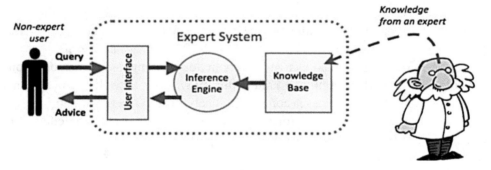

A unique knowledge representation formalism is used in the knowledge base to store the domain-specific knowledge. In a learning system shell or builder tool, one or more predefined formalisms for representing domain knowledge are used for encoding.

Additionally, here is a matching inference engine that can work through the information that is represented in this formalism. Only domain-specific knowledge must be supplied and articulated in the knowledge-picture formalism in instruction to construct an authentic learning system. The ability to develop a '*knowledge base*' independently of the '*inference engine*' has several benefits. For example, errors and deficiencies can be readily fixed without requiring significant alterations to the program text. A *knowledge base* can be established and improved incrementally. The ability to replace a particular knowledge base (KB) with a KB on a different subject result in a completely different learning system, which is an additional benefit of explicitly separating knowledge from inference.

Learning systems are developed by reviewing several information sources, including databases, textbooks & human learnings. A learning system constructor is a highly skilled individual who carries out this kind of work; they are called knowledge engineers. Knowledge acquisition is the procedure of gathering and organizing information about a certain problem topic. Knowledge elicitation is the process of obtaining knowledge through interviews with domain learners. Choosing an appropriate knowledge-representation formalism to provide the domain knowledge to the processor (computer) in an encoded format is one aspect of a knowledge engineer's job.

1.4. Types of AI Based Learning Systems in Education

In the education sector, learning systems can help with a range of tasks, from administrative work to personalized learning. Here are a few examples:

Intelligent Tutoring System (ITS)- These systems give students individualized teaching and feedback according to their unique requirements and development (Dutt and Ahuja, 2024). As an example, by giving students customized feedback and making adjustments based on their performance, Carnegie Learning's Cognitive Tutor assists students in teaching and comprehending mathematical topics (Nagori & Trivedi, 2014).

Adaptive Learning Systems- Based on the learner's abilities and preferences, these systems modify the instruction's content and pace. As an example, *Knewton* is an adaptive learning stage that supports pupils learn by tailoring the material to their specific needs and regions of greatest difficulty (Kara & Sevim, 2013).

Educational Recommender Systems- These systems make recommendations for learning materials, classes, or activities depending on the interests and profile of the learner (Garcia-Martinez, 2013). For example, Netflix-style recommendation systems for educational content, like Smart Sparrow, suggest reading materials and educational activities based on each student's unique profile.

Automated Grading Systems- These systems evaluate homework, tests, and quizzes using artificial intelligence (AI), giving students more timely and reliable feedback (Marcus et al., 2023). As an example, *Gradescope* is a platform that speeds up and gives instructors insights into grading by using machine learning algorithms to help with the process.

Administrative Decision Support Systems- Educational institutions might benefit from these systems' assistance with administrative duties including scheduling, resource allocation, and enrollment planning (Byrne & Twinomurinzi, 2012). As an Example, *CollegePlannerPro* is a tool that helps guidance counselors help students with the college planning and admission process.

Plagiarism Detection Systems- These programs use a large database of scholarly and internet materials to match student work to find instances of plagiarism (Ugo et al., 2020). As an Example, to help teachers verify that student submissions are original, *Turnitin* is a plagiarism detection application that is frequently used in educational settings.

Career Guidance Learning Systems- These methods offer individualized career counseling and advice based on a person's goals, interests, and abilities (Supriyanto et al. 2019). As an example, the website *Naviance* benefits learners to prepare for his future academic and professional endeavors, explore career alternatives, and create goals.

Learning Analytics Systems- These technologies provide insights into learning patterns and performance by analyzing vast datasets created by students' interactions with educational platforms (Mian, 2022). For example, the 'Canvas Learning Management System' has learning analytics tools that support teachers in monitoring student participation, identifying students who are at-risk, and enhancing their teaching methods.

On different features and context these learning systems also named as, Knowledge based learning systems (KBS), Decision Supports systems, Artificial Intelligence (AI) based learning systems, Inference Engines, Rule based learning systems (Clancey & Letsinger, 1981), Frame based learning systems, automated reasoning systems (Bonacina & Martelli, 2006), knowledge systems, Cognitive systems, Intelligence systems (Chahar et al. 2014), Learning advisors, Problems solving systems, Artificial learnings, and Heuristics systems etc. These terms can be used interchangeably in a variety of situations, and the language chosen may alter depending on how much emphasis is placed on particular system characteristics or applications. These above illustrations highlight how learning systems can be used in the field of education to improve administrative, instructional, and learning activities. The application of AI technology in education is still developing, providing creative answers to the various demands of teachers and pupils (Supriyanto et al., 2018).

1.5. Importance of Biology Education and AI Integration for Secondary level Students

Biology is essential for secondary students, providing a foundational understanding critical for advanced studies in areas such as medicine, environmental science, and biotechnology. It enhances critical thinking, analytical skills, and problem-solving abilities through scientific methodologies like observing, hypothesizing, experimenting, and drawing conclusions. Additionally, a strong knowledge of biology improves health literacy, empowering students to make informed health and lifestyle choices. Furthermore, it raises environmental awareness, fostering responsible behavior towards conservation and sustainability.

The integration of Artificial Intelligence (AI) in biology education significantly improves learning outcomes by tailoring educational content to each student's needs. AI-powered adaptive learning systems adjust difficulty levels based on individual progress, ensuring a solid understanding of fundamental concepts before moving on to more complex topics. Interactive simulations and virtual labs offer hands-on learning experiences, enabling students to conduct experiments and visualize biological processes without physical resources. Intelligent tutoring systems provide immediate feedback and additional resources to help with challenging concepts.

AI also analyzes student performance data, allowing educators to customize instructional strategies and interventions. Moreover, AI driven immersive learning experiences using augmented reality (AR) and virtual reality (VR) make abstract biological concepts more tangible and engaging. These technologies enhance collaboration and communication among students, improving teamwork and organizational skills. By automating assessments, AI offers immediate feedback, streamlining the learning process. Thus, integrating AI in secondary biology education not only personalizes and enriches the learning experience but also equips students with essential skills and knowledge for their future academic and career paths (Hwang et al., 2020; Zawacki-Richter et al., 2019; García & Fernández, 2018).

Example, the authors develop an AI-based learning system based on six chapters of biology from the NCERT science book for 9th grade used in Indian schools, chapters entitled: *The Fundamental Unit of Life - Cell, Tissue, Diversity of Living Organisms, Why Do We Fall Ill?, Natural Resources, and Improvement in Food Resources*. The National Council of Educational Research and Training (NCERT), set up in 1961, is an autonomous organization that advises the Indian government on enhancing school education quality. The content of these chapters is verified by educational experts, then divided into sub-content. The study material is presented to students in a question-answer format with forward and backward chaining. The authors include subject-related content, diagrams, educational games (such as jigsaw puzzles, jumble words, and content-based puzzles). For assessment, the authors develop three levels of questions, from lower-order thinking skills to higher-order thinking skills. These levels show an increase in complexity/difficulty among the questions. The difficulty level depends on the teacher's choice, type of assessment, and syllabus covered for that topic. As an outcome, this chapter adds to the conversation around AI in education by providing a real-world illustration of an AI-based learning system for content instruction. There are numerous empirical evidence found after reviewing the literature. These evidences are in the fields of student achievement, improved learning outcomes, reduced teacher workload, enhanced learning engagement and personalization, support for marginalized/diversified learners, support in automatic grading, and content proofing. The authors also observed educational implications that directly support learners, teachers, administration, and other stakeholders.

Design and Developmental Phase of an AI Based Learning System

A complicated and iterative process, including establishing the system's objectives, implementing, testing, and maintaining it, goes into creating an AI based learning system. Here is a step-by-step breakdown of the creation of AI based learning systems:

1. **Problem Analysis and Specify the Objectives:** The first step in creating a prototype of an AI based learning system is to analyze the problem. Here, the teacher or developer examined the learning issues experienced by students taking different courses and content and attempted to make the learning process enjoyable and fascinating using self-paced learning.
2. **Knowledge Acquisition:** This is the 1st stage of the developmental process, through which the developers acquire relevant knowledge from specialists (teachers, subject matter learnings, or other relevant resources like journals, internet material, books, etc.). For the knowledge phase of this segment, data must be verified by the experts and developed in order to answer the user's problem or question.
3. **Knowledge Representation:** Cases, rules, and frames are all part of this step. It separates the entire piece of content into smaller chunks or segments before encoding the information into set patterns or rules. In this instance, the developer represents the topic using the software MATLAB (numeric computing and programming platform); see figure no. 2. Example: The chapters of the biology curriculum from the IXth grade are used (The author takes six chapters of biology from NCERT science book).

Figure 2. Existing .m files (Chapters)

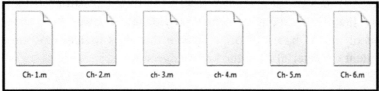

4. **Developmental Phase:** The knowledge base and inference engine are included in this phase. With the aid of the knowledge acquisition and knowledge representation stages, the knowledge base is produced in this phase. Rules are created during the knowledge base phase, such as the IF condition and THEN actions. These guidelines are presented as a chain or a series. Example: "IF X THEN Y," "IF Y THEN Z," where the condition is "IF X IS GREATER THAN Y, THEN Y IS GREATER THAN Z," and the conclusion is "IF X THEN Z."

Here, the developer can create phases, or the knowledge basis for any curriculum. Standard books should be used as the foundation for any subject that offers the same platform (equality) of knowledge in the majority of schools. The developer can create an AI based learning system program for all of the chapters based on the "IF and THEN" pattern, where the "IF" kind of program frame delivers the material in the form of questions (shown in figure 3). The knowledge base portion can be delivered to the students in the "IF" (questions) and "THEN" (response) type frames. The answers to the questions of biology can be created in the "THEN" frames (shown in figures 3 and 4).

Figure 3. Pointers of Knowledge base in query form

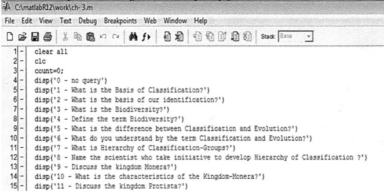

The learning system's inference engine element introduces decision-making capabilities and aids in issue resolution. The learner's question or uncertainty is analyzed by the inference engine, which provides the answer. In essence, it is the component of the AI based learning system that uses logical reasoning to infer unique content or material from the knowledge store.

Figure 4. Pointers of Knowledge base in answer form

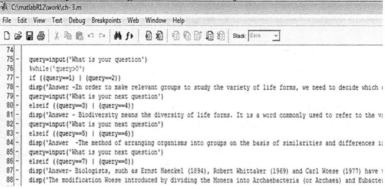

The inference engine uses 2 kinds of binding modes: backward chaining (everything must be stated in direction to achieve the goals) and forward chaining (asserts new facts). Both sorts of modes should be employed by the developer. Example: The AI based learning system's progress is seen in Figures 5, 6, and 7.

Figure 5. Function/run feature of system

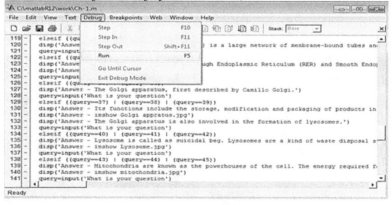

Figure 6. Query feature of learning system

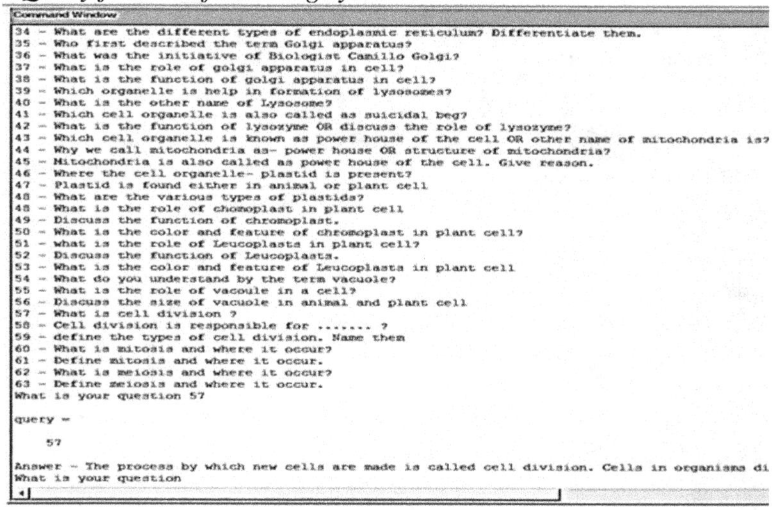

Figure 7. Explanation portion of AI based learning system

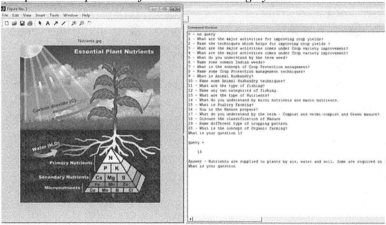

5. **Evaluation Phase:** The AI-based learning system's evaluation functionality is its special selling point. The assessment framework includes a variety of objects to gauge knowledge, such as fill-in sheets, educational games, word crosses, and Google Forms. The learners would advance to a different level depending on their responses. The pupils at levels 1, 2, and 3 would be guided gradually by a

learning system with built-in AI logic. The content will essentially be repeated and studied again if the pupils don't reach the necessary level. Figure 8 depicts the part on assessment.

Figure 8. AI based assessments

```
94   disp('Answer - Oxygen cycle refers to the movement of oxygen through the atmosphere (air), biosphere (plants and animal
95   imshow('Oxygen-Cycle.jpg')
96   query= input('What is your question')
97   elseif ((query==29)) | (query==30))
98   disp('Answer - Ozone layer depletion is the gradual thinning of the earth's ozone layer in the upper atmosphere caused
99   end
100  end
101
102  id1='https://docs.google.com/forms/d/e/1FAIpQLSfIF6U_ixPRhP6BYr5SNmn-CvOSGPghJy5T4rZPT8CITGUR5A/viewform?usp=sf_link ';
103  id2='https://docs.google.com/forms/d/e/1FAIpQLSdGplZgH1jPrJArTgOE9oEaUuHq_iEPf4ZZFpBRcamD8tF5hA/viewform?usp=sf_link ';
104  id3='https://docs.google.com/forms/d/e/1FAIpQLSc7xnGJx9vhN_KxxoT2EX1gIyPJfeOxAumSQPpEeslCFNddfg/viewform?usp=sf_link ';
105  sheetname1='My Sheet1';
106  sheetname2='My Sheet2';
107  sheetname3='My Sheet3';
108
109  %Level 1
110  url_name1=sprintf('https://docs.google.com/forms/d/e/1FAIpQLSfIF6U_ixPRhP6BYr5SNmn-CvOSGPghJy5T4rZPT8CITGUR5A/viewform?
111  sheetdata1=web(url_name1);
112  if sheetdata1>=5      %Level 2
113      url_name2=sprintf('https://docs.google.com/forms/d/e/1FAIpQLSdGplZgH1jPrJArTgOE9oEaUuHq_iEPf4ZZFpBRcamD8tF5hA/viewf
114  sheetdata2=web(url_name2);
115  end
116
117  if sheetdata2>=5      %Level 3
118      url_name3=sprintf('https://docs.google.com/forms/d/e/1FAIpQLSc7xnGJx9vhN_KxxoT2EX1gIyPJfeOxAumSQPpEeslCFNddfg/viewf
119  sheetdata3=web(url_name3);
120  end
```

6. **Refinement Phase:** This phase is vital for any type of work. This phase ensures the correctness of work and heightens product credibility at an approval level. For example, in this AI based learning system, the evaluation phase is done with the help of subject learnings, language learnings, technical learnings, and related students. Learnings evaluated the whole process of working with the system (input, process, and output). After the evaluation, some corrections and suggestions can be incorporated. This phase provides the final touch for the AI based learning system. The developer should correct all kinds of errors, add suggestions and feedback, refine the work, and make it presentable with the support of related learning.

2.0. EMPIRICAL EVIDENCES

Enhancement of Students Achievement: Research by Luckin et al. (2016) demonstrated that AI-driven personalized learning systems have the potential to significantly improve students' academic performance in subjects like mathematics. Their study utilized an Intelligent Tutoring System (ITS) that tailored instruction and feedback to individual student needs, leading to higher scores on standardized assessments compared to traditional teaching methods.

Improved Learning Outcomes with Adaptive Systems: Kulik and Fletcher (2016) conducted a meta-analysis that underscored the effectiveness of adaptive learning technologies. They found that these systems, which adjust content and pace according to students' learning needs, contributed to enhanced learning outcomes, particularly in complex subjects such as biology and physics.

Reduction of Teacher Workload: Holmes et al. (2019) highlighted the potential of AI to alleviate teachers' administrative burdens. Their research indicated that AI tools, such as automated grading and instant feedback systems, could streamline tasks, allowing educators to focus more on direct teaching and student interaction.

Enhanced Engagement and Personalization: According to Graesser et al. (2018), AI driven educational systems significantly increase student engagement and motivation by providing personalized learning experiences. This approach not only improves retention rates but also enhances academic performance.

Support for Marginalized Groups: Pedro et al. (2019) explored how AI technologies can offer more equitable educational opportunities for marginalized groups, such as refugees and individuals with disabilities. Their findings underscored AI's capability to provide tailored learning pathways that cater to diverse learning needs, thereby promoting inclusivity in education.

Reliability of Automated Grading: Valenti et al. (2003) investigated automated grading systems and found them to be consistent and reliable in assessing student work, offering scalability without compromising accuracy when compared to human graders.

3.0. EDUCATIONAL IMPLICATIONS

There are some related cases of the implications for education: A Learning System with AI as a Platform for different stakeholders of Education

- It can be hired as a help tool to generate learning practices that foster flexibility, communication, critical thinking, problem-solving skills, and original thought in students.
- More student understanding of the specific subject will produce motivated learners.
- Students will be motivated and engaged, and learning will become less boring.
- It will enhance pupils' ability to recall information, remember it, and apply it to practical situations.

- For pupils who struggle with sustained attention, it will be a pleasurable method of learning.
- It can solve the issue of insufficient and incompetent teachers being available at various locations or schools.
- Reduce the burden of content load for teachers.
- For parents, it provides support for their children in education

4.0. CONCLUSION

In educational forums and conferences, there is a lot of discussion on learning in the twenty-first century. The primary goal of this in the majority of nations is to prepare people for the problems that lie ahead in life. It is imperative to concentrate on conducive learning environments in light of this aspect (Balakrishnan et al., 2016). In previous years, the instructor had complete control over the teaching-learning procedure through the usage of demonstration, lectures, and other techniques. Subsequently, the focus turned to student-centered approaches, such as heuristic, project, and activity methods. Since technology integration is the most effective learning strategy under the current circumstances, it is extensively emphasized in the system of educational policy. One of the best tools available to educators or researchers for sparking children's interest in science is an AI based learning system. The motivation, interest, and engagement level of students is raised in the classroom via an AI based learning system (Azzam and Charles, 2024). Enhancing visual skills and using the value of technology in practical settings are the main goals in order to benefit learners to become extra thoughtful (reflective) thinkers and better communicators with others (Zirawaga, 2017). By keeping learning engaging, it also helps learners maintain their mental tranquilly. The "special" environment may be created and influenced by educational games that are part of an AI based learning system (Howard-Jones, 2011). As a result of adjusting instruction and learning activities to each learner's unique needs, AI based Learning system can significantly enhance learner engagement and motivation, boost learning efficiency, and take into account the diversity of learners. AI based learning system has the ability to empower teachers and students and revolutionize education in the digital age when the correct tactics are put in place. Whatever technology does, one thing is for sure: it will require constant redefining and adjusting of our methods of teaching (Duha, 2023).

REFERENCES

Al-Ars, Z. T., & Al-Bakry, A.AL-Ars. (2019). A web/mobile decision support system to improve medical diagnosis using a combination of K-Mean and fuzzy logic. *Telkomnika*, 17(6), 3145–3154. DOI: 10.12928/telkomnika.v17i6.12715

Azzam, A., & Charles, T. (2024). A Review of Artificial Intelligence in K-12 Education. Open. *Journal of Applied Sciences*, 14(8), 2088–2100. DOI: 10.4236/ojapps.2024.148137

Balakrishnan, M., & Gananathan, M. Nadarajah, Vellasamy S. & George, E. G. W. (2016). Enhancement of Higher Order Thinking Skills among Teacher Trainers by Fun Game Expert Approach World Academy of Science, Engineering and Technology. *International Journal of Educational and Pedagogical Sciences*, 10(12).

Bonacina, M. P., & Martelli, A. (2006). Automated reasoning. *Intelligenza Artificiale.*, 3, 14–20.

Bonnet, A. (1985). *Artificial Intelligence, Promise and Performance*. Prentice Hall Int.

Buchanan, B. G. (1986). Expert systems: Working systems and the research literature. *Expert Systems: International Journal of Knowledge Engineering and Neural Networks*, 3(1), 32–51. DOI: 10.1111/j.1468-0394.1986.tb00192.x

Byrne, E., & Twinomurinzi, H. (2012). Facilitating administrative decision-making using Decision Support Systems. e-Leadership Conference on Sustainable e-Government and e- Business InnovationsE-LEADERSHIP. 1-7. DOI: 10.1109/e-Leadership.2012.6524707

Chahar, R., Chandiok, A., & Chaturvedi, D. K. (2014). Intelligent analysis of the effect of Internet system in society. [IJCI]. *International Journal on Cybernetics & Informatics*, 3(3). Advance online publication. DOI: 10.5121/ijci.2014.3302

Chandiok, A., & Chaturvedi, D. K. (2018). Cognition Functionality based Question Answering System. International Journal of Computer Applications, 179(20) (0975- 8887).

Chandiok, A., & Chaturvedi, D. K. (2018). CIT: Integrated cognitive computing and cognition agent technologies based cognitive architecture for human-like functionality in artificial system. Biologically Inspired Cognitive Architectures. 2212-683X https://doi.org/.DOI: 10.1016/j.bica.2018.07.020

Clancey, W. J., & Letsinger, R. (1981). NEOMYCIN: Reconfiguring a Rule-Based Expert System for Application to Teaching. *International Joint Conference on Artificial Intelligence*.

Copeland, B. (2018). MYCIN. Encyclopedia Britannica. https://www.britannica.com/technology/MYCIN

Duha, M. S. U. (2023). ChatGPT in Education: An Opportunity or a Challenge for the Future? *TechTrends*, 67(3), 402–403. DOI: 10.1007/s11528-023-00844-y

Dutt, S., & Ahuja, N. J. (2024). *An intelligent HCI based tutoring system for child-centric learning environment*. Multimedia Tools App., DOI: 10.1007/s11042-024-20052-x

Felix, C. V. (2020). The Role of the Teacher and AI in Education. Sengupta, E., Blessinger, P. and Makhanya, M.S. (Ed.). *International Perspectives on the Role of Technology in Humanizing Higher Education (Innovations in Higher Education Teaching and Expert*, Vol. 33), Emerald Publishing Limited, (pp. 33–48). DOI: 10.1108/S2055-364120200000033003

García, E., & Fernández, C. (2018). The impact of AI in education. *Journal of Education and Learning*, 7(3), 201–208. DOI: 10.5539/jel.v7n3p201

Garcia-Martinez, S., & Hamou-Lhadj, A. (2013). Educational Recommender Systems: A Pedagogical-Focused Perspective. In Tsihrintzis, G., Virvou, M., & Jain, L. (Eds.), *Multimedia Services in Intelligent Environments. Smart Innovation, Systems and Technologies* (Vol. 25). Springer., DOI: 10.1007/978-3-319-00375-7_8

Grabusts, P. (2020). Fuzzy Logic Learning Methods In Student Education. *Society. Integration. Education.Proceedings of the International Scientific Conference, 4*, 438-448. https://doi.org/DOI: 10.17770/sie2020vol4.4840

Graesser, A. C., Hu, X., & Sottilare, R. A. (2018). Intelligent Tutoring Systems. In Hattie, J., & Anderman, E. M. (Eds.), *International Guide to Student Achievement* (pp. 267–270). Routledge.

Grosz, B. J., & Stone, P. (2018). A century-long commitment to assessing artificial intelligence and its impact on society. *Communications of the ACM*, 61(12), 68–73. DOI: 10.1145/3198470

Gupta, Y. P. (1990). Various aspects of expert systems: applications in manufacturing, *Technovation*, 10(7), (pp.487-504), ISSN 0166-4972, DOI: 10.1016/0166-4972(90)90027-H

Haseski, H. I. (2019). What do Turkish pre-service teachers think about artificial intelligence? *International Journal of Computer Science Education in Schools*, 3(2), 3–23. Advance online publication. DOI: 10.21585/ijcses.v3i2.55

Holmes, W., Bialik, M., & Fadel, C. (2019). *Artificial Intelligence in Education: Promises and Implications for Teaching and Learning*. Center for Curriculum Redesign.

Howard-Jones, P. A., Demetriou, S., Bogacz, R., Yoo, J. H., & Leonards, U. (2011). Toward a science of expert games. *Mind, Brain and Education : the Official Journal of the International Mind, Brain, and Education Society*, 5(1), 33–41. DOI: 10.1111/j.1751-228X.2011.01108.x

Humble, N., & Mozelius, P. (2019). Artificial Intelligence in Education-a Promise, a Threat or a Hype? In European Conference on the Impact of Artificial Intelligence and Robotics 2019 (ECIAIR 2019), Oxford, UK (pp. 149–156). Academic Conferences and Publishing International Limited.

Hwang, G. J., Sung, H. Y., Chang, S. C., & Huang, X. C. (2020). A learning style perspective to investigate the necessity of developing adaptive learning systems. *Journal of Educational Technology & Society*, 23(2), 148–161.

Ichsan, I. Z., Rahmayanti, H., Purwanto, A., Sigit, D. V., Miarsyah, M., & Gomes, P. W. P. (2020). HOTS-AEPCOVID-19 and ILMIZI learning model: The 21st-Century environmental learning in senior high school. [Jurnal Pendidikan Biologi Indonesia]. *JPBI*, 6(2), 265–272. DOI: 10.22219/jpbi.v6i2.12161

Kara, N., & Sevim, N. (2013). Adaptive Expert Systems: Beyond Teaching Machines. *Contemporary Educational Technology*, 4(2), 108–120. DOI: 10.30935/cedtech/6095

Kochmar, Ekaterina, Vu, Dung, Belfer, Robert, Gupta, Varun, Serban, Iulian, & Pineau, Joelle. (2020). *Automated Personalized Feedback Improves Learning Gains in An Intelligent Tutoring System*. .DOI: 10.1007/978-3-030-52240-7_26

Kulik, J. A., & Fletcher, J. D. (2016). Effectiveness of Intelligent Tutoring Systems: A Meta-Analytic Review. *Review of Educational Research*, 86(1), 42–78. DOI: 10.3102/0034654315581420

Kushnir, N., Osypova, N., Valko, N., & Kuzmich, L. (2020). Model of an Education Robotics Course for Natural Sciences Teachers. *CEUR workshop Proceeding*. Vol- 2740/20200322.pdf.

Lansdown, J., & Roast, C. (1987). The Possibilities and Problems of Knowledge-Based Systems for Design. *Environment and Planning. B, Planning & Design*, 14(3), 255–266. DOI: 10.1068/b140255

Luckin, R., Holmes, W., Griffiths, M., & Forcier, L. B. (2016). *Intelligence Unleashed: An Argument for AI in Education*. Pearson.

Manyika, J., Chui, M., Miremadi, M., Bughin, J., George, K., Willmott, P., & Dewhurst, M. (2017). *A future that works: Automation, employment, and productivity*. McKinsey Global Institute.

Marcus, M., Neil, C. C., Michael Kölling, B., & Miaojing, S. (2023). Automated Grading and Feedback Tools for Programming Education. *Systematic Reviews*, 1(1). Advance online publication. DOI: 10.1 145/nnnnnnn.nnnnnnn

Matsuzaka, Y., & Yashiro, R. (2023). AI-Based Computer Vision Techniques and Expert Systems. *AI*, 4(1), 289–302. DOI: 10.3390/ai4010013

Mian, Y., Khalid, F., Qun, A., & Ismail, S. (2022). Expert Analytics in Education, Advantages and Issues: A Systematic Literature Review. *Creative Education*, 13(9), 2913–2920. DOI: 10.4236/ce.2022.139183

Mohammed, P. S., & Watson, E. (2019). Towards Inclusive Education in the Age of Artificial Intelligence: Perspectives, Challenges, and Opportunities. *In Artificial Intelligence and Inclusive Education* (pp. 1-15). DOI: DOI: 10.1007/978-981-13-8161-4_2

Mohammed, P. S., & Watson, E. N. (2019). Towards inclusive education in the age of artificial intelligence: perspectives, challenges, and opportunities. In Knox, J., Wang, Y., & Gallagher, M. (Eds.), *Artificial Intelligence and Inclusive Education. Perspectives on Rethinking and Reforming Education*. Springer., DOI: 10.1007/978-981-13-8161-4_2

Nabella, E., Zaini, Muhammad, & Ajizah, Aulia. (2020). Development of Worksheets for High School Biology Student-Based on Critical Thinking Skills on the Circulation System Concept. *BIO-INOVED: Jurnal Biologi-Inovasi Pendidikan*. 2. 47. .DOI: 10.20527/bino.v2i1.7980

Nagori, V., & Trivedi, B., (2014). Types of Expert System. *Comparative Study Asian Journal of Computer and Information Systems*, 2(2), ISSN: 2321 – 5658.

Newell, A., & Simon, H. A. (1963). *GPS, a program that simulates human thought*, in: E.A. FEIGENBAUM, J. FELDMAN (eds.), *Computers and Thought*, McGraw-Hill, New York.

Örücü, S., & Selek, M. (2020). Design and validation of rule-based expert system by using kinect v2 for real-time athlete support. *Applied Sciences (Basel, Switzerland)*, 10(2), 1–24. DOI: 10.3390/app10020611

Pedro, F., Subosa, M., Rivas, A., & Valverde, P. (2019). *Artificial intelligence in education: Challenges and opportunities for sustainable development.* UNESCO.

Rojas, J. A., Espitia, H. E., & Bejarano, L. A. (2021). Design and Optimization of a Fuzzy Logic System for Academic Performance Prediction. *Symmetry*, 2021(13), 133. DOI: 10.3390/sym13010133

Roll, I., & Wylie, R. (2016). Evolution and revolution in artificial intelligence in education. *International Journal of Artificial Intelligence in Education*, 26(2), 582–599. DOI: 10.1007/s40593-016-0110-3

Salekhova, L., Nurgaliev, A., Zaripova, R., & Khakimullina, N. (2013). The Principles of Designing an Expert System in Teaching Mathematics. *Universal Journal of Educational Research*, 1(2), 42–47. DOI: 10.13189/ujer.2013.010202

Sekeroglu, B., Dimililer, K., & Tuncal, K. (2019). Artificial intelligence in education: application in student performance evaluation. *Dilemas Contemporáneos: Educación. Política y Valores*, 7(1), 1–21.

Shaw, M. L. G., & Gaines, B. R. (1992). The Synthesis of Knowledge Engineering and Software Engineering. In P. Loucopoulos (Ed.), Advanced Information Systems Engineering. Springer-Verlag., LNCS 593.

Shiwani, S. M., & Chaturvedi, D. K. (2021). Historical perspective of Artificial Intelligence based expert system. 44th National Systems Conference (NSC), Systems for Sustainable Healthcare Habitats (pp. 187-190). https://www.sysi.org/downloads/NSC-2021-Proceedings.pdf

Supriyanto, G., Widiaty, I., Gafar Abdullah, A., & Mupita, J. (2018). Application of expert system for education. *IOP Conference Series. Materials Science and Engineering*, 434, 012304. DOI: 10.1088/1757-899X/434/1/012304

Supriyanto, G., Widiaty, I., Gafar Abdullah, A., & Riksa Yustiana, Y. (2019). Application expert system career guidance for students. *Journal of Physics: Conference Series*, 1402(6), 066031. DOI: 10.1088/1742-6596/1402/6/066031

Tawafak, R., Alfarsi, G., & Iqbal Malik, S. (2022). An Application of Heuristic and Meta Dendral Expert System. ITM Web of Conferences. 42. 001009. DOI: 10.1051/itmconf/20224201009

Ugo, C., Ikerionwu, C., & Obi, N. (2020). Plagiarism Detection Systems. [IJSRP]. *International Journal of Scientific and Research Publications*, 10(3), 9969. DOI: 10.29322/IJSRP.10.03.2020.p9969

Valenti, S., Neri, F., & Cucchiarelli, A. (2003). An Overview of Current Research on Automated Essay Grading. *Journal of Information Technology Education*, 2(1), 319–330. DOI: 10.28945/331

Wogu, I. A. P., Misra, S., Olu-Owolabi, E. F., Assibong, P. A., & Udoh, O. D. (2018). Artificial intelligence, artificial teachers and the fate of learners in the 21st century education sector: Implications for theory and practice. *International Journal of Pure and Applied Mathematics*, 119(16), 2245–2259.

Zaporozhko, V., Shardakov, V., & Parfenov, D. (2020). Fuzzy model for evaluating the results of online learning. *IOP Conference Series. Materials Science and Engineering*, 734(1), 012150. DOI: 10.1088/1757-899X/734/1/012150

Zawacki-Richter, O., Marín, V. I., Bond, M., & Gouverneur, F. (2019). Systematic review of research on artificial intelligence applications in higher education – where are the educators? *International Journal of Educational Technology in Higher Education*, 16(1), 39. DOI: 10.1186/s41239-019-0171-0

Zhang, L., & Sun, Y. (2024). Integrating AI into biology education: Pedagogical strategies and student outcomes. *Computers & Education*, 190, 104603. DOI: 10.1016/j.compedu.2023.104603

Zirawaga, V. S., Olusanya, A. I., & Maduku, T. (2017). Gaming in Education: Using Games as a Support Tool to Teach History. Journal of Education and Practice. 8(15), ISSN 2222-1735 (Paper) ISSN 2222-288X (Online).

Chapter 8
Reshaping Assessment Horizons AI's Evolutionary Impact on Traditional Methods

C. Indu
Lovely Professional University, India

Prem Lata Gautam
Lovely Professional University, India

Mehak Malhotra
Lovely Professional University, India

Akshat Jain
Lovely Professional University, India

ABSTRACT

The incorporation of Artificial Intelligence (AI) in educational evaluation signifies a revolutionary transition from conventional techniques to automated systems driven by sophisticated algorithms. AI frees up teachers to concentrate on individualized instruction by streamlining tasks like item creation and feedback provision. Intelligent tutoring programs tailor lessons to each student's needs and increase interest by personalizing the learning process. But there are issues that need to be carefully considered, like algorithmic bias and privacy concerns. Working together, engineers, legislators, and educators can fully utilize AI's potential while reducing its perils. Continued research is necessary to improve algorithms and guarantee their effectiveness in a variety of scenarios. Beyond its immediate uses, AI-driven

DOI: 10.4018/979-8-3693-3944-2.ch008

evaluation helps to design educational policies that support critical thinking and lifetime learning, as well as evidence-based decision-making.

INTRODUCTION

In the field of education, student performance evaluations have long been a vital component of the teaching and learning process. Traditionally, assessments have mostly involved paper-based tests and manual grading, in which teachers carefully examine each student's comprehension and competency with the content. Although these techniques have proven useful over time, they are not without drawbacks. For example, manual grading is subjective and time-consuming, which might result in inconsistent evaluation results. Furthermore, conventional tests frequently lack the flexibility required to take individual requirements and a variety of learning styles into account (Darling-Hammond et al., 2010).

However, with the advent of artificial intelligence (AI) in educational evaluation in recent years, a paradigm change has taken place. With its capacity to swiftly and accurately complete complicated tasks and analyze enormous volumes of data, artificial intelligence (AI) presents a viable replacement for conventional evaluation techniques. Teachers may use AI to transform the way student performance is assessed by incorporating it into assessment processes (Siemens and Long, 2011).

The idea of using artificial intelligence (AI) in educational assessment includes a variety of cutting-edge methods and tools designed to improve the effectiveness, precision, and scalability of assessment procedures. Fundamentally, the goal of AI-driven assessment is to use automated processes and sophisticated algorithms to expedite every facet of review, from creating items to providing comments (Koedinger and Corbett, 2006).

The potential of AI-driven evaluation to offer students individualized learning experiences is one of its main benefits. Intelligent tutoring systems can assess individual learning styles and modify course materials to suit each student's specific requirements and inclinations. In addition to increasing student engagement, this individualized approach promotes mastery-based learning, which allows students to advance at their speed and get a better comprehension of the subject matter (Shaun et al., 2014).

Furthermore, by giving teachers insightful data on student performance and learning patterns, AI-driven evaluation has the power to revolutionize teaching methods. Teachers may better adjust their educational tactics by gaining a deeper knowledge of their students' strengths and shortcomings by analyzing the data supplied by AI-powered exams. There are certain difficulties with using AI in educational evaluation, though. AI systems must prioritize inclusion, openness, and justice by carefully addressing ethical aspects such as algorithmic bias and privacy concerns. Furthermore, to fully explore AI's potential in assessment and minimize any unforeseen repercussions, research and development must continue (Jandrić, 2017; Aydın, 2024; Heffernan and Heffernan, 2014).

We will go into great depth on the ways that artificial intelligence is changing the face of educational assessment in this chapter. We will look at the educational effects, ethical issues, and practical implications of AI-driven assessment based on theoretical frameworks and empirical study findings. In the end, we will offer insights into how researchers, educators, administrators, and tech developers might use AI to improve student assessment while maintaining the values of equality and justice (Anderson et al., 1995).

PARADIGM SHIFT

How student performance is assessed has undergone a significant paradigm change with the introduction of Artificial Intelligence (AI) into educational evaluation. Significant modifications to traditional assessment methods characterize this transition, especially when compared to manual grading procedures and paper-based tests of the past (Shute and Zapata-Rivera, 2012).

The approach to accuracy and efficiency that AI-driven evaluation takes sets it apart from conventional techniques in several important ways. The administration, delivery, and scoring of traditional paper-based tests can take a significant amount of time and money. Teachers have to create, print, and distribute test materials. They also have to personally mark each student's response, which may take a lot of time and effort. By automating certain duties, AI-driven evaluation, on the other hand, simplifies these processes. By creating test items, administering tests online, and promptly analyzing student replies, AI systems can lighten the workload of teachers and provide students feedback more quickly (Flogie and Aberšek, 2022).

Furthermore, a degree of scalability that is difficult to accomplish with traditional approaches is provided by AI-driven evaluation. Teachers are constrained by things like physical space, printing expenses, and time limits when administering traditional paper-based examinations. On the other hand, AI-powered evaluation systems can handle more students at once and offer immediate feedback to every student, wherever they may be. Teachers may evaluate student performance more effectively and efficiently because of its scalability, especially in large or online learning contexts (Zheng and Zheng, 2021).

The capacity of AI-driven assessment to offer individualized learning experiences sets it apart from conventional techniques in a big way. A one-size-fits-all method of assessment is usually provided via traditional paper-based exams, where every student is given the same set of questions and grading standards. AI-driven evaluation systems, on the other hand, can adjust to the unique demands and preferences of each learner. Real-time analysis of student replies by intelligent algorithms can pinpoint areas of strength and weakness and adjust future questions or lesson plans appropriately. In addition to increasing student engagement, this individualized approach promotes mastery-based learning, which allows students to advance at their speed and get a better comprehension of the subject matter (D'Mello and Graesser, 2012).

Additionally, instructors may gain important insights about student performance and learning trends using AI-driven assessment tools. Beyond a grade or score, traditional methods of evaluation frequently yield little information about students' knowledge. In contrast, educators may recognize patterns, trends, and areas for development with the help of comprehensive data and reports generated by AI-driven assessment tools. Teachers may make well-informed judgments regarding curriculum design, individualized interventions, and instructional tactics to assist student learning by analyzing this data. The use of artificial intelligence (AI) in educational evaluation signifies a noteworthy divergence from conventional approaches, providing enhancements in efficacy, precision, expandability, and customization. Artificial intelligence driven assessment systems have the power to revolutionize the way student performance is assessed and eventually improve the learning process for both students and teachers by automating activities, giving immediate feedback, and creating personalized learning experiences (Anderson et al., 1995).

EFFICIENCY, ACCURACY, AND SCALABILITY

The use of Artificial Intelligence (AI) in educational evaluation processes yields several benefits, such as increased efficacy, precision, and expandability. These enhancements represent a substantial shift from conventional evaluation techniques, providing teachers and students with a more efficient and successful means of assessing performance (Siemens and Long, 2011).

First of all, AI helps to make the evaluation process more efficient. Conventional approaches frequently entail laborious chores, including creating, producing, and distributing test materials in addition to manually scoring student answers. Conversely, a lot of these jobs are automated by AI, which saves teachers a ton of time and money. For instance, AI systems may produce test questions based on preset standards, saving teachers from having to start from scratch when creating questions. In addition to shortening the assessment period, this automated item production procedure guarantees uniformity in exam item difficulty and relevancy (Shute and Zapata-Rivera, 2012).

Furthermore, AI makes evaluation results more accurate. Human errors can occur during manual grading procedures, which might provide inconsistent evaluation findings. Assessment systems can more accurately and impartially evaluate student replies by utilizing AI algorithms, which lowers the possibility of inconsistent grades. AI-powered systems, for example, can use natural language processing methods to evaluate written answers and grade them according to predetermined standards. In addition to increasing the accuracy of assessment results, this computerized grading procedure gives pupils more precise performance feedback (Shaun et al., 2014).

In addition, AI-powered evaluation systems have unmatched scalability, supporting several students at once and giving each one immediate feedback. Physical space, printing expenses, and time constraints are only a few of the constraints that sometimes impede traditional paper-based tests. On the other hand, tests can be given online using AI-enabled assessment platforms, enabling students to finish them from any internet-connected place. In online learning contexts, where teachers may need to evaluate a sizable student cohort asynchronously, this scalability is very helpful. Furthermore, real-time assessment data analysis by AI algorithms may produce comprehensive reports and insights into patterns in student performance. These analytics provide teachers the ability to pinpoint areas in which they need to improve and modify their lesson plans to better suit the varied requirements of their pupils (Koedinger and Corbett, 2006).

There are several benefits to incorporating AI into educational assessment processes, such as increased scalability, accuracy, and efficiency. Artificial intelligence (AI)-driven assessment tools simplify the assessment process and give teachers and students insightful performance data by automating operations like item creation, grading, and feedback supply. These developments mark a substantial improvement in educational evaluation, empowering teachers to choose teaching and learning tactics with greater knowledge and improving students' overall educational experiences (Su et al., 2023).

Pedagogical Implications

Artificial intelligence (AI) has the potential to significantly alter teaching and learning practices through its incorporation into evaluation procedures in the educational system. AI-driven assessment contributes to a more efficient and student-centered learning environment by promoting personalized learning experiences, improving teaching strategies, and supporting mastery-based learning (Koedinger and Corbett, 2006).

To begin with, AI-driven assessment enables customized learning experiences by modifying course materials to suit every student's unique requirements and preferences. To provide individualized interventions and assistance, intelligent algorithms evaluate student performance data to pinpoint areas of strength and weakness. Adaptive learning systems, for instance, employ AI to dynamically modify the degree of difficulty and speed of learning activities according to students' proven competency levels. In addition to improving student engagement, this individualized approach promotes greater comprehension and retention of the material (Siemens and Long, 2011).

Additionally, AI-driven assessment improves education by giving teachers insightful data about student learning styles and the efficacy of their lessons. Teachers can better understand their students' learning requirements and modify their teaching tactics by analyzing the data produced by AI-powered exams. For example, learning analytics dashboards give teachers access to up-to-date data on student achievement, enabling them to spot problematic pupils and provide individualized guidance. Furthermore, recommendation systems driven by AI make relevant recommendations for learning materials and activities based on the learning profiles of students, assisting teachers in creating more interesting and productive learning environments (Flogie and Aberšek, 2022).

Additionally, mastery-based learning—where students are encouraged to advance at their speed and develop a thorough comprehension of the subject matter—is supported by AI-driven evaluation. Specifically, intelligent tutoring systems are essential in this area since they offer personalized, adaptive training based on each student's distinctive learning path. These systems scaffold learning activities to build upon existing knowledge, give prompt feedback on students' replies, and, when needed, offer focused remediation. AI-driven assessment encourages a mastery-oriented approach to learning, which gives students the confidence to take charge of their education and pursue ongoing development (Anderson et al., 1995).

There are several pedagogical benefits to AI-driven assessment, including improved teaching strategies, individualized learning opportunities, and support for mastery-based learning. Realizing these advances is largely dependent on intelligent tutoring systems driven by artificial intelligence (AI), which offers customized, adaptive training tailored to each student's unique needs. Deep knowledge and lifelong learning may be fostered in more effective, engaging, and student-centered learning environments that educators can develop as they continue to use AI technology in assessment processes (D'Mello and Graesser, 2012).

Ethical Considerations

There are several practical challenges, ethical concerns, and pedagogical implications associated with integrating Artificial Intelligence (AI) into educational assessment processes that need to be carefully considered. Firstly, algorithmic bias is a major issue, as AI systems may unintentionally reinforce or magnify biases that are already present in the training data. For instance, if past assessment data disproportionately favors certain demographic groups, AI-driven assessment systems may unintentionally disadvantage students from underrepresented backgrounds. Secondly, this raises questions about fairness and equity related to educational assessment (Su et al., 2023).

Students' data, including their performance metrics and learning behaviors, must be handled with the utmost care to protect their privacy rights. Teachers and technology developers must implement strong data protection measures and adhere to strict privacy regulations to safeguard student confidentiality. Privacy consequences are another important factor to take into account when using AI-driven assessment. As these systems collect and analyze vast amounts of student data, there is a risk of privacy breaches and unauthorized access to sensitive information (Végh and Gubo, 2022).

Equity concerns can also surface in AI-driven assessment if some students are disadvantaged because they do not have access to technology or do not possess digital literacy skills. Students from low-income socioeconomic backgrounds or those living in rural areas might not have the resources to fully participate in online assessments, which could result in differences in educational outcomes. Proactive measures to guarantee equal access to technology and support for all students are needed to address these equity concerns. Beyond its practical challenges and ethical implications, AI-driven assessment has pedagogical ramifications as well. An overreliance on AI systems could result in a loss of human judgment and teacher-student interactions during the assessment process. Although AI algorithms can automate certain tasks and offer valuable insights, they should be used in conjunction with human judgment in educational assessment, with educators playing a crucial role in the interpretation of assessment data, the provision of contextualized feedback, and the creation of meaningful learning experiences for students (Huang et al., 2021).

Prioritizing inclusion, openness, and justice in AI-driven evaluation procedures is essential for tackling these issues. By putting techniques like varied training data, algorithmic audits, and bias detection tools into practice, educators and software developers may actively reduce algorithmic prejudice. For stakeholders to develop confidence and trust in AI-driven evaluation systems, transparency in their development and application is crucial. Education professionals may encourage accountability and guarantee fairness in the assessment process by being transparent about the workings of AI algorithms and the assessment criteria (Diakopoulos, 2016).

AI-driven assessment in the classroom has pedagogical ramifications, practical challenges, and ethical issues that need to be carefully considered. To preserve the values of inclusion, openness, and fairness, challenges like algorithmic bias, privacy ramifications, and equity concerns need to be addressed. It is the joint duty of educators and tech developers to carefully and morally handle these issues, making sure that AI-driven assessment procedures provide fair and fulfilling learning opportunities for every student (Jandrić, 2017).

Suggestion for Stakeholders

A variety of stakeholders, including educators, policymakers, and technology developers, must work together and give serious thought to how to integrate artificial intelligence (AI) into educational evaluation. To guarantee the moral use of AI and advance its effectiveness in evaluation procedures, the following useful recommendations are provided:

For Educators:

- **Ongoing Professional Development:** To become acquainted with AI-driven assessment tools and procedures, educators can take advantage of continuing professional development opportunities and training. They will be able to successfully incorporate AI into their lessons while upholding pedagogical integrity thanks to this (Darling-Hammond and Richardson, 2009).
- **Critical Assessment of AI Systems:** To make sure AI-driven assessment tools support learning objectives and core values, educators should conduct a critical assessment of these tools. They ought to evaluate the fairness, validity, and dependability of AI algorithms, as well as how these systems affect the educational experiences of their students (Holmes et al., 2023).
- **Human Oversight and Interpretation:** Teachers should continue to play a major part in the assessment process even when AI technologies can automate some assessment chores. They ought to evaluate assessment results, offer contextualized comments, and make defensible judgments by fusing their professional knowledge with AI-generated insights (Hilton and Pellegrino, 2012).

For Legislators:

- **Regulatory Frameworks:** To ensure the ethical application of AI in educational evaluation, legislators should create and execute regulatory frameworks. These frameworks have to cover topics like algorithmic bias, data privacy, and equality to guarantee that AI-driven evaluation procedures respect the values of justice and openness (Pasquale, 2015).
- **Data Protection Laws:** To preserve students' privacy rights in AI-driven assessments, legislators should pass strong data protection legislation. These regulations should include procedures for accountability and enforcement in

addition to providing explicit standards for the gathering, storing, and use of student data (Végh and Gubo, 2022).
- **Ethical Standards and Guidelines:** To create ethical standards and guidelines for the use of AI in assessment, legislators should collaborate with stakeholders in education. These guidelines ought to support ethical AI techniques and offer direction for resolving issues with bias, accountability, and transparency (Holmes and Miao, 2023).

For Technology Developers:

- **Bias Detection and Mitigation:** When creating AI-driven evaluation systems, technology developers should incorporate bias detection and mitigation strategies. To provide fair and equal assessment results for every student, they should carry out comprehensive audits of AI algorithms to locate and resolve any potential sources of bias (Mittelstadt et al., 2016).
- **Transparency and Explainability:** When designing and implementing AI-driven evaluation systems, technology developers should give priority to transparency and explainability. To help teachers and students comprehend and have faith in the technology, they had to offer detailed documentation on the operation of AI algorithms, the data sources utilized for training, and the evaluation standards (Selwyn, 2019).
- **User-Centered Design:** Educators and students should be included in the development process by technology developers using a user-centered design approach. To better understand end users' wants, preferences, and concerns, they should ask for input from them. Then, using this feedback, they should iteratively improve AI-driven evaluation tools (Jandrić, 2017).

Teachers, policymakers, and tech developers must work together and take the initiative to successfully integrate AI into educational evaluation. Through adherence to these pragmatic recommendations and prioritization of ethical issues, stakeholders may effectively negotiate the intricacies of AI-driven assessment, guaranteeing effectiveness and fostering favorable educational consequences for every student.

Application and Difficulties

Artificial intelligence (AI) has enormous potential to change educational methods and enhance student results when it is included in assessment procedures. Its potential is accompanied, yet, by several difficulties and restrictions that need to be properly taken into account (Kengam, 2020).

The use of automated grading systems for objective assessments, such as multiple-choice questions or short-answer replies, is one prominent application of artificial intelligence in assessment. These systems analyze and assess student responses using natural language processing algorithms, giving teachers and students immediate feedback. For instance, grading systems like Gradescope and Turnitin use AI to speed up the process, saving teachers a great deal of time and giving students feedback sooner (Romero and Ventura, 2010).

Furthermore, personalized assessment experiences catered to each student's requirements and learning trajectory are provided via AI-powered adaptive learning systems. Based on students' learning preferences, skills, and weaknesses, these systems constantly modify the instructional content by analyzing student performance data using machine learning algorithms. To encourage deeper engagement and mastery-based learning, adaptive learning systems such as DreamBox and Knewton, for example, offer personalized learning pathways that adjust in real time to students' progress (Koedinger and Corbett, 2006).

But in addition to their potential advantages, AI-driven evaluation systems have several drawbacks. The possibility of algorithmic bias, in which AI systems unintentionally reinforce or magnify preexisting prejudices found in the training data, is a major challenge. AI-driven evaluation systems may inadvertently penalize students from underrepresented backgrounds, for example, if past assessment data disproportionately benefits particular demographic groups. This would result in unfair outcomes. Additionally, it is still a concern to guarantee the validity and reliability of assessment results driven by AI. To guarantee the accuracy and impartiality of assessment results human oversight and validation are still necessary, even though AI algorithms are capable of processing vast amounts of data and carrying out intricate tasks quickly and precisely. To provide comprehensive assessments of students' learning, educators need to critically assess the efficacy of AI-driven assessment tools and take into account their limitations (Miller, 2019).

Although there are obstacles to overcome, several case studies demonstrate the potential benefits of AI-driven assessment tools in educational environments. For instance, a Stanford University study found that AI-driven grading systems for short-answer responses showed similar accuracy to human graders, especially in subjects like computer science and mathematics. Similarly, adaptive learning platforms, such as Carnegie Learning's MATHia, have been demonstrated to significantly improve student performance and engagement in mathematics education. To sum up, the use of artificial intelligence (AI) in educational evaluation procedures has a plethora of possible uses for enhancing effectiveness, customization, and student achievements. However, to guarantee the moral and efficient application of AI-driven evaluation tools, issues like algorithmic bias, validity, and dependability must be properly addressed. Teachers and legislators may gain a better understanding of the potential and constraints of artificial intelligence (AI) in assessment and make well-informed judgments on its application in educational settings by critically analyzing case studies and real-world examples of AI technologies in use (Stein et al., 1999).

Implications for Practice and Policy

The use of artificial intelligence (AI) for evaluation in education has important ramifications for educational policy and practice. AI technologies have the potential to have a significant impact on curriculum design, assessment policies, and teaching strategies as they become more widely used in assessment procedures. First of all, by fostering individualized learning experiences and bolstering mastery-based learning, the integration of AI in assessment has the potential to transform instructional strategies. Large volumes of student data may be analyzed by AI-driven evaluation systems to determine each student's unique learning preferences and needs, allowing teachers to adjust their lesson plans. For instance, AI-powered adaptive learning platforms may dynamically modify the curriculum in response to student performance, offering focused assistance and enrichment activities. In addition to increasing student engagement, this individualized approach gives teachers the confidence to accommodate a range of learning styles and skill levels in the classroom (Koedinger and Corbett, 2006).

Additionally, by encouraging the creation of competency-based education models, the use of AI in assessment may affect curriculum design. AI-driven assessment systems enable teachers to create curricular pathways that prioritize the development and application of skills by measuring students' knowledge of certain learning objectives and competencies. With the emphasis now being placed on competence demonstration rather than seat time, competency-based education allows students to advance at their speed and reach higher levels of comprehension (Darling-Hammond and Ifill-Lynch, 2006).

A push towards integrating AI-driven assessment tools into standardized testing frameworks may result from educators and policymakers realizing the potential of AI to expedite assessment processes and enhance the reliability of assessment outcomes. For instance, AI-powered proctoring systems can monitor students during online exams to prevent cheating and ensure test integrity, which could lead to changes in assessment policies regarding test administration and security protocols. Moreover, the adoption of AI in assessment is likely to influence assessment policies at the institutional and governmental levels (Berland et al., 2014).

AI in assessment does offer certain advantages, but there are drawbacks as well that need to be taken into account when developing educational practices and policies. AI-driven evaluation procedures must carefully manage ethical issues about algorithmic bias, data privacy, and equity to respect the values of justice and openness. To reduce the possibility of biases and inequities in educational results, educators and legislators should give inclusiveness and equality priority when developing and deploying AI-driven evaluation systems (Siemens and Gasevic, 2012)

There are a variety of wider ramifications of AI in assessment for educational practice and policy. While AI technologies present chances to improve curriculum design, assessment procedures, and teaching strategies, they also present ethical issues and obstacles that need to be taken into account. Through cautious maneuvering through these ramifications and giving ethical values priority, educators and legislators may leverage AI's promise to revolutionize assessment procedures and enhance learning results for every student (West, 2018).

CONCLUSION

An important turning point in the evolution of evaluation methods is the incorporation of Artificial Intelligence (AI) into educational assessment, which ushers in a new era of efficiency, accuracy, and scalability. This chapter has examined the various ways that artificial intelligence (AI) might impact assessment procedures, including how it could change curriculum design, teaching strategies, and assessment guidelines (Means, 2020).

The revolutionary influence of AI on teaching methods—especially in advancing personalized learning experiences and bolstering mastery-based learning—is one of the main topics covered. With the use of AI-driven assessment technologies, teachers may successfully address a variety of learning styles and increase student engagement by customizing their lesson plans to each student's requirements and preferences. Furthermore, by gauging students' knowledge of certain learning objectives and competencies, AI supports competency-based education models, allowing teachers to create curricular pathways that emphasize the development and application of skills (Berland et al., 2014).

Additionally, assessment policies at the institutional and governmental levels are impacted by the incorporation of AI into assessment procedures. The possibility of AI to expedite assessment procedures and enhance the dependability of assessment results is becoming more and more apparent to educators and legislators. AI-powered proctoring systems, for instance, may keep an eye on students taking online tests to stop cheating and guarantee test integrity. This might result in modifications to assessment regulations concerning test administration and security procedures (West, 2018).

But in addition to the advantages that AI in evaluation offers, some issues and problems need to be taken into account. It is important to carefully navigate the ethical issues of algorithmic bias, data privacy, and equality to make sure that AI-driven evaluation procedures maintain the values of justice and openness. To reduce the possibility of biases and inequities in educational results, educators and legislators should give inclusiveness and equality priority when developing and deploying AI-driven evaluation systems (Siemens and Gasevic, 2012).

It is clear from considering the significant turning point in the evolution of assessment methods that the use of AI in educational assessment signifies a paradigm change. There are unmatched prospects to improve the efficacy, accuracy, and scalability of assessment procedures with AI-driven assessment. AI-driven assessment technologies let teachers make data-driven decisions and enhance learning outcomes for every student by automating activities, giving immediate feedback, and facilitating personalized learning experiences. In general, there are significant ramifications for educational practice and policy from the use of AI in educational evaluation. Teachers and legislators need to take advantage of AI's benefits as well as the ethical issues and practical difficulties that come with implementing this technology as it continues to progress. We can establish more efficient, fair, and student-centered learning environments that equip students for success in the twenty-first century by using the revolutionary potential of AI-driven assessment (Koedinger and Corbett, 2006).

FUTURE DIRECTIONS

In terms of future developments, AI-driven evaluation seems promising for ongoing innovation and practice transformation in education. The future of educational evaluation is expected to be shaped by emerging technology and research areas, but there may also be obstacles that need to be overcome.

An important development in AI-driven assessment is the growing use of adaptive learning tools. These systems use AI algorithms to dynamically modify the curriculum according to the demands and performance of the students. We anticipate seeing further developments in adaptive learning systems in the future, along with improved personalization and customization features. Furthermore, advancements in assessment efficiency and accuracy will be fueled by research on adaptive assessment techniques such as dynamic item production and adaptive testing algorithms.

The use of multimodal data sources in AI-driven evaluation is another new trend. Additional data sources for evaluating student involvement, attention, and emotional states are being investigated, including technologies like voice recognition, facial identification, and eye tracking. Assessment systems that use these multimodal data streams may be able to offer more comprehensive evaluations of student performance by offering deeper insights into the learning processes and behaviors of students.

Furthermore, improvements in natural language processing (NLP) methods for text analysis and automated essay grading are probably in store for the future of AI-driven evaluation. Written replies can be analyzed by NLP algorithms, which can offer comments on their grammar, coherence, and relevance to the material. We should expect more accuracy and dependability in automated grading systems as NLP technologies advance, which will lighten the load on teachers and give students feedback more quickly.

Notwithstanding these developments, several possible obstacles might influence how AI-driven evaluation develops in the future. Ensuring the ethical application of AI technology is a difficulty, especially when dealing with algorithmic bias and data privacy concerns. Clear moral standards and legal frameworks are required to control the creation and application of AI-driven evaluation systems as they proliferate.

Furthermore, worries regarding the dehumanization of education and the loss of human judgment in the evaluation process may arise from the assessment process's growing dependence on AI. Teachers need to find a way to use AI tools to improve productivity and effectiveness without sacrificing the human component of instruction.

Furthermore, the spread of AI-driven evaluation systems has the potential to worsen already-existing educational disparities, especially for pupils from underprivileged or marginalized areas. To promote justice and inclusion in educational assessment, it is imperative to solve major obstacles such as ensuring equal access to AI-driven assessment tools and tackling digital literacy and technological infrastructure concerns.

Future developments in multimodal assessment, automated grading systems, and personalized learning are all promising for AI-driven evaluation. However achieving the full potential of AI in educational evaluation would need tackling issues with equality, human judgment, and ethics. Educators and legislators may leverage artificial intelligence (AI) to develop more efficient, fair, and student-centered assessment procedures by keeping an eye out for new developments and taking proactive measures to overcome obstacles.

REFERENCES

Anderson, J. R., Corbett, A. T., Koedinger, K. R., & Pelletier, R. (1995). Cognitive tutors: Lessons learned. *Journal of the Learning Sciences*, 4(2), 167–207. DOI: 10.1207/s15327809jls0402_2

Aydın, İ. N. A. Y. E. T. (2024). Eğitim Teknolojisinde Etik Sorunlar. *Kastamonu Eğitim Dergisi*, 32(2).

Berland, M., Baker, R. S., & Blikstein, P. (2014). Educational data mining and learning analytics: Applications to constructionist research. Technology. *Knowledge and Learning*, 19(1-2), 205–220. DOI: 10.1007/s10758-014-9223-7

D'Mello, S., & Graesser, A. (2012). Dynamics of affective states during complex learning. *Learning and Instruction*, 22(2), 145–157. DOI: 10.1016/j.learninstruc.2011.10.001

Darling-Hammond, L., Adamson, F., & Abedi, J. (2010). *Beyond basic skills: The role of performance assessment in achieving 21st century standards of learning*. Stanford Center for Opportunity Pollcy in Education.

Darling-Hammond, L., & Ifill-Lynch, O. (2006). If They'd Only Do Their Work! *Educational Leadership*, 63(5), 8–13.

Darling-Hammond, L., & Richardson, N. (2009). Research review/teacher learning: What matters. *Educational Leadership*, 66(5), 46–53.

Diakopoulos, N. (2016). Accountability in algorithmic decision making. *Communications of the ACM*, 59(2), 56–62. DOI: 10.1145/2844110

Flogie, A., & Aberšek, B. (2022). *Artificial intelligence in education*. Active Learning-Theory and Practice.

Heffernan, N. T., & Heffernan, C. L. (2014). The ASSISTments ecosystem: Building a platform that brings scientists and teachers together for minimally invasive research on human learning and teaching. *International Journal of Artificial Intelligence in Education*, 24(4), 470–497. DOI: 10.1007/s40593-014-0024-x

Hilton, M. L., & Pellegrino, J. W. (Eds.). (2012). *Education for life and work: Developing transferable knowledge and skills in the 21st century*. National Academies Press.

Holmes, W., Bialik, M., & Fadel, C. (2023). *Artificial intelligence in education*. Globethics Publications.

Holmes, W., & Miao, F. (2023). *Guidance for generative AI in education and research*. UNESCO Publishing.

Huang, J., Saleh, S., & Liu, Y. (2021). A review on artificial intelligence in education. *Academic Journal of Interdisciplinary Studies*, 10(3).

Jandrić, P. (2017). *Learning in the age of digital reason*. Springer. DOI: 10.1007/978-94-6351-077-6

Kengam, J. (2020). Artificial intelligence in education. *Research Gate*, 18, 1–4.

Koedinger, K. R., & Corbett, A. (2006). Cognitive tutors: Technology bringing learning sciences to the classroom. na.

Means, B. (2020). Learning Online; What research tells us about whether, when wnd how.

Miller, T. (2019). Explanation in artificial intelligence: Insights from the social sciences. *Artificial Intelligence*, 267, 1–38. DOI: 10.1016/j.artint.2018.07.007

Mittelstadt, B. D., Allo, P., Taddeo, M., Wachter, S., & Floridi, L. (2016). The ethics of algorithms: Mapping the debate. *Big Data & Society*, 3(2), 2053951716679679. DOI: 10.1177/2053951716679679

Pasquale, F. (2015). *The black box society: The secret algorithms that control money and information*. Harvard University Press. DOI: 10.4159/harvard.9780674736061

Romero, C., & Ventura, S. (2010). Educational data mining: A review of the state of the art. IEEE Transactions on Systems, Man, and Cybernetics [applications and reviews]. *Part C*, 40(6), 601–618.

Selwyn, N. (2019). What's the problem with learning analytics? *Journal of Learning Analytics*, 6(3), 11–19. DOI: 10.18608/jla.2019.63.3

Shaun, R., De Baker, J., & Inventado, P. S. (2014). *Educational Data Mining and Learning Analytics*.

Shute, V. J., & Zapata-Rivera, D. (2012). Adaptive educational systems. *Adaptive technologies for training and education*, 7(27), (pp.1-35).

Siemens, G., & Gasevic, D. (2012). Guest editorial-learning and knowledge analytics. *Journal of Educational Technology & Society*, 15(3), 1–2.

Siemens, G., & Long, P. (2011). Penetrating the fog: Analytics in learning and education. *EDUCAUSE Review*, 46(5), 30.

Stein, M. K., Smith, M. S., & Silver, E. (1999). The development of professional developers: Learning to assist teachers in new settings in new ways. *Harvard Educational Review*, 69(3), 237–270. DOI: 10.17763/haer.69.3.h2267130727v6878

Su, J., Ng, D. T. K., & Chu, S. K. W. (2023). Artificial intelligence (AI) literacy in early childhood education: The challenges and opportunities. *Computers and Education: Artificial Intelligence*, 4, 100124. DOI: 10.1016/j.caeai.2023.100124

Végh, L., & Gubo, Š. (2022). Assessment of Algorithmic and Logical Thinking of First-and Second-Year Computer Science Students at J. Selye University in Academic Years 2019/20 and 2021/22. In *ICERI2022 Proceedings* (pp. 1888-1895IATED.

West, D. M. (2018). *The future of work: Robots, AI, and automation*. Brookings Institution Press.

Zheng, L., & Zheng, L. (2021). Learning analytics for computer-supported collaborative learning design. *Data-driven design for computer-supported collaborative learning: Design matters*, (pp.31-43).

Chapter 9
Machine Learning Integration to Analyze Student Behavior in an Online Digital Learning System

Somdeep Das
Management Development Institute, Murshidabad, India

Pinaki Pratim Acharjya
 https://orcid.org/0000-0002-0305-2661
Haldia Institute of Technology, India

ABSTRACT

This chapter highlights the various means of digital learning systems, its impact on the school level students of various age groups, the psychology of learning and its behavioral impact on their outcome, and Prognostic Analysis of the behavior on the ISCED level 1 students. This chapter also put forth the significance of not only establishing the technological transformation as a 'change' of Education System, but also carefully designing a holistic learning environment for future, specifically the cognitive and emotional engagement of students of the age group ranging from 6-12 years whose behavioral aspects varies with their varied levels of education.

DOI: 10.4018/979-8-3693-3944-2.ch009

1. INTRODUCTION

In recent times technology has transformed the education system, the way students learn, and the teachers teach. The online digital learning system (ODLS) is the trend which is evolving rapidly over the traditional learning systems. The success of digital learning system, which is enhanced and powered by technology relies on the digital interfaces/platforms, the availability of internet connectivity, internet-enabled devices, and the readiness of learners and teachers.

Online teaching and online delivery of courses have become the main advantages of ODLS as it is leading to a revolution by exposing the world-class education system to the students. Unlike traditional systems, instead of physical classrooms, virtual classrooms make the platform for teaching and learning environment. Virtual classrooms provide flexibility which is beyond time and space. As a result, majority of students can register themselves in these online curriculums (Hussian et al., 2018). Through the integrated software portals, students can track their performance and interact with their teachers. In a similar way the parents can also track the performance, behavior, and attendance of their wards and interact with their teachers. The online pedagogical system provides a significant paradigm shift in the education system and has brought students, parents, and teachers together at one platform.

1.1 Key Users of Digital Platform: Teachers From Kindergarten to ISCED Level-3, College Professors and Students, and Tutors

The digital interface/ platform: Digital learning platforms provides an interactive interface for students to explore lesson content in virtual environment facilitated by digital equipment. Here, digital equipment can refer to software applications and devices both. These platforms essentially leverage lessons with significantly amalgamate with multimedia contents, videos, animations, photos, and audio recordings. These platforms provide self-evaluation basis learning which further enables students with an opportunity to do and redo their activity to achieve excellence. Digital learning platforms have the potential to be an effective learning tool for students at many levels of education. Hence the key benefits of these interfaces can be summarized as:

- Multimedia learning experiences for students
- Differentiate instruction automatically based on student ability
- Self-evaluation of students' progress
- Virtual xercises
- No barrier of a physical Classroom
- Student-Teacher-Parent involvement

- Cheaper

Digital Learning Platforms integrating with Software and Services like various management and information systems along with document creation software builds a robust online environment for learning. LMSs (Learning Management Systems) work with other educational platforms, like SISs (Student Information Systems) and other document creation software which further provide the virtual learning environment for students and teachers. While SISs digitally maintain the documentation part of the student information, LMS performs the dissemination of the courses through the online platform (Villagrá-Arnedo et al., 2016; Hussain et al., 2019) Whereas Document creation software enable instructors to create their own lessons often allow the user to upload files from document creation software.

Figure 1. Shows Digital Interface integrated with software and services in an Online Environment

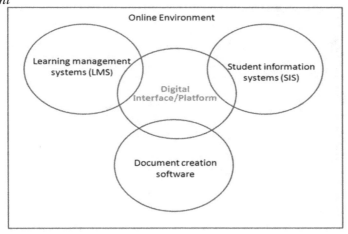

The education progression has been immensely transformed by the advent of innovative digital tools, applications, and devices. In the learner's perspective the evolution of ed-tech sector has made the delivery process to be accessed from everyplace and anytime. These ed-tech sectors are more engaging, entertaining and exploring. With the arrival of 4G internet at affordable rates, and affordable Smartphone access to technology to retrieve course content has profoundly impacted the online digital courses. The leading population of new learners are accessing the internet from their Smartphone which is a perfect, customized and business empowered stage for online training. Further, various online Education Technology applications (Edtech), Massive Open Online Courses (MOOCs) (Hussain et al., 2019; Bonafini et al., 2017), Web based education platforms, and cloud-based communication platforms can be easily accessible on Smart phones besides tablets and laptops. The interpretation of statistic (*Forecast number of smartphone connections in 2025, by country,* 2019) shows that China has more than 850 million users of smartphones as represented in (Fig.2) and which is more than any nation in the world. In terms of more users of smartphones, India stands second in the ranking, but not exactly half the same number of as China. The figure (Fig.3) shows the year wise growth of smartphone users by country.

Figure 2. Shows high and increasing Smartphone penetration

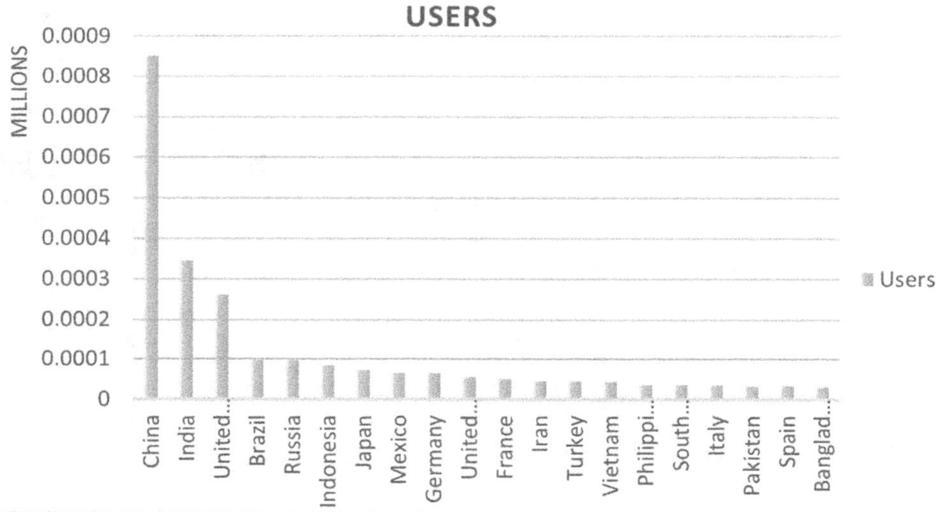

Figure 3. Shows year wise increase in Smartphone users

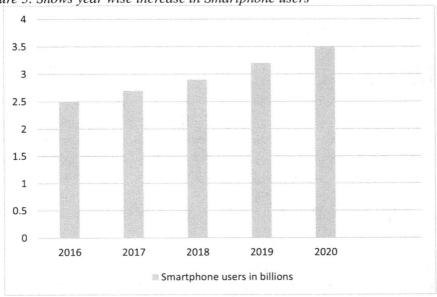

The significance and popularity of ODLS can be visualized in two phases, first Pre- Covid19 and post Covid19 outbreak. Before the pandemic hit the global scenario resulting in shutdown of schools, colleges and Universities to contain the outbreak of Covid19, ODLS was gaining pace and popularity for self-motivated learners, executive learners and tertiary education level students for honing skills in specific courses. Whereas Digital Learning Systems like Smart Classroom, Flipped Classroom (Cheng et al., 2018), Use of Video etc. were moderately popular in primary and secondary level schools.

Post Covid19, the scenario has changed. ODLS has become a necessity for students from Primary level education to professional level learning. The traditional physical classroom curriculums are converted into online courses, and virtual classroom solutions to allow millions of students to continue learning from their homes. Online education is transforming the domain of education, connecting students to global learning platforms, and making learning more dynamic. Apart from this, few decisive factors affecting the students were also observed in online learning like motivational factors to learn, factors related to the learning platform/ interface and the factors related to the new teaching and learning procedures (Bahati et al., 2017) Different cloud based online platform like Zoom, Webex and so forth integrated with LMS like open source learning management frameworks like Moodle are developing as virtual learning foundation of ODLS, though Google classroom (*Remote*

Learning During COVID-19: Lessons from Today, Principles for Tomorrow, n.d.) itself facilitates the services of online learning management system.

Increasing internet penetration, time constraints faced by students, geographical challenges in attending physical classes, and the low expense involved in online training are the primary drivers of the digital learning sector. Going forward, there would be a convergence of digital and physical worlds, as the internet becomes more flexible and accessible to everyone.

In the backdrop of Covid-19, while these ODLS are gaining popularity, certain challenges are also associated with online learning systems (Hussain et al., 2018; 2019) as there is no direct communication between student and teacher. Dearth of student motivation and related concern in various course activities and course information makes the most critical challenges of this learning environment. With the emergence of internet-based learning platforms it has become easier to monitor student performance by the teachers. The log data can be used to study and analyze the performances of students. Learning Management Systems (LMSs), Massive Open Online Courses (MOOC), and Digital Electronics Education and Design Suite (DEEDS) (Hussain et al., 2018) are some of the most looked after web-based learning platforms. Albeit various models were verified based on MOOC, most of them covered only the behavioral aspect of learning engagement, as opposed to the multidimensional parts of association in learning (Jung and Lee, 2018). However, research has shown that there is an interrelation among educational data mining, psychology, and education. It has established that students' active involvement and approach considerably impact learning (Käser et al., 2017).

Many studies are carried out to predict the students' performance in their conduct in the classroom. Unlike (Bahati et al., 2017), this states that the strength of relationship between student engagement and their respective performance in online courses is positive but weakly related. Predictive analytics helps instructors to monitor students' behavior in terms of utilization level of course contents and student's evaluation scores as they are directly associated with student's involvement level (Hussain et al., 2019). On the other hand, analytics facilitates the students by providing them with suitable suggestions and solutions to enhance the learning performance by collecting data and further analyzing the collected data (Hussain et al., 2019; Leitner et al., 2017).

In this research a variety of machine learning algorithms are used for prognostic analysis of the student's behavior under certain conditions and building the model. The presented study focuses on building a machine learning model to comprehend the student's behavior and classification under ODLS.

The works related to the use of Machine Learning is to help the teacher to generate better models and learning methodologies applied in the online digital learning environments. The analysis result allows the teachers to avail preemptive solutions for their teaching approaches towards the students. Various LMSs are facilitating in capturing this data for the teachers.

2. BACKGROUND STUDY

To understand the impact of ODLS on the behavior of school level students we need to first classify the various age groups of students ranging from 6-18 years old in an Internationally recognized standard and then we need to understand the psychological aspects of those classified age groups with respect to their memory processes, cognitive development and maturity levels. After classifying the different age group levels, prognostic analysis can be done on each of them using Supervised Algorithm to understand the psychological behavior towards ODLS and the behavioral impact on their performance.

2.1. International Classification of Education Levels

ISCED is intended to fill in as a system to categorize educational activity as characterized in curriculum and the subsequent capabilities into universally concurred classifications. The fundamental ideas and meanings of ISCED are in this manner expected to be universally substantial and complete of the full scope of instruction frameworks. "The International Standard Classification of Education" (ISCED) is a part of the "United Nations International Family of Economic and Social Classifications" and received officially by the General Conference of UNESCO Member States (Schneider, 2013; *ISCED 2011*, 2012). ISCED is considered to be the reference standard for classification of education curriculums by various education levels and age groups of students.

Table 1. Classification of various ISCED Levels

Level	School	Grades	Age range	Duration (yrs)
ISCED Level 0	Early Childhood Development		0-3	
	Pre Primary Education	KG	3-6	

continued on following page

Table 1. Continued

Level	School	Grades	Age range	Duration (yrs)
ISCED Level 1	Primary education	Grade-1	6-7	6
		Grade-2	7-8	
		Grade-3	8-9	
		Grade-4	9-10	
		Grade-5	10-11	
		Grade-6	11-12	
ISCED Level 2	Lower Secondary	Grade-7	12-13	2-5
		Grade-8	13-14	
		Grade-9	14-15	
		Grade-10	15-16	
ISCED Level 3	Upper Secondary	Grade-11	16-17	3
		Grade-12	17-18	
ISCED Level 4	Post Secondary	-	18-21	2-3
ISCED Level 5	Short cycle Tertiary education	-	18-20	2
ISCED Level 6	Bachelor's or equivalent	-	18-21	3-4
ISCED Level 7	Master's or equivalent	-	21-23	2

Table 1, summarizes various levels of education system spanning from ISCED Level-0 to ISCED Level-7 with respective age range, grades and duration taken to complete the level.

We consider the ISCED Level (1-3) in our study, since this belongs to the pure School level classification. With this we can classify the basic education into twelve years of duration which includes a Primary Education of six years duration, Lower Secondary Education of four years of duration, and Upper Secondary Education of two years duration.

The former ISCED level (0) has learning pedagogy planned for younger children ranging in the age group of 0 to 6 years, while another is planned for ISCED levels (5-8).

2.2. Behavioral Phenomena

To further justify the psychological behavior of these age groups as mentioned in the "Primary", "Lower" "Secondary", and "Upper Secondary" level education system, we need to understand the various stages involved in the cognitive development and learning with respect to cognitive and educational psychology.

The cognitive stage theory states the gradual phase by phase process of the ability to think rationally and methodically (*Cognitive Development: The Theory of Jean Piaget,* n.d.). Cognitive development refers to the transformation in the progression whereas cognition alludes to perception and processing of memory (Babakr et al., 2019).

Table 2. Summary of Jean Piaget Theory

Stage No	Stage	Ability	Age group (in years)
1	Sensorimotor	"Ability to experience the world through movement and senses." (*Cognitive Development: The Theory of Jean Piaget,* n.d.).	Birth to age 2
2	Preoperational	"Ability to symbolize activities, but the activities are considered logically inadequate" (Cognitive Development: The Theory of Jean Piaget, n.d.).	2 to 7
3	Concrete Operational	"Ability to think and understand more flexibly and logically but not up to the standard of an adult" (Cognitive Development: The Theory of Jean Piaget, n.d.).	7 to 11
4	Formal Operational	"Ability to think rationally and hypothetically and develop problem solving skills" (Cognitive Development: The Theory of Jean Piaget, n.d.).	11 and beyond

A theory developed by Jean Piaget on cognitive development illustrates the transformation in logical thinking which occurs during the growth ages of a child. As presented in Table.2, the theory further explains four phases of cognitive development (Babakr et al., 2019) and summarizes the thinking, learning, and reasoning ability of a child with respect to their age groups. It also shows how the ability of a child can vary from one phase to another in terms of cognitive development.

Psychologically, the behavior of students is one of the root drivers for their performance at a school. All psychological behavioral issues like self-motivation and self-driven attitude add to learning and it is not merely intelligence that influences learning outcomes (Kassarnig et al., 2018). Also, the learning capability of a child varies from one child to another. This ambiguity also relies on the development factor of a child. Apart from this, the cognitive development of a child is also highly influenced by the social aspect of their ecosystem. Child's interactions with their parents, teachers and peers greatly impact their intensity of thoughts and understanding (Herodotou et al., 2019). In psychological science, well-defined and established standards are used for appraisal processes to measure the students' performances (*Assessment,* 2018). A learning appraisal is often the initial phase in this progression.

As stated (Livieris et al., 2019), learning appraisal reveals the following outcomes:

- Comparison of student's age and education classification level to achieve academic success
- Strengths and weaknesses in hidden learning skills
- Positive and negative motivation
- Environmental concerns

In the online platform the behavioral aspect can be understood by the level of participation and involvement in the class and respective learning outcomes.

3. RELATED WORK

Observation of researchers depicts that the correlation between behavioral patterns and academic performance are very strong (Yao et al., 2019). In pursuance to analyzing the psychological behavior of students included in the ODLS environment, it was discovered that considerable research on predicting various behavioral patterns of students has been conducted.

Villagrá-Arnedo et al. (2016) states that use of both behavioral and learning data offers better results used by the Support Vector Machine prediction algorithm whereas diminishing the number of features does not optimize the outcome of prediction. The results showed that, in a learning environment, behavioral and learning data provides better and more stable predictions about the results of the students. It concluded that the performance of the predicting algorithm is augmented by the use of assorted significant data.

The study made by Liu and d'Aquin (2017) presents the relationship between student characteristics and their learning achievement. In this approach they used supervised learning algorithms to predict the learning achievement of students included in the virtual learning environment. Moreover, they used K-Prototypes algorithm with different K values on different sets of experiments to find the cluster of successful and unsuccessful students. They concluded that successful students are more mature and active, their upbringing is in privileged areas and have completed their higher education as compared to the weaker counterparts.

Marbouti et al. (2016) suggested course predicting models to classify weak students so as to help them get better in their performance. "Support Vector Machine", "K-Nearest Neighbors", and "Naive Bayes Classifier" are the three machine learning supervised algorithms, which were used in this study to identify the best algorithm. Among the various methods used for testing, the Naive Bayes Classifier model's performance was identified as the best. It concluded that by providing specific guidelines on creating accurate prediction models to identify weak students, the instructors and the students both can be informed in advance to improve the performance of students. However, it was found in the study that pedagogical decisions made by the teachers such as pedagogical design, assessments process, and the grading system instructions tend to limit this model on these circumstantial factors.

Hussain et al. (2018) explored the possibility of incorporating various machine learning algorithms such as an "Artificial Neural Network" (ANN), "Support Vector Machine" (SVM), "Logistic Regression" (LR), "Naïve Bayes Classifier" (NBC), and "Decision Tree" (DT). The result showed that among the above algorithms, ANN and SVM models achieved the precision of 75% in forecasting the course related complexity which a student will face in the next session. Subsequently all the models in the study were trained and found that an SVM model achieved an accuracy of up to 80%. The researchers observed that using an SVM or ANN is suitable for forecasting the performance of an individual student and can improve the performance of teaching, learning and student involvement. They observed that a studied model can identify weak students in advance and teachers can revisit designing of those digital courses for them. Such augmentation can guide teachers to identify the session complexity in advance and hence anticipate the learning behaviors of students during various coursework and exercises.

Tomas and Jayagopi (2017) analyzed the attentiveness of the students by capturing data points of various facial gestures of students. Computer vision techniques have been used for capturing data points. Further, those data points were fed into various supervised machine learning algorithms for classification and the results were tabulated. The hyper-parameters of the final model was cross validation to address the common issue of over fitting in supervised learning algorithms. "Support Vector Machine" and "Logistic Regression" algorithms were used to generate the final models. They proposed a predictive model of student's engagement in a classroom. Applying the model on the video data recorded from the classroom illustrates the state of students in terms of their being focused or unfocused and subsequently the model makes decision. They also compared machine learning algorithms and baseline evaluator to conclude that the performance of machine learning algorithms is better as compared to the later.

Hussain et al. (2019) qualified several Machine Learning algorithms to develop a model to test the result for predicting specific behavior of students on low engagement. The results demonstrated that in terms of accuracy the "J48", "Decision Tree" (DT), "JRIP", and gradient-boosted classifiers displayed better performance as compared to other tested models. On the basis of those obtained values, they conducted two experiments, one of which illustrates that DT, J48, JRIP, and GBT are the largely suitable algorithms for predicting low engagement students. Another experiment for predicting low engagement showed that the most important input variables of the dataset are clicks on specific tabs of website. The researchers concluded that proposed predictive models allow teachers to engage and ensue students in different activities.

Yao et al. (2019) identified three characteristics of student viz. diligence, orderliness and sleep patterns, which have significant correlations with academic performance. The researchers calculated the result on prediction by grouping various features which are related to academic performance. They designed and proposed a "Multi-Task Learning-to-Rank Academic Performance Prediction framework" (MTLTR-APP). Various algorithms like Ridge Regression, Decision Tree, Random Forest, RankSVM, MLP, and XGB were used and found that MTLTR-APP algorithm can perform better in predicting academic performance.

Käser et al. (2017) proposed the use of probabilistic graphical models, which significantly improve prediction accuracy. The researchers also presented student knowledge and examination strategies jointly in one model. Furthermore, they concluded that as opposed to pure performance models, enhanced models perform better results for learning. Ding et al. (2018) explored the intensity of student involvement in online forums and the impact of 'gamification' on them.

Liang et al. (2017) examined the qualities of students that impact the learning conduct and for cleaning the original dataset using the attribute reduction method. They ascertained the semblance of understudies' conduct and used the Jaccard coefficient calculation to characterize the understudies. Furthermore, they utilized three classifier models as Linear Discriminant Analysis, "Logistic Regression, and Linear Support Vector Machine.

Although most of the literature was found to be focused on higher education, the respective predictive model obtained from the behavioral phenomena observed in colleges, universities, and tertiary education can possibly show the way forward for the study and analysis on student behavior in ISCED Level 1 (i.e. Primary Education). Various behavioral patterns impacting academic performance has been identified (Kassarnig et al., 2018) such as student's active participation in the class, raising hands for queries or answers, involvement in discussion, regularly visiting the posts, and presence in class. These patterns can be classified as the key attributes of the study.

4. METHODOLOGY

Our aim is to analyze behavioral patterns of ISCED level 1 students in an online digital learning environment. The public domain dataset (www.kagggle.com) has been taken. Data preprocessing and analyses are performed using Python 3.7.6.

4.1 Data Preprocessing

Pre-processing plays an important role in Machine learning. The main purpose of preprocessing is to convert the raw dataset into suitable form so that we can find the most suitable input variables which are mostly connected to the students' behavioral aspects. As suggested in (Kassarnig et al., 2018), we can prepare our dataset in the category of age group of 6-12. Also, from (Babakr et al., 2019), we can classify this age group in ISCED level 1. The dataset does not consist of any attribute mentioning the age group. Hence, the dataset is prepared by grouping the Grade attribute from Grade-1 to Grade-6 (age group of 1-12). First, this prepares the dataset into our desired ISCED level 1 age group of students, which also defines the Primary Education students' age group. Student performance is another feature which is understood by the Grade classification attribute of the dataset. Different Grade classification levels and their respective values are Low-Grade (0 to 69), Middle-Grade (70 to 89), High-Grade (90 to 100). Further, these levels are represented as L, M, and H respectively. This preprocessing does not imply any logical change in the dataset.

Figure 4. Schematic diagram of the prognostic model

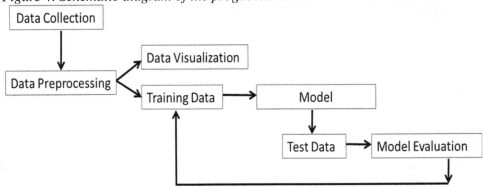

4.2 Feature Selection

Feature selection is a method which selects an appropriate subset of attributes from the original attribute which can proficiently depict the input variables (Hussain et al., 2018). The performance of the learning model depends on the input variable i.e. the feature selection. In our dataset there are many attributes which may be irrelevant for classification purposes and may impact the model negatively. This issue can be resolved by selecting input variable from the dataset which may describe the student's characteristics appropriately and further can be utilized to predict the performance of student.

In our study we extracted a few of those features which may impact in predicting students' performance. We extracted features (raised hands, visited resources, viewing announcements, and discussions) from the dataset, which may be termed as the behavioral features. This seems relevant for understanding the students' engagement during the class. To do this feature selection we used Exploratory Data Analysis (EDA). Other features may also be separately used to understand the impact on students' performance.

4.3 Visualization

Data visualization primarily gives an idea of the data and shows different parameters and provides qualitative understanding of the dataset and can help in identifying various patterns and relationships against each other. Here, in Fig. 5 we have used the histogram to show each of the identified parameters from the preprocessed dataset to indicate the behavioral features of students. The scattered matrix presented in Fig.6 shows statistical overview of different behavioral input parameters against each other.

Figure 5. Histogram showing each identified behavior values

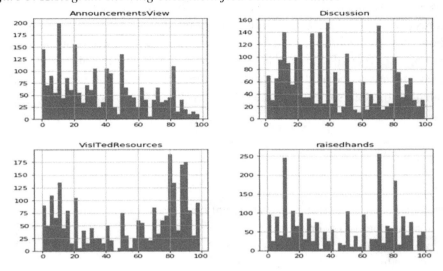

Figure 6. Scattered Plot showing different behavioral inputs

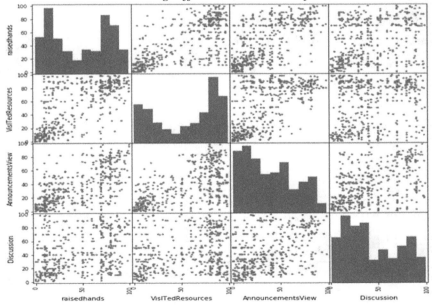

We can make predictions about one variable from another if there is a relationship between two variables. Further to identify the strength of association between two features of behavior, Pearson *r* correlation is applied between the student's behavior. It shows how the features are correlated to one another. Pearson *r* correlation is the most popular types of correlation, used to compute the degree of the relationship between linearly associated variables (Nettleton, 2014). The following is the formula to calculate the Pearson *r* correlation:

$$r_{xy} = \frac{n\sum x_i y_i - \sum x_i \sum y_i}{\sqrt{n\sum x_i^2 - (\sum x_i)^2}\sqrt{n\sum y_i^2 - (\sum y_i)^2}}$$

r_{xy} = Pearson r correlation coefficient between x and y
n = number of observations
x_i = value of x (for ith observation)
y_i = value of y for ith observation)

In terms of the strength of relationship, a correlation of −1 indicates negative correlation. A correlation of +1 indicates positive correlation. A weaker relationship between two variables is depicted by the correlation coefficient value tending to 0.

Figure 7. Correlation graph of features

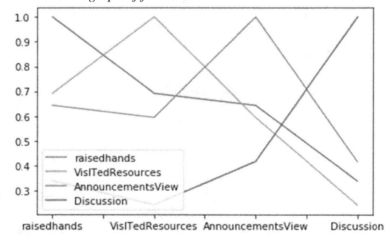

Table 3. Correlation of features

	Raised Hands	Visited Resources	Announcements View	Discussion
Raised Hands	1.000000	0.639584	0.587896	0.234832
Visited Resources	0.639584	1.000000	0.518894	0.155941
Announcements View	0.587896	0.518894	1.000000	0.426953
Discussion	0.234832	0.155941	0.426953	1.000000

Applying Pearson r correlation, it is clear from fig. 7 and Table. 3, the best correlated features are raised hands and visited resources.

Furthermore, a K-means algorithm is applied on a new dataset extracted with the behavioral features from the original dataset to create the cluster of students. An elbow method is used to find the best k, as k=7 for K-means algorithm. The student clustering is done in three groups Low, Mid and High. Figure 8 shows the scatter plot of students clustering. From this visualization, it can be observed that there are three clusters represented by 3 colors. Each cluster has its own centroid.

Figure 8. Clustering of students with behavior

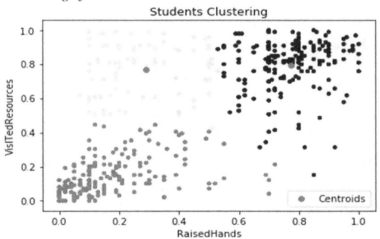

4.4. Model Construction

To predict each student's behavior and respective performance in an ODLS, we use several widely used machine learning algorithms, viz. K-Nearest Neighbors, Logistic Regression, Support Vector Machine and Decision Tree. Based on the performance of the classifier algorithms we can suggest the best model for this study.

SVM is a supervised learning method which can perform both linear classification as well as non-linear classification unlike LR which is only used for binary classification (Tomas and Jayagopi, 2017). DT is a popular algorithm for classification as well as regression whereas KNN is a classification algorithm generally used to predict categorical value.

Now we first split our preprocessed data into the training dataset and testing dataset. Then input the training dataset to each of the algorithms to train the model and construct the model. Thereafter, the defined model is tested with the test dataset for attaining the utmost accuracy. The predictive model is then evaluated with evaluation matrixes for maximum accuracy and will be deployed in the proposed system.

4.5. Model Evaluation

To quantify the accuracy of the algorithm we use confusion matrix. The confusion matrix is used to illustrate the performance of each classifier algorithm applied on a group of test data for which true values are known. By performing this we put the model into its performance evaluation state. Confusion matrix provides the quantitative information with four values, TP (True positive), FP (False positive), FN (False Negative), and TN (True Negative). All the number of values (TP+TN+FP+FN) in the matrix represents the amount of data in the test data. Fig. 9 shows the formation of a confusion matrix. These four parameters of performance evaluation of a model, i.e. accuracy, precision, recall, and F1 score are used to evaluate the effectiveness of a model.

Figure 9. A simple confusion matrix construct

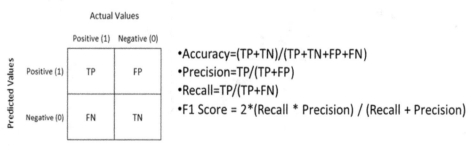

- Accuracy=(TP+TN)/(TP+TN+FP+FN)
- Precision=TP/(TP+FP)
- Recall=TP/(TP+FN)
- F1 Score = 2*(Recall * Precision) / (Recall + Precision)

To evaluate the performance of our models we find the confusion matrix for each of the tested models built with KNN, SVM, LR, and DT. Figures 10, 11, 12 and 13 shows the confusion matrixes of each of the performing algorithms. Also, it shows the respective values of performance evaluation parameters accuracy, precision, recall, and F1 score.

Figure 10. Confusion Matrix of KNN Model and Performance Chart

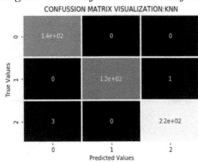

```
KNN:
              precision   recall  f1-score   support

           H       0.98     1.00      0.99       136
           L       0.87     0.99      1.00       126
           M       0.44     0.99      0.99       218

    accuracy                          0.99       480
   macro avg       0.99     0.99      0.99       480
weighted avg       0.99     0.99      0.99       480
```

Figure 11. Confusion Matrix of SVM Model and Performance Chart

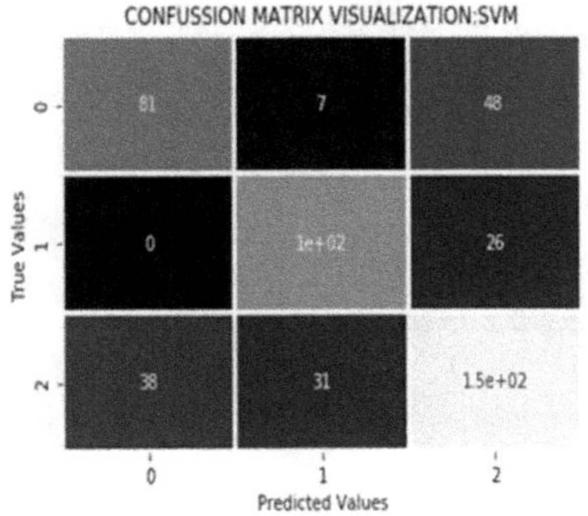

```
SVM:
              precision   recall  f1-score   support

           H       0.68     0.60      0.64       136
           L       0.87     0.87      0.76       126
           M       0.67     0.68      0.68        15

    accuracy                          0.69       480
   macro avg       0.69     0.69      0.69       480
weighted avg       0.69     0.69      0.69       480
```

Figure 12. Confusion Matrix of LR Model and Performance Chart

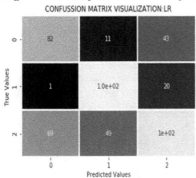

Figure 13. Confusion Matrix of with DT Model and Performance Chart

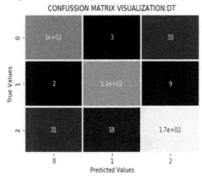

Table 4. Summary of the Accuracy of tested Models

Sl No	Algorithms	Accuracy	F1 Score
1	K-Nearest Neighbors (KNN)	0.99	0.99
2	Logistic Regression (LR)	0.60	0.59
3	Support Vector Machine (SVM)	0.69	0.69
4	Decision Tree (DT)	0.80	0.80

Hence from the above table 4, it is found that the best model is with the KNN classifier algorithm having accuracy 0.99.

5. CONCLUSION

The presented research focused on analysis of psychological behavior of ISCED level 1 students who are using the Online Digital Learning System (ODLS). The study highlights the various means of digital learning systems. It focuses on building a machine learning model to understand the student's behavior and impact on their performance under ODLS environment. The model was trained using various machine learning classifier algorithms. The test results in terms of accuracy suggest KNN as the best model amongst others. The result concludes with the accuracy of the LR model as 0.99.

6. FUTURE SCOPE

Future work may be carried out for the behavioral study and impact of ODLS on students' performance on **ISCED** level 2 and **ISCED** level 3 students. Furthermore, models of this research can be used in order to predict the gender wise behavior aspects of students separately for various levels of education. These outcomes can be improved later on when more data are accessible, however they are sufficient to distinguish learning issues and propensities. This prognostic model may also be referred to for the analysis of student behavior in the post Covid-19 scenario.

REFERENCES

https://www.melbournechildpsychology.com.au/blog/educational-psychology-how-it-helps-learning, accessed on April, 21st, 2020

https://mhrd.gov.in/sites/upload_files/mhrd/files/statistics-new/ESAG-2018.pdf, accessed on May, 15th, 2020

https://www.mospi.gov.in/national-statistical-office-nso, accessed on May, 15th, 2020

https://www.dqindia.com/powered-by-govt-it-spending-india-to-become-second-largest-it-marketin-apac-region-by-2018, accessed on May, 15th, 2020

https://www.kaggle.com, accessed on May, 8th, 2020

Assessment. (2018). American Psychological Association. Retrieved from https://www.apa.org/ed/schools/teaching-learning/top-twenty/principles/assessment, accessed on April, 20th, 2020

Babakr, Z. H., Mohamedamin, P., & Kakamad, K. (2019). Piaget's Cognitive Developmental Theory: Critical Review. *Education Quarterly Eeview*, 2(3), 517–524.

Bahati, B., Uno, F., & Tedre, M. (2017). Can student engagement in online courses predict performance on online knowledge surveys? *International Journal of Learning, Teaching and Educational Research*, 16(3), 73–87.

Blundell, C., Lee, K. T., & Nykvist, S. (2016). Digital learning in schools: Conceptualizing the challenges and influences on teacher practice. *Journal of Information Technology Education*, 15, 535–560.

Bonafini, F. C., Chae, C., Park, E., & Jablokow, K. W. (2017). How much does student engagement with videos and forums in a MOOC affect their achievement? *Online Learning : the Official Journal of the Online Learning Consortium*, 21(4), 223–240. DOI: 10.24059/olj.v21i4.1270

Cheng, L., Ritzhaupt, A. D., & Antonenko, P. (2018, October). Effects of the flipped classroom instructional strategy on students' learning outcomes: A meta-analysis. *Educational Technology Research and Development*, 67(4), 793–824. DOI: 10.1007/s11423-018-9633-7

Chiu, T. K., Jong, M. S. Y., & Mok, I. A. (2020). Does learner expertise matter when designing emotional multimedia for learners of primary school mathematics? *Educational Technology Research and Development*, 68(5), 2305–2320.

Cognitive Development: The Theory of Jean Piaget. (n.d.). SUNY. Retrieved from https://courses.lumenlearning.com/suny-educationalpsychology/chapter/cognitive-development-the-theory-of-jean-piaget, accessed on April, 20th, 2020

Ding, L., Er, E., & Orey, M. (2018). An exploratory study of student engagement in gamified online discussions. *Computers & Education*, 120, 213–226. DOI: 10.1016/j.compedu.2018.02.007

Forecast number of smartphone connections in 2025, by country. (2019). Statista. Retrieved from https://www.statista.com/statistics/982135/smartphone-connections-by-country, accessed on May, 10th, 2020

Herodotou, C., Rienties, B., Boroowa, A., Zdrahal, Z., & Hlosta, M. (2019, October). A large-scale implementation of predictive learning analytics in higher education: The teachers' role and perspective. *Educational Technology Research and Development*, 67(5), 1273–1306. DOI: 10.1007/s11423-019-09685-0

Holmes, N. (2018). Holmes, "Engaging with assessment: Increasing student engagement through continuous assessment,". *Active Learning in Higher Education*, 19(1), 23–34. DOI: 10.1177/1469787417723230

Hussain, M., Zhu, W., Zhang, W., & Abidi, S. M. R. (2018). Student Engagement Predictions in an e-Learning System and Their Impact on Student Course Assessment Scores. *Computational Intelligence and Neuroscience*, 2018(1), 6347186. DOI: 10.1155/2018/6347186 PMID: 30369946

Hussain, M., Zhu, W., Zhang, W., Abidi, S. M. R., & Ali, S. (2019). Using machine learning to predict student difficulties from learning session data. *Artificial Intelligence Review*, 52(1), 381–407. DOI: 10.1007/s10462-018-9620-8

ISCED. 2011. (2012). UNESCO Institute for Studies. Retrieved from https://uis.unesco.org/sites/default/files/documents/international-standard-classification-of-education-isced-2011-en.pdf, accessed on April, 21st, 2020

https://en.unesco.org/covid19/educationresponse/globalcoalition, June, 1st, 2020

Jung, Y., & Lee, J.Jung and J. Lee. (2018). Learning engagement and persistence in massive open online courses (MOOCS). *Computers & Education*, 122, 9–22. DOI: 10.1016/j.compedu.2018.02.013

Käser, T., Hallinen, N. R., & Schwartz, D. L. (2017) Modeling exploration strategies to predict student performance within a learning environment and beyond. In: 17th International conference on learning analytics and knowledge 2017, pp 31–40. "DOI: 10.1145/3027385.3027422

Kassarnig, V., Mones, E., Bjerre-Nielsen, A., Sapiezynski, P., Dreyer Lassen, D., & Lehmann, S. (2018, December). Academic performance and behavioral patterns. *EPJ Data Science*, 7(1), 10. DOI: 10.1140/epjds/s13688-018-0138-8

Leitner, P., Khalil, M., & Ebner, M. (2017). In Peña-Ayala, A. (Ed.), *"Learning analytics in higher education—a literature review," in Learning Analytics:Fundaments, Applications, and Trends: A View of the CurrentState of the Art to Enhance E-Learning* (pp. 1–23). Springer.

Liang, K., Zhang, Y., He, Y., Zhou, Y., Tan, W., & Li, X. (2017). Online Behavior Analysis-Based Student Profile for Intelligent E-Learning. *Journal of Electrical and Computer Engineering*, 2017, 1–7. DOI: 10.1155/2017/9720396

Liu, S., & d'Aquin, M. (2017, April). Unsupervised learning for understanding student achievement in a distance learning setting. In *2017 IEEE Global Engineering Education Conference (EDUCON)* (pp. 1373-1377). IEEE.

Livieris, I. E., Drakopoulou, K., Tampakas, V. T., Mikropoulos, T. A., & Pintelas, P. (2019, April). Predicting Secondary School Students' Performance Utilizing a Semi-supervised Learning Approach. *Journal of Educational Computing Research*, 57(2), 448–470. DOI: 10.1177/0735633117752614

Manwaring, C., Larsen, R., Graham, C. R., Henrie, C. R., & Halverson, L. R. (2017). andL. R. Halverson, "Investigating student engagement in blended learning settings using experience sampling and structural equation modelling,". *The Internet and Higher Education*, 35, 21–33. DOI: 10.1016/j.iheduc.2017.06.002

Marbouti, F., Diefes-Dux, H. A., & Madhavan, K. (2016). Models for early prediction of at-risk students in a course using standards-based grading. *Computers & Education*, 103, 1–15. DOI: 10.1016/j.compedu.2016.09.005

ME, M. R. V., Umamageshwari, S., & Unnimaya, D. An intelligent approach to predict the student behaviour and performance.

Mutahi, J., Kinai, A., Bore, N., Diriye, A., & Weldemariam, K. (2017, March). Studying engagement and performance with learning technology in an African classroom. In *Proceedings of the Seventh International Learning Analytics & Knowledge Conference* (pp. 148-152). DOI: 10.1145/3027385.3027395

Nettleton, D. (2014). Selection of variables and factor derivation. Commercial data mining, 79-104.

Remote Learning During COVID-19: Lessons from Today, Principles for Tomorrow. (n.d.). World Bank Group. Retrieved from https://www.worldbank.org/en/topic/edutech/brief/how-countries-are-using-edtech-to-support-remote-learning-during-the-covid-19-pandemic

Scagnoli, N. I., Choo, J., & Tian, J. (2017). 'Students' insights on the use of video lectures in online classes'. *British Journal of Educational Technology.* Advance online publication. DOI: 10.1111/bjet.12572

Schneider, S. L. The International Standard Classification of Education 2011. In: Elisabeth Birkelund G, editor. Comparative Social Research [Internet]. Emerald Group Publishing Limited; 2013 p. 365–79. Available from: https://www.emerald.com/insight/content/doi/10.1108/S0195-6310(2013)0000030017/full/html

Sun, A., & Chen, X. (2016). Online Education and Its Effective Practice: A Research Review. *Journal of Information Technology Education*, 15, 157–190. DOI: 10.28945/3502

Thomas, C., & Jayagopi, D. B. (2017, November). Predicting student engagement in classrooms using facial behavioral cues. In *Proceedings of the 1st ACM SIGCHI international workshop on multimodal interaction for education* (pp. 33-40).

Tick, A. (2018, June). Research on the Digital Learning and E-learning Behaviour and Habits of the Early Z Generation. In 2018 IEEE 22nd International Conference on Intelligent Engineering Systems (INES) (pp. 000033-000038). IEEE.

. Villagrá-Arnedo, C. J., Gallego-Durán, F. J., Compañ, P., Llorens Largo, F., & Molina-Carmona, R. (2016). Predicting academic performance from behavioral and learning data.

Yao, H., Lian, D., Cao, Y., Wu, Y., & Zhou, T. (2019). Predicting academic performance for college students: A campus behavior perspective. [TIST]. *ACM Transactions on Intelligent Systems and Technology*, 10(3), 1–21. DOI: 10.1145/3299087

Chapter 10
Research Study Results:
Integrating Artificial Intelligence Into a Higher Education Course

Luanne M. Amato
https://orcid.org/0000-0003-1403-4343
Holy Family University, USA

Christine Schoettle
Holy Family University, USA

ABSTRACT

Artificial Intelligence (AI) became known as a technological breakthrough in the 1990s but its impact on higher education was minimal. In the current academic climate, AI is now considered a significant force that affects students, faculty, and administrators, but with a dearth of information validated by research, on how to respond. This chapter details a pilot mixed methods research study that examines the education and use of AI, in the form of chatbots, in a live course. The chapter provides a background of AI, the current experience of administrators, faculty, and students, and introduces the research objectives, questions, population, and process. This chapter provides insights of students and faculty based on a survey and a focus group to validate the need for informed professional development for faculty and ethics training for students in order that they may successfully navigate AI in higher education course work.

DOI: 10.4018/979-8-3693-3944-2.ch010

INTRODUCTION

Artificial intelligence (AI), originally introduced to the general public as a part of the science fiction film genre, is transforming business processes across the globe (Guan, et. al., 2020). AI, also identified as Machine/Computational Intelligence is designed to perform tasks that mimic human brain function especially in areas of learning, reasoning, and error detection (Wang et al., 2021). AI first entered into the higher education scene in the 1970s, but administrators and academics paid little attention to its capabilities or future ramifications until its evolution over the last ten years (Guan et al., 2020). Only recently, with the increased use of chatbots for plagiarism, college faculty have become aware of the negative aspects of AI technology and based on misinformation, reactions are volatile and unrealistic. Faculty have displayed resistance to understanding the positive aspects of AI tools and resources and feel helpless in combating the increasing incidences of ethical violations by students. As a result, the attitude for banning the use of AI for source citation has become one solution proposed to remedy this issue.

AI use in the form of chatbots admittedly can increase cheating opportunities for all students but ignorance of practices to mitigate cheating, and increased knowledge of AI benefits has delayed acceptance. The banning of this type of technology is unenforceable since AI chatbot detection software has also evolved to mask its use when researching for an assignment. AI chatbots can be used virtually anywhere and are undetected by plagiarism software.

Usually, to support claims, researchers indicate outcomes of past research, quantitative and qualitative, to validate ideas or discover alternatives. There is little research, either quantitative or qualitative, at this point that could help bolster the positive aspects of using AI technology or provide best practices as a guide. This chapter relates the initiation, deployment, and outcomes of a mixed methods research study conducted to address the issue of AI misuse and mistrust with results adapted to support best practices.

This chapter has five objectives:

- To provide background information explaining the faculty and student experiences when encountering AI.
- Introduction of the mixed methods research study, the problem, its objectives, research questions, population, and explanation of the process.
- Identification of results based on student and faculty insights.
- Explanation of how the pilot research study has informed professional development, and student understanding of how to integrate AI technology into assignments and the ethical implications associated with its usage.

BACKGROUND

According to Bill Gates, Artificial Intelligence is poised to "change the world" (Donvan, 2023), but its implementation can be a double-edged sword. AI in higher education is here to stay; how educators manage its use will determine if AI is a blessing or curse.

The Faculty Experience

The COVID-19 pandemic first introduced AI technology as a viable resource when instructors sought to find adaptable methods of instructions when forced into an online environment (Nagro, 2021). However, as learning returned to normal, a vast majority of faculty breathed a sigh of relief as they went back to their traditional and long-standing lesson plans and course designs. Once the urgency disappeared, faculty resisted the continuity of using AI that would disrupt standard practice and add challenges to their pedagogy. Now, a few years post pandemic, AI is disrupting the academic landscape, but this time it is driven by student knowledge and use. AI usage has become entrenched by the student population (especially chatbots) since it lessens anxiety when trying to complete assignments and if used for cheating, is almost undetectable. As a result, faculty no longer have the option to choose to use AI. Faculty must accept the technology and increase their knowledge of the best practices for its use.

Successful integration of AI technology into higher education courses design and implementation is contingent on the acceptance of faculty. Acceptance of emerging technology allows for course design and instruction within "smarter" learning environments, since modern technology is able to capture and adapt innovative educational trends sooner (Wang et al., 2021). According to one quantitative research study there are five factors affecting faculty perceptions: anxiety, self-efficacy, attitude (behavior intention), perceived ease of use, and perceived usefulness. Researchers Wang, Liu, and Tu (2021) utilized the Technology Acceptance Model (TAM) and reported outcomes on the influence of these factors through the analysis of data using SPSS software. They are as follows:

- There is a positive correlation between self-efficacy and perceived ease of use and attitudes toward use.
- A positive self-efficacy can also influence perceived usefulness and perceived ease of use (Wang et. al., 2021)

Another influence for acceptance relates to professional development and training in AI tools and resources. Training materials on using AI in course design and other functions is in its infancy especially due to the rapid evolution of the technology. However, faculty is hopeful since AI tools are evolving to include assistance with creation of curriculum and learning outcomes, formative and summative assessments, and meaningful rubrics that will optimally reduce workload (Ogurlu & Mossholder, 2023). Best practices in instructional methodology suggest that the instructor must be confident in their subject knowledge in order to successfully integrate new resources into learning activities. Therefore, meaningful, and available professional development and training opportunities are of critical importance to successful acceptance and adaptation of AI tools and resources.

The Student Experience

Per academic research, the overarching goal for students when using AI, especially in the form of chatbots is to elevate their educational experience. AI tools and resources are meant to support improved engagement, efficiencies in course design, and broaden student perspectives on concepts related to their course of study (Antony & Ramnath, 2023). In February 2024, 1,250 undergraduate students replied to a poll designed to gauge their attitudes on using AI in academics. The results were:

- Fifty-three percent have used chatbots to help to understand concepts.
- Thirteen percent used chatbot content but only 5% copied and pasted without editing.
- Thirty-five percent were unaware that the output may contain incorrect information including statistics or citations.
- Sixty-three percent believe their institution has a policy related to using AI.
- Thirty percent believe their institutions should provide recommendations about the best AI tools and resources to use.
- Only twenty-two percent are satisfied with academic support when using AI.
- Seventy-three percent agree that AI is now part of their future lives and will continue to use it after graduation (Freeman & HEPI, 2024).

Another result of the student poll is related to diversity and its effect on AI usage. Administrators and researchers are recognizing the emergence of a digital divide in accessing and utilizing AI tools and resources. An overwhelming majority of students (58%) using AI are from a privileged background or of Asian descent. In order to narrow the digital divide, it is suggested that academic institutions provide internet capabilities and premium AI tools, which have a price tag, to their marginalized populations (Freeman & HEPI, 2024).

ChatGPT, first released in November 2022, was one of the first AI tools that students embraced to assist with writing assignments, especially since the version was free and available. Almost immediately faculty recognized issues regarding the lack of authenticity in student writing and the struggle to maintain academic integrity (Ogurlu & Mossholder, 2023). Research outcomes and data from a prior research study identify that students are unaware of the definition of plagiarism and there is confusion and emotional distress when an accusation of cheating is directed at a student, especially when a grade is in jeopardy. One study outcome reported students, when accused of academic dishonesty when using AI, adamantly professed that the breach was unintentional stating that they were unclear about the rules governing citations and plagiarism (Stone, 2023). A critical focal point of the student experience for this study revolved around ethics, the definition of plagiarism, and covered topics of cheating when citing sources.

RESEARCH STUDY OVERVIEW

In the Spring of 2023, two researchers from a University in the northeastern section of the United States, received a mini grant to explore the challenges related to the AI revolution exploding on college campuses across the globe. The researchers created a pilot study that investigated the student perception of AI tools in the form of chatbots, how to incorporate these tools into creating assignments, and to determine student understanding of the ethical challenges associated with the use of AI technology, especially in citing research. The study also allowed for consideration of the faculty experience in facilitating a course where students used AI with the goal to understand the cause of faculty reluctance to perceive AI tools and resources in a positive light. The timeline for the grant extended through the Fall 2023 semester with a final report that covered the outcomes of the study with multiple presentation dates in early 2024. These outcomes included the impact on student learning and future implications. Also, part of the mandate of a mini grant award was the creation of professional development material based on the research results that benefit the university's administration in policy creation and faculty in adapting course design to meet the obstacles created by AI, specifically when grading student assignments. One unexpected outcome from the study was the compilation of best practices in education using AI specifically related to educating faculty about the positive outcomes for everyone using AI. These best practices are part of an IGI Global publication, *Creative AI Tools and Ethical Implications in Teaching and Learning* (Amato & Schoettle, 2023).

Research Study

The researchers, to meet the objectives of the mini grant, created a pilot research study that incorporated a redesign of an active course, CMIS 220, Management of Information Systems conducted during the Fall 2023 semester. The redesign consisted of the following course assignments related to the design and use of AI:

- Initial instructions directed the students to use an AI chatbot of their choice. The course suggested ChatGPT because it is free and available.
- Written assignments requiring a chatbot output as a first submission; second submission required the student to revise the chatbot content with updated references and written in their own words.
- Discussion board topics requiring student research originating with the use of chatbots, and then revised with additional resources and updated in their own words. Also required were response discussion posts with three other students on the research topic.
- Inclusion of a two-part module exploring ethics which provided education on plagiarism and how to avoid it. After completion of the educational module, students were required to take an assessment with 80% as a minimum passing score. Students could retake the assessment until they reach the 80% threshold.

There were seven CMIS 220 courses held during the Fall 2023 semester, taught by four faculty members. Instruction in four of the courses was in an online format, and three were face to face. After the conclusion of the courses, an anonymous survey was deployed online to all students enrolled in the seven courses, with participation optional. In addition, the researchers hosted a focus group with faculty who taught the course. The survey and focus group questions were constructed through the use of ChatGPT and further revised by the researchers. The survey and focus group questions are located in Appendix A and B.

Research Questions and Rationale

- RQ1: How can we as educators utilize AI in our coursework to support student learning outcomes and discourage plagiarism?
- RQ2: How can we teach our students to use AI effectively and efficiently to improve their comprehension, effectively complete their assignments, and avoid plagiarism?

Rationale: The impact of AI to the higher education environment is significant but also recent. There is a scarcity of quantitative or qualitative research to assist educators in developing courses that integrate AI seamlessly. This mixed methods study was created to assist faculty in designing courses that will educate students on how to use AI resources and tools to complete assignments ethically and effectively. The best practices endorsed by this study will provide professional development opportunities for faculty and provide guidance on how to use AI resources and tools.

Process

The data collected for this research was based on two artifacts: a student survey and a faculty focus group. The researchers selected the student survey because the University is equipped to notify the appropriate student population by email and guarantee anonymity. The student survey was deployed through Qualtrics and in order to ensure anonymity, compiled by a third-party administrator, who then passed the results to the researchers. The focus group questions were sent in an email to faculty who taught the class in the Fall 2023 semester, in advance of the actual focus group meeting. The researchers chose the focus group because they have easy access to the instructors since they were faculty from the School of Business and Technology. The questions for the student survey and faculty focus group were compiled using AI software (ChatGPT) initially and then revised by the researchers. Before implementation, the University's Institutional Review Board (IRB) approved the research study process and student and faculty survey questions.

The second assessment of results was a review of the ethics scores from the week four ethics testing. The week four ethics module included education and examples on how a student can uphold academic integrity by citing sources correctly. In the redesigned course, students were directed to a website that contained instructional information and the certification test. Students were emailed the results of the assessment, which was then uploaded to an assignment box in Canvas for grading. Since the assignment required a minimum score of 80%, and students must repeat the educational process and testing until they reached the threshold, the researchers expected that the scoring was an indicator of student success in understanding what actions constitute plagiarism.

Results

Student Survey

The return on student surveys resulted in a small sample size of sixteen respondents out of 120 surveys deployed. Please see Appendix A in Table 1 for a copy of the survey. The survey consisted of ten questions with the first nine requiring answers using a Likert scale with five choices (strongly agree, agree, neutral, disagree, strongly disagree). The tenth question was open-ended asking students for any additional comments or suggestions about their experience using AI resources. Please see Appendix C for a summary of responses for questions one through nine in graph form and free text responses for question 10. (See Figure 1, Figure 2, Figure 3, Figure 4, Figure 5, Figure 6, Figure 7, Figure 8, Figure 9 in Appendix C). The last question's (question ten in Table 3) feedback was reviewed and summarized by the researchers.

The Ethics Module

In week four of a fifteen-week series, students were directed to access and review information from the Indiana University Plagiarism Tutorials and Tests ethics educational website about how to cite sources without plagiarizing. The website is located at (https://plagiarism.iu.edu/index.html). After the review students participated in a certification exam to assess their knowledge and understanding of plagiarism based on the concepts provided in the review. Students were sent an email with their score at completion of the assessment, which they uploaded to the assignment dropbox for grading and verification. The minimum score allowed to pass the test was 80% and students were allowed unlimited access to retake the exam as needed to meet the threshold. Only one student could not complete the test with an 80% score.

Faculty Focus Group

Due to the uncertainty when creating and grading assignments in the AI environment, administrators and faculty need authentic and meaningful assessment criteria to help design anti-cheating assignments and build their own assessment rubrics (Al Amoush & Farhat, 2023). The faculty focus group process provides an opportunity for experts in their field to share their knowledge, experiences, successes, and failures.

During the focus group exercise, several themes emerged that raised flags of concern during the course. These concerns are identified as: clarity of assignment directions, lack of proficiency when using AI, AI resource availability, professional development, student engagement, and ethics. The faculty involved in the focus group also included comments regarding any future applications of courses using AI. (Please see Table 2 for the Focus Group questions using a Likert Scale).

DISCUSSION

Student Survey

Do surveys accurately assess outcomes? Prior research explores the value of using surveys as an evaluation tool and raises questions as to whether survey responses are a reliable source of data and a basis for accurate decision making (Tek Lama et al., (2015). In a 2015 study the researchers concluded that higher education students, when answering survey questions, often select responses at random, and do not read or clearly understand the question, although admittedly there is little research that validates this claim (Tek Lama et al., 2015).

The researchers for this study decided, despite the published drawbacks, to utilize an anonymous survey to gauge student reaction to the educational tools included in the redesigned course that increased their awareness and utilization of AI. One noted limitation of the survey specific to this research was the lack of engagement by all faculty. The course was taught using different resources across the seven offerings, with a mix and match of assignments deemed usable by the instructor. A few instructors resisted providing any instruction on how to use AI, because they believed they were educating their students on how to cheat. Therefore, all students did not have the same experience in completing the course work.

Since the open-ended question resulted in positive feedback and appreciation for the inclusion of how to use an AI tool to help with research in the course, researchers concluded that students who responded to the survey were only those positively impacted by the course. It is also important to note that all students utilized the free version of ChatGPT to complete their assignments.

Faculty Focus Group

The faculty focus group, based on their AI course experience, was instrumental in highlighting the various themes that should be addressed and turned into action plans for administrators in higher education. Overall, the group highlighted the developing landscape of AI integration in education and the necessity for ongoing adaptation and learning for administrators, faculty, and students.

The first concern raised was in the clarity of assignment directions. According to comments raised by students in class, the directions were unclear with more clarification needed for the word "revise." At first, students thought they were prompted to take the AI generated output and edit the output. The faculty changed the wording of the directions to "write in your own words" which helped clarify what the students needed to do to complete the assignment. Other comments offered were that the assignments were over simplified and needed more rigor.

The second concern raised was the lack of knowledge about AI when accessing the tools to complete assignments. Faculty suggested that students should have an awareness of the resource's limitations before completing assignments. Known limitations for AI tools include understanding context, cannot assess, or provide emotion, inaccurate source citations, and inaccuracies in information. The free version of ChatGPT (3.5) (suggested for use by the course) restricts word count to approximately 750 words and the information is not current beyond 2021. Another commentary suggested was for faculty to demonstrate the use of an AI tool with a shared prompt. A shared prompt is defined as several students using the same wording as input for the same AI tool and comparing output. When students use a shared prompt, they can easily recognize the variability in results thus demonstrating the need to validate sources.

The third concern raised was the availability of AI resources. All students do not have the same access to internet capabilities or extra funds to purchase more updated versions. For example, the free version of ChatGPT 3.5 is accurate up to 2021. The newer versions (ChatGPT 4 & 4.5) cost $.16 to $.99 per day depending on the plan and have expanded features but the accuracy date for exploring information is reported the same as 2021. There is concern that as chatbots evolve, their range of information will also increase, but at a steeper price.

The fourth concern raised was the availability of meaningful professional development for instructors. There are various AI tools and resources available for use in educational settings, but lack of understanding adds to the reluctance of instructors to utilize the tools. For this study, the instructors were not provided any additional instruction, although the University's instructional design staff offers optional training opportunities. Going forward after the study's completion and as part of the professional development plan, the researchers are creating a list of recommended AI resources, with cost and reviews included in the information, which will reside in a university web page for faculty reference.

The fifth concern raised was regarding student engagement. The faculty stated that it was difficult to foster student engagement when there is a lack of instructor understanding of the basic capabilities of AI. In order to entice students to participate, instructors must be comfortable with the material they are presenting. Faculty do not want to appear unprepared or lack the knowledge when delivering a lesson to their students. Additionally, teaching AI concepts requires an editing of curriculum and pedagogy to include more engagement exercises, which faculty are reluctant to do (Tag 2012).

The sixth concern addressed the ethics surrounding the utilization of AI, emphasizing the importance of students' knowledge of plagiarism. Educators have verbalized the concern that grading has become more of a policing - checking assignments to determine if an AI tool was used and results copied without revision or proper citation. However, faculty are reluctant to admit that the design of an assignment contributes to the plagiarism problem. The traditionalist teacher who uses the same material every semester which includes a rote answer to a concept question, is fostering the opportunity for misuse of AI. The prevailing remedy in AI to mitigate cheating is to modify assignments that are then graded for student interpretation, creativity, presentation, and team efforts and creation of those that will promote critical thinking strategies (Hale, 2018). Faculty often cite their unwillingness to revise assignments is prompted by time constraints and the extra work needed to update their course offerings.

Finally, the instructors discussed the future implications of AI in higher education. Faculty felt that it is essential to develop an interdisciplinary course on AI that would enable students to understand AI's application and use beyond a single course. Another suggestion was to integrate AI into all courses across all disciplines in order to develop a standard for faculty to follow and thus reduce confusion. AI is rapidly becoming part of the global requirement for students to secure any type of job post-graduation; therefore, higher education is mandated to include a curriculum that supports an AI learning outcome.

Impact on Student Learning

From the results of the surveys, the researchers concluded that the study had a direct impact on student learning. The course redesign and inclusion of how to ethically use a new technological tool has, according to student input, improved learning not only in the CMIS220 class but has been transferable to other courses at the university. The faculty also reported, through the results of the focus group, the need for faculty to increase their knowledge of the availability of AI tools, how to select the most useful, and how to employ the tools and resources in course design and in the classroom to increase student learning especially in ethical use.

Limitations

There were limitations to the study that included 1) a small response rate for the student survey (approximately 12%), 2) miscommunication about type of assignments that should be included in the course, and 3) some faculty resistance to AI learning objectives.

There were over one hundred students in the seven classes, but the response rate for the survey was 12%. Students at this university historically do not answer survey requests, especially when there is no incentive included. The researchers were to provide the revised syllabus which included the AI assignments to the instructors, but three of the faculty did not receive the updated copy. Even though a Canvas shell was provided with the revised assignments, those instructors did not follow all of the assignment structure and reverted to past material from other semesters. They cherry-picked only those AI concepts they felt important to highlight in the class. Finally, some faculty resisted student education in the use of AI tools in the form of chatbots, expressing their concern that students who were unaware of the availability of AI chatbots, once the capabilities became known, would use the technology to cheat. These faculty favored the creation of policies that specifically prohibited the use of AI in any writing assignment.

Future Application of Results

The onset of AI on higher education campuses has highlighted the need for a more targeted approach to professional development for administrators and faculty. Part of the mini grant award was the responsibility of the researchers to communicate the results of the study in the form of education for administrators, faculty, and staff. Based on the results of the research study, with input from the University's chief design officer, the researchers initiated three forms of professional development to fulfill the requirements of the mini grant.

- Quarterly presentations on applicable course designs integrating AI that were tested during the research study.
- Listing of applicable AI Resources and Tools specific to higher education with associated information that includes cost, website, summary of features, and reviews. There is a plethora of information available about the myriad of AI tools and resources available, but little is known about what resources provide the best fit.
- The researchers authored and published - by IGI Worldwide - a chapter related to best practices using artificial intelligence ethically and responsibly. (Using artificial intelligence ethically and responsibly: Best practices in high-

er education. *in Creative AI Tools and Ethical Implications in Teaching and Learning.* IGI Publications, 2023).

The CMIS 220 course is a core course for degree completion in the Management/Marketing curriculum. The researchers are also instructors for the CMIS 220 course and, for the future, will continue to build and revise the design and assignments based on newer AI tools and resources.

CONCLUSION

In the 21st Century global environment a wide mix of persons who shape our global economies and business practices have provided input into the future of AI.

- "ChatGPT is scary good. We are not far from dangerously strong AI." ~Elon Musk (The Best ChatGPT quotes, 2023).
- ChatGPT is incredibly limited, but good enough at some things to create a misleading impression of greatness ………. we have lots of work to do on robustness and truthfulness." ~Sam Altman, CEO OpenAI. Twitter 12/10/22 (The Best ChatGPT quotes, 2023).
- "ChatGPT is a chatbot that can write essays with advanced language skills, reply to questions similar to human conversation, write code, and reminds us of all that artificial intelligence is changing the world as we speak." ~Dave Waters (The Best ChatGPT quotes, 2023).

These observations, and others, although there is a difference in the perceived impact of AI - all provide the same message. AI has become an integral part of the global human landscape and as a result, a critical component of learning in higher education. The researchers of the pilot study presented in this chapter, hope to use its outcomes to continue the conversation and encourage future qualitative and quantitative studies to examine and provide meaningful and up-to-date guidance for application of AI tools and resources, keeping pace as the technology evolves.

REFERENCES

Al Amoush, S., & Farhat, A. (2023). The power of authentic assessment in the age of AI. Faculty Focus online. Retrieved from https://www.facultyfocus.com/articles/educational-assessment/the-power-of-authentic-assessment-in-the-age-of-ai/

Amato, L., & Schoettle, C. (2023). Using artificial intelligence ethically and responsibly: Best practices in higher education. In Keengwe, J. (Ed.), *Creative AI Tools and Ethical Implications in Teaching and Learning* (pp. 19–31). IGI Global Publications. DOI: 10.4018/979-8-3693-0205-7.ch002

Antony, S., & Ramnath, R. (2023). A phenomenological exploration of students' perceptions of AI chatbots in higher education. *IAFOR Journal of Education*, 11(2), 7–38. DOI: 10.22492/ije.11.2.01

Donvan, J. (2023, February 24). *Will ChatGPT Do More Harm Than Good?* [Open to Debate Podcast, NPR]. Retrieved from https://opentodebate.org/debate/will-chatgpt-do-more-harm-than-good/

Freeman, J. (2024). *Provide or Punish? Students' Views on Generative AI in Higher Education. HEPI Policy Note 51.* Higher Education Policy Institute.

Guan, C., Mou, J., & Jiang, Z. (2020). Artificial intelligence innovation in education: A twenty-year data-driven historical analysis. *International Journal of Innovation Studies*, 4(4), 134–147. DOI: 10.1016/j.ijis.2020.09.001

Hale, M. (2018). Thwarting plagiarism in the humanities classroom: Storyboards, scaffolding, and a death fair. *The Journal of Scholarship of Teaching and Learning*, 18(4), 86–110. DOI: 10.14434/josotl.v18i4.23174

Lama, Tek, Arias, P., Mendoza, K., & Manahan, J. (2015). Student evaluation of teaching surveys: Do students provide accurate and reliable information? *E-Journal of Social & Behavioural Research in Business*, 6(1), 30–39.

Nagro, S. A. (2021). The role of artificial intelligence techniques in improving the behavior and practices of faculty members when switching to elearning in light of the COVID-19 crisis. *International Journal of Education and Practice*, 9(4), 687–714. DOI: 10.18488/journal.61.2021.94.687.714

Ogurlu, U., & Mossholder, J. (2023). The perception of ChatGPT among educators: Preliminary findings. [RESSAT]. *Research in Social Sciences & Technology*, 8(4), 196–215. DOI: 10.46303/ressat.2023.39

Stone, A. (2023). Student perceptions of academic integrity: A qualitative study of understanding, consequences, and impact. *Journal of Academic Ethics*, 21(3), 357–375. DOI: 10.1007/s10805-022-09461-5 PMID: 36466717

The Best ChatGPT Quotes. (2023). Supply Chain Today, homepage. Retrieved from https://www.supplychaintoday.com/best-chatgpt-quotes/

Wang, Y., Liu, C., Tu, Y.-F. (2021). Factors affecting the adoption of ai-based applications in higher education: An analysis of teachers' perspectives using structural equation modeling. educational technology & society, 24 (3), 116– 129.

ADDITIONAL READING

AI and ChatGPT Resources for Higher Education. (n.d.). Alchemy. Retrieved from https://alchemy.works/ai-chatgpt-resources/.

How can educators respond to students presenting AI-generated content as their own? (n.d.). OpenAI. Retrieved from https://help.openai.com/en/articles/8313351-how-can-educators-respond-to-students-presenting-ai-generated-content-as-their-own

Smyers, L. (2023, October 9). Advancing opportunities for AI in higher education. Microsoft. Retrieved from https://educationblog.microsoft.com/en-us/2023/10/advancing-opportunities-for-ai-in-higher-education

Soto, M. (2023, May 26). The paradigm shift: How artificial intelligence is reshaping the world as "things will never be the same". LinkedIn. Retrieved from https://www.linkedin.com/pulse/paradigm-shift-how-artificial-intelligence-reshaping-world-soto/

KEY TERMS AND DEFINITIONS

Academic Integrity: A commitment to the demonstration of honest and ethical behavior.
Chatbot: A computer software program that simulates human conversations.
ChatGPT: An AI chatbot brand that mimics human responses.
Institutional Review Board: A peer group that reviews research studies to ensure that they meet ethical standards, follow institutional procedures, and protect all participants from harm.

Plagiarism: Use of another author's work with full knowledge, without a proper citation.

Professional Development Plan: A formal document that serves as an outline for career goals and includes strategies to achieve them.

APPENDIX A: STUDENT SURVEY QUESTIONNAIRE

1 = Strongly Disagree, 2 = Disagree, 3 = Neutral, 4 = Agree, and 5 = Strongly Agree.

Table 1. Student Survey Questionnaire using Likert Scale

1. The instructions for using AI tools were clear and understandable.
2. The incorporation of AI resources enhanced my understanding of course concepts.
3. AI tools improved my overall learning experience in this course.
4. The use of AI resources positively impacted my engagement with the course material.
5. The integration of AI resources made the course content more interesting and relevant.
6. The AI tools and platforms used in the course were user-friendly and intuitive.
7. I would like to see more courses incorporate AI resources to enhance the learning experience.
8. I am aware of the ethical considerations associated with the use of AI resources in this course.
9. The AI-supported rubrics provided a fair and accurate evaluation of my knowledge reflected in the grading.
10. Please provide any additional comments or suggestions regarding your experience with AI resources in this course.

APPENDIX B: FOCUS GROUP QUESTIONNAIRE

Appendix B: CMIS 220: Fall 2023 Focus Group Questions:
Instructions: This focus group will discuss the merits of using AI in course design and delivery. We will not discuss individual students or use their names.

Table 2. Focus Group Questions designed by ChatGPT

Criteria	Questions
Overall Experience	How would you describe your overall experience with this course?
	In what ways do you believe AI resources enhanced or detracted from the teaching and learning experience?
Content & Relevance	How effectively did the AI resources align with the course content and learning objectives?
	Did the AI resources offer new perspectives or insights that traditional materials did not?
Student Engagement	Were there any challenges or barriers that students encountered when interacting with AI resources?
Pedagogical Impact	How did the integration of AI resources affect your teaching methods or instructional approach?
Technical Aspects	How user-friendly were the AI tools or platforms you used? Did they require significant technical skills to navigate?
Assessment & Feedback	Were you able to utilize AI rubrics for evaluating student progress or providing timely feedback? If yes, how effective was this approach?
Professional Development	How has your experience with AI resources influenced your perspective on integrating technology into future courses?
Future Implementation	Would you consider using AI resources again in future courses? Why or why not?
	Are there specific improvements or enhancements you would like to see in AI resources to better support teaching and learning?
Student Perspectives	Have you gathered any feedback from students regarding their experiences with AI resources? If so, what were their observations and opinions?

APPENDIX C: RESULTS OF STUDENT SURVEY QUESTIONNAIRE: QUESTIONS 1 – 10

Figure 1.

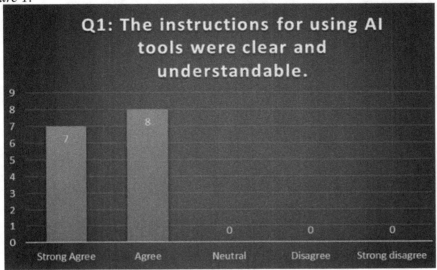

Figure 2.

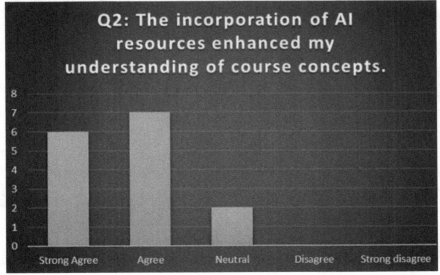

Figure 3.

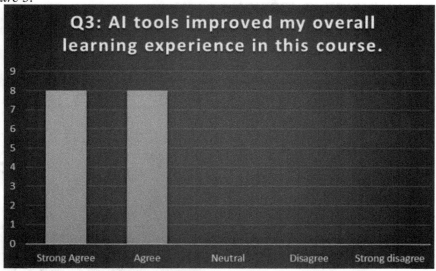

Figure 4.

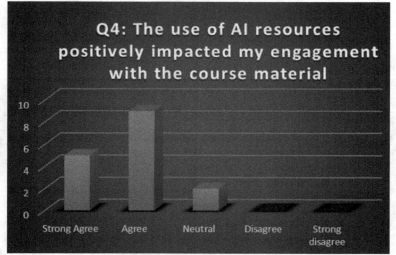

Figure 5.

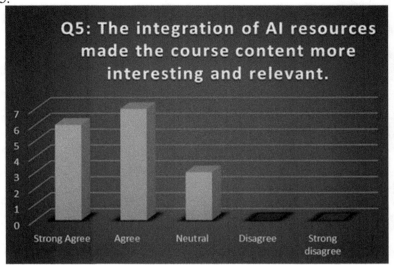

Figure 6.

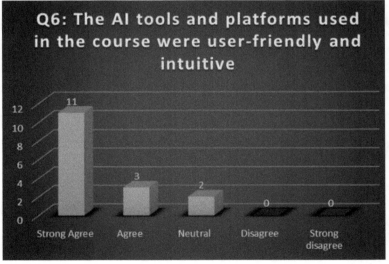

Figure 7.

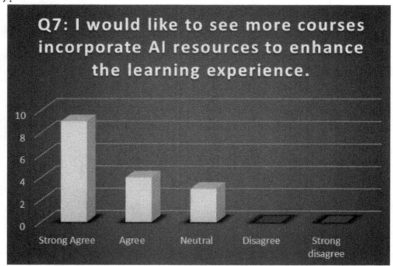

Figure 8.

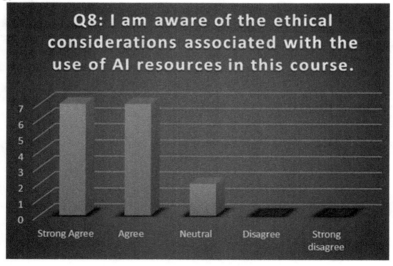

Figure 9.

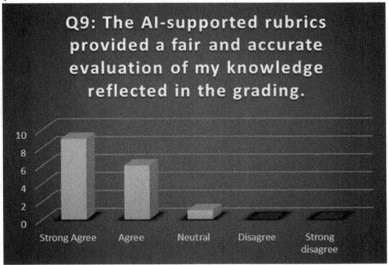

Table 3. Q10: (Open Ended) Please provide any additional comments or suggestions regarding your experience with AI resources in this course.

The AI is impressive and may as well be the new google, but this feels different then what I am used to.
I thought it was a creative way of teaching a class about AI.
AI was explained very well to use and I think AI helped me get a better understanding on how it is used and it helped me when I was confused about a topic or did not fully understand.
It was something new and very interesting.
Thank you for an enjoyable semester
Great class

Chapter 11
Artificial Intelligence and Language Learning:
Methods, Tools, and Challenges

Ana Rita Costa
ESTGA, Portugal

Sandra Vieira Vasconcelos
 https://orcid.org/0000-0003-4062-331X
UNIAG, ESHT, Polytechnic Institute of Porto, Portugal

Ana Balula
 https://orcid.org/0000-0001-8287-258X
University of Aveiro, Portugal

ABSTRACT

Artificial Intelligence (AI) has shifted from an emerging trend to a mainstream topic in education, impacting various educational settings, including teacher training. This chapter emphasizes the need to equip teachers with competencies to integrate AI into their practices, particularly in foreign language teaching and learning. By compiling a comprehensive list of AI platforms and tools, the authors aim to support teachers by offering options that can be tailored to different learning designs and outcomes, moving away from "one size fits all" solutions. The chapter provides an annotated list of AI tools, highlighting their features, applications, benefits, and limitations. Referencing Mollick and Mollick's (2023) approaches to AI in education, it includes language chatbots, generative AI, machine translation, and personalized textbooks, showcasing practical examples and reflecting on recent trends. As a result, the chapter seeks to inform and inspire future initiatives in language learning and teaching, helping other practitioners to effectively incorporate AI into their practices.

DOI: 10.4018/979-8-3693-3944-2.ch011

INTRODUCTION

Once described as an emerging trend in Education, Artificial Intelligence (AI) has indisputably become a mainstream topic within this scope and is currently having a profound impact on a wide range of educational settings, including teacher training. As a result, it has become paramount to not only understand whether and how teachers are keeping pace with this transformation, but also to equip them with the necessary competences to include AI in their teaching practices.

Focusing on foreign language teaching and learning, this chapter aims to support practitioners and teacher trainers, by putting together a comprehensive list of platforms and tools that can promote and support the use of AI in teaching and learning settings. Rather than relying on "one size fits all" solutions, the authors explore different options that can inform and complement current approaches and be tailored to meet a wide range of learning designs and outcomes. Drawing from experience and an extensive literature and best practice review, this annotated list focus on key features of each tool and will consider different categories, showcasing different ways AI tools can support language learning, namely the use of language chatbots, generative AI platforms, machine translation and personalized textbooks.

In addition to taking into account recent trends and scenarios in language learning, describing the key features of each platform/tool and reflecting on their perceived applicability, affordances and shortcomings, this description is based on Mollick and Mollick's (2023) approaches for using AI, considering its different roles and uses in educational settings.

Acknowledging the potential of AI within the scope of foreign language teaching and learning, and the ensuing benefits and challenges, this chapter will, therefore, showcase practical examples, which can be replicated by practitioners and teachers in training, ultimately contributing to inform future language learning and teaching initiatives.

BACKGROUND

AI, abbreviated from "artificial intelligence", encompasses technologies aimed at streamlining tasks that traditionally require human intellect. The journey of AI spans several decades, going back to Alan Turing's groundbreaking publication, "Computing Machinery and Intelligence," which introduced the fundamental query regarding machine cognition (Martinez *et al.*, 2019).

AI technologies are revolutionizing numerous sectors worldwide, including medicine, agriculture, energy, manufacturing, transportation, logistics, human resources, and national security, leading to significant transformations in the economy, workforce, education, and global competitiveness (Martinez *et al.*, 2019). Moreover, AI's influence extends to shaping public awareness and everyday activities, as evidenced by the proliferation of commonplace applications such as wearable fitness trackers, customer service chatbots, online shopping product recommendations, security cameras, music playlist suggestions, email categorization features, and many others.

Over the last two decades AI has become a staple of education, with its use having been extensively documented and reviewed by different researchers and practitioners (Zhai *et al.*, 2021; Holmes & Tuomi, 2022; Tahiru, 2021; Ng *et al.*, 2023) and teachers becoming increasingly familiar with prevalent AI technologies and their integration into learning systems (Baker, 2000; Humble & Mozelius, 2022). These encompass adaptive learning, intelligent tutoring systems, AI-powered transcribing capabilities, advanced assessment and proctoring technologies, analytics, and big data utilization, among others. However, until recently, AI's function in these contexts was mostly limited to background support systems primarily aimed at automation, standing in contrast with other educational technology tools that users directly interact with for their tasks. With the emergence and widespread development of generative AI, these tools have become more versatile, showcasing what some authors describe as an "unprecedented shift" (Saheb & Saheb, 2023) in education, particularly when it comes to their potential to enhance and personalize learning experiences (Abunaseer, 2023).

Generative AI tools, commonly known as large language models, possess remarkable speed and proficiency in generating language, images, and computer code. Their emergence brings new functionalities, expanding the scope of behind-the-scenes operations to broad public utilization. Moreover, they foster an environment in which teachers and policymakers are urged to embrace potentially transformative advantages. This transition requires adapting to the changes instigated by generative AI across educational technology and broader educational systems (Humble & Mozelius, 2022). With the ability to rapidly generate text-based responses, virtual images or artwork based on keywords, compose music from text, and potentially handle a range of other tasks, generative AI tools demonstrate remarkable efficiency. This potential challenges conventional perceptions of traditional teaching, learning practices, and creativity, reshaping our understanding of current educational methods. As a result, regardless of the growing concerns surrounding generative AI tools, they embody an inevitable reality, which is prompting educational systems to adjust and reconfigure teaching practices while contemplating new assessment paradigms.

The initial response within the education sector to the emergence of generative AI tools was characterized by panic (Martinez *et al.*, 2019). Even though the sudden availability of tools capable of producing human-like outputs was enthusiastically embraced by students, it was initially rebutted or ignored by many educational institutions. Subsequently, there was a phase of disparagement towards AI tools, accompanied by numerous attempts to discredit them and mitigate their impact. This resulted in a period of active resistance, with institutions going insofar as banning AI tools and resorting to traditional pen and paper exams to prevent their use (Michel-Villarreal *et al.*, 2023). Eventually, a sense of resigned acceptance prevailed, with a few enthusiasts having begun to explore ways to leverage AI tools, utilizing them for creating materials and offering personalized feedback.

Presently, numerous educational institutions acknowledge the permanence of AI tools, focusing on staying abreast of both their potential risks and the learning benefits they provide (UNESCO, 2019). Despite the apprehension surrounding these generative AI tools, it represents an unavoidable reality which challenges the educational systems to adapt and (re)construct teaching practices and reconsider a new assessment paradigm.

AI FOR LANGUAGE LEARNING: TOOLS AND METHODS

Just as online education revolutionized language learning, the evolution of AI technology is leading in a new educational era within this scope. As the integration of AI into language learning is steadily increasing, it has become imperative for teachers to prepare for, adapt to and embrace this transformative reality, which includes being able to understand and cope with a plethora of new applications and tools as, for instance, language learning chatbots, generative AI in language learning, machine translation and tailored textbooks.

Chatbots

Language learning chatbots can be invaluable tools in the language acquisition process given that they provide learners with a platform for developing language competences in a comfortable and non-intimidating environment (Zhang *et al.*, 2013). Learners can engage in conversations with the chatbot anytime and anywhere, without the fear of judgment or embarrassment, allowing them to build confidence and fluency gradually. Another advantage of language learning chatbots is their ability to simulate real-life conversational scenarios. By engaging in dialogue with the chatbot, learners can practice various language functions, such as greetings, asking for directions, making requests, and expressing opinions, in contextually relevant situations. This immersive learning experience helps learners develop practical language skills that are applicable in everyday life. Moreover, language learning chatbots offer tailored responses based on the learner's input, allowing for personalized learning experiences (Ifelebuegu, Kulume & Cherukut, 2023). The adaptive nature of this tool enables learners to focus on areas they need to improve, receive targeted feedback, and track their progress over time. Additionally, chatbots are available 24/7 and can provide immediate feedback, highlighting errors in grammar, pronunciation, or vocabulary usage, thus facilitating more effective learning.

Generative AI

In what concerns the use of generative AI in Language Learning, which leverage advanced algorithms found in models like GPT-3, they enhance language learning by generating text that closely resembles human speech (Chang, 2023). Though traditional beliefs emphasize the importance of engaging with native speakers for comprehensive language acquisition, AI advancements are quickly narrowing this gap by replicating genuine speech and dialogues more accurately. This technology creates immersive language experiences through interactive conversations and dynamic content generation, fostering an environment conducive to improving language proficiency naturally and in context. These systems replicate real-world dialogues, providing personalized feedback and customized learning experiences that adjust to individual needs and learning pace.

Machine Translation

Besides improving the quality of translations, the use of AI technologies like neural machine translation can also aid in the understanding of foreign languages. Methods such as "machine translation as a bad model", students gain valuable insights into the nuances of language usage and develop a deeper understanding of grammar and syntax, ultimately contributing to their overall proficiency in the target language.

Personalized Textbooks

Finally, by acknowledging the diverse learning paces and preferences among individuals, personalized textbooks dynamically adjust to learners' progress and needs. This adaptability is particularly beneficial for teachers, who can input content into an AI platform to generate customized textbooks tailored to specific schools, courses, or student groups. This innovative and flexible approach allows artificial intelligence to accommodate a variety of learning styles. By presenting students' perspectives on relevant issues, controversies, or problems related to the theme and arguments supporting a specific position, a comparison and contrast with existing approaches pertaining to the chapter's specific topic and the main theme of the book can be made.

Hence, from language learning chatbots providing personalized practice to generative AI enhancing immersion and machine translation aiding comprehension, AI tools offer diverse benefits for language learning. As teachers embrace these advancements, they can foster a more engaging and effective language learning experience for students, ultimately shaping the future of education.

The integration of AI into education holds immense potential for improving teaching methodologies and learning outcomes. According to Mollick and Mollick (2023), seven key methods for using AI's capabilities in language education can be considered, i.e. AI as mentor, tutor, coach, teammate, learner, simulator and tool (see Figure 1).

Figure 1. Seven key methods for using AI's capabilities in language education

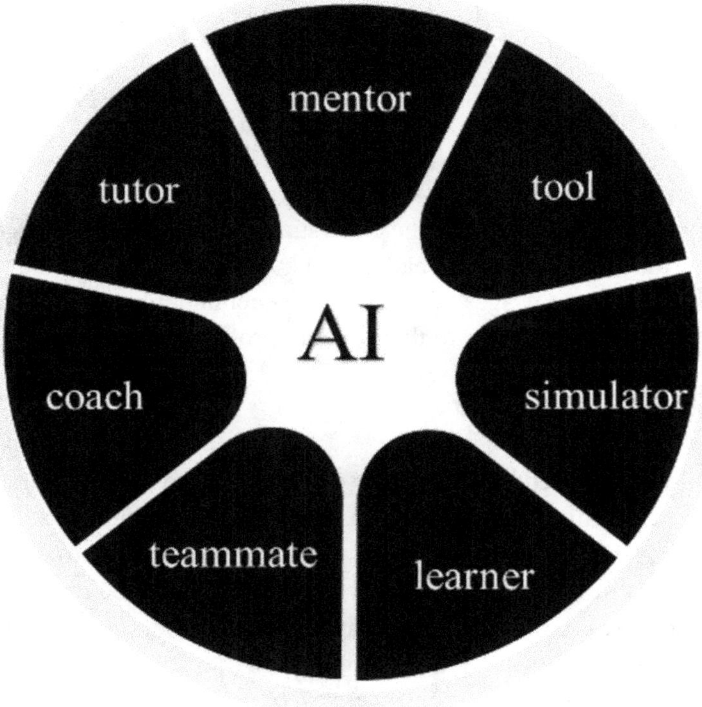

Source: Mollick and Mollick (2023)

According to the authors, incorporating AI chatbots as mentors can greatly benefit students by offering frequent, instantaneous, and adaptable feedback. For example, students can utilize chatbots to receive feedback on essay structures or to identify errors in programming code. However, it is crucial to emphasize the importance of critically evaluating the feedback provided by chatbots, both for teachers and students. The practice of tutoring, aimed at enhancing skills through personalized attention in small group or one-on-one settings, has been shown to be effective for learning (Kraft, Schueler, Loeb & Robinson, 2021). Skilled tutors often employ questioning techniques, collaborative problem-solving, and tailored instruction to assist their students. AI chatbots can complement tutoring services by serving as supplementary resources. For instance, users can instruct chatbots to provide explanations and analogies for concepts tailored to personal or academic interests, or to pose open-ended questions that foster deeper thinking. It is worth noting that the effectiveness of chatbots may vary across subjects, so teachers should experiment with them and evaluate their utility before integrating them extensively.

Metacognitive skills offer students benefits such as understanding learning processes, identifying knowledge gaps, and developing effective study techniques. For example, both teachers and students can utilize chatbots as a coach to reflect on experiences during group projects or to brainstorm ways to improve study habits. It is advisable to initially practice metacognitive routines without the assistance of chatbots to compare results and optimize their effectiveness. Furthermore, it is important to acknowledge that the coaching style or tone of chatbots may not be suitable for everyone.

Effective teamwork involves leveraging individual skills, providing social support, and embracing diverse perspectives, leading to enhanced performance and a richer learning experience (Hackman, 2011). AI can fulfill various roles within a team setting. For instance, teams can use AI to synthesize ideas, create action item timelines, or offer alternative perspectives or critiques of team ideas. There are numerous apps designed to support time and team management, which not only benefit language learning but also serve as valuable assets for students' future careers.

Furthermore, engaging in activities like organizing knowledge, teaching concepts to others, and responding to inquiries not only aids in reinforcing one's understanding of a topic but also enhances learning. Students can benefit from the concept of learning by teaching, making it valuable to have them teach a chatbot as part of their real-world practice. This approach holds particular significance for teacher training. For instance, you could instruct a chatbot to adopt the role of a learner and pose questions related to a specific topic, such as teaching the simple past tense. Experiment with various prompts, refining them to ensure the chatbot provides helpful responses.

Often, the ability to apply skills and knowledge in diverse contexts requires abstract thinking, problem-solving skills, and self-awareness. Deliberate practice, including activities like role-playing, is essential for developing these transferable skills. AI chatbots can play a pivotal role in facilitating such activities by generating scenarios, participating in role-playing exercises, and offering constructive feedback. For example, you can direct the chatbot to create a realistic ethical dilemma relevant to your field or to role-play as a patient or client in a scenario.

Finally, as the teacher's role frequently extends beyond pedagogical duties to encompass various aspects of their profession, the versatility of AI chatbots can also be relevant. Chatbots can assist in tasks such as lesson planning and activity creation, drafting peer observation reports, or generating other types of reports. Additionally, they can automate tasks like grading online tests, providing insights into students' strengths and areas needing improvement. The challenge then is to determine how AI can enhance the teacher training process and contribute to professional development, rather than merely replacing traditional tasks.

AI INTEGRATION IN LANGUAGE LEARNING: PLANNING, TEACHING AND GIVING FEEDBACK

In various sectors, including education, AI is being explored to enhance professionals' productivity and efficiency. Generative AI holds promise in helping teachers across multiple tasks, including lesson planning, resource creation, student feedback, and assessment support. This section will offer insights into employing AI for crafting teaching materials, covering the entire process from initial planning to practical implementation. In addition to a literature review, it is based on hands-on experience and structured observation throughout the 2023-24 school year, aiming to reflect the current educational landscape. As a result, it can be expected to become outdated in little time. Notwithstanding, the suggested AI tools should be perceived as examples, with practitioners being challenged to explore more updated versions of the ones presented in this section.

Planning

When planning a lesson plan, teachers can resort to various AI tools to streamline their process. These range from sophisticated paid platforms like LessonPlans.ai (https://www.lessonplans.ai/), Education Copilot (https://educationcopilot.com/), and Learnt.ai (https://learnt.ai/), to user-friendly free options such as Google Gemini (https://gemini.google.com/app) to OpenAI's ChatGPT (https://openai.com/index/chatgpt/). Many paid platforms offer free trial periods, allowing teachers to explore different options before committing to a subscription. However, it is important to note that "free" tools often require users to share personal information, so teachers should exercise caution in this regard.

When employing a generative AI tool such as ChatGPT or Google Gemini, it is advisable to start by defining a role and specific learning context. Once these parameters are set, the tool generates a variety of materials and activities tailored to the given context. These may include prompts for classroom warm-up discussions, vocabulary exercises, reading comprehension tasks, debates, and homework assignments. Additionally, the suggested lesson plan provides estimated teaching times for each activity. Teachers may need to refine their prompts and actively engage with the tool to generate more ideas.

While these generative AI tools can help in lesson plan creation, the structure of these lessons tends to exhibit repetition and a lack of creativity and diversity. To unlock more innovative teaching ideas from AI, teachers may need to explore more in-depth by providing more specific and detailed prompts or exploring alternative paid tools.

For reading comprehension exercises, ChatGPT and Google Gemini may recommend selecting an article from an online newspaper and creating your own comprehension activity. However, if requested, they often produce simplistic activities that may not align with your students' proficiency levels.

Other AI tools specialize in generating reading comprehension exercises from specific texts. Examples include QuestionWell (https://www.questionwell.org/), Formative AI (https://www.formative.com/), and Conker (https://www.conker.ai/), which can produce a variety of questions effortlessly. Simply input the chosen article, and the AI will generate essential questions, learning objectives, and align multiple-choice questions. Similarly, for listening comprehension exercises, various AI tools like Quizizz AI (https://quizizz.com/home/quizizz-ai?lng=en) or Twee (https://twee.com/) can swiftly create exercises based on YouTube videos. However, it is essential for teachers to verify the quality of the output, especially concerning the difficulty level of the items suggested by these tools.

Lesson plans generated by ChatGPT or Google Gemini often feature collaborative projects, which can serve as valuable pedagogical resources. To explore such options, request guidelines from the tool, and you'll receive detailed instructions on implementing this type of activity.

Teaching

As previously discussed in this chapter, AI tools offer significant potential for language teaching. This section will feature practical examples of utilizing generative AI to develop teaching activities that students can engage with both in and outside of the classroom context.

To enhance students' communication skills, consider creating debate groups using AI with Parlay Genie (https://new.parlayideas.com/), a discussion prompt generator. This tool generates thought-provoking questions for learners, drawing from specific topics, YouTube videos, or articles.

Additionally, you can encourage students to interact with influential figures from any historical period using Hello History (https://www.hellohistory.ai/). This tool facilitates realistic conversations with historical figures, providing students with an opportunity to engage in lifelike dialogues. For instance, students can practice forming questions by interacting with their favorite historical personalities.

Another engaging activity for students involves utilizing AI Chatbots such as ChatGPT or Google Gemini for a writing task. Students can be tasked with writing an essay on a given topic and then employing generative AI to review and correct their work. This can be followed by students presenting their findings to the class and engaging in a debate on the opportunities and challenges posed by AI.

In terms of grammar exploration, students can leverage AI to explore specific areas of grammar. For example, students could research a specific verb tense, such as the past simple. After studying the verb tense, students can share how it was addressed by AI with the rest of the class. This discussion can be followed by a discussion on their findings and the obstacles faced during the activity.

Students can also use tools that incorporate speech recognition to practice pronunciation and verb conjugation, as it is possible to listen to your speech and receive feedback on accuracy and fluency.

Another instructional activity you can carry out with students involves research projects in which they are tasked with finding and selecting the most suitable language learning app and presenting it to their peers. Through this assignment, students are prompted to explore various free apps available online, test their functionalities, and ultimately recommend the most fitting option, thereby fostering critical thinking skills.Providing students with the option to choose the AI tool they wish to use not only assesses their proficiency in using such tools but also allows teachers to discover new tools that can enhance language learning.

While this section focus primarily on generative AI text output tools, it is worth noting that there is a variety of other tools that focus on generating output in alternative formats, including images, video, audio, code, and even music.

Giving Feedback

AI has proven valuable for creating materials and designing tasks and activities for learners. Additionally, AI can provide feedback to learners, either in conjunction with the teacher or independently. A range of new tools and applications are being developed to offer instant feedback on pronunciation, grammar, and vocabulary. Some language learning applications use speech recognition to suggest corrections, which is beneficial for learners, while others can determine the level of a text according to the Common European Framework of Reference for Languages (CEFR). Some examples of tools that can help teachers prepare feedback for learners are Grammarly (https://www.grammarly.com/) and gotFeedback (https://www.gotfeedback.com/).

Grammarly assists teachers and/or students in checking writing assignments. It uses AI to identify mistakes in grammar, spelling, style, and tone, enabling faster and more frequent feedback preparation. Similarly, GotFeedback is designed to provide students with feedback. Users can select specific aspects for feedback, such as narrative structure, details, claims, or evidence, or customize the prompt themselves. Users can upload a .doc or .pdf file or paste in text. The platform will then provide an evaluation that teachers can give to students, or that students can use while drafting their texts.

Closely related to preparing feedback for learners is assessment. Initial reactions to AI have caused many educational institutions to panic, prompting the revision of assessment practices. The impact of these changes will vary depending on the educational context: online exams will need significant rethinking, while face-to-face exams may remain largely unaffected.

Academic integrity must be discussed with learners, as teachers need to clearly define what is acceptable and what is not acceptable. They must decide how much students can use AI and for what types of academic tasks. Importantly, teachers who understand AI's capabilities and limitations will be better equipped to make these decisions.

Here are several ideas and recommendations for redesigning assessed writing tasks in light of AI advancements:

- The more teachers know their students, the easiest it gets to identify authenticity of the work they present. Familiarity with the students' work helps identify if submitted work is genuinely theirs. Collect in-class writing samples to better spot inconsistencies.
- Pose complex, hypothetical questions without straightforward answers. While this may require higher language proficiency, it can effectively challenge students and reduce AI assistance.

- Assign tasks based on very recent local events. This makes it harder for AI to generate responses while allowing students to demonstrate their learning.
- Focus on Personal Experience. Design essay questions that require students to relate their answers to their personal experiences or class activities.
- Encourage peer and self-assessment, where students reflect on the differences in their evaluations. This is particularly useful for formative assessments.
- Provide a mix of images and text for students to write about. This complexity makes it harder for AI to generate accurate responses.
- Have students generate responses using AI, then critically evaluate and improve upon them. This also raises awareness of AI limitations and show students they teachers know how to identify AI generated text.
- If you suspect a piece of writing isn't a student's own work, discuss it with them. Ask them to explain their writing and process, which also enhances their oral skills.

As AI continues to evolve, these strategies will need regular updates. Staying informed about the latest developments will equip teachers with the necessary strategies to adapt accordingly. Moreover, the more you are familiar with AI, the easier it gets to identify AI generated text, so make sure you explore AI tools and their potentialities and last but not least ask better questions.

Challenges for Teachers

A multitude of AI tools has become accessible to the general public since late 2022, offering both promising opportunities and significant concerns for teachers. While these tools have greatly enhanced students' access to information, there is a valid concern that students may miss out on developing crucial intellectual abilities if they bypass the process of gathering, synthesizing, and crafting their own written assignments.

Teachers contend with a great number of writing tasks daily, often struggling to accurately assess them. The authenticity of student-produced work becomes a pressing issue, as it is challenging to determine whether a given piece of writing originates from the students themselves or if it is generated by artificial intelligence. Figure 2 includes some clues for teachers to navigate this challenge more effectively.

Figure 2. Clues for AI integration in learning

> **Clues for AI integration in learning**
>
> - Familiarize yourself with AI tools
> - Do not rely on AI-Generated text detection
> - Encourage personal opinion or experience
> - Stimulate reflexive, critical, or emotional insights
> - Encourage experience-based learning and active engagement
> - Foster critical thinking and application skills
> - Emphasize referencing and bibliographic correctness
> - Pose challenges beyond AI's capabilities

In fact, it is increasingly relevant for teachers to become acquainted with the latest iterations of AI tools – the more they understand their functionalities, the better equipped they will be to discern AI-generated texts. Notably, unless specifically requested, AI-generated texts often follow a consistent format (introduction, main topics, and conclusion) and various AI-generated text detectors, such as GPTZERO (https://gptzero.me/), can help confirm whether your students' texts were produced using an AI tool. However, these tools only provide a probability of AI creation; therefore, to rely solely on them

may not be the most effective approach. Given the ever-evolving nature of digital technology, a possibility would be to consider adapting the learning tasks to accommodate this digital landscape rather than merely verifying if students have copied/pasted the content of assignments. Moreover, when assigning writing tasks related to class topics, teachers can incorporate a subjective dimension by prompting students to share their personal opinions or recall relevant experiences. Later, if you have doubts about the authenticity of a text, you can request students to further develop their opinions or experiences to verify the integrity of their assignments. AI text generators are very good at synthesizing information; instead, teachers can design tasks that require critical analysis of quotes or the exploration of connections between different topics and challenge students to demonstrate critical thinking, emotional intelligence, collaborative skills, or other cross-cutting competences.

Thus, it is important to challenge students to go beyond rote memorization by asking them to critically analyze quotes, relate disparate topics, or connect classroom concepts to real-world scenarios. By incorporating these reflective and analytical elements into assignments, teachers empower students to apply their knowledge in diverse contexts. Moreover, by emphasizing the relevance of classroom learning to real-life situations, teachers inspire students to become active participants in their own learning journey, fostering a deeper appreciation for the subject matter and its broader implications in the world around them. Besides, students can also engage in experiential learning, and work upon specific personal experiences. By inviting students to express their own thoughts, they not only deepen their understanding of the subject matter but also cultivate critical thinking competences. Encouraging students to relate the topics to real-life situations, such as local news or current events, can also contribute to bridge the gap between classroom concepts and the practicalities of everyday life, fostering a deeper understanding and relevance to the material being studied.

Teachers can also ensure that students provide references and adhere strictly to recommended bibliography requirements. Unlike humans, AI typically doesn't attribute information or select recommended sources. While AI can gather information from various sources, it lacks the ability to choose appropriate bibliographies. For instance, if students are tasked with analyzing a specific article, AI may struggle to summarize and cite the required text, particularly if it is presented in .jpg format. Thus, capitalizing on the limitations of AI, teachers can challenge students with tasks that AI cannot easily accomplish. Assignments involving the critical analysis of texts in formats that cannot be copied and pasted into an AI text generator, such as .jpg images, can pose significant challenges for students. By designing tasks that require skills beyond AI's current capabilities, teachers can foster resilience and critical thinking skills in their students.

Summing up, as AI continues to evolve, it offers unprecedented opportunities to enrich language learning and education as a whole. By understanding and leveraging the strengths and limitations of AI, teachers can create a more engaging, effective, and personalized learning experience. Embracing these technological advancements, educators can not only enhance traditional teaching methods but also equip students with the critical thinking and analytical skills necessary to thrive in an increasingly digital world.

Future Research Directions

Albeit comprehensive, the list of tools provided within the scope of this chapter is still incipient, covering mostly reading and writing skills. Moreover, as the use of AI gradually becomes the norm, challenges pertaining to ethics and privacy will become even more relevant, and will require a more in-depth analysis. Drawing from this premise, in the near future, the authors expect to update the current list, not only to feature different applications for AI in language education, but also by discussing how these tools can be combined with more traditional teaching and learning approaches. This integration will be key to understand the potentially transformative effects of AI.

In order to achieve this goal, in addition to expanding and refining their review, authors will resort to questionnaires and focus groups, as to better understand the challenges faced by practitioners, and expand the range of practical examples provided. Based on these perceptions it will also be possible to outline tool-specific merits and shortcomings, thus providing a clearer outline of current teaching and learning landcsapes.

CONCLUSION

Artificial Intelligence has now become a central topic with significant impacts across various educational settings. Consequently, it is essential to assess how teachers are adapting to this transformation and to ensure they possess the necessary skills to integrate AI into their teaching practices.

This chapter has presented some recent trends and scenarios in language teaching and learning, in an attempt to discuss the advantages and challenges posed by AI in this context. It has presented and describe the key features of some platforms and tools, reflecting on their applicability, advantages, and limitations. Additionally, it has also incorporated Mollick and Mollick's (2023) approaches for using AI in various educational roles and settings, as a way to understand the different roles that AI can play in the context of education.

This chapter specifically aimed to support both practitioners and teacher teachers by compiling a comprehensive list of AI platforms and tools that can enhance teaching and learning environments. Instead of advocating for a "one size fits all" approach, the authors attempted to present a range of options designed to complement and inform existing methodologies, adaptable to diverse learning designs and outcomes. The annotated list, informed by extensive experience and a thorough review of literature and best practices, categorizes various AI tools that support language teaching and learning.

Recognizing the potential of AI in foreign language teaching and learning, along with its benefits and challenges, this chapter provided practical examples that can be replicated by practitioners and teachers in training.

ACKNOWLEDGMENT

This work is financially supported by National Funds through FCT – Fundação para a Ciência e a Tecnologia, I.P., under the projects: UIDB/00194/2020 (https://doi.org/10.54499/UIDB/00194/2020), UIDP/00194/2020 (https://doi.org/10.54499/UIDP/00194/2020) and the DIGI PROF: Transparent Assessment for Online Learning by Digitally Competent Professors (ERASMUS+ Project, ref. 2021-1-LT01-KA220-HED-000031154).

REFERENCES

Abunaseer, H. (2023). The use of generative AI in education: Applications, and impact. *Technology and the Curriculum: Summer 2023*.

Baker, M. (2000). The roles of models in Artificial Intelligence and education research: A prospective view. *International Journal of Artificial Intelligence in Education*, 11, 122–143.

Chang, C., & Kidman, G. (2023). The rise of generative artificial intelligence (AI) language models - challenges and opportunities for geographical and environmental education. *International Research in Geographical and Environmental Education*, 32(2), 85–89. DOI: 10.1080/10382046.2023.2194036

Escalante, J., Pack, A., & Barrett, A. (2023). AI-generated feedback on writing: Insights into efficacy and ENL student preference. *International Journal of Educational Technology in Higher Education*, 20(1), 57. DOI: 10.1186/s41239-023-00425-2

Hackman, J. (2011). *Collaborative intelligence: Using teams to solve hard problems*. Berrett-Koehler Publishers.

Holmes, W., & Tuomi, I. (2022). State of the art and practice in AI in education. *European Journal of Education*, 57(4), 542–570. DOI: 10.1111/ejed.12533

Humble, N., & Mozelius, P. (2022). The threat, hype, and promise of artificial intelligence in education. *Discover Artificial Intelligence*, 2(22), 22. Advance online publication. DOI: 10.1007/s44163-022-00039-z

Ifelebuegu, A., Kulume, P., & Cherukut, P. (2023). Chatbots and AI in Education (AIEd) tools: The good, the bad, and the ugly. *Journal of Applied Learning and Teaching*, 6(2), 1–14. DOI: 10.37074/jalt.2023.6.2.29

Klimova, B., Pikhart, M., Benites, A. D., Lehr, C., & Sanchez-Stockhammer, C. (2023). Neural machine translation in foreign language teaching and learning: A systematic review. *Education and Information Technologies*, 28(1), 663–682. DOI: 10.1007/s10639-022-11194-2

Kraft, M., Schueler, B., Loeb, S., & Robinson, C. (2021). *Accelerating student learning with High-dosage tutoring: Guide for local education agencies.* Annenberg Institute for School Reform at Brown University.

Martinez, D., Malyska, N., Streilein, B., Caceres, R., Campbell, W., Dagli, C., Gadepally, V., Greenfeld, K., Hall, R., King, A., Lippmann, R., Miller, B., Reynolds, D., Richardson, F., Sahin, C., Tran, A., Trepagnier, P., & Zipkin, J. (2019). *Artificial intelligence: Short history, present developments, and future outlook.* Massachusetts Institute of Technology.

Michel-Villarreal, R., Vilalta-Perdomo, E., Salinas-Navarro, D. E., Thierry-Aguilera, R., & Gerardou, F. S. (2023). Challenges and opportunities of generative AI for higher education as explained by ChatGPT. *Education Sciences*, 13(9), 856. DOI: 10.3390/educsci13090856

Mollick, E. R., & Mollick, L. (2023). *Assigning AI: Seven Approaches for Students, with Prompts. SSRN.* http://dx.doi.org/DOI: 10.2139/ssrn.4475995

Ng, D. T. K., Lee, M., Tan, R. J. Y., Hu, X., Downie, J. S., & Chu, S. K. W. (2023). A review of AI teaching and learning from 2000 to 2020. *Education and Information Technologies*, 28(7), 8445–8501. DOI: 10.1007/s10639-022-11491-w

Saheb, T., & Saheb, T. (2023). Topical review of artificial intelligence national policies: A mixed method analysis. *Technology in Society*, 74, 102316. DOI: 10.1016/j.techsoc.2023.102316

Tahiru, F. (2021). AI in education: A systematic literature review. *Journal of Cases on Information Technology*, 23(1), 1–20. DOI: 10.4018/JCIT.2021010101

UNESCO. (2019). *Digital Library, Artificial intelligence in education: challenges and opportunities for sustainable development.* https://unesdoc.unesco.org/ark:/48223/pf0000366994

Zhai, X., Chu, X., Chai, C. S., Jong, M. S. Y., Istenic, A., Spector, M., Liu, J.-B., Yuan, J., & Li, Y. (2021). A Review of Artificial Intelligence (AI) in Education from 2010 to 2020. *Complexity*, 2021(1), 1–18. DOI: 10.1155/2021/8812542

Zhang, S., Shan, C., Lee, J., Che, S., & Kim, J. (2023). Effect of chatbot-assisted language learning: A meta-analysis. *Education and Information Technologies*, 28(11), 15223–15243. DOI: 10.1007/s10639-023-11805-6

KEY TERMS AND DEFINITIONS

AI Simulation: system that mimics human behaviors and/or situations based on existing data and complex algorithms.

Artificial Intelligence: Often described as machines that can think like humans, it refers to computer systems and applications that can process large amounts of data and perform tasks that traditionally require human intelligence. These include (but are not limited to) visual perception, speech recognition and translation, with systems arguably being able to make decisions and create new knowledge based on existing information.

Chatbot: software designed to simulate conversation with human users, especially over the internet. Chatbots equipped with AI often use technique such as natural language processing to create automatic responses to users' questions.

Common European Framework of Reference (CEFR): Communicative language competences: competences which empower a person to act using specifically linguistic means.

Mentoring: the process of advising and or training someone, usually carried out by someone more experienced, acting as a counselor. In AI-based mentoring this process is technology-driven, with systems providing personalized guidance to learners using machine learning algorithms.

Personalized Learning: customized learning strategies and material which adapts to individual needs and profiles. Within the scope of AI, it is often referred to as adaptive learning, relying on data analysis that makes it possible to create personalized learning paths for each student.

Tutoring: Instruction in a particular subject. AI tutoring refers to computer-based systems that to create a personalized learning experience and human-like lessons, usually without human intervention.

Chapter 12
Exploring the Role of Artificial Intelligence in Second Language Acquisition:
A Focus on English Learning

Ines Rodrigues
https://orcid.org/0000-0001-7540-6994
Instituto Superior de Ciências Empresariais e Turismo, Portugal

ABSTRACT

As technology advances, the integration of Artificial Intelligence (AI) in education is prompting a paradigm shift. This chapter explores AI's impact on English as a second language (ESL) acquisition, focusing on its role in developing listening, writing, reading, and speaking skills among students in Portugal. The study highlights the importance of considering students as active participants in shaping their learning environments and ensuring their perspectives influence educational practices. Data were gathered through an online questionnaire targeting secondary school students from public schools in Portugal. Although AI is still emerging in Portuguese schools, students generally view AI-powered tools positively for both English learning and daily tasks. Importantly, they do not see AI as compromising the teacher's role, recognizing the irreplaceable value of empathy and human connection. The study calls for further research into students' perceptions of AI in education.

DOI: 10.4018/979-8-3693-3944-2.ch012

1. INTRODUCTION

English has established itself as the global lingua franca, playing a significant role in today's globalised world, particularly in international communication, diplomacy, and commerce. Its dominance on the internet and in media further underscores its importance as a vital tool for accessing a vast array of information, entertainment, and academic resources. For many, mastering English is not just an academic pursuit but a necessity for professional advancement and global interaction.

However, Learning English as a second language (ESL) poses significant challenges for non-native speakers. These challenges include difficulties in pronunciation due to interference from native accents, mastering new vocabulary, and understanding complex grammatical structures. Achieving fluency requires consistent practice, motivation, and a significant investment of time. The challenge of maintaining motivation, coupled with the need for regular practice, can make language acquisition a daunting task.

In response to these challenges, Artificial Intelligence (AI) offers innovative solutions that have the potential to transform language learning. By providing personalised learning experiences, adaptive content, and real-time feedback, AI can make the process of learning English more efficient, engaging, and tailored to individual needs. The rapid advancement of AI technologies, particularly during the COVID-19 pandemic, has accelerated their integration into educational settings, making these tools more accessible than ever before.

While the mainstream integration of AI in education might seem recent, sometimes at a pace that is hard to keep up with, particularly with the rise of applications like ChatGPT, the integration of AI in our daily lives is not new. The concept of machines exhibiting intelligent behaviour dates back to the pioneering work of Alan Turing, often regarded as the father of modern computer science (Joshi, A., 2024). Over the years, AI has evolved from basic applications, like chess-playing programmes, to sophisticated personal assistants such as Siri and Alexa, and now, to advanced educational tools capable of transforming language learning.

In Portugal, significant strides have been made in promoting digital literacy and integrating technology into education. Public schools now ensure that every student has access to a digital device, fostering a more connected and technological learning environment. Additionally, comprehensive training programmes are underway to equip teachers with the skills necessary to incorporate digital tools effectively into their teaching practices. However, the success of these initiatives depends not only on the availability of technology, but also on how students perceive and interact with these tools.

Nevertheless, the question remains: where do students stand in this digital revolution?

We have previously argued (Rodrigues, 2017) that involving students in addressing educational challenges enhances their sense of belonging and respect within the school environment. Listening to students' voices provides invaluable insights into what impacts them the most and offers perspectives that can lead to meaningful improvements in educational practices. The work of Jean Rudduck and others (Rudduck & Flutter, 2000) further supports this, highlighting the importance of student feedback in driving educational reform. Student voice has many benefits to the education system and affords young people the opportunity to talk about what helps and what hinders their learning. By understanding students' perspectives, particularly in the context of AI integration, educators can better evaluate the efficacy of these technologies in enhancing language learning.

Thus, this study seeks to explore the transformative potential of AI in ESL learning from the students' perspective. It aims to assess how AI-driven tools influence various language acquisition skills, including listening, speaking, reading, and writing. Moreover, it examines the benefits, challenges, and concerns associated with these technologies, as perceived by the students who are their primary users. Through this exploration, the study contributes to the ongoing discourse on AI in education, offering insights that can inform educators, researchers, and policymakers in their efforts to harness the full potential of AI in language learning.

2. CHALLENGES OF TRADITIONAL METHODS IN THE CLASSROOM

Before the advent of digital educational tools, and even before the widespread use of the internet, students were primarily taught using what are now referred to as "traditional methods". These methods relied heavily on textbooks, posters, flashcards, transparencies and in the early 2000s, PowerPoint presentations were considered cutting-edge.

With the emergence of digital tools targeted at education, new strategies were introduced. However, despite the proliferation of modern educational technology, many teachers continue to rely on these traditional methods for various reasons (Richards & Rogers, 2014). One reason is familiarity; many teachers have been trained in and have long used traditional methods may find more comfort in sticking to what they know. Additionally, schools may have established routines and limited resources can make it difficult for schools to adopt new teaching strategies or adapt to new approaches. The integration of innovative methods typically requires investment in technology and professional development, both of which may be constrained by budget limitations, leading school boards to make difficult choices about where to allocate funds (Kravchenko et al, 2024). Furthermore, both teachers and students may resist change due to fear of the unknown, with teachers lacking access to professional development opportunities that could help them transition to new approaches, making it more challenging to move away from traditional methods.

Traditional methods usually rely on memorisation, drills, and teacher-centred instruction, which can lead to student disengagement and boredom (Richards & Rogers, 2014). Also, these methods often tend to prioritise reading and writing skills, at the expense of speaking and listening, which are crucial for language acquisition. Furthermore, traditional approaches tend to follow rigid curricula and teaching materials, leaving little or no room for personalisation based on student's individual needs, interests, learning styles and paces. Moreover, traditional methods often prioritise grammar over communicative fluency, which combined with a lack of attention to cultural diversity, often results in an education that is neither relevant nor inclusive.

As we can see, traditional methods of teaching English have several limitations. These methods often lack practicality and fail to connect teaching content with real-world and social demand (Li, Yun, 2022). For instance, traditional classrooms in many countries, including Portugal, often operate within an exam-oriented educational system that prioritises rote learning and standardized testing, further complicating the situation, as teachers focus heavily on adhering to textbooks and preparing students for standardised exams. This approach leaves little room for creativity or adaptation to individual student needs. Adding to this, some students have weak learning ability and may experience difficulties in reaching the expected level of progress.

Addressing these challenges requires a shift towards more communicative, learner-centred approaches, that integrate authentic materials and real-life contexts, promoting active student participation, and incorporating technology that can lead to more dynamic and personalised experiences and enhance learning outcomes. By embracing AI and other digital resources, teachers can better meet the diverse needs of language learners, creating more dynamic, interactive, and personalised learning experiences that support their needs and preferences.

Despite any reasons, it is crucial for educators and educational institutions to explore and embrace new teaching methods that better prepare students for the rapidly changing world. By incorporating more engaging activities and leveraging AI tools, teachers can create learning environments that are not only more effective but also more aligned with the demands of the modern world.

3. THE RISE OF AI IN LANGUAGE LEARNING

The integration of AI in language learning represents one of the most significant developments in educational technology in recent years. While the roots of AI in education can be traced back to earlier efforts in computer-assisted language learning, the 21st century has witnessed a rapid evolution in the capabilities and applications of AI, transforming how languages are taught and learned.

The concept of using computers to aid language learning is not new. As early as the 1960s and 1970s, educators and researchers were exploring the potential of computers to provide language practice, feedback, and instruction through programs such as PLATO and the Dartmouth Time-Sharing System (Warschauer, 2000). These early systems were rudimentary by today's standards but laid the groundwork for the development of more sophisticated AI-driven tools.

By the late 20th century, the landscape of language learning began to shift with the introduction of more interactive and adaptive programmes. These programmes incorporated elements of AI, such as natural language processing and speech recognition, to provide more personalised and responsive learning experiences. However, it wasn't until the last decade that AI truly began to revolutionise language education, driven by advancements in machine learning, big data, and cloud computing.

AI has revolutionised language learning by offering innovative tools and applications that adapt to individual learners' needs. Language learning apps like Duolingo, Babbel or Rosetta Stone employ AI algorithms to tailor lessons to individual learners' proficiency levels, learning styles, and progress. These platforms employ interactive exercises that adapt in real-time, providing immediate feedback and reinforcement, which are crucial for effective language acquisition. To illustrate this, Vesselinov & Grego (2012) assessed the effectiveness of Duolingo and found that 34 hours of Duolingo were equivalent to a semester of university-level language education. Their study provides empirical evidence of how AI can accelerate language acquisition through personalised and interactive learning experiences. Similarly, Babbel integrates AI to offer lessons that focus on practical language skills, such as conversational fluency, by adapting content based on the user's native language and learning preferences.

Furthermore, speech recognition technology, another significant AI application, provides real-time feedback on pronunciation, intonation, grammar, punctuation, and writing styles, helping learners refine their listening skills (Sun, W. 2023). Tools like Google's speech-to-text and speech recognition features in language learning apps provide real-time feedback on pronunciation, allowing learners to practice and refine their speaking abilities in a low-pressure environment. This instant feedback mechanism not only helps in correcting errors but also builds confidence in using the language in real-world scenarios.

The impact of AI on language learning extends beyond just technological innovation. AI-driven tools have demoed access to quality language education, making it more accessible to learners across the globe. With AI, language learning has become more flexible and available to people regardless of their location, time constraints, or financial resources. This is particularly important in regions where access to qualified language instructors is limited or where traditional educational resources are scarce.

Moreover, AI enables a level of personalisation that was previously unattainable in traditional classroom settings. By continuously analysing learner performance data, AI can identify specific areas where a student is struggling and provide targeted exercises to address those weaknesses. This individualised approach helps to accelerate learning, as students receive the exact support they need when they need it.

The inclusivity of AI-powered language tools also deserves attention. These tools can support learners with diverse needs, including those with learning disabilities, by offering customizable learning experiences. Besides, they can be more inclusive and accessible to all students, including those who speak different languages, serving as an additional support system for English language learners and teachers (Gawate, 2019).

Research conducted by Hwang et al. (2019) highlights how the design of engaging activity layouts can significantly improve ESL students' motivation to learn and speaking accuracy. These findings underscore the importance of thoughtful activity design in maximising students' speaking accuracy and motivation.

However, Yang & Kyun (2022) identify three major challenges in the area of AI-supported language learning. The first is the lack of empirical research about the pedagogical effects of students' interaction with AI-supported language learning, as well as their attitudes towards AI technology. While AI tools are widely used, there is still a need for systematic studies that explore how these technologies impact learning outcomes over time and how they compare with traditional teaching methods. And although research in AI for education is growing, more systematic reviews and empirical studies are needed to fully understand its impact (Liang et al, 2021).

The second challenge is the technological barrier faced by many schools and students, which has imposed some difficulties in adopting AI in language learning. While AI tools have made language learning more accessible, the digital divide means that not all students have equal access to these technologies. This inequality can exacerbate educational disparities, particularly in underprivileged communities where access to the internet and digital devices is limited.

The third challenge involves overcoming teachers' concerns about the potential depersonalization of education with the increased reliance on AI. Language learning is inherently a social activity, and the interaction with a human teacher or peers provides cultural and emotional context that AI cannot fully replicate (Godwin-Jones,

2019). Therefore, while AI offers powerful tools for language learning, it should be seen as a complement to, rather than a replacement for, human interaction in the educational process.

Belda-Medina and Calvo-Ferrer (2022) highlight a crucial issue in their research, emphasizing the need to revise the English as a Second Language (ESL) curriculum to better align with the rapid advancements in AI technology. Their study underscores the growing gap between teachers' current digital skills and the evolving applications of AI in language education. As AI becomes increasingly integrated into educational settings, the importance of equipping teachers with the necessary skills and knowledge to effectively utilize these tools is paramount. By being aware of the potential drawbacks or challenges associated with AI, such as issues related to privacy, bias, or the over-reliance on technology, teachers can implement AI in a way that maximises its benefits while mitigating potential risks.

The present study aims to tackle these challenges, by exploring the use of AI in ESL classrooms from the students' perspective, providing valuable insights that contribute to the ongoing discussion on the evolving role of AI in language education.

4. THE PRESENT STUDY

4.1 Significance of the Study

In the realm of education, it is imperative that students' voices are not only heard, but also valued and prioritised in decision-making processes that directly impact them. Theoretical frameworks such as Student Voice Theory (Fielding, M., 2001; Cook-Sather, A., 2006) and Critical Pedagogy (Freire, P., 1968) underscore the importance of empowering students as active participants in their own learning and educational environments. Recognising and integrating students' perspectives can yield numerous benefits, including fostering a sense of ownership, increasing engagement, and empowering them, which can, in turn, lead to enhanced academic performance, motivation, and overall well-being. Moreover, ethical considerations demand that students' rights as stakeholders in the educational process be respected, ensuring their autonomy, dignity, and agency are upheld (Maitumeleng, N., 2017). By embracing student voice and incorporating it into educational practices, we can create more inclusive, responsive, and student-centred learning environments that better meet the diverse needs and aspirations of all learners.

In light of the transformative potential of AI in education, understanding students' perceptions becomes crucial in assessing the adoption and integration of AI in the English classroom. As AI continues to reshape current approaches to second language teaching and learning, this study's primary objective is to investigate and analyse its impact on the process of learning English as a second language from the students' perspective. Specifically, the research aims to assess how AI-driven tools and platforms influence the acquisition of various language skills, including listening, speaking, reading, and writing, as well as to identify the benefits, challenges, and concerns associated with these technologies.

In this new educational landscape, the role of the teacher is also evolving. Therefore, the study will explore students' views on the future role of teachers in an AI-augmented learning environment. By gathering insights directly from students, this research seeks to provide a comprehensive understanding of their experiences, preferences, and perceptions regarding the integration of AI technologies in their education. The findings are intended to contribute to the broader discourse on the effectiveness and implications of AI in language learning, offering valuable insights to educators, researchers, and policymakers about the potential benefits and challenges as perceived by students, who are the end-users of these technologies.

Furthermore, the study holds the potential to raise students' awareness of AI's capabilities in fostering autonomous language learning, while also supporting them in identifying personalised learning methods. For teachers, understanding students' perspectives toward AI could lead to the development of more tailored instructional materials and strategies that align with the students' needs and preferences. Lastly, this study is of considerable importance as it addresses a significant gap in the literature by providing insights into the impact of AI on ESL learning within the Portuguese context, where such research is currently lacking.

4.2 Data and Participants

This study collected data from 100 secondary school students enrolled in both regular and vocational courses in public schools across Portugal, all of whom are learning English as a second language. The questionnaire used for data collection was distributed through an online forum accessible to teachers, with clear instructions specifying that the study was intended exclusively for students in public schools.

A key characteristic of this study is that none of the participants had prior exposure to AI within their school environment. Instead, their experiences with AI tools and technologies were limited to autonomous use at home. This factor is critical to the research, as it ensures that the findings reflect students' independent interactions with AI, free from formal educational guidance or influence. This autonomy allows the study to capture authentic insights into how students perceive and use AI in their language learning process outside of the structured school environment.

While this research focuses on public school students, we acknowledge that private schools might yield different results due to factors such as students' socioeconomic status or parents' educational backgrounds. These differences could influence students' experiences and perceptions of AI in education. Additionally, public schools typically serve a more diverse student population, potentially enhancing the generalisability of our findings. Future research could explore these contrasts to provide a more comprehensive understanding of how different educational environments impact the integration of AI in language learning.

Before starting data collection, the objectives of the research were thoroughly explained to the participants. They were informed that their personal information would remain confidential, ensuring their privacy and anonymity. Moreover, it was emphasised that participation in the study was entirely voluntary and not a mandatory class assignment. Consequently, the respondents were students who chose to participate out of their own interest.

To gain insights into students' familiarity and usage of AI, a questionnaire with single-choice, multiple-choice and open questions was developed using AI-driven assistance. Specifically, ChatGPT, an AI language model and chatbot, was used to help formulate thoughtful and relevant questions and improve the ones that were defined according to the different sections, thereby enhancing the quality of the research survey. The contribution of AI in designing the questionnaire is duly acknowledged here.

Questionnaires provide a relatively quick and efficient way of gathering large amounts of information from a sample of individuals. In this study, the questionnaire was distributed via Google Forms to 100 students and comprised 25 questions divided into 4 categories: a) demographic information; b) awareness and usage of AI in language learning; c) effectiveness and impact; d) future expectations. To collect quantitative data, a 5-point Likert scale was employed, with options ranging from Very Effective = 5 to Not Effective at All = 1. The questionnaire also included four open-ended questions designed to capture students' perceptions and deeper insights into their experiences with AI (see Table 1).

Table 1. Open questions and explanation

Questions	Explanation
B7. What have you used chatbots for?	Provides information about the tasks and activities done by students using a chatbot.
C4. How effective do you find AI tools in saving time for daily learning tasks? Justify.	Provides information about their understanding on the practical applications of AI, the contexts it is used, and its effectiveness
D4. Do you believe AI can replace human language teachers? Justify.	Provides information about students' thoughts on their future classroom and the role of the teachers in their learning process.
D6. Would you recommend AI language learning tools to others? Justify.	Provides information on if and why students' would recommend the use of AI to their peers.

The primary aim of the questionnaire was to understand how students use AI in their schoolwork and assess its utility, effectiveness, and impact on acquiring and developing language skills. Additionally, it sought to measure students' perceptions of the future role of language teachers in an educational landscape increasingly influenced by AI. Given that AI is still in its early stages of integration into Portuguese schools, this study also aimed to explore students' visions for the future of their educational environment as AI technology continues to develop and spread.

This research is exploratory in nature, focusing on the diversity of students' understandings and conceptions of AI rather than examining how these perceptions may be linked to background variables such as gender, academic performance, or socioeconomic status. By examining students' perceptions, this study aims to provide an initial insight into the students' perspectives on AI in language learning, which can serve as a foundation for more in-depth research in the future, as well as valuable insights for educators, policymakers, and researchers.

5. FINDINGS AND DISCUSSION

In this section the findings of the study are discussed under the themes of the questionnaire and presented in tables. The tables are then analysed from the perspectives of students and based on the relevant theories.

5.1. Section A: Students' Demographic Information

The study involved 100 participants aged between 15 and 19 years. The majority were 15 years old, comprising 53 students, while only three participants were at the upper age limit of 19. These students were enrolled in the 10th, 11th and 12th grades. The sample was even split by gender, with 50 male students, and 50 were female students. All participants were native speakers of Portuguese, though one student identified as a speaker of Brazilian Portuguese, which is a distinct variety of the Portuguese language native to Brazil. This linguistic detail is worth noting, as it may subtly influence language learning experiences and perceptions, especially in a study focused on ESL.

All participants were enrolled in English as a second language classes, yet a division was observed between the types of courses they attended. Specifically, 76 students were enrolled in regular academic courses, while 24 were pursuing vocational courses. This distinction in educational pathways is significant and warrants further exploration. The discrepancy in the number of respondents from regular versus vocational tracks could be indicative of varying levels of engagement or interest in the study's subject matter.

Vocational students might perceive the questionnaire, which focuses on language learning and related topics, as less pertinent to their immediate educational goals and future careers. This perception could lead to lower motivation to participate or to engage fully with the questionnaire. The voluntary nature of participation in the study may have further amplified this disparity, as students who do not see the direct relevance of the topic to their studies might opt out or provide less thoughtful responses.

This assumption is not without basis; it finds support in some of the responses to the open-ended questions included in the questionnaire. These responses suggest that vocational students, in particular, may view language learning - and by extension, the study - as less central to their educational experience. This attitude could reflect a broader trend where vocational education students prioritise practical skills directly linked to their future professions over academic subjects like English, which they might not perceive as immediately useful.

Therefore, the demographic makeup of the respondents, particularly the imbalance between regular and vocational students, provides a crucial context for interpreting the study's findings. It highlights potential differences in engagement and motivation that could influence the overall results, especially in how different groups of students perceive and approach language learning. Future studies could benefit from exploring these differences more explicitly, perhaps by tailoring questionnaires to better align with the specific interests and motivations of vocational students or by investigating the factors that drive their engagement with academic subjects like ESL.

5.2. Section B: Students' Conceptions of the Level of Awareness and Usage of AI in Language Learning

This section delves into the students' awareness and usage of AI-driven tools, with a particular focus on their application in language learning. Question B1 aimed to determine whether students had prior experience with AI-driven tool or applications, without narrowing the scope to language-specific tools. Given that AI is relatively new to the educational community in Portugal, it was not our intention to limit it immediately to tools specifically designed for learning languages.

The results indicated that a significant majority of the respondents, 75 out of 100, had already used some form of AI-driven tool or applications. However, 18 students reported never having used such tools, and 7 were uncertain about their experiences. The ambiguity among students regarding their use of AI technologies underscores a broader challenge in distinguishing between AI-based and non-AI applications. As Long & Magerko (2020) note, the pervasive integration of AI into modern technologies often makes it difficult for users to identify whether an application employs AI. For example, personal assistants such as Siri or Alexa have been in the market for a long time; yet, many users interact with them without fully realising the underlying AI that powers these interactions. Therefore, it is understandable that students may not be aware of the nature of the technology they have used. This phenomenon is reflected in the responses; for instance, although student 16 claimed to have never used an AI-driven tool, when asked to list the AI tools they might have used, student 16 wrote ChatGPT (Table 2).

The findings also reveal that AI chatbots, particularly ChatGPT, are becoming increasingly integrated into students' daily lives. Notably, 75% of the students reported using ChatGPT, suggesting that chatbots are rapidly gaining traction as accessible and useful tools. This widespread adoption indicates a growing comfort with AI-driven technologies among students, even if they are not fully aware of the AI components at play.

Narrowing the questionnaire to language learning, when students were asked about the learning applications or software they had used and what they had used them for, one stood out (Table 3). 52% of students reported that they had already used Duolingo mostly to learn a new language, as expressed by student 9, "to learn a new language for a trip (Italian) and improving English skills", or by student 43, "to learn languages and to better understand and communicate in those languages". Duolingo's appeal lies in its gamified approach to language learning, which combines visual, audio, and grammar exercises to engage users in an interactive manner. As noted by Azzahara et al. (2023), Duolingo's gamified structure significantly enhances vocabulary acquisition, making learning both fun and effective.

Other applications, like Gamma, were mentioned by 15% of students, predominantly for school-related work, as stated by students 5, 6, 73 or 75. This application, while not strictly a language learning tool, seems to be leveraged for academic purposes, reflecting its versatility in supporting various aspects of students' educational experiences. Meanwhile, a smaller number of students (6%) indicated using ChatGPT as a language learning tool, which aligns with its broader usage trends.

Table 2. Question B2: List the tools you have used

ChatGPT	75 students
Duolingo	10 students
Gamma	8 students
Siri	3 students
Alexa	2 students
No answer	25 students

Table 3. Question B3: Which of the following AI language learning apps or software have you used?

Babel	8 students	Lingostar	1 student
Busuu	3 students	Rosetta Stone	0 students
D-ID	1 student	TalkPal	3 students
Duolingo	52 students	Other	6 students
Gamma	15 students	None of the above	28 students

Further analysis of the students' responses regarding the use of chatbots such as ChatGPT or CoPilot reveals that 30% of the students primarily utilised these tools for schoolwork. This finding is consistent with prior research by Solak (2024), which identified ChatGPT as a helpful resource for completing homework and assignments. However, many students were more detailed on their responses. The following excerpts illustrate the use of chatbots such as ChatGPT or CoPilot beyond mere homework assistance.

Table 4. Question B7: Statements related to the general use of chatbots

S7: for schoolwork when allowed
S11: Help with school homeworks, help to simplify a topic to study for a test, give ideas
S12: I have used it to search for information, to write texts and in a school assessment where it was required to use chat gpt
S29: Fact checking and resuming information
S41: To do a research about the laws of Newton
S44: having a little silly fun time

Based on their responses, it appears that students use chatbots for a variety of purposes, namely, for simplifying complex topics, fact-checking, summarizing information, and conducting research. For example, they use chatbots for schoolwork and homework assistance (S7, S11, S41), to simplify topics for study (S11), for fact-checking and summarising information (S29), or even to do some research (S41). They also mentioned using it to improve their writing skills and boost creativity, as some students use chatbots to help with writing tasks and to generate ideas (S11, S12). These uses highlight the potential of AI-driven chatbots to serve as multifaceted educational tools, aiding students in tasks that range from improving writing skills to generating creative ideas. Despite this, a few students also mentioned using chatbots for entertainment, as indicated by S44, who mentioned using it for "having a little silly fun time."

However, the integration of chatbots into educational practices is not without its challenges. Solak (2024) also raised concerns about the reliability of the tool, referring that they can sometimes provide inaccurate or misleading information.

This issue is particularly relevant when students rely on chatbots for "giving ideas," "writing texts," or "resuming information," as these tasks can foster a certain degree of academic laziness, as suggested by Alharbi (2023). Alharbi argues that students may become overly dependent on chatbots, leading to superficial learning without the critical engagement that comes from researching multiple sources.

Moreover, the responses also reflect a lack of consensus within the educational community regarding the use of AI tools. For instance, while student 7 mentioned using it when it is allowed, student 12 noted that its use was required for an assessment. This disparity highlights the varying degrees of acceptance and integration of AI within different educational settings. In fact, integrating AI in the classroom may be seen as an opportunity, but it can also be challenging. On one hand, many teachers still lack sufficient understanding of AI technologies and without proper training on the use of AI in the classroom, they may struggle to integrate AI pedagogically, potentially leading to either over-reliance on or resistance to these tools. On the other hand, they might not often find the right balance between traditional approaches and AI-driven scenarios, ending up discouraging its use in the classroom (Alharbi, 2023).

Finally, the ethical implications of AI usage in education cannot be overlooked. According to Su & Yang (2023), the deployment of tools like ChatGPT in classrooms raises important ethical concerns. These include the potential for AI to mislead or manipulate students, particularly if the information provided is not accurate. If AI use is not carefully monitored, it could lead to misconceptions and faulty learning outcomes, thereby compromising educational integrity.

5.3. Section C: Students' Conceptions of the Effectiveness and Impact of AI in ESL Learning

This section explores students' perceptions of how effective and impactful AI tools are in learning English as a second language. The data collected provides insights into which language skills students believe AI can enhance, how effective they find these tools in improving their language abilities, and their views on the role of AI in managing daily learning tasks.

In question C1 students were asked to identify which language skills they believed AI could effectively improve. The results are presented in table 5.

Table 5. Question C1: Which language skills do you think AI can effectively improve? (Select all that apply)

Skills	Reading	Listening	Writing	Speaking
Students	49	44	65	48

The data suggests that students perceive AI as most effective in improving writing skills (65 students), data suggests that most students believe AI can effectively improve their writing skills, followed by reading (49 students), speaking (48 students), and listening (44 students) skills. This preference for writing improvement could be due to the interactive nature of AI in text-based applications. These tools require students to engage in written communication, which not only helps them practice their writing by writing prompts, but also enhances their reading skills through interaction with generated content. Furthermore, the immediate feedback and suggestions for improvement provided by AI tools (Li, 2022; Sun, 2023) reinforce this belief. However, it would be beneficial to explore how these student perceptions align with the actual capabilities and limitations of AI in enhancing language skills.

The students' perceptions of AI's effectiveness in improving their language skills and in saving time on daily learning tasks were assessed in questions C2 and C3 (tables 6 and 7).

Table 6. Question C2: How effective do you find AI tools in improving your language skills?

Scale	1	2	3	4	5
Students	9	6	30	47	8

Table 7. Question C3: How effective do you find AI tools in saving time for daily learning tasks?

Scale	1	2	3	4	5
Students	3	9	21	42	25

Most students rated the effectiveness of AI in improving language skills as 4, indicating a belief that AI tools are somewhat effective. However, only a small number of students (8) rated these tools as very effective (5). In contrast, when asked about the effectiveness of AI in saving time for daily learning tasks, a higher proportion of students (25) rated it as very effective (5). This discrepancy suggests that while students acknowledge the utility of AI tools in managing and organising learning tasks, their confidence in AI's ability to directly enhance language skills is reduced.

This finding could imply that students view AI more as a facilitator of learning efficiency rather than as a primary tool for language acquisition. The perception that AI is better suited for managing tasks rather than developing complex language skills may reflect the current state of AI technology, which excels in providing quick, accurate responses but might not yet fully replace traditional learning methods (Javaid et al, 2023).

To gain deeper insights, students were asked to elaborate on their ratings in question C4. Table 8 presents a sample of their responses.

Table 8. Question C4: How effective do you find AI tools in saving time for daily learning tasks?

Scale	Sample of Students' Answers
5	S29: The best way to improve your language skills is to read, listen and write about said language. Through AI, you can find material to improve your language more efficiently and adjust stuff that would require a higher level of understanding to your own personal level of understanding. S46: They can help us to improve (in my case) the speaking and reading and can make a for a example a text better than us in a few seconds S51: AI has the creativity and the database to explore less used words or specific words or ideas and it can also make people find words to express ideas in better ways S56: it makes it easier to communicate in English with other people or even other languages, it makes us more autonomous to learn more. S59: I talk a lot With chatbots in English and I think That improved my skills, and it's practical and we can use the AI whenever we want. S98: I think it helps because it doesn't take up a lot of time, instead of researching I can just write there and it will give me the answers right away
4	S8: It can improve my language skills by correcting my grammar. It can save me time because it can write me texts(ChatGPT) that can help do the work faster. S12: AI helps in improving my language skills because of apps like Duolingo and saves time for daily learning tasks because it is faster to ask something in a site like chat gpt than looking for it on the internet or in a book. S21: I think AI it's an amazing choice for people who want to learn a new language but don't have the time to take a normal course. But, AI tools still have a lot to improve to be perfect in efficiency. S58: AI is really quick and direct in their answers, you ask the question and instead of seeing lots of sites the AI gives the whole answer quickly, so it saves a lot of time. S59: I talk a lot With chatbots in English and I think That improved my skills, and it's practical and we can use the AI whenever we want. S63: it helps to learn more things and it's very effective if you want to save time, sometimes it can give you wrong information, but for example for simple things it's really useful.
3	S4: AI is a way of doing those things, but there are better options. S9: I don't think you can really become fluent in a language only by doing a course in an AI tool, but certainly you can learn a lot of things. S41: I think AI on one hand can be very helpful when used correctly but on the other hand it is a way of not doing their work for some students. S71: In my experience, I believe that AI wouldn't have a very big effect on my language skills, although I have only tried using AI with English. I think that it can help you save a lot of time with proof-reading, making sentences more concise and cohesive, among other aspects.
2	S68: I believe that AI has not had an impact in my learning of English, mostly because when I learnt it, most of it still wasn't an actual tool for the public. AI can help daily life by saving some time in tasks where you might need all of your attention.
1	S7: I don't think AI could be helpfull in these situations. S55: I've never used AI to study languages, so I cannot consider it effective or not in improving my skills. S77: It's not something I need or use often.

The responses indicate that most students find AI tools effective, particularly in saving time on daily tasks. They appreciate AI's ability to adapt learning materials to individual needs (S29), the efficiency in providing quick responses (S98), and the potential for AI to enhance specific language skills like vocabulary and speaking through continuous interaction (S51, S59). However, there is also recognition of AI's current limitations (S21), such as its inability to fully replace traditional learning methods (S4) and concerns about the potential misuse of AI in academic settings (S41).

However, students refer that AI still has room for improvements, recognising its limitations (S21) which can be overcome with the advancement in technology, according to Solak (2024). Some students believe that AI can be helpful, but that there are better options available (S4), suggesting that they recognise the value of traditional learning methods alongside AI tools. Many express their scepticism about learning a foreign language using AI tools (S9) and feeling that AI hasn't significantly impacted their language learning (S68), which can be an indicator that they should be used as a supplement rather than a replacement for traditional learning methods.

In addition, these are 11th grade students that had been studying English since 3rd grade, which suggests that this could also be due to a lack of exposure to AI tools during their language learning path. Moreover, others raise concerns about AI being used to avoid doing some work (S41). This suggests a concern about the potential misuse of AI tools in a school setting. Lastly, some students haven't used AI for language learning and cannot affirm its effectiveness, nor find it helpful (S55), which suggests a need for more exposure and understanding of the benefits AI can bring to language learning.

While most students find AI tools effective in saving time for daily learning tasks, opinions diverge, as students acknowledge the need for further improvement in AI tools. The analysis also highlights the importance of using AI tools as a complement to traditional learning methods rather than a replacement. It also emphasises the need for responsible use of AI tools in school settings to avoid misuse or abuse.

The final question in this section, C5, asked students to evaluate the usefulness of various AI features in language learning. They were given eight options to choose from (table 9).

Table 9. Question C5: How do you think AI tools can help you improve your language skills?

Aspects of Language Learning	Students
Providing personalised exercises and lessons based on my individual learning style.	50%
Assisting in improving my pronunciation through voice recognition technology.	41%
Offering real-time feedback on my spoken language, helping me refine my accent.	34%
Facilitating interactive conversations with chatbots or virtual tutors.	33%
Correcting grammar and writing style to enhance my written communication.	54%

continued on following page

Table 9. Continued

Aspects of Language Learning	Students
Suggesting vocabulary and sentence structures to improve writing proficiency.	53%
Providing audio versions of written content to enhance reading skills.	30%
Making language learning more engaging and enjoyable.	46%
Keeping me motivated through gamification and interactive elements.	35%
Other	6%

This question provides an insight into what students value most in language learning tools, highlighting areas that may be most beneficial to focus on for teachers. The data suggests that students highly value features that enhance the accuracy and appropriateness of their written communication, as evidenced by the high percentages for grammar correction (54%) and vocabulary suggestions (53%). These findings highlight a strong preference for tools that support and refine writing skills, which aligns with earlier findings that students see AI as particularly effective in improving their writing.

Students also appreciate personalised learning experiences (50%) and features that make the learning process more engaging (46%). These preferences indicate that students value AI's ability to tailor the learning experience to their individual needs, which can increase motivation and make learning more enjoyable. The use of gamification and interactive elements is also valued by a significant portion of students (35%), further emphasising the importance of maintaining interest and motivation in language learning. In addition, the immediate feedback given, the opportunity to practise their speaking skills in an environment that is free of peer pressure by using interactive conversations with chatbots or virtual tutors can provide students the practice they need to become more comfortable and fluent in the language.

On the other hand, a small percentage of students (6%) felt that AI could not help them in any of the areas listed. Their justifications suggest that these students either have specific learning needs that AI tools currently do not address or have yet to see the benefits of integrating AI into their language learning process.

The data collected in this section reveals that while students generally find AI tools effective in enhancing their language learning, particularly in improving writing skills and saving time on daily tasks, they also recognise the limitations of these tools. Students value AI features that provide personalised and accurate feedback, facilitate efficient learning, and make the process more engaging. However, there is still a need for further development in AI technology to fully address the diverse needs of language learners.

Furthermore, the findings suggest that AI should be viewed as a complement to traditional learning methods rather than a replacement. The effectiveness of AI in language learning seems to depend on its ability to integrate seamlessly into existing educational frameworks, providing students with the tools they need to enhance their language skills while also recognising the importance of human interaction and traditional teaching methods.

As AI technology continues to evolve, it will be crucial to address the concerns raised by students and ensure that these tools are used responsibly and effectively in educational settings. This will involve not only improving the capabilities of AI tools. since the lack of quality of AI-powered apps, particularly while learning a second language, can be a major problem and a barrier (Moulieswaran & Prasantha Kumar, 2023), but also educating students and teachers on how to use these tools to their fullest potential.

5.4. Section D: Students' Future Expectations of AI in ESL Learning

The final section of the questionnaire sought to understand students' expectations for the future use of AI in language learning. The responses reveal a growing demand for AI-based tools to be more personalised, interactive, and adaptable to individual learning needs. This aligns with previous findings and highlights the evolving expectations students have as they become more familiar with AI technology.

Table 10. Question D1: What features do you hope future AI-based language tools will have?

Future AI-based language tools features	Students
Adapting content to individual learning styles	63%
Adding more interactive elements to engage learners.	49%
Incorporating spoken and written simulations for practical experience.	40%
Adapting content based on user preferences.	48%
Making the user interface more user-friendly.	41%
Incorporating user feedback for continuous improvement.	41%
Ensuring inclusivity in design and content.	24%
Other	5%

The data in Table 10 underscores students' desire for future AI-based language tools to be more personalised and engaging. The most significant demand, expressed by 63% of students, is for AI tools that adapt content to individual learning styles. This finding highlights the importance of personalised learning experiences, a trend also noted by Tapalova & Zhiyenbayeva (2022), who found that students value the tailored learning opportunities offered by AI-powered platforms.

Closely following this, 49% of students expressed a need for more interactive elements in these tools. This suggests that students not only want content tailored to their needs but also seek more dynamic and engaging learning experiences. The desire for content that adapts based on user preferences (48%) further emphasises the importance of customisation in AI tools, enabling students to learn at their own pace and according to their specific interests.

Practical experience is also a key expectation, with 40% of students hoping for the incorporation of spoken and written simulations. This reflects a demand for AI tools that provide real-world practice opportunities, allowing students to apply their language skills in authentic contexts. Such features could significantly enhance the effectiveness of AI tools in helping students achieve fluency and confidence in a new language.

Moreover, 41% of students emphasised the need for a user-friendly interface and the incorporation of user feedback for continuous improvement. This suggests that students are not only focused on the educational content but also on the usability of the tools. They want an intuitive experience that evolves based on their input, making the tools more responsive to their changing needs.

While ensuring inclusivity in design and content was the least chosen feature (24%), it remains crucial. Inclusive design is essential for making AI-based language tools accessible to all students, particularly those with special needs. This aspect, though less highlighted by the students, should be a priority in the development of future AI tools to ensure equitable access to quality language education.

Only 5% of students selected "Other," with some expressing that they had never used AI for language learning. This lack of exposure aligns with previous findings and highlights the need for increased awareness and usage of AI tools in educational settings.

Based on their answers, we can conclude that the development of future AI-based language tools should prioritise personalisation, interactivity, practical and user-friendly experiences, continuous improvement, and inclusivity. By focusing on these areas, AI developers can create effective and engaging language learning tools that meet the needs and preferences of these diverse students, contributing to better language acquisition outcomes.

The last question was about the possibility of teachers being replaced by AI, and the students' justification (tables 11 and 12).

Table 11. Question D5: Do you believe AI can replace human language teachers?

	Students
Yes	13%

continued on following page

Table 11. Continued

	Students
No	49%
I have no opinion on that	38%

Table 12. Question D6: Justify your answer

	Students' Answers
Yes	S28: If the AI is good enough, it can teach any language to anyone and language teachers would be rendered useless. S27: They can give classes that will help improve the language the students are learning, as AI knows everything, it can be programmed to give classes. S46: I think AI can explain as good as teachers. S88: It's smarter than teachers.
No	S8: It can not replace a teacher because it's a very limited tool and can't have the affection that the teachers have with their students. S10: Human teaching creates a connection between the people and helps to make the learning process easier most of the time, and human interaction is really needed these days. S29: Human teachers can provide a type of interaction that AI cannot replicate. S37: I think learning with human beings it's more successful because the person it's right in front of you, it's more personal, they can listen to your pronunciation and correct you. S43: I don't think AI could ever reach the level of human empathy and understanding for the struggles other people might have while learning new languages. S53: In no way AI would be able to replace the effort and emotion of a real teacher, because a person is much more responsive to someone that is really there, to help, to congratulate, to teach and to correct any mistakes that might happen. S54: It's a controversial topic. In my opinion, we would be out of our minds if we substitute real human teachers with IA. In my personal case, when learning whatever, I like to have conversations with real teachers. It makes me feel comfortable and I learn better. S68: There is a need for empathy when you teach something. Even I'd AI can make personalised lessons for everybody, it still can't replace the need for human connection between teachers and students. S73: AI can help us develop our language skills but it's not perfect and it doesn't teach us how to talk like natives.

The prospect of AI replacing human language teachers elicited mixed responses, with only 13% of students believing that AI could fully take over the role of a teacher. These students seem to place high confidence in the capabilities of AI, likely influenced by their positive experiences with AI-based tools or perhaps due to dissatisfaction with traditional teaching methods (S28, S27, S46, S88). We can also see here the misconception that "AI knows everything" (S27).

However, the majority of students (49%) do not believe that AI can replace human teachers. Their justifications underscore the irreplaceable human elements in teaching, such as emotional connection (S8, S53), empathy, and personalised activities and feedback (S37, S53, S68). Students like S8 and S43 emphasised the importance of the emotional bond between teachers and students, something that AI, regardless of its sophistication, is unlikely to replicate. This aligns with the argument by Cope

(2021) that AI, while powerful, cannot match the human intelligence required for effective teaching, particularly in terms of understanding and responding to the nuances of human emotions and interactions.

Interestingly, 38% of students expressed uncertainty or had no opinion on the matter. This significant percentage could originate from various factors, such as a lack of exposure to AI in educational contexts, limited digital literacy, or simply uncertainty about the future capabilities of AI. This ambivalence suggests a need for more informed discussions and experiences with AI in education, helping students form more concrete opinions.

In conclusion, while there is some openness to the idea of AI playing a more significant role in language education, there remains considerable scepticism about its ability to fully replace human teachers, as also stated by Kovalenko & Baranivska (2024). The future of AI in language education will likely depend on its ability to complement rather than replace human instruction, particularly in replicating the human aspects of teaching that students find most valuable. The integration of AI in education must also consider ethical implications, and the ongoing legislative developments will play a crucial role in shaping its future use in schools.

6. LIMITATIONS AND IMPLICATIONS FOR FUTURE RESEARCH

While this study provides valuable insights into students' perceptions of AI in learning English as a second language, it is important to acknowledge its limitations. The data was collected exclusively from public schools and secondary-level classes in Portugal, which, while offering a focused view of this demographic, may not fully represent the broader population or other educational contexts. For instance, the experiences of students in private schools or those in different countries might differ significantly due to varying socioeconomic backgrounds, access to resources, and curriculum designs. Future research should consider comparative studies across these different contexts to provide a more comprehensive understanding of AI's role in language learning, as previous research has identified variations in attitudes towards AI in 5th and 6th grade students (Mertala et al, 2022).

Furthermore, the exploratory nature of this study meant that it did not delve into the possible correlations between students' perceptions and their background variables such as gender, digital and technological skills, socioeconomic status, or specific interests and hobbies. Prior research has suggested that these factors can significantly influence students' engagement with and attitudes toward digital tools (Selwyn et al., 2020). For example, students from higher socioeconomic backgrounds may have greater access to technology, thereby developing more advanced digital skills, which could affect their interaction with AI-based learning tools. Therefore, future studies should explore these correlations to better understand how these variables impact students' use and perception of AI in language learning, potentially contributing to more equitable educational practices.

Another limitation relates to the ethical and legislative landscape surrounding AI in education. As the study was being conducted, the European Union was in the process of establishing the European AI Office to oversee the implementation of the AI Act, which aims to ensure that AI technologies are developed and used in ways that respect human dignity and rights, fostering collaboration, innovation and research in AI among the various stakeholders. However, the AI Act currently addresses risks primarily related to the scoring of tests and exams, leaving gaps in the educational area like plagiarism and ethical practices, which are of concern to educators and students alike (Stavytska et al, 2024).

Challenges and ethical considerations stress the need for a balanced and responsible integration of AI tools into language learning environments. The overall attitude towards its use is positive, but prudence is recommended in addressing potential drawbacks. Future research should investigate students' perspectives on these ethical and social implications of AI in language learning, such as privacy concerns, data security, and the impact on teacher-student interactions. Understanding these issues will be crucial in developing policies that promote the responsible use of AI in educational settings.

Finally, while AI offers significant potential for transforming language learning, its implementation in educational systems is still in its early stages, especially in Portugal. As AI continues to evolve, its impact on learning English as a second language will likely grow, presenting both opportunities and challenges. The positive perceptions of students highlighted in this study suggest that AI can play a transformative role in language education, but this potential must be worked thoughtfully. Future research should continue to explore how AI can be integrated into language learning in ways that complement traditional teaching methods, enhance student engagement, and improve learning outcomes.

In conclusion, the relationship between AI and ESL education is promising, with the potential to revolutionise how languages are taught and learned, where language learning is not just a skill but an enriching and personalised journey. By continuing to research from the students' perspective, educators, researchers, and policymakers can gain a deeper understanding of the opportunities, challenges, and implications of integrating AI into ESL classrooms, ultimately enhancing language learning experiences and outcomes for all learners.

REFERENCES

Alharbi, W. (2023). *AI in the Foreign Language Classroom: A Pedagogical Overview of Automated Writing Assistance Tools*. Hindawi Education Research International., DOI: 10.1155/2023/4253331

Azzahara, T., Muliati, A., & Sakkir, G. (2023). The effect of using the Duolingo application as a medium in improving students' vocabulary mastery. *Journal of Technology in Language Pedagogy*, 2(3), 523–539.

Belda-Medina, J., & Calvo-Ferrer, J. (2022). Using Chatbots as AI Conversational Partners in Language Learning. *Applied Sciences (Basel, Switzerland)*, 12(7), 1–16. DOI: 10.3390/app12178427

Cook-Sather, A. (2006). Sound, presence, and power: "Student voice" in educational research and reform. *Curriculum Inquiry*, 36(4), 359–390. DOI: 10.1111/j.1467-873X.2006.00363.x

Cope, B. K., Kalantzis, M., & Searsmith, D. (2021). Artificial intelligence for education: Knowledge and its assessment in AI-enabled learning ecologies. *Educational Philosophy and Theory*, 53(12), 1229–1245. DOI: 10.1080/00131857.2020.1728732

Fielding, M. (2001). Beyond the rhetoric of student voice: New departures or new constraints in the transformation of 21st century schooling? *Forum for Promoting 3-19 Comprehensive Education*, 43(2), 100–112. DOI: 10.2304/forum.2001.43.2.1

Freire, P. (2017). *Pedagogy of the oppressed*. Penguin Classics.

Gawate, S. (2019). Artificial Intelligence (AI) Based Instructional Programs in Teaching-Learning of English Language. *International Journal of English Language, Literature and Translation Studies (IJELR)*, 6(6).

Godwin-Jones, R. (2019). In a world of SMART technology, why learn another language? *Journal of Educational Technology & Society*, 22(2), 4–13. https://www.jstor.org/stable/26819613

Hwang, W.-Y., Manabe, K., Cai, D.-J., & Ma, Z.-H. (2019). Collaborative Kinesthetic English Learning With Recognition Technology. *Journal of Educational Computing Research*, •••, 946–977.

Javaid, . (2023). *Unlocking the opportunities through ChatGPT Tool towards ameliorating the education system* (Vol. 3-2). BenchCouncil Transactions on Benchmarks, Standards and Evaluations., DOI: 10.1016/j.tbench.2023.100115

Joshi, A. (2024). Machine Intelligence. In *Artificial Intelligence and Human Evolution*. Apress., DOI: 10.1007/978-1-4842-9807-7_6

Kovalenko, I., & Baranivska, N. (2024). Integrating Artificial Intelligence in English Language Teaching: Exploring the potential and challenges of AI tools in enhancing language learning outcomes and personalized education. *European Socio-Legal and Humanitarian Studies*, (1), 86–95. DOI: 10.61345/2734-8873.2024.1.9

Kravchenko, H., Ryabova, Z., Kossova-Silina, H., Zamojskyj, S., & Holovko, D. (2024). Integration of information technologies into innovative teaching methods: Improving the quality of professional education in the digital age. *Data and Metadata*, 3, 431. DOI: 10.56294/dm2024431

Li, Y. (2022). Teaching mode of oral English in the age of artificial intelligence. *Frontiers in Psychology*, 13, 953482. DOI: 10.3389/fpsyg.2022.953482 PMID: 35936279

Liang, J. C., Hwang, G. J., Chen, M. R. A., & Darmawansah, D. (2021). Roles and research of artificial intelligence in language education: An integrated bibliographic analysis and systematic review approach. *Interactive Learning Environments*. Advance online publication. DOI: 10.1080/10494820.2021.1958348

Long, D., & Magerko, B. (2020). What is AI literacy? Competencies and design considerations. In *Proceedings of the 2020 CHI conference on human factors in computing systems*. pp. 1-16. DOI: 10.1145/3313831.3376727

Mertala, P., Fagerlund, J., & Calderon, O. (2022). Finnish 5th and 6th grade students' pre-instructional conceptions of artificial intelligence (AI) and their implications for AI literacy education. *Computers and Education: Artificial Intelligence*, 3, 1–11. DOI: 10.1016/j.caeai.2022.100095

Moulieswaran, N., & Prasantha Kumar, N. S. (2023). Investigating ESL Learners' Perception and Problem towards Artificial Intelligence (AI) -Assisted English Language Learning and Teaching. *World Journal of English Language*, 13(5), 290–297. DOI: 10.5430/wjel.v13n5p290

Nthontho, M. (2017). Children as stakeholders in education: Does their voice matter? *South African Journal of Childhood Education*, 7(1), 1–7. DOI: 10.4102/sajce.v7i1.434

Richards, J. C., & Rodgers, T. S. (2014). *Approaches and Methods in Language Teaching* (3rd ed.). Cambridge University Press. DOI: 10.1017/9781009024532

Rodrigues, I. (2017). Rethinking Educational Research on School Disengagement Through Students' Voices. *New Trends and Issues Proceedings on Humanities and Social Sciences, 4*(6), 01–10. DOI: 10.18844/prosoc.v4i6.2905

Rudduck, J., & Flutter, J. (2000). Pupil participation and pupil perspective: "Carving a new order of experience.". *Cambridge Journal of Education*, 30(1), 75–89. DOI: 10.1080/03057640050005780

Selwyn, N., Cordoba, B. G., Andrejevic, M., & Campbell, L. (2020). *AI for good: Australian public attitudes towards AI and society*. Monash University.

Solak, E. (2024). Revolutionizing Language Learning: How ChatGPT and AI are changing the Way we Learn Languages. *International Journal of Technology in Education.*, 7(2), 353–372. DOI: 10.46328/ijte.732

Stavytska, I., Shalova, N., Korbut, O. (2024). Exploring the impacts and techniques of teaching with artificial intelligence tools. *Перспективи та інновації науки. Педагогіка, психологія*, медицина, DOI: 10.52058/2786-4952-2024-6(40)-40-47

Su, J., & Yang, W. (2023). Unlocking the Power of ChatGPT: A Framework for Applying Generative AI in Education. *ECNU Review of Education*, 6(3), 355–366. DOI: 10.1177/20965311231168423

Sun, W. (2023). The impact of automatic speech recognition technology on second language pronunciation and speaking skills of EFL learners: A mixed methods investigation. *Frontiers in Psychology*, 14, 1210187. DOI: 10.3389/fpsyg.2023.1210187 PMID: 37663357

Tapalova, O., & Zhiyenbayeva, N. (2022). Artificial intelligence in education: AIEd for personalised learning pathways. *Electronic Journal of e-Learning*, 20(5), 639–653. DOI: 10.34190/ejel.20.5.2597

Vesselinov, R., & Grego, J. (2012). *Duolingo effectiveness study*. City University of New York.

Warschauer, M. (2000). The Changing Global Economy and the Future of English Teaching. *TESOL Quarterly*, 34(3), 511–535. DOI: 10.2307/3587741

Yang, H., & Kyun, S. (2022). The current research trend of Artificial Intelligence in language learning: A systematic empirical literature review from an activity theory perspective. *Australasian Journal of Educational Technology*, 38(5), 180–210. DOI: 10.14742/ajet.7492

Compilation of References

AACSB. (2024). AACSB Accreditation. Available at: https://www.aacsb.edu/educators/accreditation Accessed on May 12, 2024.

Abunaseer, H. (2023). The use of generative AI in education: Applications, and impact. *Technology and the Curriculum: Summer 2023*.

Adeshola, I., & Adepoju, A. P. (2023). The opportunities and challenges of ChatGPT in education. *Interactive Learning Environments*, •••, 1–14. DOI: 10.1080/10494820.2023.2253858

Aggarwal, D. (2023). Integration of Innovative Technological Developments and AI with Education for an Adaptive Learning Pedagogy. *China Petroleum Processing and Petrochemical Technology Catalyst Research*, 23(2), 709–714. DOI: 10.5281/zenodo.7778371

Aguinis, H., Beltran, J. R., & Cope, A. (2024). How to use generative AI as a human resource management assistant. *Organizational Dynamics*, 53(1), 101029. DOI: 10.1016/j.orgdyn.2024.101029

Ahmed, Z., Tariq, A., Tahir, M. J., Tabassum, M. S., Bhinder, K. K., Mehmood, Q., Malik, M., Aslam, S., Asghar, M. S., & Yousaf, Z. (2022). Knowledge, attitude, and practice of artificial intelligence among doctors and medical students in Pakistan: A cross-sectional online survey. *Annals of Medicine and Surgery (London)*, 76. Advance online publication. DOI: 10.1016/j.amsu.2022.103493 PMID: 35308436

Akaev, A. A., & Rudskoi, A. I. (2017). Economic potential of breakthrough technologies and its social consequences. In Devezas, T., Leitão, J., & Sarygulov, A. (Eds.), *Industry 4.0. Studies on entrepreneurship, structural change and industrial dynamics*. Springer., DOI: 10.1007/978-3-319-49604-7_2

Akgun, S., & Greenhow, C. (2022). Artificial intelligence in education: Addressing ethical challenges in K-12 settings. *AI and Ethics*, 2(3), 431–440. DOI: 10.1007/s43681-021-00096-7 PMID: 34790956

Akyol, S., & Alataş, B. (2012). Güncel Sürü Zekası Optamizasyon Algoritmaları. *Nevşehir Bilim ve Teknoloji Dergisi,* 1(1).

Al Amoush, S., & Farhat, A. (2023). The power of authentic assessment in the age of AI. Faculty Focus online. Retrieved from https://www.facultyfocus.com/articles/educational-assessment/the-power-of-authentic-assessment-in-the-age-of-ai/

Al Lily, A. E., Ismail, A. F., Abunasser, F. M., & Alqahtani, R. H. A. (2020). Distance education as a response to pandemics: Coronavirus and Arab culture. *Technology in Society*, 63, 101317. DOI: 10.1016/j.techsoc.2020.101317 PMID: 32836570

Al-Ars, Z. T., & Al-Bakry, A.AL-Ars. (2019). A web/mobile decision support system to improve medical diagnosis using a combination of K-Mean and fuzzy logic. *Telkomnika*, 17(6), 3145–3154. DOI: 10.12928/telkomnika.v17i6.12715

Alcı, B., & ve Altun, S. (2007). Lise Öğrencilerinin Matematik Dersine Yönelik Özdüzenleme Ve Bilişüstü Becerileri Cinsiyete Sınıfa Ve Alanlara Göre Farklılaşmakta Mıdır?.*Çukurova Üniversitesi Sosyal Bilimler Enstitüsü Dergisi,* 16(1).

Alexan, A. I., Osan, A. R., & Oniga, S. (2012, October). Personal assistant robot. In Design and Technology in Electronic Packaging (SIITME)*, 2012 IEEE 18th International Symposium for IEEE.* (pp. 69-72). DOI: 10.1109/SIITME.2012.6384348

Alghamdi, S. A., & Alashban, Y. (2023). Knowledge, attitudes and practices towards artificial intelligence (AI) among radiologists in Saudi Arabia. *Journal of Radiation Research and Applied Sciences*, 16(2), 100569. Advance online publication. DOI: 10.1016/j.jrras.2023.100569

Alharbi, W. (2023). *AI in the Foreign Language Classroom: A Pedagogical Overview of Automated Writing Assistance Tools*. Hindawi Education Research International., DOI: 10.1155/2023/4253331

Ali, M., Aini, M. A., & Alam, S. N. (2024). Integrating technology in learning in madrasah: Towards the digital age. [INJOE]. *Indonesian Journal of Education*, 4(1), 290–304.

Ali, W. (2020). Online and remote learning in higher education institutes: A necessity in light of COVID-19 pandemic. *Higher education studies*, 10(3), (pp.16-25). https://doi.org/DOI: 10.5539/hes.v10n3p16

Aljanabi, M., Ghazi, M., Ali, A. H., & Abed, A. (2023). ChatGPT: Open possibilities. *Iraqi Journal for Computer Science and Mathematics*, 4(1), 62–64. DOI: 10.52866/20ijcsm.2023.01.01.0018

Al-khresheh, M. H. (2024). Bridging technology and pedagogy from a global lens: Teachers' perspectives on integrating ChatGPT in English language teaching. *Computers and Education: Artificial Intelligence*, 6, 100218. DOI: 10.1016/j.caeai.2024.100218

Al-Medfa, M. K., Al-Ansari, A. M., Darwish, A. H., Qreeballa, T. A., & Jahrami, H. (2023). Physicians' attitudes and knowledge toward artificial intelligence in medicine: Benefits and drawbacks. *Heliyon*, 9(4), e14744. Advance online publication. DOI: 10.1016/j.heliyon.2023.e14744 PMID: 37035387

Altunbey, F., & Alataş, B. (2015). Sosyal ağ analizi için sosyal tabanlı yapay zekâ optimizasyon algoritmalarının incelenmesi. *International Journal of Pure and Applied Sciences*, 1(1).

Álvarez-Herrero, J. F. (2024). Opinion of Spanish Teachers About Artificial Intelligence and Its Use in Education. In *IoT, AI, and ICT for Educational Applications: Technologies to Enable Education for All* (pp. 163–172). Springer Nature Switzerland. DOI: 10.1007/978-3-031-50139-5_8

Amato, L., & Schoettle, C. (2023). Using artificial intelligence ethically and responsibly: Best practices in higher education. In Keengwe, J. (Ed.), *Creative AI Tools and Ethical Implications in Teaching and Learning* (pp. 19–31). IGI Global Publications. DOI: 10.4018/979-8-3693-0205-7.ch002

Anderson, J. C., & Gerbing, D. W. (1984). The effect of sampling error on convergence, improper solutions, and goodness-of-fit indices for maximum likelihood confirmatory factor analysis. *Psychometrika*, 49(2), 155–173. DOI: 10.1007/BF02294170

Anderson, J. R., Corbett, A. T., Koedinger, K. R., & Pelletier, R. (1995). Cognitive tutors: Lessons learned. *Journal of the Learning Sciences*, 4(2), 167–207. DOI: 10.1207/s15327809jls0402_2

Anon. 2021. "Family Educational Rights and Privacy Act (FERPA)." Retrieved June 18, 2024 (https://www2.ed.gov/policy/gen/guid/fpco/ferpa/index.html)

Anon. 2024. "Computation Used to Train Notable Artificial Intelligence Systems." Our World in Data. Retrieved June 17, 2024 (https://ourworldindata.org/grapher/artificial-intelligence-training-computation)

Antony, S., & Ramnath, R. (2023). A phenomenological exploration of students' perceptions of AI chatbots in higher education. *IAFOR Journal of Education*, 11(2), 7–38. DOI: 10.22492/ije.11.2.01

Apps, J. W. (1990). *Study skills for today's college student*. McGraw-Hill, Inc.

Arnon, S., & Reichel, N. (2007). Who is the ideal teacher? Am I? Similarity and difference in perception of students of education regarding the qualities of a good teacher and of their own qualities as teachers. *Teachers and Teaching*, 13(5), 441–464. DOI: 10.1080/13540600701561653

Assessment. (2018). American Psychological Association. Retrieved from https://www.apa.org/ed/schools/teaching-learning/top-twenty/principles/assessment, accessed on April, 20th, 2020

Aydin, Ö. (2022). OpenAI ChatGPT Generated Literature Review: Digital Twin in Healthcare. Available online at: https://papers.ssrn.com/sol3/papers.cfmabstract_id = 4308687 (accessed April 10, 2024).

Aydın, İ. N. A. Y. E. T. (2024). Eğitim Teknolojisinde Etik Sorunlar. *Kastamonu Eğitim Dergisi*, 32(2).

Ayeni, O. O., Al Hamad, N. M., Chisom, O. N., Osawaru, B., & Adewusi, O. E. (2024). AI in education: A review of personalized learning and educational technology. *GSC Advanced Research and Reviews*, 18(2), 261–271. DOI: 10.30574/gscarr.2024.18.2.0062

Azzahara, T., Muliati, A., & Sakkir, G. (2023). The effect of using the Duolingo application as a medium in improving students' vocabulary mastery. *Journal of Technology in Language Pedagogy*, 2(3), 523–539.

Azzam, A., & Charles, T. (2024). A Review of Artificial Intelligence in K-12 Education. Open. *Journal of Applied Sciences*, 14(8), 2088–2100. DOI: 10.4236/ojapps.2024.148137

Baako, I., & Abroampa, W. K. (2023). Research trends on ICT integration in Education: A bibliometric analysis. In *Cogent Education* (Vol. 10, Issue 2). Taylor and Francis Ltd. DOI: 10.1080/2331186X.2023.2281162

Babakr, Z. H., Mohamedamin, P., & Kakamad, K. (2019). Piaget's Cognitive Developmental Theory: Critical Review. *Education Quarterly Eeview*, 2(3), 517–524.

Baber, H., Nair, K., Gupta, R., & Gurjar, K. (2023). The beginning of ChatGPT – a systematic and bibliometric review of the literature. *Information and Learning Science*, 125(7/8), 587–614. DOI: 10.1108/ILS-04-2023-0035

Baeza-Yates, Ricardo . (2018). Bias on the web. *Commun.* ACM 61, 6 (May 2018), (pp.54–61). DOI:Https://Doi.Org/10.1145/3209581

Bahati, B., Uno, F., & Tedre, M. (2017). Can student engagement in online courses predict performance on online knowledge surveys? *International Journal of Learning, Teaching and Educational Research*, 16(3), 73–87.

Bai, X. (2024). THE ROLE AND CHALLENGES OF ARTIFICIAL INTELLIGENCE IN INFORMATION TECHNOLOGY EDUCATION. *Pacific International Journal*, 7(1), 86–92. DOI: 10.55014/pij.v7i1.524

Baker, M. (2000). The roles of models in Artificial Intelligence and education research: A prospective view. *International Journal of Artificial Intelligence in Education*, 11, 122–143.

Baker, R. S., Inventado, P. S., & Corbett, A. T. (2017). *"Educational Data Mining and Learning Analytics." Cambridge Handbook of the Learning Sciences* (2nd ed.). Cambridge University Press.

Balakrishnan, M., & Gananathan, M. Nadarajah, Vellasamy S. & George, E. G. W. (2016). Enhancement of Higher Order Thinking Skills among Teacher Trainers by Fun Game Expert Approach World Academy of Science, Engineering and Technology. *International Journal of Educational and Pedagogical Sciences*, 10(12).

Barbosa, S., Cosley, D., Sharma, A., & Cesar Jr, Roberto M. (2016). Averaging gone wrong: Using time-aware analyses to better understand behavior. *InProceedings of the 25th International Conference on World Wide Web*. 829–841. DOI: 10.1145/2872427.2883083

Barbour, M. K., & Hodges, C. B. (2024). Preparing teachers to teach online: A critical issue for teacher education. *Journal of Technology and Teacher Education*, 32(1), 5–27. https://www.learntechlib.org/primary/p/223927/

Baykara, M., Gürtürk, U., Atasoy, B., & Perçin, İ. (2017). "Augmented reality based mobile learning system design in preschool education'', 72-77. *2017 International Conference on Computer Science and Engineering (UBMK)*. IEEE. DOI: 10.1109/UBMK.2017.8093560

Belanche, D., Casalo, L. V., & Flavian, C. (2019). Artificial intelligence in FinTech: Understanding robo-advisors adoption among customers. *Industrial Management & Data Systems*, 119(7), 1411–1430. DOI: 10.1108/IMDS-08-2018-0368

Belda-Medina, J., & Calvo-Ferrer, J. (2022). Using Chatbots as AI Conversational Partners in Language Learning. *Applied Sciences (Basel, Switzerland)*, 12(7), 1–16. DOI: 10.3390/app12178427

Berger, A. L., Della Pietra, V. J., & Della Pietra, S. A. (1996). A Maximum Entropy Approach to Natural Language Processing. *Computational Linguistics*, 22(1), 39–71.

Berland, M., Baker, R. S., & Blikstein, P. (2014). Educational data mining and learning analytics: Applications to constructionist research. Technology. *Knowledge and Learning*, 19(1-2), 205–220. DOI: 10.1007/s10758-014-9223-7

Bhutoria, A. (2022). Personalized education and artificial intelligence in United States, China, and India: A systematic review using a human-in-the-loop model. *Computers and Education: Artificial Intelligence*, 3, 1–18. DOI: 10.1016/j.caeai.2022.100068

Bicknell, K., Brust, C., Settles, B., Svrcek, M., & Brock, D. C. (2023). How Duolingo's AI learns what you need to learn. *Accessed*, (Apr), 25.

Biggs, J. (2001). Enhancing Learning: A Matter of Style or Approach. Ed.: Robert J. Sternberg ve Li - Fang Zhang. Perspectives on Thinking, Learning and Cognitive Styles. Lawrance Erlbaum Associates, Mahwah, ss.73 - 102.

Biggs, J. (1996). Enhancing teaching through constructive alignment. *Higher Education*, 32(3), 347–364. DOI: 10.1007/BF00138871

Binns, R., Veale, M., Van Kleek, M., & Shadbolt, N. (2020). The Ethics of AI in Education: A Review of Current Practices. *Journal of Educational Technology*, 15(2), 123–138.

Blundell, C., Lee, K. T., & Nykvist, S. (2016). Digital learning in schools: Conceptualizing the challenges and influences on teacher practice. *Journal of Information Technology Education*, 15, 535–560.

Bojanowski, Piotr, Edouard Grave, Armand Joulin, and Tomas Mikolov. 2017. "Enriching Word Vectors with Subword Information."

Bonacina, M. P., & Martelli, A. (2006). Automated reasoning. *Intelligenza Artificiale.*, 3, 14–20.

Bonafini, F. C., Chae, C., Park, E., & Jablokow, K. W. (2017). How much does student engagement with videos and forums in a MOOC affect their achievement? *Online Learning : the Official Journal of the Online Learning Consortium*, 21(4), 223–240. DOI: 10.24059/olj.v21i4.1270

Bonnet, A. (1985). *Artificial Intelligence, Promise and Performance.* Prentice Hall Int.

Boomsma, A. (1985). Nonconvergence, improper solutions, and starting values in Lisrel maximum likelihood estimation. *Psychometrika*, 50(2), 229–242. DOI: 10.1007/BF02294248

Boser, U. (2013). *Are Schools Getting a Big Enough Bang for Their Education Technology Buck?* Center for American Progress.

Bostrom, N., & Yudkowsky, E. (2014). The ethics of artificial intelligence *The Cambridge handbook of artificial intelligence*. Cambridge: Cambridge University Press.

Botelho, A., Baral, S., Erickson, J. A., Benachamardi, P., & Heffernan, N. T. (2023). Leveraging Natural Language Processing to Support Automated Assessment and Feedback for Student Open Responses in Mathematics. *Journal of Computer Assisted Learning*, 39(3), 823–840. DOI: 10.1111/jcal.12793

Boulay, B. (2022). Artificial Intelligence in Education and Ethics. In *Handbook of Open, Distance and Digital Education* (pp. 1–16). Springer Nature Singapore. DOI: 10.1007/978-981-19-0351-9_6-2

Bozkurt, A., Karadeniz, A., Baneres, D., Guerrero-Roldán, A. E., & Rodríguez, M. E. (2021). Artificial intelligence and reflections from educational landscape: A review of AI studies in half a century. *Sustainability (Basel)*, 13(2), 1–16. DOI: 10.3390/su13020800

Braga, D., Coelho, L., & Fernando Gil, V. R. (2007). "Homograph Ambiguity Resolution in Front-End Design for Portuguese TTS Systems." Pp. 1761–64 in *Proc.* [International Speech Communication Association.]. *Interspeech*, •••, 2007.

Breiman, L. (2001). *Machine Learning*, 45, (pp.5–32), Random Forests.

Browne, M. W., & Cudeck, R. (1993). Alternative ways of assessing model fit. In K. A. Bollen ve S. Long (Der.) *Testing structural equation models* (pp. 131–161). Sage Publications.

Buchanan, B. G. (1986). Expert systems: Working systems and the research literature. *Expert Systems: International Journal of Knowledge Engineering and Neural Networks*, 3(1), 32–51. DOI: 10.1111/j.1468-0394.1986.tb00192.x

Bukar, U. A., Sayeed, M. S., Razak, S. F. A., Yogarayan, S., & Sneesl, R. (2024). Decision-making framework for the utilization of generative artificial intelligence in education: A case study of ChatGPT. *IEEE Access : Practical Innovations, Open Solutions*, 12, 95368–95389. DOI: 10.1109/ACCESS.2024.3425172

Burgstahler, S. (2015). *Universal Design in Higher Education* (2nd ed.). Harvard Education Press.

Butler, K. A. (1987). *Learning Styles - Personel Exploration and Practical Applications*. The Learner's Dimension.

Buyukozturk, Ş., Kilic Cakmak, E., Akgun, Ö. E., Karadeniz, Ş., & Demirel, F. (2021). *Scientific research methods in education*. Pegem Academy.

Büyüköztürk, Ş., Kılıç-Çakmak, E., Akgün, Ö., Karadeniz, Ş., & Demirel, F. (2020). *Bilimsel araştırma yöntemleri*. Pegem Akademi.

Byrne, E., & Twinomurinzi, H. (2012). Facilitating administrative decision-making using Decision Support Systems. e-Leadership Conference on Sustainable e-Government and e- Business InnovationsE-LEADERSHIP. 1-7. DOI: 10.1109/e-Leadership.2012.6524707

Can 2016. Kişisel Asistan Teknolojisi. https://www.derinogrenme.com/2016/12/28/kisisel-asistan-teknolojisi/ Erişim tarihi: 10.04.2018.

Canfora, G., Di Sorbo, A., Emanuele, E., Forootani, S., & Visaggio, C. A. 2018. "A Nlp-Based Solution to Prevent from Privacy Leaks in Social Network Posts." Pp. 1–6 in *Proceedings of the 13th International Conference on Availability, Reliability and Security, ARES '18*. New York, NY, USA: Association for Computing Machinery. DOI: 10.1145/3230833.3230845

Carroll, A. (1998). *How to Study Better and Faster - Using Your Learning Styles and Strengths-. J*. Weston Walch Publisher.

Castellan, N. J.Jr. (1987). Computers and the shape of the future: Implications for teaching and learning. *Education and Computing*, 3(1-2), 39–48. DOI: 10.1016/S0167-9287(87)80483-1

Chahar, R., Chandiok, A., & Chaturvedi, D. K. (2014). Intelligent analysis of the effect of Internet system in society. [IJCI]. *International Journal on Cybernetics & Informatics*, 3(3). Advance online publication. DOI: 10.5121/ijci.2014.3302

Chan, C. K. Y. (2024a). Introduction to Artificial Intelligence in Higher Education. In Chan & Colloton (eds) Generative AI in Higher Education: The ChatGPT Effect (1st ed.). Routledge, (pp.1-23). https://doi.org/DOI: 10.4324/9781003459026-1

Chan, C. K. Y. (2024b). Redesigning Assessment in the AI Era. In Chan & Colloton (eds) Generative AI in Higher Education: The ChatGPT Effect (1st ed.). Routledge, (pp.87-127). DOI: 10.4324/9781003459026-4

Chan, C. K. Y., & Colloton, T. (2024). *Generative AI in Higher Education: The ChatGPT Effect* (1st ed.). Routledge., DOI: 10.4324/9781003459026

Chandiok, A., & Chaturvedi, D. K. (2018). CIT: Integrated cognitive computing and cognition agent technologies based cognitive architecture for human-like functionality in artificial system. Biologically Inspired Cognitive Architectures. 2212-683X https://doi.org/.DOI: 10.1016/j.bica.2018.07.020

Chandiok, A., & Chaturvedi, D. K. (2018). Cognition Functionality based Question Answering System. *International Journal of Computer Applications*, 179(20) (0975- 8887).

Chang, C., & Kidman, G. (2023). The rise of generative artificial intelligence (AI) language models - challenges and opportunities for geographical and environmental education. *International Research in Geographical and Environmental Education*, 32(2), 85–89. DOI: 10.1080/10382046.2023.2194036

Chassignol, M., Khoroshavin, A., Klimova, A., & Bilyatdinova, A. (2018). Artificial Intelligence trends in education: A narrative overview. *Procedia Computer Science*, 136, 16–24. DOI: 10.1016/j.procs.2018.08.233

Cheng, L., Ritzhaupt, A. D., & Antonenko, P. (2018, October). Effects of the flipped classroom instructional strategy on students' learning outcomes: A meta-analysis. *Educational Technology Research and Development*, 67(4), 793–824. DOI: 10.1007/s11423-018-9633-7

Chen, J., & Lin, J. (2023). Artificial intelligence as a double-edged sword: Wielding the power principles to maximize its positive effects and minimize its negative effects. *Contemporary Issues in Early Childhood*, 25, 1. DOI: 10.1177/14639491231169813

Chen, L., Chen, P., & Lin, Z. (2020). Artificial Intelligence in Education: A Review. *IEEE Access : Practical Innovations, Open Solutions*, 8, 75264–75278. DOI: 10.1109/ACCESS.2020.2988510

Chen, Y., Jensen, S., Albert, L. J., Gupta, S., & Lee, T. (2023). Artificial intelligence (AI) student assistants in the classroom: Designing chatbots to support student success. *Information Systems Frontiers*, 25(1), 161–182. DOI: 10.1007/s10796-022-10291-4

Chintalapati, S., & Pandey, S. K. (2022). Artificial intelligence in marketing: A systematic literature review. *International Journal of Market Research*, 64(1), 38–68. DOI: 10.1177/14707853211018428

Chiu, T. K., Jong, M. S. Y., & Mok, I. A. (2020). Does learner expertise matter when designing emotional multimedia for learners of primary school mathematics? *Educational Technology Research and Development*, 68(5), 2305–2320.

Chiu, T. K., Xia, Q., Zhou, X., Chai, C. S., & Cheng, M. (2022). Systematic literature review on opportunities, challenges, and future research recommendations of artificial intelligence in education. *Computers and Education: Artificial Intelligence*, 4(100118), 1–15. DOI: 10.1016/j.caeai.2022.100118

Chocarro, R., Cortinas, M., & Marcos-Matas, G. (2021). Teachers' attitudes towards chatbots in education: A technology acceptance model approach considering the effect of social language, bot proactiveness, and users' characteristics. *Educational Studies*, •••, 1–19. DOI: 10.1080/03055698.2020.1850426

Choi, S., Jang, Y., & Kim, H. (2023). Influence of pedagogical beliefs and perceived trust on teachers' acceptance of educational artificial intelligence tools. *International Journal of Human-Computer Interaction*, 39(4), 910–922. DOI: 10.1080/10447318.2022.2049145

Chong, Man Yan Miranda. 2013. "A Study on Plagiarism Detection and Plagiarism Direction Identification Using Natural Language Processing Techniques."

Chowdhury, S., Dey, P., Joel-Edgar, S., Bhattacharya, S., Rodriguez-Espindola, O., Abadie, A., & Truong, L. (2023). Unlocking the value of artificial intelligence in human resource management through AI capability framework. *Human Resource Management Review*, 33(1), 100899. DOI: 10.1016/j.hrmr.2022.100899

Cingi, H. (1994). *Sampling method.* Hacettepe University press.

Civaner, M. M., Uncu, Y., Bulut, F., Chalil, E. G., & Tatli, A. (2022). Artificial Intelligence in Medical Education: A Cross-Sectional Needs Assessment. *BMC Medical Education*, 22(1), 772. DOI: 10.1186/s12909-022-03852-3 PMID: 36352431

Clancey, W. J., & Letsinger, R. (1981). NEOMYCIN: Reconfiguring a Rule-Based Expert System for Application to Teaching. *International Joint Conference on Artificial Intelligence*.

Clarke, K. A. (2005). The phantom menace: Omitted variable bias in econometric research. *Conflict Management and Peace Science*, 22(4), 341–352. DOI: 10.1080/07388940500339183

Coccia, M. (2019). Why do nations produce science advances and new technology? *Technology in Society*, 59, 101124. DOI: 10.1016/j.techsoc.2019.03.007

Coelho, L., & Reis, S. (2023). Enhancing Learning Experiences Through Artificial Intelligence: Classroom 5.0. In *Fostering Pedagogy Through Micro and Adaptive Learning in Higher Education: Trends, Tools, and Applications*. IGI Global. DOI: 10.4018/978-1-6684-8656-6.ch008

Cognitive Development: The Theory of Jean Piaget. (n.d.). SUNY. Retrieved from https://courses.lumenlearning.com/suny-educationalpsychology/chapter/cognitive-development-the-theory-of-jean-piaget, accessed on April, 20th, 2020

Cohen, P. R., & Feigenbaum, E. A. (Eds.). (2014). *The handbook of artificial intelligence* (Vol. 3). Butterworth-Heinemann.

Colloton, T. (2024). Strengths and Weaknesses in Embracing ChatGPT in Curriculum Design. In Chan & Colloton (eds) Generative AI in Higher Education: The ChatGPT Effect (1st ed.). Routledge, (pp.44-86). https://doi.org/DOI: 10.4324/9781003459026-3

Combéfis, S. (2022). Automated Code Assessment for Education: Review, Classification and Perspectives on Techniques and Tools. *Software*, 1(1), 3–30. DOI: 10.3390/software1010002

Conneau, Alexis, Khandelwal, Kartikay, Goyal, Naman, Chaudhary, Vishrav, Wenzek, Guillaume, Guzmán, Francisco, Grave, Edouard, Ott, Myle, Zettlemoyer, Luke, & Stoyanov, Veselin. 2020. *"Unsupervised Cross-Lingual Representation Learning at Scale."*

Cook-Sather, A. (2006). Sound, presence, and power: "Student voice" in educational research and reform. *Curriculum Inquiry*, 36(4), 359–390. DOI: 10.1111/j.1467-873X.2006.00363.x

Cope, B. K., Kalantzis, M., & Searsmith, D. (2021). Artificial intelligence for education: Knowledge and its assessment in AI-enabled learning ecologies. *Educational Philosophy and Theory*, 53(12), 1229–1245. DOI: 10.1080/00131857.2020.1728732

Copeland, B. (2018). MYCIN. Encyclopedia Britannica. https://www.britannica.com/technology/MYCIN

Coskun, F., & Gulleroglu, H. D. (2021). Yapay zekanın tarih içindeki gelişimi ve eğitimde kullanılması. [JFES]. *Ankara University Journal of Faculty of Educational Sciences*, 54(3), 947–966. DOI: 10.30964/auebfd.916220

Costa, E. B., Fonseca, B., Santana, M. A., de Araújo, F. F., & Rego, J. (2017). Evaluating the effectiveness of educational data mining techniques for early prediction of students' academic failure in introductory programming courses. *Computers in Human Behavior*, 73, 247–256. DOI: 10.1016/j.chb.2017.01.047

Creswell, J. W. (2014). *A concise introduction to mixed methods research*. SAGE publications.

D'Mello, S., & Graesser, A. (2012). Dynamics of affective states during complex learning. *Learning and Instruction*, 22(2), 145–157. DOI: 10.1016/j.learninstruc.2011.10.001

Dahri, N. A., Yahaya, N., Al-Rahmi, W. M., Vighio, M. S., Alblehai, F., Soomro, R. B., & Shutaleva, A. (2024). Investigating AI-based academic support acceptance and its impact on students' performance in Malaysian and Pakistani higher education institutions. *Education and Information Technologies*, •••, 1–50. DOI: 10.1007/s10639-024-12599-x

Danks, D., & London, A. J. (2017). Algorithmic bias in autonomous systems. *In Proceedings of the International Joint Conference on Artificial Intelligence.*, 4691–4697.

Darling-Hammond, L., Adamson, F., & Abedi, J. (2010). *Beyond basic skills: The role of performance assessment in achieving 21st century standards of learning*. Stanford Center for Opportunity Pollcy in Education.

Darling-Hammond, L., & Ifill-Lynch, O. (2006). If They'd Only Do Their Work! *Educational Leadership*, 63(5), 8–13.

Darling-Hammond, L., & Richardson, N. (2009). Research review/teacher learning: What matters. *Educational Leadership*, 66(5), 46–53.

Davenport, T., Guha, A., Grewal, D., Bressgott, T., & Davenport, T. (2020). How artificial intelligence will change the future of marketing. *Journal of the Academy of Marketing Science*, 48(1), 24–42. DOI: 10.1007/s11747-019-00696-0

Dayanik, E., Vu, N. T., & Padó, S. (2022). Bias Identification and Attribution in NLP Models With Regression and Effect Sizes. *Northern European Journal of Language Technology*, 8(1). Advance online publication. DOI: 10.3384/nejlt.2000-1533.2022.3505

de Queiroz, D. C., do Nascimento, J. L. G., de Oliveira Nunes, P. H., Gomes, A. M. P., de Souza, J. T., & de Oliveira, I. N. (2024). Artificial intelligence in education: An overview of distance education courses. *Revista de Gestão Social e Ambiental*, 18(5), e08125–e08125. DOI: 10.24857/rgsa.v18n5-169

De Vocht, J. (1994). *Experiments for the Characterization of Hypertext Structures. Yayınlanmamış Yüksek Lisans Tezi*. Eindhoven Univ. Of Technology.

Delgado, A. J., Wardlow, L., McKnight, K., & O'Malley, K. (2015). Educational technology: A review of the integration, resources, and effectiveness of technology in K-12 classrooms. *Journal of Information Technology Education*, 14, 397–416. http://www.jite.org/documents/Vol14/JITEv14ResearchP397416Delgado1829.pdf. DOI: 10.28945/2298

Demir, O. (2019). Sürdürülebilir kalkınma için yapay zeka. In Telli, G. (Ed.), *Yapay zeka ve gelecek* (pp. 44–63). Doğu Kitapevi.

Deng, X., & Yu, Z. (2023). A meta-analysis and systematic review of the effect of Chatbot technology use in sustainable education. *Sustainability (Basel)*, 15(4), 2940. DOI: 10.3390/su15042940

Denny, P., Prather, J., Becker, B. A., Finnie-Ansley, J., Hellas, A., Leinonen, J., Luxton-Reilly, A., Reeves, B. N., Santos, E. A., & Sarsa, S. (2024). Computing Education in the Era of Generative AI. *Communications of the ACM*, 67(2), 56–67. DOI: 10.1145/3624720

Devlin, Jacob, Chang, Ming-Wei, Lee, Kenton, & Toutanova, Kristina. 2019. "BERT: Pre-Training of Deep Bidirectional Transformers for Language Understanding."

Diakopoulos, N. (2016). Accountability in algorithmic decision making. *Communications of the ACM*, 59(2), 56–62. DOI: 10.1145/2844110

Ding, L., Er, E., & Orey, M. (2018). An exploratory study of student engagement in gamified online discussions. *Computers & Education*, 120, 213–226. DOI: 10.1016/j.compedu.2018.02.007

Dockterman, D. (2018). Insights from 200+ Years of Personalized Learning. *NPJ Science of Learning*, 3(1), 1–6. DOI: 10.1038/s41539-018-0033-x PMID: 30631476

Dogan, M. E., Goru Dogan, T., & Bozkurt, A. (2023). The use of artificial intelligence (AI) in online learning and distance education processes: A systematic review of empirical studies. *Applied Sciences (Basel, Switzerland)*, 13(5), 3056. DOI: 10.3390/app13053056

Dogan, N. (2019). Measurement and evaluation in education Ankara: Pegem academy.

Donvan, J. (2023, February 24). *Will ChatGPT Do More Harm Than Good?* [Open to Debate Podcast, NPR]. Retrieved from https://opentodebate.org/debate/will-chatgpt-do-more-harm-than-good/

Druga, S., & Ko, A. J. (2021). "How do children's perceptions of machine intelligence change when training and coding smart programs?", In *Interaction design and children*, (pp. 49–61).

Du Boulay, B. (2016). Artificial intelligence as an effective classroom assistant. *IEEE Intelligent Systems*, 31(6), 76–81. DOI: 10.1109/MIS.2016.93

Duha, M. S. U. (2023). ChatGPT in Education: An Opportunity or a Challenge for the Future? *TechTrends*, 67(3), 402–403. DOI: 10.1007/s11528-023-00844-y

Dunn, K., & Dunn, R. (1986). The Look of Learning Styles. *Early Years*, 8, 46–52.

Dutt, S., & Ahuja, N. J. (2024). *An intelligent HCI based tutoring system for child-centric learning environment.* Multimedia Tools App., DOI: 10.1007/s11042-024-20052-x

Dwivedi, Y. K., Kshetri, N., Hughes, L., Slade, E. L., Jeyaraj, A., Kar, A. K., Baabdullah, A. M., Koohang, A., Raghavan, V., Ahuja, M., Albanna, H., Albashrawi, M. A., Al-Busaidi, A. S., Balakrishnan, J., Barlette, Y., Basu, S., Bose, I., Brooks, L., Buhalis, D., & Wright, R. (2023). "So what if ChatGPT wrote it?" Multidisciplinary perspectives on opportunities, challenges and implications of generative conversational AI for research, practice and policy. *International Journal of Information Management*, 71, 102642. DOI: 10.1016/j.ijinfomgt.2023.102642

Ebrahimi, Sayna. 2024. "LANISTR: Multimodal Learning from Structured and Unstructured Data."

EDUCAUSE. (2019). *EDUCAUSE Horizon Report 2019: Higher Education Edition.*

Ekizce, H. N., Anılan, B., & Atalay, N. (2022). Pre-service science teachers' levels of awareness of industry 4.0 concepts. *Journal of Innovative Research in Teacher Education*, 3(2), 192–208. DOI: 10.29329/jirte.2022.464.9

Elhajjar, S. (2024). The current and future state of the marketing management profession. *Journal of Marketing Theory and Practice*, 32(2), 233–250. DOI: 10.1080/10696679.2023.2166535

Elhajjar, S., Karam, S., & Borna, S. (2020). Artificial intelligence in marketing education programs. *Marketing Education Review*, 31(1), 2–13. DOI: 10.1080/10528008.2020.1835492

Elkhatat, A. M., Elsaid, K., & Almeer, S. (2023). Evaluating the Efficacy of AI Content Detection Tools in Differentiating between Human and AI-Generated Text. *International Journal for Educational Integrity*, 19(1), 1–16. DOI: 10.1007/s40979-023-00140-5

Encyclopedia Britannica. (1991). *Encyclopedia Britannica Verlag.*

Ennam, A. (2024). Assessing Covid-19 pandemic-forced transitioning to distance e-learning in Moroccan universities: An empirical, analytical critical study of implementality and achievability. *Journal of North African Studies*, 29(1), 153–177. DOI: 10.1080/13629387.2021.1937138

Ertel, W. (2018). *Introduction to artificial intelligence.* Springer.

Ertel, W. (2018). *Introduction to Artificial Intelligence.* Springer.

Escalante, J., Pack, A., & Barrett, A. (2023). AI-generated feedback on writing: Insights into efficacy and ENL student preference. *International Journal of Educational Technology in Higher Education*, 20(1), 57. DOI: 10.1186/s41239-023-00425-2

Etlican, G. (2012). X ve y kuşaklarının online eğitim teknolojilerine karşı tutumlarının karşılaştırılması (Doctoral dissertation).

European Commission. (2022). Ethical guidelines on the use of artificial intelligence (AI) and data in teaching and learning for Educators. Retrieved November 11, 2022, from https://education.ec.europa.eu/news/ethical-guidelines-on-the-use-of-artificial-intelligence-and-data-in-teaching-and-learning-for-educators

Ezzaim, A., Dahbi, A., Aqqal, A., & Haidine, A. (2024). AI-based learning style detection in adaptive learning systems: A systematic literature review. *Journal of Computers in Education*, (pp.1-39). https://doi.org/DOI: 10.1007/s40692-024-00328-9

Fatemi, F. (2020). Bridging the gender gap in AI. *Forbes*. https://www.forbes.com/sites/falonfatemi/2020/02/17/bridging-the-gender-gap-in-ai/

Fatima, S., Desouza, K. C., & Dawson, G. S. (2020). National strategic artificial intelligence plans: A multi-dimensional analysis. *Economic Analysis and Policy*, 67, 178–194. DOI: 10.1016/j.eap.2020.07.008

Felder, R. M. (1996). Matters of style. *ASEE Prism*, 6(4), 18–23.

Felix, C. V. (2020). The Role of the Teacher and AI in Education. Sengupta, E., Blessinger, P. and Makhanya, M.S. (Ed.). *International Perspectives on the Role of Technology in Humanizing Higher Education (Innovations in Higher Education Teaching and Expert*, Vol. 33), Emerald Publishing Limited, (pp. 33–48). DOI: 10.1108/S2055-364120200000033003

Feng, X., Wei, Y., Pan, X., Qiu, L., & Ma, Y. (2020). Academic Emotion Classification and Recognition Method for Large-Scale Online Learning Environment—Based on A-CNN and LSTM-ATT Deep Learning Pipeline Method. *International Journal of Environmental Research and Public Health*, 17(6), 1941. DOI: 10.3390/ijerph17061941 PMID: 32188094

Ferreira, R., Gregório, P., Coelho, L., & Reis, S. S. 2023. "Natural Language Processing and Cloud Computing in Disease Prevention and Management." (Pp. 217–40) in *Exploring the Convergence of Computer and Medical Science Through Cloud Healthcare*. IGI Global.

Fetzer, J. H. (1990). What is artificial intelligence? *In: Artificial Intelligence: Its Scope and Limits*. (Vol. 4). Studies in Cognitive Systems, Springer, Dordrecht. https://doi.org/https://doi.org/10.1007/978-94-009-1900-6_1

Fielding, M. (2001). Beyond the rhetoric of student voice: New departures or new constraints in the transformation of 21st century schooling? *Forum for Promoting 3-19 Comprehensive Education*, 43(2), 100–112. DOI: 10.2304/forum.2001.43.2.1

Fietta, V., Zecchinato, F., Stasi, B. D., Polato, M., & Monaro, M. (2022). Dissociation between users' explicit and implicit attitudes toward artificial intelligence: An experimental study. *IEEE Transactions on Human-Machine Systems*, 52(3), 481–489. DOI: 10.1109/THMS.2021.3125280

Figueiredo, M. M. (2019). Artificial Intelligence acceptance: morphological elements of the acceptance of Artificial Intelligence. (Doctoral dissertation). http://hdl.handle.net/10400.14/28555

Firat, M. (2023). What ChatGPT means for universities: Perceptions of scholars and students. *Journal of Applied Learning and Teaching*, 6(1). Advance online publication. DOI: 10.37074/jalt.2023.6.1.22

Fitria, T. N. (2021, December). Artificial intelligence (AI) in education: Using AI tools for teaching and learning process. In *Prosiding Seminar Nasional & Call for Paper STIE AAS* (Vol. 4, No. 1, pp. 134-147).

Flogie, A., & Aberšek, B. (2022). *Artificial intelligence in education*. Active Learning-Theory and Practice.

Forecast number of smartphone connections in 2025, by country. (2019). Statista. Retrieved from https://www.statista.com/statistics/982135/smartphone-connections-by-country, accessed on May, 10th, 2020

Fraenkel, J. R., Wallen, N. E., & Hyun, H. H. (2012). *How to design and evaluate research in education*. McGraw-hill.

Freedman, J. L., Sears, D. O., & Carlsmith, J. M. (1993). *Social psychology*. Prentice Hall.

Freeman, J. (2024). *Provide or Punish? Students' Views on Generative AI in Higher Education. HEPI Policy Note 51.* Higher Education Policy Institute.

Freire, P. (2017). *Pedagogy of the oppressed*. Penguin Classics.

Friedman, B., & Nissenbaum, H. (1996). Bias in computer systems. *ACM Trans. Inf. Syst. 14, 3 (July 1996), (pp.330–347). DOI:*Https://Doi.Org/10.1145/230538.230561

Gabriska, D., & Pribilová, K. (2023). Artificial intelligence in education, issues and potential of use in the teaching process. *2023 21st International Conference on Emerging eLearning Technologies and Applications (ICETA)*, (pp.141-146). https://doi.org/DOI: 10.1109/ICETA61311.2023.10344286

Galindo-Domínguez, H., Delgado, N., Losada, D., & Etxabe, J. M. (2024). An analysis of the use of artificial intelligence in education in Spain: The in-service teacher's perspective. *Journal of Digital Learning in Teacher Education*, 40(1), 41–56. DOI: 10.1080/21532974.2023.2284726

Gall, M. D., Gall, J. P., Jacobsen, D. R., & Bullock, T. L. (1990). *Tools fo r Learning*. ASCD Publication.

García, E., & Fernández, C. (2018). The impact of AI in education. *Journal of Education and Learning*, 7(3), 201–208. DOI: 10.5539/jel.v7n3p201

Garcia-Martinez, S., & Hamou-Lhadj, A. (2013). Educational Recommender Systems: A Pedagogical-Focused Perspective. In Tsihrintzis, G., Virvou, M., & Jain, L. (Eds.), *Multimedia Services in Intelligent Environments. Smart Innovation, Systems and Technologies* (Vol. 25). Springer., DOI: 10.1007/978-3-319-00375-7_8

García-Méndez, S., de Arriba-Pérez, F., & María del Carmen, S.-L. (2024). A Review on the Use of Large Language Models as Virtual Tutors. *Science & Education*. Advance online publication. DOI: 10.1007/s11191-024-00530-2

García, P., Amandi, A., Schiaffino, S., & Campo, M. (2007). Evaluating Bayesian networks' precision for detecting students' learning styles. *Computers & Education*, 49(3), 794–808. DOI: 10.1016/j.compedu.2005.11.017

Gawate, S. (2019). Artificial Intelligence (AI) Based Instructional Programs in Teaching-Learning of English Language. *International Journal of English Language, Literature and Translation Studies (IJELR)*, 6(6).

Gillespie, N., Lockey, S., & Curtis, C. (2021). Trust in artificial intelligence: A five country study. https://doi.org//DOI: 10.14264/e34bfa3

Gilmartin, E., Cowan, B. R., Vogel, C., & Campbell, N. (2018). Explorations in Multiparty Casual Social Talk and Its Relevance for Social Human Machine Dialogue. *Journal on Multimodal User Interfaces*, 12(4), 297–308. DOI: 10.1007/s12193-018-0274-2

Gimpel, H., Hall, K., Decker, S., Eymann, T., Lämmermann, L., Mädche, A., & Vandrik, S. (2023). Unlocking the power of generative AI models and systems such as GPT-4 and ChatGPT for higher education: A guide for students and lecturers (No. 02-2023). *Hohenheim Discussion Papers in Business, Economics and Social Sciences*. https://nbn-resolving.de/urn:nbn:de:bsz:100-opus-21463

Godwin-Jones, R. (2019). In a world of SMART technology, why learn another language? *Journal of Educational Technology & Society*, 22(2), 4–13. https://www.jstor.org/stable/26819613

Godwin-Jones, Robert. 2021. "Big Data and Language Learning: Opportunities and Challenges."

Golan, R., Reddy, R., Muthigi, A., & Ramasamy, R. (2023). Artificial Intelligence in Academic Writing: A Paradigm-Shifting Technological Advance. *Nature Reviews. Urology*, 20(6), 327–328. DOI: 10.1038/s41585-023-00746-x PMID: 36829078

González-Calatayud, V., Prendes-Espinosa, P., Roig-Vila, R., & Carpanzano, E. (2021). applied sciences Review Artificial Intelligence for Student Assessment: A Systematic Review. *Applied Sciences (Basel, Switzerland)*, 5467. Advance online publication. DOI: 10.3390/app

Goodwin, L. D. (1999). The role of factor analysis in the estimation of construct validity. *Measurement in Physical Education and Exercise Science*, 3(2), 85–100. DOI: 10.1207/s15327841mpee0302_2

Gordon, M., Daniel, M., Ajiboye, A., Uraiby, H., Xu, N. Y., Bartlett, R., Hanson, J., Haas, M., Spadafore, M., Grafton-Clarke, C., Gasiea, R. Y., Michie, C., Corral, J., Kwan, B., Dolmans, D., & Thammasitboon, S. (2024). A Scoping Review of Artificial Intelligence in Medical Education: BEME Guide No. 84. *Medical Teacher*, 46(4), 446–470. DOI: 10.1080/0142159X.2024.2314198 PMID: 38423127

Gosling, S. D., & Mason, W. (2015). Internet research in psychology. *Annual Review of Psychology*, 66(1), 877–902. DOI: 10.1146/annurev-psych-010814-015321 PMID: 25251483

Grabusts, P. (2020). Fuzzy Logic Learning Methods In Student Education. *Society. Integration. Education.Proceedings of the International Scientific Conference, 4*, 438-448. https://doi.org/DOI: 10.17770/sie2020vol4.4840

Graesser, A. C., Chipman, P., Haynes, B. C., & Olney, A. (2018). Autotutor and ALEKS: A Personalized, Conversational Agent Tutoring System. *International Journal of Artificial Intelligence in Education*, 28(1), 39–62.

Graesser, A. C., Hu, X., & Sottilare, R. A. (2018). Intelligent Tutoring Systems. In Hattie, J., & Anderman, E. M. (Eds.), *International Guide to Student Achievement* (pp. 267–270). Routledge.

Grosz, B. J., & Stone, P. (2018). A century-long commitment to assessing artificial intelligence and its impact on society. *Communications of the ACM*, 61(12), 68–73. DOI: 10.1145/3198470

Grzybowski, A., Pawlikowska–Łagód, K., & Lambert, W. C. (2024). A history of artificial intelligence. *Clinics in Dermatology*, 42(3), 221–229. DOI: 10.1016/j.clindermatol.2023.12.016 PMID: 38185196

Guan, C., Mou, J., & Jiang, Z. (2020). Artificial intelligence innovation in education: A twenty-year datadriven historical analysis. *International Journal of Innovation Studies*, 4(4), 134–147. DOI: 10.1016/j.ijis.2020.09.001

Gunawan, K. L., Kaniawati, I., & Setiawan, W. (2021). The responses to artificial intelligence in teacher integrated science learning training program. *Journal of Physics: Conference Series*, 2098(1), 012034. Advance online publication. DOI: 10.1088/1742-6596/2098/1/012034

Gunay, D., & Sisman, B. (2019). *Bilgi ve egitim teknolojileri okuryazarlığı.* , In *Egitimde ve endustride 21. yüzyil becerileri* (ss. 257-275Ankara: Pegem Akademi.

Gupta, A. K., Aggarwal, V., Sharma, V., & Naved, M. (2024). Education 4.0 and Web 3.0 technologies application for enhancement of distance learning management systems in the post–COVID-19 era. In *the role of sustainability and artificial intelligence in education improvement* (pp. 66-86Chapman and Hall/CRC.

Gupta, Y. P. (1990). Various aspects of expert systems: applications in manufacturing, *Technovation,* 10(7), (pp.487-504), ISSN 0166-4972, DOI: 10.1016/0166-4972(90)90027-H

Gurol, M. (1990). Eğitim aracı olarak bilgisayar ilişkin öğretmen görüş ve tutumları. (Unpublished Master's Thesis). Fırat Üniversitesi, Elazığ.

Guvercin, A. (2006). Examining the depression levels of the mothers and their children who see an earthquake according to some variables. https://www.proquest.com/dissertations-theses/depremzede-anneler-ve-çocuklarının-depresyon/docview/2564166661/se-2

Hackman, J. (2011). *Collaborative intelligence: Using teams to solve hard problems.* Berrett-Koehler Publishers.

Hale, M. (2018). Thwarting plagiarism in the humanities classroom: Storyboards, scaffolding, and a death fair. *The Journal of Scholarship of Teaching and Learning*, 18(4), 86–110. DOI: 10.14434/josotl.v18i4.23174

Harris, A., & Jones, M. (2019). Virtual Reality and Augmented Reality in Teacher Training: An Innovative Approach. *Journal of Educational Technology & Society*, 22(3), 34–45.

Haseski, H. (2019). What Do Turkish Pre-Service Teachers Think About Artificial Intelligence? *Int. J. Comput. Sci. Educ. Sch.*, 3(2), 3–23. DOI: 10.21585/ijcses.v3i2.55

Hauk, N., Hüffmeier, J., & Krumm, S. (2018). Ready to be a silver surfer? A meta-analysis on the relationship between chronological age and technology acceptance. *Computers in Human Behavior*, 84, 304–319. DOI: 10.1016/j.chb.2018.01.020

Heffernan, N. T., & Heffernan, C. L. (2014). The ASSISTments ecosystem: Building a platform that brings scientists and teachers together for minimally invasive research on human learning and teaching. *International Journal of Artificial Intelligence in Education*, 24(4), 470–497. DOI: 10.1007/s40593-014-0024-x

Herodotou, C., Rienties, B., Boroowa, A., Zdrahal, Z., & Hlosta, M. (2019, October). A large-scale implementation of predictive learning analytics in higher education: The teachers' role and perspective. *Educational Technology Research and Development*, 67(5), 1273–1306. DOI: 10.1007/s11423-019-09685-0

Hilton, M. L., & Pellegrino, J. W. (Eds.). (2012). *Education for life and work: Developing transferable knowledge and skills in the 21st century*. National Academies Press.

Holmes, N. (2018). Holmes, "Engaging with assessment: Increasing student engagement through continuous assessment,". *Active Learning in Higher Education*, 19(1), 23–34. DOI: 10.1177/1469787417723230

Holmes, W., Bialik, M., & Fadel, C. (2019). *Artificial Intelligence in Education: Promises and Implications for Teaching and Learning*. Harvard Education Press.

Holmes, W., & Miao, F. (2023). *Guidance for generative AI in education and research*. UNESCO Publishing.

Holmes, W., & Tuomi, I. (2022). State of the art and practice in AI in education. *European Journal of Education*, 57(4), 542–570. DOI: 10.1111/ejed.12533

Howard-Jones, P. A., Demetriou, S., Bogacz, R., Yoo, J. H., & Leonards, U. (2011). Toward a science of expert games. *Mind, Brain and Education : the Official Journal of the International Mind, Brain, and Education Society*, 5(1), 33–41. DOI: 10.1111/j.1751-228X.2011.01108.x

Hrastinski, S., Olofsson, A. D., Arkenback, C., Ekström, S., Ericsson, E., Fransson, G., Jaldemark, J., Ryberg, T., Öberg, L.-M., Fuentes, A., Gustafsson, U., Humble, N., Mozelius, P., Sundgren, M., & Utterberg, M. (2019). Critical imaginaries and reflections on artificial intelligence and robots in postdigital K-12 education. *Postdigital Science and Education*, 1(2), 427–445. DOI: 10.1007/s42438-019-00046-x

https://en.unesco.org/covid19/educationresponse/globalcoalition, June, 1st, 2020 https://mhrd.gov.in/sites/upload_files/mhrd/files/statistics-new/ESAG-2018.pdf, accessed on May, 15th, 2020

https://www.dqindia.com/powered-by-govt-it-spending-india-to-become-second-largest-it-marketin-apac-region-by-2018, accessed on May, 15th, 2020

https://www.kaggle.com, accessed on May, 8th, 2020

https://www.melbournechildpsychology.com.au/blog/educational-psychology-how-it-helps-learning, accessed on April, 21st, 2020

https://www.mospi.gov.in/national-statistical-office-nso, accessed on May, 15th, 2020

Huang, J., Saleh, S., & Liu, Y. (2021). A review on artificial intelligence in education. *Academic Journal of Interdisciplinary Studies*, 10(3).

Huang, W., Hew, K. F., & Fryer, L. K. (2022). Chatbots for Language Learning—Are They Really Useful? A Systematic Review of Chatbot-Supported Language Learning. *Journal of Computer Assisted Learning*, 38(1), 237–257. DOI: 10.1111/jcal.12610

Humble, N., & Mozelius, P. (2019). Artificial Intelligence in Education-a Promise, a Threat or a Hype? In European Conference on the Impact of Artificial Intelligence and Robotics 2019 (ECIAIR 2019), Oxford, UK (pp. 149–156). Academic Conferences and Publishing International Limited.

Humble, N., & Mozelius, P. (2022). The threat, hype, and promise of artificial intelligence in education. *Discover Artificial Intelligence*, 2(22), 22. Advance online publication. DOI: 10.1007/s44163-022-00039-z

Hung, C.-T., Wu, S.-E., Chen, Y.-H., Soong, C.-Y., Chiang, C.-P., & Wang, W.-M. (2024). The Evaluation of Synchronous and Asynchronous Online Learning: Student Experience, Learning Outcomes, and Cognitive Load. *BMC Medical Education*, 24(1), 326. Advance online publication. DOI: 10.1186/s12909-024-05311-7 PMID: 38519950

Hussain, M., Zhu, W., Zhang, W., & Abidi, S. M. R. (2018). Student Engagement Predictions in an e-Learning System and Their Impact on Student Course Assessment Scores. *Computational Intelligence and Neuroscience*, 2018(1), 6347186. DOI: 10.1155/2018/6347186 PMID: 30369946

Hussain, M., Zhu, W., Zhang, W., Abidi, S. M. R., & Ali, S. (2019). Using machine learning to predict student difficulties from learning session data. *Artificial Intelligence Review*, 52(1), 381–407. DOI: 10.1007/s10462-018-9620-8

Hussin, A. A. (2018). Education 4.0 made simple: Ideas for teaching. *International Journal of Education and Literacy Studies*, 6(3), 92–98. DOI: 10.7575/aiac.ijels.v.6n.3p.92

Hwang, G. J., Sung, H. Y., Chang, S. C., & Huang, X. C. (2020). A learning style perspective to investigate the necessity of developing adaptive learning systems. *Journal of Educational Technology & Society*, 23(2), 148–161.

Hwang, W.-Y., Manabe, K., Cai, D.-J., & Ma, Z.-H. (2019). Collaborative Kinesthetic English Learning With Recognition Technology. *Journal of Educational Computing Research*, ●●●, 946–977.

Ichsan, I. Z., Rahmayanti, H., Purwanto, A., Sigit, D. V., Miarsyah, M., & Gomes, P. W. P. (2020). HOTS-AEPCOVID-19 and ILMIZI learning model: The 21st-Century environmental learning in senior high school. [Jurnal Pendidikan Biologi Indonesia]. *JPBI*, 6(2), 265–272. DOI: 10.22219/jpbi.v6i2.12161

Ifelebuegu, A., Kulume, P., & Cherukut, P. (2023). Chatbots and AI in Education (AIEd) tools: The good, the bad, and the ugly. *Journal of Applied Learning and Teaching*, 6(2), 1–14. DOI: 10.37074/jalt.2023.6.2.29

Introna, L., & Nissenbaum, H. (2000). Defining the Web: The politics of search engines. *Computer 33,* 1 *(Jan. 2000), (pp.54–62). DOI:*Https://Doi.Org/10.1109/2.816269

Irshad, H. (2020). Attitude of university students and teachers towards instructional role of artificial intelligence. *International Journal of Distance Education and E-Learning (IJDEEL)*. 5(2). https://doi.org/DOI: 10.36261/ijdeel.v5i2.1057

ISCED. 2011. (2012). UNESCO Institute for Studies. Retrieved from https://uis.unesco.org/sites/default/files/documents/international-standard-classification-of-education-isced-2011-en.pdf, accessed on April, 21st, 2020

Jandrić, P. (2017). *Learning in the age of digital reason*. Springer. DOI: 10.1007/978-94-6351-077-6

Jaskari, M.-M. (2024). Academic Design Thinking Pedagogy as an Approach to Foster Sustainability Skills in Higher Education. In Goi, C. (Ed.), *Teaching and Learning for a Sustainable Future: Innovative Strategies and Best Practices* (pp. 69–90). IGI Global., DOI: 10.4018/978-1-6684-9859-0.ch004

Javaid, . (2023). *Unlocking the opportunities through ChatGPT Tool towards ameliorating the education system* (Vol. 3-2). BenchCouncil Transactions on Benchmarks, Standards and Evaluations., DOI: 10.1016/j.tbench.2023.100115

Jeong, H., Han, S. S., Kim, K. E., Park, I. S., Choi, Y., & Jeon, K. J. (2023). Korean dental hygiene students' perceptions and attitudes toward artificial intelligence: An online survey. *Journal of Dental Education*, 87(6), 804–812. Advance online publication. DOI: 10.1002/jdd.13189 PMID: 36806223

Jiang, S. (2019). Rejecting surveillance cameras on campus. *Teachers'. Perspectives*, 2019(12), 2.

Johnson, L., Adams Becker, S., & Cummins, M. (2016). *The NMC Horizon Report: 2016 Higher Education Edition*. New Media Consortium.

Jonassen, ve, H. D., & Grobowski, B. L. (1999). *Handbook of Individual Differences, Learning and Instruction*. Lawrance Erlbaum Associates.

Joshi, A. (2024). Machine Intelligence. In *Artificial Intelligence and Human Evolution*. Apress., DOI: 10.1007/978-1-4842-9807-7_6

Judijanto, L., Atsani, M. R., & Chadijah, S. (2024). Trends in the development of artificial intelligence-based technology in education. *International Journal of Teaching and Learning*, 2(6), 1722–1723. https://injotel.org/index.php/12/article/view/197

Jung, Y., & Lee, J.Jung and J. Lee. (2018). Learning engagement and persistence in massive open online courses (MOOCS). *Computers & Education*, 122, 9–22. DOI: 10.1016/j.compedu.2018.02.013

Kagitcibasi, C. (1999). *New person and people*. Evrim publishing.

Kamalov, F., Santandreu Calonge, D., & Gurrib, I. (2023). New era of artificial intelligence in education: Towards a sustainable multifaceted revolution. *Sustainability (Basel)*, 15(16), 12451. DOI: 10.3390/su151612451

Kaplan, E. Joseph ve Daniel A. Kies. (1995). Teaching Styles and Learning Styles. *Journal of Instructional Psychology*, 22(1), 29–34.

Kaplan, Ronald M. 2004. "Lexical Functional Grammar A Formal System for Grammatical Representation."

Kara, N., & Sevim, N. (2013). Adaptive Expert Systems: Beyond Teaching Machines. *Contemporary Educational Technology*, 4(2), 108–120. DOI: 10.30935/cedtech/6095

Karasar, N. (2002). *Scientific research method*. Nobel publishing.

Käser, T., Hallinen, N. R., & Schwartz, D. L. (2017) Modeling exploration strategies to predict student performance within a learning environment and beyond. In: 17th International conference on learning analytics and knowledge 2017, pp 31–40. "DOI: 10.1145/3027385.3027422

Kassarnig, V., Mones, E., Bjerre-Nielsen, A., Sapiezynski, P., Dreyer Lassen, D., & Lehmann, S. (2018, December). Academic performance and behavioral patterns. *EPJ Data Science*, 7(1), 10. DOI: 10.1140/epjds/s13688-018-0138-8

Katz, J. E., & Graveman, R. F. (1991). Privacy Issues of a National Research and Education Network. *Telematics and Informatics*, 8(1), 71–120. DOI: 10.1016/S0736-5853(05)80096-6

Kaya, F., Aydin, F., Schepman, A., Rodway, P., Yetisensoy, O., & Demir-Kaya, M. (2022). The roles of personality traits, AI anxiety, and demographic factors in attitudes toward artificial intelligence. *International Journal of Human-Computer Interaction*. Advance online publication. DOI: 10.1080/10447318.2022.2151730

Keefe, J. W. (1990). *Learning Style Profile Handbook* (Vol. II). Developing Cognitive Skills. National Association of Secondary School Principals.

Keles, A. (2007). Artificial intelligence and web based intelligent tutoring system design in learning teaching process and "An application in mathematics teaching". (Doctoral Dissertation). Atatürk University. Erzurum.

Kengam, J. (2020). Artificial intelligence in education. *Research Gate*, 18, 1–4.

Khalifa, M., & Albadawy, M. (2024). Using Artificial Intelligence in Academic Writing and Research: An Essential Productivity Tool. *Computer Methods and Programs in Biomedicine Update*, 5, 100145. DOI: 10.1016/j.cmpbup.2024.100145

Khare, K., Stewart, B., & Khare, A. (2018). Artificial intelligence and the student experience: An institutional perspective. *IAFOR Journal of Education*, 6(3).

Kilic, S. (2014). Effect size. *Journal of Mood Disorders*, 4(1), 44–46. DOI: 10.5455/jmood.20140228012836

Kim, S. W., & Lee, Y. (2020). Attitudes toward artificial intelligence of high school students' in Korea. *Journal of the Korea Convergence Society*, 11(12), 1–13. DOI: 10.15207/JKCS.2020.11.12.001

Kizilcec, R. F., Reich, J., Yeomans, M., Dann, C., Brunskill, E., Lopez, G., & Tingley, D. (2020). Scaling up behavioral science interventions in online education. *Proceedings of the National Academy of Sciences of the United States of America*, 117(26), 14900–14905. DOI: 10.1073/pnas.1921417117 PMID: 32541050

Klimova, B., Pikhart, M., Benites, A. D., Lehr, C., & Sanchez-Stockhammer, C. (2023). Neural machine translation in foreign language teaching and learning: A systematic review. *Education and Information Technologies*, 28(1), 663–682. DOI: 10.1007/s10639-022-11194-2

Kline, R. B. (2016). *Principles and practice of structural equation modelling*. Guilford Press.

Kochmar, Ekaterina, Vu, Dung, Belfer, Robert, Gupta, Varun, Serban, Iulian, & Pineau, Joelle. (2020). *Automated Personalized Feedback Improves Learning Gains in An Intelligent Tutoring System*. .DOI: 10.1007/978-3-030-52240-7_26

Koc, N., & Celik, B. (2015). The impact of number of students per teacher on student achievement. *Procedia: Social and Behavioral Sciences*, 177, 65–70. DOI: 10.1016/j.sbspro.2015.02.335

Koedinger, K. R., & Corbett, A. (2006). Cognitive tutors: Technology bringing learning sciences to the classroom. na.

Koklu, N., Buyukozturk, S., & Bokeoglu, C. O. (2007). *Statistic for Social Sciences*. Pegem.

Kolb, D. A. (1984). *Experiential Learning: Experience as The Source of Learning and Development*. Prentice-Hall.

Kong, S. C., Cheung, W. M. Y., & Zhang, G. (2021). Evaluation of an artificial intelligence literacy course for university students with diverse study backgrounds. *Computers and Education: Artificial Intelligence*, 2, 100026. DOI: 10.1016/j.caeai.2021.100026

Koufakou, A., Garciga, J., Paul, A., Morelli, J., & Frank, C. 2022. "Automatically Classifying Emotions Based on Text: A Comparative Exploration of Different Datasets." Pp. 342–46 in 2022 IEEE 34th International Conference on Tools with Artificial Intelligence (ICTAI). DOI: 10.1109/ICTAI56018.2022.00056

Kovalenko, I., & Baranivska, N. (2024). Integrating Artificial Intelligence in English Language Teaching: Exploring the potential and challenges of AI tools in enhancing language learning outcomes and personalized education. *European Socio-Legal and Humanitarian Studies*, (1), 86–95. DOI: 10.61345/2734-8873.2024.1.9

Koyuncu, M. (2009). Fuzzy querying in intelligent information systems. In *International Conference on Flexible Query Answering Systems* (pp. 536-547). Springer, Berlin, Heidelberg. DOI: 10.1007/978-3-642-04957-6_46

Kraft, M., Schueler, B., Loeb, S., & Robinson, C. (2021). *Accelerating student learning with High-dosage tutoring: Guide for local education agencies*. Annenberg Institute for School Reform at Brown University.

Kravchenko, H., Ryabova, Z., Kossova-Silina, H., Zamojskyj, S., & Holovko, D. (2024). Integration of information technologies into innovative teaching methods: Improving the quality of professional education in the digital age. *Data and Metadata*, 3, 431. DOI: 10.56294/dm2024431

Kulik, C.-L. C., & Fletcher, J. D. (2016). Effectiveness of Intelligent Tutoring Systems: A Meta-Analysis. *Review of Educational Research*, 86(3), 430–456. DOI: 10.3102/0034654315581420

Kurban, T. (2006). *Kablosuz Taşinabilir Uzaktan Sağlik İzleme Sistemi: Mobil Sağlik Danişmanı*. Yayınlanmamış Yüksek Lisans Tezi.

Kushnir, N., Osypova, N., Valko, N., & Kuzmich, L. (2020). Model of an Education Robotics Course for Natural Sciences Teachers. *CEUR workshop Proceeding*. Vol- 2740/20200322.pdf.

Lama, Tek, Arias, P., Mendoza, K., & Manahan, J. (2015). Student evaluation of teaching surveys: Do students provide accurate and reliable information? *E-Journal of Social & Behavioural Research in Business*, 6(1), 30–39.

Lansdown, J., & Roast, C. (1987). The Possibilities and Problems of Knowledge-Based Systems for Design. *Environment and Planning. B, Planning & Design*, 14(3), 255–266. DOI: 10.1068/b140255

Legg, S., & Hutter, M. (2007). A collection of definitions of intelligence. *Frontiers in Artificial Intelligence and applications* (Vol. 157).

Leitner, P., Khalil, M., & Ebner, M. (2017). In Peña-Ayala, A. (Ed.), *"Learning analytics in higher education—a literature review," in Learning Analytics: Fundaments, Applications, and Trends: A View of the CurrentState of the Art to Enhance E-Learning* (pp. 1–23). Springer.

Leta, F. (2023). Ethics in Education: Exploring the Ethical Implications of Artificial Intelligence Implementation. *Ovidius University Annals, Economic Sciences Series*, XXIII(1), 413–421. DOI: 10.61801/OUAESS.2023.1.54

Liang, J. C., Hwang, G. J., Chen, M. R. A., & Darmawansah, D. (2021). Roles and research of artificial intelligence in language education: An integrated bibliographic analysis and systematic review approach. *Interactive Learning Environments*. Advance online publication. DOI: 10.1080/10494820.2021.1958348

Liang, K., Zhang, Y., He, Y., Zhou, Y., Tan, W., & Li, X. (2017). Online Behavior Analysis-Based Student Profile for Intelligent E-Learning. *Journal of Electrical and Computer Engineering*, 2017, 1–7. DOI: 10.1155/2017/9720396

Libovický, Jindřich, Rosa, Rudolf, & Fraser, Alexander. 2019. "How Language-Neutral Is Multilingual BERT?"

Lin, Y., & Yu, Z. (2024). A bibliometric analysis of artificial intelligence chatbots in educational contexts. *Interactive Technology and Smart Education*, 21(2), 189–213. DOI: 10.1108/ITSE-12-2022-0165

Liu, S., & d'Aquin, M. (2017, April). Unsupervised learning for understanding student achievement in a distance learning setting. In *2017 IEEE Global Engineering Education Conference (EDUCON)* (pp. 1373-1377). IEEE.

Liu, Y., Chen, L., & Yao, Z. (2022). The application of artificial intelligence assistant to deep learning in teachers' teaching and students' learning processes. *Frontiers in Psychology*, 13, 929175. DOI: 10.3389/fpsyg.2022.929175 PMID: 36033031

Livieris, I. E., Drakopoulou, K., Tampakas, V. T., Mikropoulos, T. A., & Pintelas, P. (2019, April). Predicting Secondary School Students' Performance Utilizing a Semi-supervised Learning Approach. *Journal of Educational Computing Research*, 57(2), 448–470. DOI: 10.1177/0735633117752614

Li, Y. (2022). Teaching mode of oral English in the age of artificial intelligence. *Frontiers in Psychology*, 13, 953482. DOI: 10.3389/fpsyg.2022.953482 PMID: 35936279

Long, D., & Magerko, B. (2020, April). What is AI literacy? Competencies and design considerations. In *Proceedings of the 2020 CHI Conference on Human Factors in Computing Systems* (pp. 1–16). DOI: 10.1145/3313831.3376727

Loranger, A. L. (1994). The study strategies of successful and unsuccessful high school students. *Journal of Reading Behavior*, 26(4), 347–360. DOI: 10.1080/10862969409547858

Luckin, R., & Holmes, W. (2016). Intelligence unleashed: An argument for AI in education.

Luckin, R., Holmes, W., Griffiths, M., & Forcier, L. B. (2016). *Intelligence Unleashed: An Argument for AI in Education*. Pearson.

Maestrales, S., Zhai, X., Touitou, I., Baker, Q., Schneider, B., & Krajcik, J. (2021). Using Machine Learning to Score Multi-Dimensional Assessments of Chemistry and Physics. *Journal of Science Education and Technology*, 30(2), 239–254. DOI: 10.1007/s10956-020-09895-9

Magalhães, R., Oliveira, A., Terroso, D., Vilaça, A., Veloso, R., Marques, A., Pereira, J., & Coelho, L. (2024). Mixed Reality in the Operating Room: A Systematic Review. *Journal of Medical Systems*, 48(1), 76. DOI: 10.1007/s10916-024-02095-7 PMID: 39145896

Maghsudi, S., Lan, A., Xu, J., & van Der Schaar, M. (2021). Personalized education in the artificial intelligence era: What to expect next. *IEEE Signal Processing Magazine*, 38(3), 37–50. DOI: 10.1109/MSP.2021.3055032

Ma, L., & Sun, B. (2020). Machine learning and AI in marketing–connecting computing power to human insights. *International Journal of Research in Marketing*, 37(3), 481–504. DOI: 10.1016/j.ijresmar.2020.04.005

Mannuru, N. R., Shahriar, S., Teel, Z. A., Wang, T., Lund, B. D., Tijani, S., Pohboon, C. O., Agbaji, D., Alhassan, J., Galley, J. K. L., Kousari, R., Ogbadu-Oladapo, L., Saurav, S. K., Srivastava, A., Tummuru, S. P., Uppala, S., & Vaidya, P. (2023). Artificial intelligence in developing countries: The impact of generative artificial intelligence (AI) technologies for development. *Information Development*, 02666669231200628. Advance online publication. DOI: 10.1177/02666669231200628

Mantello, P., Ho, M. T., Nguyen, M. H., & Vuong, Q. H. (2021). Bosses without a heart: Socio-demographic and cross-cultural determinants of attitude toward Emotional AI in the workplace. *AI & Society*, •••, 1–23. DOI: 10.1007/s00146-021-01290-1 PMID: 34776651

Manwaring, C., Larsen, R., Graham, C. R., Henrie, C. R., & Halverson, L. R. (2017). andL. R. Halverson, "Investigating student engagement in blended learning settings using experience sampling and structural equation modelling,". *The Internet and Higher Education*, 35, 21–33. DOI: 10.1016/j.iheduc.2017.06.002

Manyika, J., Chui, M., Miremadi, M., Bughin, J., George, K., Willmott, P., & Dewhurst, M. (2017). *A future that works: Automation, employment, and productivity*. McKinsey Global Institute.

Maphoto, K. B., Sevnarayan, K., Mohale, N. E., Suliman, Z., Ntsopi, T. J., & Mokoena, D. (2024). Advancing students' academic excellence in distance education: Exploring the potential of generative AI integration to improve academic writing skills. Open Praxis, 16(2), 142-159. https://search.informit.org/doi/10.3316/informit.T2024041000014190886861950

Marais, P. (2016). We can't believe what we see": Overcrowded classrooms through the eyes of student teachers. *South African Journal of Education*, 36(2), (pp.1–10). https://hdl.handle.net/10520/EJC189909. DOI: 10.15700/saje.v36n2a1201

Marbouti, F., Diefes-Dux, H. A., & Madhavan, K. (2016). Models for early prediction of at-risk students in a course using standards-based grading. *Computers & Education*, 103, 1–15. DOI: 10.1016/j.compedu.2016.09.005

Marcinkowski, F., Kieslich, K., Starke, C., & Lünich, M. (2020). Implications of AI (un-) fairness in higher education admissions: the effects of perceived AI (un-) fairness on exit, voice and organizational reputation. *InProceedings of the 2020 Conference on Fairness, Accountability, and Transparency*, 122–130. DOI: 10.1145/3351095.3372867

Marcus, M., Neil, C. C., Michael Kölling, B., & Miaojing, S. (2023). Automated Grading and Feedback Tools for Programming Education. *Systematic Reviews*, 1(1). Advance online publication. DOI: 10.1 145/nnnnnnn.nnnnnnn

Mariano, J., Marques, S., Ramos, M. R., Gerardo, F., Cunha, C. L., Girenko, A., Alexandersson, J., Stree, B., Lamanna, M., Lorenzatto, M., Mikkelsen, L. P., Bundgård-Jørgensen, U., Rego, S., & de Vries, H. (2022). Too old for technology? Stereotype threat and technology use by older adults. *Behaviour & Information Technology*, 41(7), 1503–1512. DOI: 10.1080/0144929X.2021.1882577

Martin, B. A., Jin, H. S., Wang, D., Nguyen, H., Zhan, K., & Wang, Y. X. (2020). The influence of consumer anthropomorphism on attitudes towards artificial intelligence trip advisors. *Journal of Hospitality and Tourism Management*, 44, 108–111. DOI: 10.1016/j.jhtm.2020.06.004

Martinez, D., Malyska, N., Streilein, B., Caceres, R., Campbell, W., Dagli, C., Gadepally, V., Greenfeld, K., Hall, R., King, A., Lippmann, R., Miller, B., Reynolds, D., Richardson, F., Sahin, C., Tran, A., Trepagnier, P., & Zipkin, J. (2019). *Artificial intelligence: Short history, present developments, and future outlook*. Massachusetts Institute of Technology.

Martinovic, D., & Ralevich, V. (2007). Privacy Issues in Educational Systems. *International Journal of Internet Technology and Secured Transactions*, 1(1/2), 132. DOI: 10.1504/IJITST.2007.014838

Mathew, A. N., Rohini, V., & Paulose, J. (2021). NLP-based personal learning assistant for school education. *Iranian Journal of Electrical and Computer Engineering*, 11(5), 4522–4530. DOI: 10.11591/ijece.v11i5.pp4522-4530

Matsuzaka, Y., & Yashiro, R. (2023). AI-Based Computer Vision Techniques and Expert Systems. *AI*, 4(1), 289–302. DOI: 10.3390/ai4010013

Mccarthy, J. (2004). WHAT IS ARTIFICIAL INTELLIGENCE? http://www-formal.stanford.edu/jmc/

McCarthy, J., Minsky, M. L., Rochester, N., & Shannon, C. E. (2006). A Proposal for the Dartmouth Summer Research Project on Artificial Intelligence.

ME, M. R. V., Umamageshwari, S., & Unnimaya, D. An intelligent approach to predict the student behaviour and performance.

Means, B. (2020). Learning Online; What research tells us about whether, when wnd how.

Mertala, P., Fagerlund, J., & Calderon, O. (2022). Finnish 5th and 6th grade students' pre-instructional conceptions of artificial intelligence (AI) and their implications for AI literacy education. *Computers and Education: Artificial Intelligence*, 3, 1–11. DOI: 10.1016/j.caeai.2022.100095

Mian, Y., Khalid, F., Qun, A., & Ismail, S. (2022). Expert Analytics in Education, Advantages and Issues: A Systematic Literature Review. *Creative Education*, 13(9), 2913–2920. DOI: 10.4236/ce.2022.139183

Miao, F., Holmes, W., Huang, R., & Zhang, H. (2021). *AI and education: A guidance for policymakers*. UNESCO Publishing.

Michel-Villarreal, R., Vilalta-Perdomo, E., Salinas-Navarro, D. E., Thierry-Aguilera, R., & Gerardou, F. S. (2023). Challenges and opportunities of generative AI for higher education as explained by ChatGPT. *Education Sciences*, 13(9), 856. DOI: 10.3390/educsci13090856

Mikolov, Tomas, Chen, Kai, Corrado, Greg, & Dean, Jeffrey. 2013. "Efficient Estimation of Word Representations in Vector Space."

Miller, T. (2018). "Ethics of Artificial Intelligence and Robotics." *Stanford Encyclopedia of Philosophy*. Retrieved from https://plato.stanford.edu

Miller, T. (2019). Explanation in artificial intelligence: Insights from the social sciences. *Artificial Intelligence*, 267, 1–38. DOI: 10.1016/j.artint.2018.07.007

Minsky, M. (1995). *Smart machines. The third culture.* Simon & Shuster.

Mittelstadt, B. D., Allo, P., Taddeo, M., Wachter, S., & Floridi, L. (2016). The ethics of algorithms: Mapping the debate. *Big Data & Society*, 3(2), 2053951716679679. DOI: 10.1177/2053951716679679

Modi, P. J., Veloso, M., Smith, S. F., & Oh, J. (2005). Cmradar: A personal assistant agent for calendar management. In *Agent-Oriented* [Springer, Berlin, Heidelberg.]. *Information Systems*, II, 169–181.

Mohammed, P. S., & Watson, E. (2019). Towards Inclusive Education in the Age of Artificial Intelligence: Perspectives, Challenges, and Opportunities. *In Artificial Intelligence and Inclusive Education* (pp. 1-15). DOI: DOI: 10.1007/978-981-13-8161-4_2

Mollick, E. R., & Mollick, L. (2023). *Assigning AI: Seven Approaches for Students, with Prompts. SSRN.* http://dx.doi.org/DOI: 10.2139/ssrn.4475995

Mon, B. F., Wasfi, A., Hayajneh, M., & Slim, A. (2023). A Study on Role of Artificial Intelligence in Education. *In 2023 International Conference on Computing, Electronics & Communications Engineering (ICCECE)* IEEE., (pp. 133–138). DOI: 10.1109/iCCECE59400.2023.10238613

Moreno, J., & Pineda, A. F. (2020). A Framework for Automated Formative Assessment in Mathematics Courses. *IEEE Access: Practical Innovations, Open Solutions*, 8, 30152–30159. DOI: 10.1109/ACCESS.2020.2973026

Morgan, G. A., Leech, N. L., Gloeckner, G. W., & Barrett, K. C. (2004). *SPSS for introductory statistics: Use and interpretation.* Psychology Press. DOI: 10.4324/9781410610539

Moulieswaran, N., & Prasantha Kumar, N. S. (2023). Investigating ESL Learners' Perception and Problem towards Artificial Intelligence (AI) -Assisted English Language Learning and Teaching. *World Journal of English Language*, 13(5), 290–297. DOI: 10.5430/wjel.v13n5p290

Mouta, A., Torrecilla-Sánchez, E. M., & Pinto-Llorente, A. M. (2024). Design of a future scenarios toolkit for an ethical implementation of artificial intelligence in education. *Education and Information Technologies*, 29(9), 10473–10498. DOI: 10.1007/s10639-023-12229-y

Müller, V. C. (2016). *Risks of artificial intelligence.* Chapman & Hall. DOI: 10.1201/b19187

Muñoz, S. A. S., Gayoso, G. G., Huambo, A. C., Tapia, R. D. C., Incaluque, J. L., Aguila, O. E. P., & Arias-Gonzales, J. L. (2023). Examining the impacts of ChatGPT on student motivation and engagement. *Social Space*, 23(1), 1–27.

Murphy, R. F. (2019). Artificial intelligence applications to support K-12 teachers and teaching: A review of promising applications, opportunities, and challenges. *Perspective* Rand Corporation. https://www.rand.org/pubs/perspectives/PE315.html

Murtaza, S. S., Lak, P., Bener, A., & Pischdotchian, A. (2016, January). How to effectively train IBM Watson: Classroom experience. In 2016 49th Hawaii International Conference on System Sciences (HICSS) (pp. 1663-1670 IEEE.

Mustard, D. B. (2003). Reexamining criminal behavior: The importance of omitted variable bias. *The Review of Economics and Statistics*, 85(1), 205–211. DOI: 10.1162/rest.2003.85.1.205

Mutahi, J., Kinai, A., Bore, N., Diriye, A., & Weldemariam, K. (2017, March). Studying engagement and performance with learning technology in an African classroom. In *Proceedings of the Seventh International Learning Analytics & Knowledge Conference* (pp. 148-152). DOI: 10.1145/3027385.3027395

Muthén, L. K., & Muthén, B. O. (2002). How to use a Monte Carlo study to decide on sample size and determine power. *Structural Equation Modeling*, 9(4), 599–620. DOI: 10.1207/S15328007SEM0904_8

Nabella, E., Zaini, Muhammad, & Ajizah, Aulia. (2020). Development of Worksheets for High School Biology Student-Based on Critical Thinking Skills on the Circulation System Concept. *BIO-INOVED: Jurnal Biologi-Inovasi Pendidikan*. 2. 47. .DOI: 10.20527/bino.v2i1.7980

Nabiyev, V. V. (2012). *Artificial Intelligence: Human-Computer Interaction*. Seçkin Yayıncılık.

Nagori, V., & Trivedi, B., (2014). Types of Expert System. *Comparative Study Asian Journal of Computer and Information Systems,* 2(2), ISSN: 2321 – 5658.

Nagro, S. A. (2021). The role of artificial intelligence techniques in improving the behavior and practices of faculty members when switching to elearning in light of the COVID-19 crisis. *International Journal of Education and Practice*, 9(4), 687–714. DOI: 10.18488/journal.61.2021.94.687.714

Nah, F. F.-H., Zheng, R., Cai, J., Siau, K., & Chen, L. (2023). Generative AI and ChatGPT: Applications, challenges, and AI-human collaboration. *Journal of Information Technology Case and Application Research*, 25(3), 277–304. DOI: 10.1080/15228053.2023.2233814

Napoleon, D., & Ramanujam, V. (2022). Education 4.0: Curriculum Development for the Educational Framework. In *Industry 4.0 Technologies for Education* (pp. 275-291). Auerbach Publications.

Narayanan, S., Ramakrishnan, R., Durairaj, E., & Das, A. (2023, November 28). (n.d.). Artificial Intelligence Revolutionizing the Field of Medical Education. *Cureus*, 15(11), e49604. DOI: 10.7759/cureus.49604 PMID: 38161821

Naveed, Humza, Khan, Asad Ullah, Qiu, Shi, Saqib, Muhammad, Anwar, Saeed, Usman, Muhammad, Akhtar, Naveed, Barnes, Nick, & Mian, Ajmal. 2024. "A Comprehensive Overview of Large Language Models."

Nematzadeh, A., Ciampaglia, G. L., Menczer, F., & Flammini, A. (2017). How algorithmic popularity bias hinders or promotes quality. *ArXiv Preprint ArXiv:1707.00574(2017)*.

Nenkova, Ani, & McKeown, Kathleen. 2011. "Automatic Summarization." *Foundations and Trends® in Information Retrieval* 5(2–3): (pp.103–233).

Nettleton, D. (2014). Selection of variables and factor derivation. Commercial data mining, 79-104.

Neuwirth, R. J. (2023). Prohibited artificial intelligence practices in the proposed EU artificial intelligence act (AIA). *Computer Law & Security Report*, 48(105798), 1–14. DOI: 10.1016/j.clsr.2023.105798

Newell, A., & Simon, H. A. (1963). *GPS, a program that simulates human thought, in:* E.A. FEIGENBAUM, J. FELDMAN (eds.), *Computers and Thought*, McGraw-Hill, New York.

Ng, D. T. K., & Chu, S. K. W. (2021). Motivating Students to Learn AI Through Social Networking Sites: A Case Study in Hong Kong. *Online Learning : the Official Journal of the Online Learning Consortium*, 25(1), 195–208. DOI: 10.24059/olj.v25i1.2454

Ng, D. T. K., Lee, M., Tan, R. J. Y., Hu, X., Downie, J. S., & Chu, S. K. W. (2023). A review of AI teaching and learning from 2000 to 2020. *Education and Information Technologies*, 28(7), 8445–8501. DOI: 10.1007/s10639-022-11491-w

Ng, D. T. K., Leung, J. K. L., Chu, S. K. W., & Qiao, M. S. (2021). Conceptualizing AI literacy: An exploratory review. *Computers and Education: Artificial Intelligence*, 2, 100041.

Ng, D. T. K., Leung, J. K. L., Su, J., Ng, R. C. W., & Chu, S. K. W. (2023). Teachers' AI digital competencies and twenty-first century skills in the post-pandemic world. *Educational Technology Research and Development*, 71(1), 137–161. DOI: 10.1007/s11423-023-10203-6 PMID: 36844361

Nishant, R., Schneckenberg, D., & Ravishankar, M. N. (2024). The formal rationality of artificial intelligence-based algorithms and the problem of bias. *Journal of Information Technology*, 39(1), 19–40. DOI: 10.1177/02683962231176842

Nizam, H., & Akın, S. S. (2014). *Sosyal medyada makine öğrenmesi ile duygu analizinde dengeli ve dengesiz veri setlerinin performanslarının karşılaştırılması.* XIX. Türkiye'de İnternet Konferansı.

North, C., & Nord, C. (2018). *Ten facts about artificial intelligence in teaching and learning*. University of California.

Nthontho, M. (2017). Children as stakeholders in education: Does their voice matter? *South African Journal of Childhood Education*, 7(1), 1–7. DOI: 10.4102/sajce.v7i1.434

Numanoglu, M. (1992). Milli eğitim bakanlığı bilgisayar destekli eğitim projesi: Bilgisayar destekli eğitim yazılımlarında bulunması gereken eğitsel özellikler. (Unpublished Master's Thesis) Ankara University. Ankara.

O'Neil, C. (2016). *Weapons of Math Destruction: How Big Data Increases Inequality and Threatens Democracy*. Crown Publishing Group.

Oblinger, D., & Oblinger, J. (2005). Is it age or IT: First steps toward understanding the net generation. Educating the net generation, 2(1–2), 20. Prensky, M. (2001). Digital Natives, Digital Immigrants Part 1. *On the Horizon*, 9(5), 1–6.

Ogurlu, U., & Mossholder, J. (2023). The perception of ChatGPT among educators: Preliminary findings. [RESSAT]. *Research in Social Sciences & Technology*, 8(4), 196–215. DOI: 10.46303/ressat.2023.39

Okello, I. (2023). Analyzing the Impacts of Artificial Intelligence on Education. *IAA Journal of Education*, 9(3), 8–13. DOI: 10.59298/IAAJE/2023/2.10.1000

Okonkwo, C. W., & Ade-Ibijola, A. (2021). Chatbots applications in education: A systematic review. *Computers and Education: Artificial Intelligence,*.

Olteanu, A., Castillo, C., Diaz, F., & Kıcıman, E. (2019). Social data: Biases, methodological pitfalls, and ethical boundaries. *Frontiers in Big Data*, 2, 13. DOI: 10.3389/fdata.2019.00013 PMID: 33693336

Onan, A., & Korukoğlu, S. (2016). Makine öğrenmesi yöntemlerinin görüş madenciliğinde kullanılması üzerine bir literatür araştırması. *Pamukkale Üniversitesi Mühendislik Bilimleri Dergisi*, 22(2), 111–122.

Ong, Q. K. L., & Annamalai, N. (2024). Technological pedagogical content knowledge for twenty-first century learning skills: The game changer for teachers of industrial revolution 5.0. *Education and Information Technologies*, 29(2), 1939–1980. DOI: 10.1007/s10639-023-11852-z

Open, A. I. (2023a). GPT-4 (June 21 version) [Large language model]. https://chat.openai.com/

Open, A. I. (2023b). ChatGPT (September 29 version) [Large language model]. https://chat.openai.com/

Open, A. I. (2024). GPT's. Accessed at May, 12, 2024. https://help.openai.com/en/collections/8475420-gpts

Örücü, S., & Selek, M. (2020). Design and validation of rule-based expert system by using kinect v2 for real-time athlete support. *Applied Sciences (Basel, Switzerland)*, 10(2), 1–24. DOI: 10.3390/app10020611

Osborne, J. W., & Fitzpatrick, D. C. (2012). Replication analysis in exploratory factor analysis: What it is and why it makes your analysis better. *Practical Assessment, Research & Evaluation*, 17(15), 1–8.

Oztemel, E. (1992). Integrating expert systems and neural networks for intelligent on-line statistical process control. (Doctoral Dissertation). University of Wales. Cardiff.

Paiva, José Carlos, José Paulo Leal, and Álvaro Figueira. 2022. "Automated Assessment in Computer Science Education: A State-of-the-Art Review." ACM Transactions on Computing Education 22(3):34:1-34:40. .DOI: 10.1145/3513140

Palvia, S., & Matta, V. (2023). Comparing Student Perceptions of In-Class, Online Synchronous, and Online Asynchronous Instruction. *World Journal on Educational Technology: Current Issues*, 15(3), 303–320. DOI: 10.18844/wjet.v15i3.8656

Park, I., Kim, D., Moon, J., Kim, S., Kang, Y., & Bae, S. (2022). Searching for new technology acceptance model under social con-text: Analyzing the determinants of acceptance of intelligent information technology in digital transformation and implications for the requisites of digital sustainability. *Sustainability (Basel)*, 14(1), 579. DOI: 10.3390/su14010579

Pasquale, F. (2015). *The black box society: The secret algorithms that control money and information*. Harvard University Press. DOI: 10.4159/harvard.9780674736061

Pedro, F., Subosa, M., Rivas, A., & Valverde, P. (2019). *Artificial intelligence in education: Challenges and opportunities for sustainable development*. UNESCO.

Pennington, J., Socher, R., & Manning, C. 2014. "GloVe: Global Vectors for Word Representation." Pp. 1532–43 in *Proceedings of the 2014 Conference on Empirical Methods in Natural Language Processing (EMNLP)*, edited by Moschitti, A., Pang, B., & Daelemans, W.. Doha, Qatar: Association for Computational Linguistics. DOI: 10.3115/v1/D14-1162

Perez, S., Massey-Allard, J., Butler, D., Ives, J., Bonn, D., Yee, N., & Roll, I. (2017). Identifying productive inquiry in virtual labs using sequence mining. In *Artificial Intelligence in Education: 18th International Conference, AIED 2017*, Wuhan, China, June 28–July 1, 2017, Proceedings 18. Springer International Publishing., (pp.287–298). DOI: 10.1007/978-3-319-61425-0_24

Perrotta, C., & Selwyn, N. (2020). Deep learning goes to school: Toward a relational understanding of AI in education. *Learning, Media and Technology*, 45(3), 251–269. DOI: 10.1080/17439884.2020.1686017

Pinto-Coelho, L., Horst-Udo, H., Jokisch, O., & Braga, D. 2009. "Towards an Objective Voice Preference Definition for the Portuguese Language." in joint SIG-IL/Microsoft Workshop on Speech and Language Technologies for Iberian Languages. Porto Salvo, Portugal.

Pirim, A. G. H. (2006). Yapay zeka. *Journal of Yaşar University*, 1(1), 81–93.

Popel, M., Tomkova, M., Tomek, J., Kaiser, Ł., Uszkoreit, J., Bojar, O., & Žabokrtský, Z. (2020). Transforming Machine Translation: A Deep Learning System Reaches News Translation Quality Comparable to Human Professionals. *Nature Communications*, 11(1), 4381. DOI: 10.1038/s41467-020-18073-9 PMID: 32873773

Popenici, S. A. D., & Kerr, S. (2017). Exploring the impact of artificial intelligence on teaching and learning in higher education. *Research and Practice in Technology Enhanced Learning*, 12(1), 22. Advance online publication. DOI: 10.1186/s41039-017-0062-8 PMID: 30595727

Porayska-Pomsta, K., Holmes, W., & Nemorin, S. (2023). The ethics of AI in education. In *Handbook of Artificial Intelligence in Education*. Edward Elgar Publishing. DOI: 10.4337/9781800375413.00038

Radford, A., & Wu, J. (2019). *R. Child, D. Luan, Dario Amodei, and I. Sutskever*. Language Models Are Unsupervised Multitask Learners.

Radford, Alec, & Narasimhan, Karthik. 2018. "Improving Language Understanding by Generative Pre-Training."

Rainer, R. K., Prince, B., Sánchez-Rodríguez, C., Splettstoesser-Hogeterp, I., & Ebrahimi, S. (2020). *Introduction to information systems*. John Wiley & Sons.

Regan, P. M., & Jesse, J. (2019). Ethical challenges of edtech, big data and personalized learning: Twenty-first century student sorting and tracking. *Ethics and Information Technology*, 21(3), 167–179. DOI: 10.1007/s10676-018-9492-2

Reidenberg, J. R., & Schaub, F. (2018). Achieving big data privacy in education. *Theory and Research in Education*, 16(3), 263–279. DOI: 10.1177/1477878518805308

Reis, S., Coelho, L., Sarmet, M., Araújo, J., & Corchado, J. M. 2023. "The Importance of Ethical Reasoning in Next Generation Tech Education." Pp. 1–10 in 2023 5th International Conference of the Portuguese Society for Engineering Education (CISPEE). DOI: 10.1109/CISPEE58593.2023.10227651

Reis, S., Guimarães, P., Coelho, F., Nogueira, E., & Coelho, L.. 2018. "A Framework for Simulation Systems and Technologies for Medical Training." Pp. 1–4 in 2018 Global Medical Engineering Physics Exchanges/Pan American Health Care Exchanges (GMEPE/PAHCE).

Remian, D. (2019). Augmenting education: ethical considerations for incorporating artificial intelligence in education.

Remote Learning During COVID-19: Lessons from Today, Principles for Tomorrow. (n.d.). World Bank Group. Retrieved from https://www.worldbank.org/en/topic/edutech/brief/how-countries-are-using-edtech-to-support-remote-learning-during-the-covid-19-pandemic

Richards, J. C., & Rodgers, T. S. (2014). *Approaches and Methods in Language Teaching* (3rd ed.). Cambridge University Press. DOI: 10.1017/9781009024532

Rich, E. (1985). *Artificial Intelligence and the Humanities* (Vol. 19, Issue 2).

Riegg, S. K. (2008). Causal inference and omitted variable bias in financial aid research: Assessing solutions. *Review of Higher Education*, 31(3), 329–354. DOI: 10.1353/rhe.2008.0010

Rodrigues, I. (2017). Rethinking Educational Research on School Disengagement Through Students' Voices. *New Trends and Issues Proceedings on Humanities and Social Sciences, 4*(6), 01–10. DOI: 10.18844/prosoc.v4i6.2905

Rogers, J. (1985). Artificial intelligence in education (panel session)., 52. https://doi.org/.DOI: 10.1145/320435.320454

Rojas, J. A., Espitia, H. E., & Bejarano, L. A. (2021). Design and Optimization of a Fuzzy Logic System for Academic Performance Prediction. *Symmetry*, 2021(13), 133. DOI: 10.3390/sym13010133

Roll, I., & Wylie, R. (2016). Evolution and revolution in artificial intelligence in education. *International Journal of Artificial Intelligence in Education*, 26(2), 582–599. DOI: 10.1007/s40593-016-0110-3

Romero, C., & Ventura, S. (2010). Educational data mining: A review of the state of the art. IEEE Transactions on Systems, Man, and Cybernetics [applications and reviews]. *Part C*, 40(6), 601–618.

Roschelle, J., Feng, M., Murphy, R. F., & Mason, C. A. (2016). Online mathematics homework increases student achievement. *AERA Open*, 2(4), 2332858416673968. DOI: 10.1177/2332858416673968

Rudduck, J., & Flutter, J. (2000). Pupil participation and pupil perspective: "Carving a new order of experience.". *Cambridge Journal of Education*, 30(1), 75–89. DOI: 10.1080/03057640050005780

Rudolph, J., Tan, S., & Tan, S. (2023). ChatGPT: Bullshit spewer or the end of traditional assessments in higher education? *Journal of Applied Learning and Teaching*, 6(1), 342–363. DOI: 10.37074/jalt.2023.6.1.9

Russel, S., & Norvig, P. (2010). *Artificial intelligence - a modern approach*. Pearson Education.

Rütti-Joy, O., Winder, G., & Biedermann, H. (2023). Building AI Literacy for Sustainable Teacher Education. *Zeitschrift für Hochschulentwicklung*, 18(4), 175–189. DOI: 10.21240/zfhe/18-04/10

Sabzalieva, E., & Valentini, A. (2023). ChatGPT and artificial intelligence in higher education: quick start guide.

Saheb, T., & Saheb, T. (2023). Topical review of artificial intelligence national policies: A mixed method analysis. *Technology in Society*, 74, 102316. DOI: 10.1016/j.techsoc.2023.102316

Salekhova, L., Nurgaliev, A., Zaripova, R., & Khakimullina, N. (2013). The Principles of Designing an Expert System in Teaching Mathematics. *Universal Journal of Educational Research*, 1(2), 42–47. DOI: 10.13189/ujer.2013.010202

Sánchez-Prieto, J. C., Cruz-Benito, J., Therón, R., & García-Peñalvo, F. J. [Francisco J.] (2019). How to Measure Teachers' Acceptance of AI-driven Assessment in eLearning. In González, M. Á. C., Sedano, F. J. R., Llamas, C. F., & García-Peñalvo, F. J. (Eds.), *Proceedings of the Seventh International Conference on Technological Ecosystems for Enhancing Multiculturality* (pp. 181–186). ACM. https://doi.org/ DOI: 10.1145/3362789.3362918

Sanh, V., Debut, L., Chaumond, J., & Wolf, T. (2020). *DistilBERT, a Distilled Version of BERT: Smaller*. Faster, Cheaper and Lighter.

Santy, Sebastin, Liang, Jenny T., Le Bras, Ronan, Reinecke, Katharina, & Sap, Maarten. 2023. "NLPositionality: Characterizing Design Biases of Datasets and Models."

Sarmet, M., Kabani, A., Coelho, L., Seabra dos Reis, S., Zeredo, J. L., & Mehta, A. K. (2023). The Use of Natural Language Processing in Palliative Care Research: A Scoping Review. *Palliative Medicine*, 37(2), 275–290. DOI: 10.1177/02692163221141969 PMID: 36495082

Scagnoli, N. I., Choo, J., & Tian, J. (2017). 'Students' insights on the use of video lectures in online classes'. *British Journal of Educational Technology*. Advance online publication. DOI: 10.1111/bjet.12572

Schepman, A., & Rodway, P. (2020). Initial validation of the general attitudes towards Artificial Intelligence Scale. *Computers in Human Behavior Reports*, 1, 100014. Advance online publication. DOI: 10.1016/j.chbr.2020.100014 PMID: 34235291

Schepman, A., & Rodway, P. (2022). The general attitudes towards artificial intelligence scale (GAAIS): Confirmatory validation and associations with personality, corporate distrust, and general trust. *International Journal of Human-Computer Interaction*. Advance online publication. DOI: 10.1080/10447318.2022.2085400

Schneider, S. L. The International Standard Classification of Education 2011. In: Elisabeth Birkelund G, editor. Comparative Social Research [Internet]. Emerald Group Publishing Limited; 2013 p. 365–79. Available from: https://www.emerald.com/insight/content/doi/10.1108/S0195-6310(2013)0000030017/full/html

Schön, E. M., Neumann, M., Hofmann-Stölting, C., Baeza-Yates, R., & Rauschenberger, M. (2023). How are AI assistants changing higher education? *Frontiers of Computer Science*, 5, 1208550. Advance online publication. DOI: 10.3389/fcomp.2023.1208550

Sekeroglu, B., Dimililer, K., & Tuncal, K. (2019). Artificial intelligence in education: application in student performance evaluation. *Dilemas Contemporáneos: Educación. Política y Valores*, 7(1), 1–21.

Selwyn, N. (2016). *Education and Technology: Key Issues and Debates*. Bloomsbury Academic.

Selwyn, N. (2019). What's the problem with learning analytics? *Journal of Learning Analytics*, 6(3), 11–19. DOI: 10.18608/jla.2019.63.3

Selwyn, N., Cordoba, B. G., Andrejevic, M., & Campbell, L. (2020). *AI for good: Australian public attitudes towards AI and society*. Monash University.

Sharma, R. C., Kawachi, P., & Bozkurt, A. (2019). The landscape of artificial intelligence in open, online and distance education: Promises and concerns. *Asian Journal of Distance Education*, 14(2), 1–2.

Shaun, R., De Baker, J., & Inventado, P. S. (2014). *Educational Data Mining and Learning Analytics*.

Shaw, M. L. G., & Gaines, B. R. (1992). The Synthesis of Knowledge Engineering and Software Engineering. In P. Loucopoulos (Ed.), Advanced Information Systems Engineering. Springer-Verlag., LNCS 593.

Shemshack, A., & Spector, J. M. (2020). A Systematic Literature Review of Personalized Learning Terms. *Smart Learning Environments*, 7(1), 33. DOI: 10.1186/s40561-020-00140-9

Shen, J., Wu, H., Reeves, P., Zheng, Y., Ryan, L., & Anderson, D. (2020). The association between teacher leadership and student achievement: A meta-analysis. *Educational Research Review*, 31, 100357. DOI: 10.1016/j.edurev.2020.100357

Sherif, M., & Sherif, C. W. (1996). Introduction to social psychology 2. (Tra. Mustafa Atakay & Aysun Yılmaz). İstanbul: Sosyal.

Shermis, Mark D., & Hamner, Ben. 2012. "Contrasting State-of-the-Art Automated Scoring of Essays: Analysis." Pp. 51–82 in *Handbook of Automated Essay Evaluation*.

Shiwani, S. M., & Chaturvedi, D. K. (2021). Historical perspective of Artificial Intelligence based expert system. 44th National Systems Conference (NSC), Systems for Sustainable Healthcare Habitats (pp. 187- 190). https://www.sysi.org/downloads/NSC-2021-Proceedings.pdf

Shute, V. J., & Zapata-Rivera, D. (2012). Adaptive educational systems. *Adaptive technologies for training and education*, 7(27), (pp.1-35).

Siemens, G., & Baker, R. S. D. (2012). Learning analytics and educational data mining: towards communication and collaboration. *InProceedings of the 2nd International Conference on Learning Analytics and Knowledge*, 252–254. DOI: 10.1145/2330601.2330661

Siemens, G., & Gasevic, D. (2012). Guest editorial-learning and knowledge analytics. *Journal of Educational Technology & Society*, 15(3), 1–2.

Siemens, G., & Long, P. (2011). Penetrating the fog: Analytics in learning and education. *EDUCAUSE Review*, 46(5), 30.

Simon, H. A. (1983). Why should machines learn? In *Machine learning*. Morgan Kaufmann., DOI: 10.1016/B978-0-08-051054-5.50006-6

Sindermann, C., Sha, P., Zhou, M., Wernicke, J., Schmitt, H. S., Li, M., Sariyska, R., Stavrou, M., Becker, B., & Montag, C. (2021). Assessing the attitude towards artificial intelligence: Introduction of a short measure in German, Chinese, and English language. *Kunstliche Intelligenz*, 35(1), 109–118. DOI: 10.1007/s13218-020-00689-0

Singil, N. (2022). Artificial intelligence and human rights. *Public and Private International Law Bulletin*, 42(1), 121–158. DOI: 10.26650/ppil.2022.42.1.970856

Solak, E. (2024). Revolutionizing Language Learning: How ChatGPT and AI are changing the Way we Learn Languages. *International Journal of Technology in Education.*, 7(2), 353–372. DOI: 10.46328/ijte.732

Somuncuoğlu, Y., & Yıldırım, A. (1998). Öğrenme stratejileri: Teorik boyutları, araştırma bulguları ve uygulama için ortaya koyduğu sonuçlar. *Eğitim ve Bilim*, 22(110).

Somyürek, S. (2014). Öğretim sürecinde z kuşağının dikkatini çekme: Artırılmış gerçeklik. *Eğitim Teknolojisi Kuram ve Uygulama*, 4(1), 63–80. DOI: 10.17943/etku.88319

Spector, J. M., & Ma, S. (2019). Inquiry and critical thinking skills for the next generation: From artificial intelligence back to human intelligence. *Smart Learning Environments*, 6(1), 1–11. DOI: 10.1186/s40561-019-0088-z

Stahl, B. C., & Wright, D. (2018). Ethics and privacy in AI and big data: Implementing responsible research and innovation. *IEEE Security and Privacy*, 16(3), 26–33. DOI: 10.1109/MSP.2018.2701164

Stavytska, I., Shalova, N., Korbut, O. (2024). Exploring the impacts and techniques of teaching with artificial intelligence tools. *Перспективи та інновації науки. Педагогіка, психологія*, медицина, DOI: 10.52058/2786-4952-2024-6(40)-40-47

Steenbergen-Hu, S., & Cooper, H. (2014). A Meta-Analysis of the Effectiveness of Intelligent Tutoring Systems on College Students' Academic Learning. *Journal of Educational Psychology*, 106(2), 331–347. DOI: 10.1037/a0034752

Stein, M. K., Smith, M. S., & Silver, E. (1999). The development of professional developers: Learning to assist teachers in new settings in new ways. *Harvard Educational Review*, 69(3), 237–270. DOI: 10.17763/haer.69.3.h2267130727v6878

Stevens, J. (2002). *Applied multivariate statistics for the social sciences.* Lawrence Erlbaurn Associates.

Stone, A. (2023). Student perceptions of academic integrity: A qualitative study of understanding, consequences, and impact. *Journal of Academic Ethics*, 21(3), 357–375. DOI: 10.1007/s10805-022-09461-5 PMID: 36466717

Su, J., Ng, D. T. K., & Chu, S. K. W. (2023). Artificial intelligence (AI) literacy in early childhood education: The challenges and opportunities. *Computers and Education: Artificial Intelligence*, 4, 100124. DOI: 10.1016/j.caeai.2023.100124

Su, J., & Yang, W. (2022). Artificial intelligence in early childhood education: A scoping review. *Computers and Education: Artificial Intelligence*, 3, 100049. DOI: 10.1016/j.caeai.2022.100049

Su, J., & Yang, W. (2023). Unlocking the Power of ChatGPT: A Framework for Applying Generative AI in Education. *ECNU Review of Education*, 6(3), 355–366. DOI: 10.1177/20965311231168423

Sun, A., & Chen, X. (2016). Online Education and Its Effective Practice: A Research Review. *Journal of Information Technology Education*, 15, 157–190. DOI: 10.28945/3502

Sunitha, D. B., & Gunavardhan, E. (2023). Artificial Intelligence based Smart Education System. *2023 4th International Conference on Electronics and Sustainable Communication Systems (ICESC)*, (pp.1346-1350). https://doi.org/DOI: 10.1109/ICESC57686.2023.10193720

Sun, L., Yin, C., Xu, Q., & Zhao, W. (2023). Artificial Intelligence for Healthcare and Medical Education: A Systematic Review. *American Journal of Translational Research*, 15(7), 4820–4828. PMID: 37560249

Sun, W. (2023). The impact of automatic speech recognition technology on second language pronunciation and speaking skills of EFL learners: A mixed methods investigation. *Frontiers in Psychology*, 14, 1210187. DOI: 10.3389/fpsyg.2023.1210187 PMID: 37663357

Sun, Z., Anbarasan, M., & Kumar, D. (2020). Design of online intelligent English teaching platform based on artificial intelligence techniques. *Computational Intelligence*, 37(3), 1166–1180. DOI: 10.1111/coin.12351

Supriyanto, G., Widiaty, I., Gafar Abdullah, A., & Mupita, J. (2018). Application of expert system for education. *IOP Conference Series. Materials Science and Engineering*, 434, 012304. DOI: 10.1088/1757-899X/434/1/012304

Supriyanto, G., Widiaty, I., Gafar Abdullah, A., & Riksa Yustiana, Y. (2019). Application expert system career guidance for students. *Journal of Physics: Conference Series*, 1402(6), 066031. DOI: 10.1088/1742-6596/1402/6/066031

Suresh, H., & Guttag, J. V. (2019). A framework for understanding unintended consequences of machine learning. *ArXiv Preprint ArXiv:1901.10002(2019)*.

Sutskever, Ilya, Vinyals, Oriol, & Le, Quoc V.. 2014. "Sequence to Sequence Learning with Neural Networks."

Tabachnick, B. G., & Fidell, L. S. (2013). *Using multivariate statistics* (6th ed.). Pearson.

Tahiru, F. (2021). AI in education: A systematic literature review. *Journal of Cases on Information Technology*, 23(1), 1–20. DOI: 10.4018/JCIT.2021010101

Tanaka, J. S. (1987). How big is big enough?": Sample size and goodness of fit in structural equation models with latent variables. *Child Development*, 58(1), 134–146. DOI: 10.2307/1130296

Tang, X., Huang, Y., Luo, W., Qian, X., & Xie, G. (2019). Personalized Recommendation for Academic Articles Based on NLP Techniques. *Frontiers in Psychology*, 10, 1543.

Tapalova, O., & Zhiyenbayeva, N. (2022). Artificial intelligence in education: AIEd for personalised learning pathways. *Electronic Journal of e-Learning*, 20(5), 639–653. DOI: 10.34190/ejel.20.5.2597

Tapan Broutın, M. S. T. (2024). Exploring Mathematics Teacher Candidates' Instrumentation Process of Generative Artificial Intelligence for Developing Lesson Plans. *Yükseköğretim Dergisi*, 14(1), 165–176.

Tasci, G., & Celebi, M. (2020). A new paradigm in education: "Artificial intelligence in higher education. *OPUS International Journal of Society Researches*, 16(29), 2346–2370. DOI: 10.26466/opus.747634

Tawafak, R., Alfarsi, G., & Iqbal Malik, S. (2022). An Application of Heuristic and Meta Dendral Expert System. ITM Web of Conferences. 42. 001009. DOI: 10.1051/itmconf/20224201009

Taylor, A., Marcus, M., & Santorini, B. (2003). The Penn Treebank: An Overview. In Abeillé, A. (Ed.), *Text, Speech and Language Technology* (Vol. 20, pp. 5–22). Springer Netherlands.

Taylor, M., Fudge, A., Mirriahi, N., & de Laat, M. (2021). *Use of digital technology in education: Literature review. Prepared for the South Australian Department for Education on behalf of The Centre for Change and Complexity in Learning*. The University of South Australia.

Tejani, A. S., Ng, Y. S., Xi, Y., & Rayan, J. C. (2024). Understanding and mitigating bias in imaging artificial intelligence. *Radiographics*, 44(5), e230067. DOI: 10.1148/rg.230067 PMID: 38635456

Tesene, M. M. (2018). Adaptable selectivity: A case study in evaluating and selecting adaptive learning courseware at Georgia State University. *Current Issues in Emerging Elearning*, 5(1), 6.

The Best ChatGPT Quotes. (2023). Supply Chain Today, homepage. Retrieved from https://www.supplychaintoday.com/best-chatgpt-quotes/

Theobald, E. J., Hill, M. J., Tran, E., Agrawal, S., Arroyo, E. N., Behling, S., Chambwe, N., Cintrón, D. L., Cooper, J. D., Dunster, G., Grummer, J. A., Hennessey, K., Hsiao, J., Iranon, N., Jones, L.II, Jordt, H., Keller, M., Lacey, M. E., Littlefield, C. E., & Freeman, S. (2020). Active learning narrows achievement gaps for underrepresented students in undergraduate science, technology, engineering, and math. *Proceedings of the National Academy of Sciences of the United States of America*, 117(12), 6476–6483. DOI: 10.1073/pnas.1916903117 PMID: 32152114

Thomas, C., & Jayagopi, D. B. (2017, November). Predicting student engagement in classrooms using facial behavioral cues. In *Proceedings of the 1st ACM SIGCHI international workshop on multimodal interaction for education* (pp. 33-40).

Tick, A. (2018, June). Research on the Digital Learning and E-learning Behaviour and Habits of the Early Z Generation. In 2018 IEEE 22nd International Conference on Intelligent Engineering Systems (INES) (pp. 000033-000038). IEEE.

Triguero, I., Molina, D., Poyatos, J., Del Ser, J., & Herrera, F. (2024). General purpose artificial intelligence systems (GPAIS): Properties, definition, taxonomy, societal implications and responsible governance. *Information Fusion*, 103, 102135. DOI: 10.1016/j.inffus.2023.102135

Troussas, C., Papakostas, C., Krouska, A., Mylonas, P., & Sgouropoulou, C. (2023). Personalized Feedback Enhanced by Natural Language Processing in Intelligent Tutoring Systems. In Frasson, C., Mylonas, P., & Troussas, C. (Eds.), *Augmented Intelligence and Intelligent Tutoring Systems* (pp. 667–677). Springer Nature Switzerland. DOI: 10.1007/978-3-031-32883-1_58

Turing, A. M., Ford, K., Glymour, C., & Hayes, P. (2009). *Computing Machinery and Intelligence*. Springer Netherlands. DOI: 10.1007/978-1-4020-6710-5_3

Tu, X., Zou, J., Su, W., & Zhang, L. (2024). What Should Data Science Education Do With Large Language Models? *Harvard Data Science Review*, 6(1). Advance online publication. DOI: 10.1162/99608f92.bff007ab

Udefi, A. M., Aina, S., Lawal, A. R., & Oluwarantie, A. I. (2023). An Analysis of Bias in Facial Image Processing: A Review of Datasets. *International Journal of Advanced Computer Science and Applications*, 14(5). Advance online publication. DOI: 10.14569/IJACSA.2023.0140593

Ugo, C., Ikerionwu, C., & Obi, N. (2020). Plagiarism Detection Systems. [IJSRP]. *International Journal of Scientific and Research Publications*, 10(3), 9969. DOI: 10.29322/IJSRP.10.03.2020.p9969

Ülgen, G. (1995). *Eğitim Psikolojisi -Birey ve Öğrenme-*. Ankara.

UNESCO. (2019). *Digital Library, Artificial intelligence in education: challenges and opportunities for sustainable development.* https://unesdoc.unesco.org/ark:/48223/pf0000366994

UNESCO. (2022). K-12 AI Curricula: A mapping of government-endorsed AI curricula. Paris, FranceUNESCO. https://unesdoc.unesco.org/ark:/48223/pf0000380602Z

Usman, F. O., Kess-Momoh, A. J., Ibeh, C. V., Elufioye, A. E., Ilojianya, V. I., & Oyeyemi, O. P.Favour Oluwadamilare UsmanAzeez Jason Kess-MomohChidera Victoria IbehAkinola Elumakin ElufioyeValentine Ikenna IlojianyaOluwaseun Peter Oyeyemi. (2024). Entrepreneurial innovations and trends: A global review: Examining emerging trends, challenges, and opportunities in the field of entrepreneurship, with a focus on how technology and globalization are shaping new business ventures. *International Journal of Science and Research Archive*, 11(1), 552–569. DOI: 10.30574/ijsra.2024.11.1.0079

Valenti, S., Neri, F., & Cucchiarelli, A. (2003). An Overview of Current Research on Automated Essay Grading. *Journal of Information Technology Education*, 2(1), 319–330. DOI: 10.28945/331

van der Wal, O., Bachmann, D., Leidinger, A., van Maanen, L., Zuidema, W., & Schulz, K. (2024). Undesirable Biases in NLP: Addressing Challenges of Measurement. *Journal of Artificial Intelligence Research*, 79, 1–40. DOI: 10.1613/jair.1.15195

VanLehn, K. (2011). The Relative Effectiveness of Human Tutoring, Intelligent Tutoring Systems, and Other Tutoring Systems. *Educational Psychologist*, 46(4), 197–221. DOI: 10.1080/00461520.2011.611369

Vartiainen, H., Tedre, M., & Valtonen, T. (2020). Learning machine learning with very young children: Who is teaching whom? *International Journal of Child-Computer Interaction*, 25, 100182. DOI: 10.1016/j.ijcci.2020.100182

Vaswani, A., Shazeer, N., Parmar, N., Uszkoreit, J., Jones, L., Gomez, A. N., Kaiser, Ł., & Polosukhin, I. 2017. "Attention Is All You Need." Pp. 6000–6010 in *Proceedings of the 31st International Conference on Neural Information Processing Systems, NIPS'17*. Red Hook, NY, USA: Curran Associates Inc.

Vavekanand, Raja. 2024. "IMPACT OF ARTIFICIAL INTELLIGENCE ON STUDENTS AND ETHICAL CONSIDERATIONS IN EDUCATION."

Vaza, R. N., Parmar, A. B., Mishra, P. S., Abdullah, I., & Velu, C. M. (2024). Security and privacy concerns in Ai-enabled IOT educational frameworks: An in-depth analysis. *Educational Administration: Theory and Practice*, 30(4), 8436–8445. DOI: 10.53555/kuey.v30i4.2742

Végh, L., & Gubo, Š. (2022). Assessment of Algorithmic and Logical Thinking of First-and Second-Year Computer Science Students at J. Selye University in Academic Years 2019/20 and 2021/22. In *ICERI2022 Proceedings* (pp. 1888-1895IATED.

Vesselinov, R., & Grego, J. (2012). *Duolingo effectiveness study*. City University of New York.

Volti, R., & Croissant, J. (2024). *Society and technological change*. Waveland press.

Vu, H. T., & Lim, J. (2022). Effects of country and individual factors on public acceptance of artificial intelligence and robotics technologies: A multilevel SEM analysis of 28-country survey data. *Behaviour & Information Technology*, 41(7), 1515–1528. DOI: 10.1080/0144929X.2021.1884288

Wang, Y., Liu, C., Tu, Y.-F. (2021). Factors affecting the adoption of ai-based applications in higher education: An analysis of teachers' perspectives using structural equation modeling. educational technology & society, 24 (3), 116– 129.

Wang, B., Rau, P. L. P., & Yuan, T. (2023). Measuring user competence in using artificial intelligence: Validity and reliability of artificial intelligence literacy scale. *Behaviour & Information Technology*, 42(9), 1324–1337. DOI: 10.1080/0144929X.2022.2072768

Wang, H., Tlili, A., Huang, R., Cai, Z., Li, M., Cheng, Z., Yang, D., Li, M., Zhu, X., & Fei, C. (2023). Examining the Applications of Intelligent Tutoring Systems in Real Educational Contexts: A Systematic Literature Review from the Social Experiment Perspective. *Education and Information Technologies*, 28(7), 9113–9148. DOI: 10.1007/s10639-022-11555-x PMID: 36643383

Wang, P. (2019). On defining artificial intelligence. *Journal of Artificial General Intelligence*, 10(2), 1–37. DOI: 10.2478/jagi-2019-0002

Wang, S., Wang, F., Zhu, Z., Wang, J., Tran, T., & Du, Z. (2024). Artificial intelligence in education: A systematic literature review. *Expert Systems with Applications*, 252, 124167. DOI: 10.1016/j.eswa.2024.124167

Wang, Y., Liu, C., & Tu, Y.-F. (2021). Factors affecting the adoption of ai-based applications in higher education: An analysis of teachers' perspectives using structural equation modeling. *Journal of Educational Technology & Society*, 24(3), 116–129. Retrieved June 8, 2023, from https://www.jstor.org/stable/27032860

Wang, Y., Wang, M., & Fujita, H. (2020). Word Sense Disambiguation: A Comprehensive Knowledge Exploitation Framework. *Knowledge-Based Systems*, 190, 105030. DOI: 10.1016/j.knosys.2019.105030

Warschauer, M. (2000). The Changing Global Economy and the Future of English Teaching. *TESOL Quarterly*, 34(3), 511–535. DOI: 10.2307/3587741

Warschauer, M., Knobel, M., & Stone, L. (2004). Technology and equity in schooling: Deconstructing the digital divide. *Educational Policy*, 18(4), 562–588. DOI: 10.1177/0895904804266469

Weber, A. S. (2016). The big student big data grab. *International Journal of Information and Education Technology (IJIET)*, 6(1), 65–70. DOI: 10.7763/IJIET.2016.V6.660

Weinstein, C.E., & MacDonald, J.D. (1986) "Why does a school psychologist need to know about learning strategies?", *Journal of School Psychology*, 24(3), (pp.257-265).

Wells, R. E. (2023). Strong AI vs. weak AI: What's the difference? Strong AI can do anything a human can do, while weak AI is limited to a specific task. LifeWire. *Retrieved August 22, 2023 from*Https://Www.Lifewire.Com/Strong-Ai-vs-Weak-Ai-7508012

West, D. M. (2018). *The future of work: Robots, AI, and automation.* Brookings Institution Press.

Williamson, B., & Piattoeva, N. (2020). Education Governance and the Role of AI: New Directions in Educational Research. *Educational Policy Review*, 29(4), 567–585.

Williams, R., Park, H., Oh, L., & Breazeal, C. (2019). PopBots. *Designing an Artificial Intelligence Curriculum for Early Childhood Education*, 33(1), 9729–9736. DOI: 10.1609/aaai.v33i01.33019729

Winkler, R., & Söllner, M. (2018). Unleashing the potential of chatbots in education: A state-of-the-art analysis. *Proceedings - Academy of Management*, 1(1), 15903. Advance online publication. DOI: 10.5465/AMBPP.2018.15903abstract

Wogu, I. A. P., Misra, S., Olu-Owolabi, E. F., Assibong, P. A., & Udoh, O. D. (2018). Artificial intelligence, artificial teachers and the fate of learners in the 21st century education sector: Implications for theory and practice. *International Journal of Pure and Applied Mathematics*, 119(16), 2245–2259.

Woods, W. A. (1970). Transition Network Grammars for Natural Language Analysis. *Communications of the ACM*, 13(10), 591–606. DOI: 10.1145/355598.362773

Wu, X., Duan, R., & Ni, J. (2024). Unveiling security, privacy, and ethical concerns of ChatGPT. *Journal of Information and Intelligence*, 2(2), 102–115. DOI: 10.1016/j.jiixd.2023.10.007

Xia, P. (2021). Design of personalized intelligent learning assistant system under artificial intelligence background. In *The 2020 International Conference on Machine Learning and Big Data Analytics for IoT Security and Privacy: SPIoT-2020*, Volume 1 (pp. 194-200). Springer International Publishing. DOI: 10.1007/978-3-030-62743-0_27

Ximei, L., Latif, Z., Danish, , Latif, S., & waraa, K. (2024). Estimating the impact of information technology on economic growth in south Asian countries: The silver lining of education. *Information Development*, 40(1), 147–157. DOI: 10.1177/02666669221100426

Xue, Y., & Wang, Y. (2022). Artificial Intelligence for Education and Teaching. *Wireless Communications and Mobile Computing*, 2022, 1–10. Advance online publication. DOI: 10.1155/2022/4750018

Xu, P., Liu, J., Jones, N., Cohen, J., & Ai, W. (2024). *The Promises and Pitfalls of Using Language Models to Measure Instruction Quality in Education*. Annenberg Institute at Brown University. DOI: 10.18653/v1/2024.naacl-long.246

Xu, W., Gao, Z., & Ge, L. (2024). New research paradigms and agenda of human factors science in the intelligence era. *Acta Psychologica Sinica*, 56(3), 363. DOI: 10.3724/SP.J.1041.2024.00363

Yang, H., & Kyun, S. (2022). The current research trend of Artificial Intelligence in language learning: A systematic empirical literature review from an activity theory perspective. *Australasian Journal of Educational Technology*, 38(5), 180–210. DOI: 10.14742/ajet.7492

Yannakoudakis, H., Briscoe, T., & Medlock, Ben. 2011. "A New Dataset and Method for Automatically Grading ESOL Texts." Pp. 180–89 in *Proceedings of the 49th Annual Meeting of the Association for Computational Linguistics: Human Language Technologies-Volume 1*.

Yao, H., Lian, D., Cao, Y., Wu, Y., & Zhou, T. (2019). Predicting academic performance for college students: A campus behavior perspective. [TIST]. *ACM Transactions on Intelligent Systems and Technology*, 10(3), 1–21. DOI: 10.1145/3299087

Yaslioglu, M. M. (2017). Factor analysis and validity in social sciences: Application of exploratory and confirmatory factor analyses. *Istanbul University Journal of the School of Business*, 46, (pp.74-85). https://dergipark.org.tr/tr/download/article-file/369427

Yeşil, S. (2009). Kültürel farklılıkların yönetimi ve alternatif bir strateji: Kültürel zeka.

Yin, X., Yu, X., Sohn, Kihyuk, Liu, Xiaoming, & Chandraker, Manmohan. (2019). Feature transfer learning for face recognition with under-represented data. *InIEEE Conference on Computer Vision and Pattern Recognition (CVPR)*, 2019. 2, 3. DOI: 10.1109/CVPR.2019.00585

Yu, H., & Guo, Y. (2023). Generative artificial intelligence empowers educational reform: Current status, issues, and prospects. []. Frontiers Media SA.]. *Frontiers in Education*, 8, 1183162. DOI: 10.3389/feduc.2023.1183162

Yüksekbilgili, Z. (2015). Türkiye'de Y Kuşağinin Yaş Araliği. *Elektronik Sosyal Bilimler Dergisi*, 14(53), 259–267.

Zadrozny, W. W., Gallagher, S., Shalaby, W., & Avadhani, A. (2015, February). Simulating IBM Watson in the classroom. In *Proceedings of the 46th ACM Technical Symposium on Computer Science Education* (pp. 72-77). DOI: 10.1145/2676723.2677287

Zaporozhko, V., Shardakov, V., & Parfenov, D. (2020). Fuzzy model for evaluating the results of online learning. *IOP Conference Series. Materials Science and Engineering*, 734(1), 012150. DOI: 10.1088/1757-899X/734/1/012150

Zaveri, P. (2023, February 3). Microsoft's landmark deal with OpenAI shows that ChatGPT is going to be the defining technology of 2023. Business Insider. Retrieved May 12, 2024, from https://www.businessinsider.com/why-generative-ai-chatgpt-the-defining-tech-of-this-year-2023-1?r=US&IR=T

Zawacki-Richter, O., Marín, V., Bond, M., & Gouverneur, F. (2019). Systematic review of research on artificial intelligence applications in higher education – where are the educators? *International Journal of Educational Technology in Higher Education*, 16(1), 39. Advance online publication. DOI: 10.1186/s41239-019-0171-0

Zeytinkaya, D. (2016). Bilişsel Stil Kullanımına Yönelik Bir Araştırma. *Journal of International Social Research*, 9(46).

Zhai, X., Chu, X., Chai, C. S., Jong, M. S. Y., Istenic, A., Spector, M., Liu, J.-B., Yuan, J., & Li, Y. (2021). A Review of Artificial Intelligence (AI) in Education from 2010 to 2020. *Complexity*, 2021(1), 1–18. DOI: 10.1155/2021/8812542

Zhai, X., Yin, Y., Pellegrino, J. W., Haudek, K. C., & Shi, L. (2020). Applying Machine Learning in Science Assessment: A Systematic Review. *Studies in Science Education*, 56(1), 111–151. DOI: 10.1080/03057267.2020.1735757

Zhang, B., & Dafoe, A. (2019). Artificial Intelligence: American attitudes and trends. *SSRN*. http://dx.doi.org/DOI: 10.2139/ssrn.3312874

Zhang, C., Schießl, J., Plößl, L., Hofmann, F., & Gläser-Zikuda, M. (2023). Acceptance of artificial intelligence among pre-service teachers: A multigroup analysis. *International Journal of Educational Technology in Higher Education*, 20(1), 49. DOI: 10.1186/s41239-023-00420-7 PMID: 36743849

Zhang, L., & Sun, Y. (2024). Integrating AI into biology education: Pedagogical strategies and student outcomes. *Computers & Education*, 190, 104603. DOI: 10.1016/j.compedu.2023.104603

Zhang, S., & Chen, X. (2022, December). Applying Artificial Intelligence into Early Childhood Math Education: Lesson Design and Course Effect. In *2022 IEEE International Conference on Teaching, Assessment and Learning for Engineering (TALE)* (pp. 635-638). IEEE. DOI: 10.1109/TALE54877.2022.00109

Zhang, S., Shan, C., Lee, J., Che, S., & Kim, J. (2023). Effect of chatbot-assisted language learning: A meta-analysis. *Education and Information Technologies*, 28(11), 15223–15243. DOI: 10.1007/s10639-023-11805-6

Zhang, T., Lu, X., Zhu, X., & Zhang, J. (2023). The contributions of AI in the development of ideological and political perspectives in education. *Heliyon*, 9(3), e13403. Advance online publication. DOI: 10.1016/j.heliyon.2023.e13403 PMID: 36879973

Zhang, Y., Qiu, C., Zhong, N., Su, X., Zhang, X., Huang, F., & Wang, L. (2021). AI education based on evaluating concentration of students in class: Using machine vision to recognize students' classroom behaviour. *InProceedings of the 2021 5th International Conference on Video and Image Processing*, 126–133. DOI: 10.1145/3511176.3511196

Zhao, S. (2021). Facial recognition in educational context. *In2021 International Conference on Public Relations and Social Sciences (ICPRSS 2021)(Pp.* 10-17*)*. Atlantis Press.

Zheng, L., & Zheng, L. (2021). Learning analytics for computer-supported collaborative learning design. *Data-driven design for computer-supported collaborative learning: Design matters*, (pp.31-43).

Zirawaga, V. S., Olusanya, A. I., & Maduku, T. (2017). Gaming in Education: Using Games as a Support Tool to Teach History. Journal of Education and Practice. 8(15), ISSN 2222-1735 (Paper) ISSN 2222-288X (Online).

About the Contributors

Ricardo Queirós é doutorado em Ciência de Computadores e Professor Adjunto na área de Informática na Escola Superior de Media Artes e Design do Instituto Politécnico do Porto onde leciona disciplinas relacionadas com programação Web e móvel. É também investigador na área da gamificação, interoperabilidade em sistemas de e-learning e aprendizagem de linguagens de programação, no Centro de Investigação em Sistemas Computacionais Avançados (CRACS), do INESC TEC Porto. É também Coordenador do Gabinete de Ensino à Distância do Centro de Inovação Pedagógica (CIP) do Politécnico do Porto. É o responsável pela International Computer Programming Education Conference (ICPEC), a primeira conferência internacional dedicada exclusivamente ao ensino da programação de computadores. Atualmente trabalha na conceção e implementação de ambientes de aprendizagem gamificados para fomentar o processo de ensino-aprendizagem de cursos de programação de computadores. É autor de mais de 100 livros e publicações científicas focados nos tópicos de ensino e investigação previamente referidos.

Mário Cruz is an Associate Professor in Foreign Language Teaching (English and Spanish), at the School of Education of the Polytechnic of Porto, where he teaches Spanish as a Foreign Language, Hispano-American Literatures and Cultures, English Teaching in Primary Education, Didactic Resources in Teaching English and supervises the pedagogical practice of future teachers. He is also an integrated researcher at inED - Center for Research and Innovation in Education at the School of Education of the Polytechnic of Porto and a collaborator at CIDTFF at the University of Aveiro. Being professionalized in recruitment groups 120 - English, 220 - Portuguese and English, 330 - English, 340 - German, 350 - Spanish and 910 - Special Education, he has worked as a teacher in public schools of basic and secondary education, since the school year of 2001-2002 until the school year 2013-2014. He also collaborated at the Paula Frassinetti School of Education (from 2003 to 2012) where he taught English Language, English Language Didactics, Information and Communication Technologies in Education, Information and Communication Technologies in Inclusive Education Contexts, Educational Technologies in English Teaching, Deep Issues of Differentiated Intervention, among other curricular units. He holds a PhD in Didactics and Professional Development from the University of Aveiro, a PhD in Linguistic Studies from the University of Vigo and a MA in Language Didactics (University of Aveiro), Teaching English and Spanish in Basic Education (Polytechnic of Porto - Escola Superior de Educação) and Teaching English and Spanish at the 3rd of Basic Education and Secondary Education (University of Aveiro). His main doctoral theses and dissertations and MA's reports focus on: critical hyper-pedagogy, the intercultural and multilingual approach, the use of technologies in the teaching-learning process and linguistic and cultural varieties. He is currently coordinator of the thematic line "Teacher Training" at inED, where he directs the research projects: "CLIL 4 U - implementation, monitoring and evaluation of bilingual teaching projects", "PEPPA 6/7 - Primary English Practice Program for Ages 6/7", "Schoolers and Scholars (SnS): Role-Playing Games (RPG) in the teaching and learning process at Primary Education" and "VarLang - Linguistic and cultural varieties in the teaching of foreign languages".

Daniela Mascarenhas is an adjunct professor at the School of Education of the Polytechnic Institute of Porto. She is involved in the training of early childhood educators and teachers of the 1st and 2nd cycle of basic education. She has published several articles and is a collaborating researcher in several research projects allocated to the research centers CeiED and inED. She is an integrated researcher in inED center. She is a trainer in several continuing education programs for teachers and educators in Portugal and São Tomé and Príncipe. Post-Doctorate in Education Sciences, in the specialty of Pedagogical Supervision, from the University of Minho (2019). Ph.D. in Education and Mathematics Didactics from the Faculty of Education Sciences of the University of Granada (2011) and validated by the University of Porto. She obtained the Diploma of Advanced Studies (DEA) in Education and Didactics of Mathematics from the Faculty of Educational Sciences of the University of Granada (2010). She graduated in Mathematics (via teaching) from the University of Minho (2003).

***

Okechukwu Amah facilitates sessions in Management Communication, Human Resources, Leadership and Human Behaviour in Organisations at Lagos Business School. He is also the Research Director at Lagos Business School. Earlier, he was a part-time lecturer at the Lagos State University, where he taught MBA students Organisational Behaviour, Organisational Theory, Business Policy and Management. He has also facilitated sessions in customised programmes for NLNG, and actively reviews articles for the annual meetings of the American Academy of Management and Southern Management Association. Dr Amah obtained his first degree in Petroleum Engineering from the University of Ibadan, MBA and PhD from the University of Benin. He started his career as a petroleum engineer with Texaco Overseas Nigeria Limited, where he held such key positions as District Petroleum Engineer and Assistant District Manager in charge of drilling, production and support services. He assumed the position of Production Manager before the company merged with Chevron Nigeria Limited. He thereafter joined Chevron Nigeria Limited, and held other pivotal positions in the organisation before moving on. Currently, Dr Amah is researching work/family conflict and facilitation, employee engagement relationships, as well as organisational citizenship and servant leadership behaviour in Nigeria. He is a member of the Society of Petroleum Engineers, Nigerian Academy of Management, American Academy of Management, Society of Human Resources Management and Southern Management Society.

Luanne Amato currently serves as an Associate Professor at Holy Family University in Philadelphia, PA where she teaches quantitative subjects and concepts in management marketing. She holds a Doctor of Education degree in Curriculum, Teaching, and Learning from Northeastern University, Boston, MA and received an MBA in International Business from Rosemont College, Bryn Mawr, PA. Student engagement and best practices in instruction are the main focus of her research, presentations, and published works. Most recently, Luanne's research has focused on Artificial Intelligence (AI) and its impact on ethics in an academic setting. She resides in Philadelphia, PA with her husband. She has five children and four grandchildren.

Feyza Aydin Bölükbaş She completed her undergraduate education at Gazi University Faculty of Education, Preschool Education Programme in 2015. In 2018, she completed her master's degree at Gazi University Institute of Educational Sciences, Department of Preschool Education. In 2018, she started her doctorate education in Gazi University Institute of Educational Sciences, Preschool Education programme and completed it in 2023. She has been working on mathematics education and science education in preschool children and taking part in projects related to technology integration in education. She is currently working as a research assistant at Aksaray University. She is currently working as a research assistant at Aksaray University, Faculty of Education, Department of Elementary Education, Department of Preschool Education.

Ana Balula holds a PhD in Multimedia in Education in the area of eteaching evaluation and an Habilitation in Education - Pedagogy and Educational Technology. She is an integrated member of the Research Centre on Didactics and Technology in the Education of Trainers (CIDTFF) and the Laboratory of Digital Contents (LCD) of the Department of Education and Psychology (DEP–UA). She has also been a member of scientific committees of international congresses and journals and has participated as a researcher in several scientific projects in her main research areas, namely: e-learning, b-learning, the use of digital technology in education, e-assessment/evaluation, Open Educational Resources (OER), Collaborative Online International Learning (COIL), English for Specific Purposes (ESP), foreign language didactics and intercultural business communication. She is Associate Professor at Águeda School of Technology and Management of the University of Aveiro (ESTGA-UA) and has been collaborating with the DEP-UA in the supervision of PhD Projects in Multimedia in Education.

Emine Bozkurt Polat was born in Kahramanmaraş in 1991, Emine BOZKURT POLAT graduated from Necmettin Erbakan University, Department of Preschool Education in 2012 and was appointed as a research assistant at Kahramanmaraş Sütçü İmam University in the same year. After completing his master's degree in Necmettin Erbakan University Preschool Education Department in 2016, he was appointed as a research assistant to Gazi University Preschool Education Department in the same year and started his doctorate education. She worked as the education coordinator at Gazi Practice Kindergarten for 1 year in the 2018-2019 academic year. The author is still working as a research assistant at Gazi University. As an academician, he has publications on technology, augmented reality, robotic coding values education in preschool children. She worked on robotic coding in her doctoral thesis.

Kadriye Selin Budak Having attained my undergraduate degree in Preschool Education from Dokuz Eylül University's Education Faculty in 2017, and subsequently earning my master's degree in Preschool Education from Pamukkale University's Educational Sciences Institute in 2018, I am currently pursuing a doctoral degree in the same field at Gazi University's Educational Sciences Institute. My research focuses on the integration of digital games and technology in preschool education, and I am actively engaged in various related projects. I am also currently serving as a lecturer at Bilecik Şeyh Edebali University

D.K. Chaturvedi, is working in Dept. of Electrical Engineering, Faculty of Engineering, D.E.I., Dayalbagh, Agra since 1989. He did his B.E. from Govt. Engineering College Ujjain, M.P. then he did his M.Tech. and Ph.D. from D.E.I. Dayalbagh in 1993 and 1998 respectively. He is gold medallist and received Young

Scientists BOYSCAST Fellowship from DST, Government of India in 2001-2002 for post doctorial research at Univ. of Calgary, Canada. He is the Fellow -The Institution of Engineers (India), Fellow - Aeronautical Society of India, Fellow –Institution of Electronics and Telecommunication Engineering, Sr. Member IEEE, USA and Member of many National and International professional bodies such as IET, U.K., ISTE, Delhi,, ISCE, Roorkee, IIIE, Mumbai and SSI etc. The Institution of Engineers (India), Kolkata, recognized his work and conferred many award like Best Paper Award, Tata Rao Medal Award, U.P. State Power Sector Award and Mossaudi Lal Award etc. ADRDE lab of DRDO conferred him life time achievement award for his valuable contributions in field of aeronautics. He is the consultant of DRDO. The Ministry of Environment and Forrest, Government of India, New Delhi has given a letter of appreciation to Prof. D.K. Chaturvedi for guiding the best M.Tech. project. His name is included in Marquis Who's Who in Engineering and Science in Asia – 2006-2007, Marquis Who's Who in Engineering and Science in America 2006-07 and Marquis Who's Who in World – 2006-2007. He did many R&D projects of MHRD, UGC, AICTE etc. and consultancy projects of DRDO. He contributed in the national mission of ICT of Govt. of India as Virtual Power Lab Developer. He has authored three books and 25 contributed chapter. He wrote more than 300 research papers in international and national peer reviewed journals, transactions and conferences. He has 15 patents. Presently He is Professor in Electrical Engineering and additional load of Head of Dept. of Footwear Technology, Faculty Training and Placement officer, D.E.I. and Advisor, IEI Students' Chapter (Elect. Engg.), Incharge, Electrical Engineering Lab.

Luis Coelho is an adjunct professor at the Engineering School of Polytechnic Institute of Porto. He is a PhD in Telecommunications and Signal Processing since 2012, and a MsC in Electronics Engineering, since 2005. As a researcher he has published several scientific articles in conferences and journals. He actively collaborates with the scientific community as participant, reviewer, organizer of scientific conferences or as journal editor. His main research interests are on image and signal processing, human-machine interaction and management, all topics with a special focus on the healthcare area.

Ana Rita Costa is an Invited Assitant Professor at Águeda Professional School of Technology and Managment and the Department of Education at the University of Aveiro. She is also a collaborating member of the Research Centre on Didactics and Technology in the Education of Trainers (CIDTFF) and at LabELing - Languages Education Laboratory of the University of Aveiro, Portugal. She has a PhD in Education: Didactics and Curriculum Development and a degree in Teaching Foreign Languages (English and German). Her main research interests are plurilingualism, curriculum development, language and cultural awareness and teacher education and English for Specific Purposes (ESP). She is the author of scientific work that was published and disseminated at national and international conferences and has been involved in the organization of national and international conferences.

Kübra Engin completed her undergraduate education in Hacettepe University Education Faculty Preschool Teaching Department in 2014. Between 2014-2016, he worked as a preschool teacher in public schools under the Ministry of National Education, and as a research assistant at Gaziosmanpaşa University Faculty of Education, Department of Pre-School Education between 2016-2017. Between 2016-2019, she completed her master's degree at Gazi University, Institute of Educational Sciences, Department of Preschool Education. She is continuing her doctorate education in the same science that she started in 2019. He is still working as a research assistant at Gazi University, Gazi Education Faculty, Preschool Education Department. His academic interests are nature education in early childhood, social and emotional learning and family education.

Minna-Maarit Jaskari, PhD, serves as a Program Manager and University Lecturer at the School of Marketing and Communication, University of Vaasa, Finland. With a current focus on AI, design thinking, marketing analytics, strategic sales management, and research methods, she contributes to the university's teaching from the bachelor to MBA levels. Her dedication to teaching has been recognized, and she strives to continuously improve her pedagogical methods. In her research, Dr. Jaskari explores higher education pedagogies, consumer research, and the impacts of music on consumers. Her findings have been shared in several academic journals, including Marketing Theory Qualitative Research: An International Journal, Nordic Journal of Business, Research in Consumer Culture Theory, Journal of Marketing Education, and Marketing Education Review. Dr. Jaskari also participates in the academic community as a member of the Journal of Marketing Education editorial board and has contributed as a guest editor for several journals. Throughout her career, Dr. Jaskari has sought to balance her roles in teaching, research, and academic service, hoping to make a positive impact on her students and the broader academic community.

Ali Mazı was born in Hatay in 1992. I completed my primary and secondary education in Hatay. I entered Kahramamaraş Sutcu Imam University in 2010. I studied in the department of elementary mathematics teaching. After completing my education, I graduated in 2014. In 2018, I completed my master's degree at Kahramanmaraş Sütçü İmam University's Department of Educational Management, Inspection, Planning and Economics. I have been working as a mathematics teacher at the Ministry of National Education since 2014. I completed my Ph.D. in 2023 at Hacettepe University Primary Education Department. My fields of study are classroom education, mathematics education and inclusive education.

Victoria Okesipe is a Research Assistant at Lagos Business School, Pan Atlantic University, where she collaborates with esteemed faculty members on interdisciplinary research projects focusing on Human Behavior, Information Technology, Artificial Intelligence, and Machine Learning. Her primary research agenda is centered on optimizing technologies for diverse stakeholders including users, customers, workers, and industries through the application of Business Data Analytics, Management, and Organization Sciences. Furthermore, Victoria's academic pursuits extend to areas such as Applied Neurophysiology, Human-Computer Interaction, and User Experience, reflecting her comprehensive approach to understanding and enhancing the human-technology interface.

Sara Reis has an MSc in Clinical Process Optimization. PhD in Bioethics / Biomedical Engineering. Polytechnic Higher Education Teacher with the category of Prof. Adjunct. Interest in the area of Biomedical Engineering, namely in the areas of Innovation and Health Management.

Inês Rodrigues is an English professor with a degree in Modern Languages and Literatures from the Faculty of Arts and Humanities University of Porto. She holds a master's degree in Adult Education and Training from the Faculty of Psychology and Educational Sciences at the University of Porto and earned an international PhD in Equity and Innovation in Education from the University of Vigo. She is certified by the Scientific-Pedagogical Council for Continuous Training, with specializations in Adult Education, Research Methodologies, Human Rights, and Educational Technologies. As an advocate for lifelong learning, she has authored English for Specific Purposes textbooks for secondary education and educational children's stories, enhancing both formal and informal education environments. Her academic and research focus lies at the intersection of education, society, and technology, particularly in the integration of artificial intelligence in educational settings. She is committed to developing innovative pedagogical resources and empowering students with 21st-century skills. Her work not only bridges technology and education but also emphasizes equity, global citizenship, and sustainability, contributing significantly to the advancement of modern educational practices.

Shiwani is currently a Senior Research Fellow in the Department of Pedagogical Sciences, Faculty of Education at Dayalbagh Educational Institute (DEI), Agra. With a robust academic background, she has pursued higher education extensively at DEI, obtaining her M.Ed. with a CGPA of 9.27, M.Phil. in Botany with a CGPA of 9.25, and an M.Sc. in Botany with a CGPA of 8.47. Since 2019, she has been working on her Ph.D. in Education, focusing on Artificial Intelligence-Based Expert Systems, Higher Order Thinking Skills, and Creative Insight. Throughout her tenure at DEI, Shiwani has made significant contributions, teaching full-time courses such as EDH 232 (Educational Psychology) and EDM-106 (School Management and Professional Ethics) while also engaging in voluntary teaching. Her scholarly work is well recognized, with numerous publications in national and international journals, including research on the impacts of education, environment challenges, and the application of expert systems to enhance learning programs. Her book "Effect of Reciprocal Teaching on Higher Order Thinking and Creativity" was published in 2023 by LAP, Lambert Academic Publishing, Germany.

Christine Schoettle currently serves as an Associate Dean for the School of Business and Technology at Holy Family University in Philadelphia, PA. She holds a Doctorate of Education degree in Educational Leadership from Gratz College, Melrose Park, PA and received an M.Ed. in Math Education from Arcadia University, Glenside, PA and an M.Ed. in Sport and Recreation Administration from Temple University, Philadelphia, PA. Best practices in teaching and utilizing new technologies in teaching are her research interests. She resides with her husband and two sons in Philadelphia, PA.

Serap Uğur graduated from an undergraduate program in "Computer Education and Instructional Technology" at Anadolu University and the master degree of the same program and doctorate degree of the Distance Education. She worked as a lecturer at the Distance Education Department of Open Education Faculty. She currently works as a Asst. Prof. at the Education Faculty. Sisman-Ugur works research and development activities&projects in fields such as e-learning content types, digital storytelling, animation, game-based learning, gamification, instructional design, crosscultural aspects, artificial intelligence, individual differences and human-computer interaction. She interested in technological singularity and transhumanism. She was Social Media Coordinator of Anadolu University Open Education System, Social Media Unit Manager of Anadolu University and Vice of Corporate Communication Coordinator of Anadolu University, Vice Coordinator Internship and Practice Courses, Coordinator of the Social Media and Digital Security Education, Research and Application Center. Uğur is currently working as Assistant Professor at Anadolu University Education Faculty.

Ilkay Ulutaş received an undergraduate degree in the Child Development and Education Teaching program at Gazi University. She completed her master's degree in child development at Ankara University and her PhD in Child Development and Education at Gazi University. In 2009, she conducted a postdoctoral study on emotional intelligence at the University College London Department of Psychology within the scope of the TUBITAK Scientist Support Department International Postdoctoral Research Scholarship Program. Her studies focus on the emotional intelligence in preschool children, Montessori education, mathematics education in early childhood education, arts in early childhood education, early childhood quality, and technology in early childhood education. She has also recently carried out projects on digital mathematics stories in early childhood education, augmented reality applications in early childhood mathematics education, and cultural heritage and technology (coding, digital storytelling) in early childhood education. She currently works as a professor at the Early Childhood Education Department at Gazi University.

Index

A

Ai-Based Learning Tools 309
Artificial Intelligence (AI) 1, 2, 3, 4, 5, 8, 9, 16, 18, 20, 21, 22, 23, 24, 25, 27, 30, 31, 32, 33, 34, 35, 36, 42, 43, 44, 46, 47, 48, 49, 50, 51, 52, 53, 54, 55, 56, 57, 59, 60, 61, 62, 63, 64, 65, 66, 68, 69, 70, 71, 72, 73, 74, 75, 76, 77, 78, 79, 80, 81, 82, 83, 84, 85, 86, 87, 90, 91, 107, 108, 109, 120, 122, 136, 137, 140, 144, 145, 146, 147, 148, 150, 153, 154, 155, 156, 157, 158, 160, 167, 169, 172, 173, 174, 179, 181, 183, 184, 185, 193, 194, 195, 196, 197, 198, 199, 200, 201, 202, 203, 204, 206, 208, 209, 210, 212, 213, 214, 215, 239, 243, 244, 245, 254, 255, 256, 257, 267, 268, 271, 278, 281, 283, 284, 285, 287, 288, 310, 311, 312

B

Business Education 96

C

Chatbot 62, 92, 98, 108, 147, 157, 244, 246, 248, 255, 257, 270, 273, 274, 284, 285, 295
ChatGPT 5, 24, 46, 47, 56, 62, 71, 84, 85, 91, 92, 93, 94, 95, 98, 104, 105, 107, 108, 109, 125, 130, 145, 194, 247, 248, 249, 251, 252, 255, 256, 257, 260, 274, 275, 276, 284, 288, 295, 298, 299, 300, 302, 310, 312

D

Digital Learning 50, 65, 217, 218, 219, 221, 222, 229, 237, 238, 241

E

Educational Practices 10, 62, 210, 287, 289, 293, 299, 309
English As A Second Language 287, 288, 293, 294, 296, 300, 308, 309
Ethics 3, 20, 23, 24, 47, 63, 65, 75, 76, 82, 84, 147, 212, 214, 243, 247, 248, 249, 250, 253, 257, 281

F

Foreign Languages 271

G

Generative AI 7, 46, 52, 62, 89, 90, 91, 92, 93, 95, 104, 105, 106, 107, 108, 109, 145, 214, 256, 267, 268, 269, 270, 271, 272, 274, 275, 276, 283, 284, 312
Generative AI Tools 7, 89, 92, 105, 269, 270, 275

H

Higher Education 3, 21, 22, 23, 24, 46, 49, 54, 55, 60, 66, 75, 80, 84, 85, 87, 89, 90, 91, 92, 94, 96, 103, 104, 105, 106, 107, 108, 109, 119, 120, 121, 130, 134, 143, 144, 145, 162, 194, 198, 226, 228, 239, 240, 243, 244, 245, 249, 251, 253, 254, 255, 256, 257, 283, 284

I

Intelligent Systems 3, 4, 8, 83, 241

L

Language Chatbots 267, 268
Language Education 272, 281, 291, 292, 293, 306, 308, 309, 311
Language Learning 6, 120, 133, 134, 136, 146, 147, 267, 268, 270, 271, 272, 273, 274, 276, 277, 280, 284, 288, 289, 291, 292, 293, 294, 295, 296,

297, 298, 299, 303, 304, 305, 306, 308, 309, 310, 311, 312
Learning Assistant 153, 154, 157, 158, 161, 163, 164, 165, 167, 168, 169, 170, 173, 174
Learning Platforms 6, 7, 8, 13, 18, 65, 73, 74, 78, 133, 157, 208, 209, 218, 219, 221, 222

M

Machine Learning 7, 24, 31, 52, 55, 61, 63, 86, 122, 124, 125, 128, 147, 151, 154, 156, 157, 158, 172, 174, 183, 208, 217, 222, 227, 229, 233, 237, 239, 285, 291
Machine Translation 124, 125, 134, 149, 267, 268, 270, 271, 272, 284
Marketing Education 108
Metaverse 153, 154, 166, 167, 168, 169, 170
Metrics 126, 127, 128, 141, 205

N

NLP 119, 120, 121, 122, 123, 124, 125, 126, 128, 129, 130, 131, 132, 133, 134, 135, 136, 137, 138, 139, 141, 142, 143, 144, 145, 150, 168, 173, 212

O

Online Digital Learning 217, 218, 222, 229, 237
OpenAI 62, 85, 89, 90, 93, 94, 97, 98, 105, 107, 109, 125, 128, 255, 257, 274

P

Personalized Learning 1, 2, 3, 6, 7, 8, 18, 23, 28, 31, 44, 47, 65, 67, 120, 134, 138, 145, 149, 157, 177, 183, 190, 191, 202, 203, 208, 210, 211, 212, 270, 280, 285
Plagiarism 92, 132, 141, 144, 184, 197, 244, 247, 248, 249, 250, 253, 256, 258, 309
preschool education 70, 75, 79, 82
Primary Schools 34
Privacy Concerns 10, 11, 16, 56, 93, 104, 136, 199, 201, 212, 309
Professional Development 7, 64, 68, 77, 80, 96, 139, 142, 143, 206, 243, 244, 246, 247, 249, 250, 252, 254, 258, 260, 274, 289, 290

R

Redesign 195, 248, 253

S

Supervised Machine Learning Algorithms 227

T

teacher candidate 80
Teacher Training 18, 69, 83, 267, 268, 273, 274
Technology Enhanced Learning 23, 54, 55

Printed in the USA
CPSIA information can be obtained
at www.ICGtesting.com
LVHW081927041124
795688LV00041B/1295